WORKS ISSUED BY
THE HAKLUYT SOCIETY

———

THE JOURNAL OF ROCHFORT MAGUIRE
1852–1854

VOLUME I

SECOND SERIES
NO. 169

CAPTAIN ROCHFORT MAGUIRE
by Stephen Pearce
National Portrait Gallery, London, no. 1214

THE
JOURNAL OF
ROCHFORT MAGUIRE
1852–1854

Two years at Point Barrow, Alaska,
aboard HMS *Plover* in the search for
Sir John Franklin

VOLUME I

EDITED BY
JOHN BOCKSTOCE

THE HAKLUYT SOCIETY
LONDON
1988

B
M 2764M
v. 1

© The Hakluyt Society 1988

ISBN 0 904180 24 7 (set of 2 volumes)
ISBN 0 904180 25 5 (Volume I)
ISSN 0072–9396

Printed in Great Britain at
the University Press, Cambridge

Published by the Hakluyt Society
c/o The Map Library
British Library, Great Russell Street
London WC1B 3DG

For Terence Armstrong

CONTENTS

ILLUSTRATIONS

MAPS

ACKNOWLEDGEMENTS

This book could not have been done without the generous help of a number of people: Lydia Black, Stephen Braund, Thomas Brower, Ernest S. Burch, Jr, John Carnahan, Annette McFayden Clark, Alan Cooke, Andrew David, John C. George, Edwin S. Hall, Jr, Todd Hansen, Clive Holland, Jonathan King, Michael Krauss, Shepard Krech, III, David Libbey, David Lyon, Robert McGhee, Emmer Mooney, The Earl and Countess of Mount Charles, Alan Pearsall, Dorothy Jean Ray, Ann Shirley, Gail Sleeman, Clara Stites, Richard Stern, James VanStone, and Hugh Wallace.

The maps were prepared by Mrs S. Gutteridge of the Department of Geography, University of Cambridge.

The National Library of Ireland has generously consented to the publication of the journal. Funding for part of the project was provided by the North Slope Borough of Alaska.

I am particularly grateful to Harry King for so cheerfully and ably assisting with the preparation of the manuscript.

Lastly, I wish to thank Terence Armstrong, to whom this volume is dedicated, for his assistance on this and many projects and for his friendship during the last twenty years.

PREFACE

The *Plover*'s voyage in search of Sir John Franklin, from 1848 to 1854, resulted in the first constant presence of Europeans in the western Arctic, and Rochfort Maguire's record of his two years at Point Barrow is, I believe, the earliest surviving account of a sustained foreign presence with the Eskimos of Northern Alaska. But Maguire's journal is more than a priceless ethnographical document: it is also a fascinating account of European men learning to cope with the dual challenges of an exotic environment and a foreign society.

I first read Rochfort Maguire's journal more than ten years ago. As I casually glanced at those pages, brimming with Maguire's tight and precise hand, I realized that here was a careful, earnest and decent man who, in the midst of a highly visible national effort, had been assigned a job of waiting, in comparative obscurity, in an unrewarding part of the Arctic while others forged ahead with geographical discoveries and the search for Franklin. Maguire had asked for a steam auxiliary exploration vessel but he received, in essence, a dumpy depot ship whereon he was to act far more as a caretaker than as a captain of discovery. With such a lacklustre prospect it is conceivable that an officer without Maguire's stability and deep sense of duty would have sunk into a miasma of gloomy routine in the dark days of Point Barrow's winters.

Maguire, however, was not this sort of man. He was careful to observe and record all things that happened to him and to his ship – and it seems to me that this was not only because he was concerned to carry out the letter and spirit of his orders but also because, despite his narrow education in the Royal Navy, he was at heart a kind and sensitive person.

Had he been merely a simple naval officer bent on the quick advancement that the Arctic service offered, his might have been a dry and lifeless account of the twenty-four months at Point Barrow. But his journal is clearly not that, and I believe it came about for two reasons: one was his curious and decent nature; the other was his close friendship with the *Plover*'s surgeon, Dr John Simpson, who was skilled as an ethnographer and as a teacher of his colleagues.

Simpson clearly was an exceptionally intelligent man who possessed a deeply curious mind in the best tradition of the great naturalists of the nineteenth century. As the *Plover*'s surgeon, Simpson had already spent one winter in eastern Siberia, another in Kotzebue Sound, and another in Port Clarence, and thus he had acquired both a fundamental sensitivity to the northern natives' culture and a working knowledge of Inupiaq, the language of the Eskimos of northwestern Alaska. His autumn in England in 1851 no doubt allowed him to probe into the accounts of other explorers who had met the Eskimos, and thus, I assume, when he rejoined his ship in 1852 he was well prepared to study a society that already deeply fascinated him. That he was successful is proved by his monograph on the western Eskimos, which is reprinted as Appendix Seven of this volume.

Simpson's breadth of learning and Maguire's gentleness clearly found a mutual spark, and, I assume, a deep respect and friendship grew between the two. Simpson's linguistic skills and understanding clearly helped Maguire grow to understand and later to tolerate and then eventually to love the Eskimos of Point Barrow, whom he first considered savages. Ultimately he left with regret, considering them friends, whose non-British ways he understood and accepted.

For their part, the Eskimos – principally the shaman 'Erk-sing-era' – must have undergone a similar growth of understanding, and these men, unlike the British, may have engendered opprobrium from their society for their friendship. They are no less the heroes of this account.

Maguire's story is a voyage of discovery in the best tradition of the Hakluyt Society's 150 years of publication. Like so many of the Hakluyt Society's volumes, it is a voyage aboard a ship – but Maguire's voyages took place aboard a ship that was stationary, a voyage of the mind undertaken by proud men of two cultures. At first antagonistic, they at the end proved to themselves and to one another that the human spirit can be both generous and genocidal. Today we can all take heart in reading what came about so improbably from 1852 to 1854 at Point Barrow.

INTRODUCTION

FOREIGN CONTACT AT POINT BARROW IN THE
NINETEENTH CENTURY

The *Plover*'s two year stay at Point Barrow as part of the Franklin search was the first extensive contact that the Eskimos of the region had had with foreigners, but although their isolation was abrutly destroyed by the search for Sir John Franklin, the distant world's advancement toward them had begun two centuries earlier. In 1648, only ten years after the Cossacks reached the Pacific Ocean, one of the most adventurous of that group, Semen Dezhnev, led the first foreign expedition through Bering Strait. Although Dezhnev and his men were the first foreigners to have visited the region, indirect contact between Alaskan Eskimos and distant peoples had been established nearly fifteen hundred years earlier by a trade in east Asian iron that passed into Alaska via Bering Strait. Nevertheless, Dezhnev's historic voyage served to intensify the Alaskans' indirect contacts; by about 1675 several trading posts were operating near the Chukchi Peninsula.[1] It was not until 1778, however, when Captain James Cook passed through Bering Strait and reached Icy Cape, that Europeans began to have a clear idea of the coast of northwestern Alaska. Nevertheless, for the rest of the eighteenth century – and until the end of the Napoleonic Wars – there were only a few foreign penetrations of the Bering Strait region.

The year 1816 marked the beginning of the end of the Eskimos' seclusion. In that year Otto von Kotzebue, sailing in search of a Northwest Passage for Tsar Alexander I, steered his ship, the *Rurik*, into Kotzebue Sound, charting the coasts that Captain Cook had avoided. His was the first of several thousand cruises that ships would make north of Bering Strait in the nineteenth century.

Before Kotzebue's voyage the Russian–American Company – the

---

[1] Fisher, 1981; Armstrong, 1965, p. 24; Golder, 1914, pp. 28–9.

1

fur trading company chartered by the Tsar to operate a monopoly in Alaska – had restricted its trading activities to southern Alaska and the Aleutian Islands. In the second decade of the nineteenth century, however, the company began to take an active interest in the northern regions of Alaska. To some extent this new interest in the North may have been a response to the increasing British fur trading activity in northwestern North America – and to the potential of territorial claims arising from these activities.

This may have been the reason why, in 1819, an American sea captain named Gray was sent north by the Russians – possibly in John Jacob Astor's brig *Sylph* – to check on the accuracy of Kotzebue's surveys. Whether Gray carried out his instructions is a matter of dispute, but he did pass through Bering Strait, anchor his ship on the north shore of the Seward Peninsula, and continue on into Kotzebue Sound in a smaller boat, while trading firearms and ammunition for furs.[1]

During the following years, 1820 and 1821, another Russian expedition reached those waters. Two vessels, under the command of M. N. Vasiliyev and G. S. Shishmarev, Kotzebue's former lieutenant, had again been sent by the Tsar in search of a northwest passage. One of the ships reached 71°06′N in the Chukchi Sea and on the way discovered Point Hope, where two settlements were observed comprising 600 people.

Of equal interest is the fact that in 1820, when the first of the Tsar's ships sailed deep into Kotzebue Sound, the Russians were concerned to find an Eskimo encampment of several hundred Eskimos, some of whom had firearms. Later, hostilities broke out and the two groups exchanged gunfire. The second Russian ship sailed into Kotzebue Sound at about this time, followed – to the Russians' surprise – by another American ship, one of Astor's brigs, the *Pedler*, commanded by William Pigot. Pigot announced to the Russians that he was on a fur trading voyage and that he carried firearms and ammunition for barter. In addition to the *Pedler* and the *Sylph*, four other American ships may have been operating in the waters near Bering Strait between 1815 and 1820.[2] Clearly, the European world was flooding into northwestern Alaska.

At the same time, Britain, at the end of the Napoleonic Wars,

[1] Foote, 1965, pp. 45–54; D. J. Ray, 1983, pp. 55–65.
[2] Howay, 1973, pp. 141–2; D. J. Ray, 1983, pp. 1–14.

found itself with a surplus of men and ships in the Royal Navy. This situation was quickly exploited by the energetic second secretary of the Admiralty, John (later Sir John) Barrow. Barrow was concerned that the Russians would discover a Northwest Passage before the English, who had been searching for it since Elizabethan times. He sent out four arctic expeditions in 1818 and 1819 and then began a more ambitious plan to discover a Northwest Passage and to chart the coasts of western arctic North America. These efforts had the support of the Hudson's Bay Company, which, like the Russian–American Company, was trying to expand its fur trading activities and territorial control in northern Alaska.

In 1825, however, Britain and Russia signed a treaty recognizing the 141st meridian as the boundary between British and Russian territories in arctic America. In 1824–5 Barrow sent out three expeditions. William Edward Parry was to try to sail through a northwest passage from the Atlantic to the Pacific, John Franklin was to lead a boat expedition down the Mackenzie River to its mouth, then west along the Alaskan coast. Both expeditions were to rendezvous in Kotzebue Sound with a third which would meet them there from the Pacific. Frederick William Beechey was to sail H.M.S. *Blossom* to the rendezvous with Franklin and Parry. He was ordered to wait for the two groups in Kotzebue Sound in 1826. If they had not arrived by the end of the summer, he was to go south and return in the summer of 1827.[1]

The *Blossom* reached Kotzebue Sound in July 1825 and continued north along the coast. At Icy Cape, Cook's farthest point of advance, Beechey, wary of probing farther and risking his ship, hoisted out the ship's barge and sent it on under the command of the *Blossom*'s master, Thomas Elson. Elson and his men became the first Europeans to see, among other features, Wainwright Inlet, Point Belcher, Point Franklin, Cape Smyth, Elson Lagoon, and finally Point Barrow, the northernmost point in Alaska.

The barge reached Point Barrow at 2 a.m. on 13 August 1826, and Elson tentatively named the point 'World's End', because he could see no land to the east, west, or north. Nuvuk, the village there, was the largest they had seen along the coast. At first two umiaks came off to them and the Eskimos seemed unsure as to whether they should approach the vessel. The sailors gave them some tobacco and

[1] Gough, 1973, p. 18; Ritchie, 1967, pp. 147–56.

3

beads, and, after they had returned to shore, other groups visited the barge. Soon the Eskimos started to steal from them, and Elson broke off contact. The aggressive behaviour of the Eskimos forced the British to conclude that it would be unsafe for them to go ashore to leave a message for Franklin.

Elson then took the barge north about a mile for astronomical observations. When the barge returned to the point, the British found twenty Eskimos waiting for them at the water's edge. They were armed with bows, arrows, and spears.[1] William Smyth, the ship's mate noted that the Eskimos thought that the English wanted to land:

they made signs for us to remain on board. They appeared quite prepared for hostilities, some of them nearly naked and, preserving a more than ordinary silence, but one spoke at a time, seemingly interrogating us with regard to our intentions. The natives kept walking abreast to us.

The barge then continued south along shore, and about 8 PM we passed a village[2] of 6 or 8 tents and 4 boats but saw neither women nor children: previous to our reaching this place we perceived them hauling their [umiaks] higher up. About 11 our friends having tired of the chase stopped and after watching us for some time longer, returned.[3]

The barge then continued south and reached the *Blossom* on 10 September in Kotzebue Sound. Although Elson had succeeded in charting more than a hundred miles of previously unknown coast, he had failed to meet Franklin or Parry.

Parry had been blocked by ice in the eastern Arctic. Franklin had descended the Mackenzie River with four boats. Then, at the head of the delta, he had divided the group into two parties to explore the Arctic coast both east and west of the river's mouth. After a tense encounter with the Mackenzie Eskimos at the western edge of the delta, he had reached Herschel Island on 17 July.

He learned from the Eskimos here that they traded annually with the 'western' Eskimos and with the Indians who lived south of the mountains for 'iron, knives and beads' and that they knew of the use of tobacco, having seen the 'western' Eskimos using it, 'but thought the flavour very disagreeable'.[4]

[1] Bockstoce, 1977, pp. 113–16.
[2] Probably the campsite of Pirginik, several miles south of Point Barrow on the sandspit.
[3] Smyth, n.d., p. 118.
[4] Franklin, 1828, pp. 130–1.

On 27 July Franklin's party passed the 141st meridian and entered Russian America. On 4 August they came upon a group of tents on a low island just to the west of today's Barter Island. Fifty-four adult Eskimos were camped there, having just completed their annual trade with the 'western' Eskimos. Franklin reached his farthest advance at the Return Islands, only 150 nautical miles from Point Barrow. On 17 August he turned back, deciding that the summer was too far advanced and that consequently further progress was dangerous. Together, his and Beechey's expeditions had succeeded in charting all but a small section of coast between Icy Cape and the Mackenzie River. Beechey returned to Kotzebue Sound the following year and continued his cartographic work. When the *Blossom* left Bering Strait in October 1827, no British vessels were to visit the region for 21 years.

Although Beechey's 1827 voyage marked a pause in exploration by British vessels, the pace of foreign contact quickened as both the Hudson's Bay Company and the Russian–American Company sought to expand the territories under their control. The Russian–American Company established trading posts at St Michael, on Norton Sound near the Yukon delta in 1833, at Nulato on the middle Yukon in 1839, and at the Unalakleet on Norton Sound in 1840 or 1841;[1] and during those years its vessels probably made several trading voyages into Kotzebue Sound as well.

In 1837 the Hudson's Bay Company began its own expansion into Alaska by sending Peter Dease and Thomas Simpson on a boat voyage to survey the coast between the farthest explorations of Beechey's and Franklin's expeditions. On 9 July 1837, Dease and Simpson left the Mackenzie delta and headed west along the Arctic coast. They passed Barter Island on the 16th and the next day in Camden Bay, possibly near Konganevik Point, encountered a large group of Mackenzie Eskimos who probably were camped there for the annual trade rendezvous with the north Alaskan Eskimos. On 24 July they passed the point where Franklin had had to turn back and entered waters where no European had ever been. They reached the Colville River, naming it after one of the members of the Hudson's Bay Company's committee. At Cape Simpson the ice prevented further progress to the west, so Thomas Simpson continued ahead on foot. On the east shore of Dease Inlet he came upon an Eskimo camp, where he was

---

[1] VanStone, 1984, p. 235; D. J. Ray, 1984.

able to rent an umiak. He noted that these were the first Eskimos who asked him for tobacco, 'of which the men, women, and even children were inordinately fond. This taste they had, of course, acquired in their indirect intercourse with the Russians; for the Esquimaux we had last parted with were ignorant of the luxury.'[1]

Simpson continued on westward in Elson Lagoon and shortly before 1 a.m. on 4 August he saw Point Barrow. He landed at Niksurak, the sandy hook halfway between the point and the settlement of Pirginik. Although the Eskimo men seemed extremely suspicious and hostile, they had no firearms. Simpson headed for the tents at Pirginik and soon a brisk trade sprang up between the two groups:

The grand article in demand here was tobacco, which, as in Dease Inlet, they call tawac, or tawacah . . . Not content with chewing and smoking it, they swallowed the fumes till they became sick, and seemed to revel in a momentary intoxication. Beads, rings, buttons, fire-steels, everything we had, were regarded as inferior to tobacco, a single inch of which was an acceptable equivalent for the most valuable article they possessed . . .

When about to embark, our paddles were missing. As these implements were essential to us, and could be of little value to the thieves, I insisted upon their being restored. After some hesitation, one of the men, stepping aside, laughingly dug them out of the sand . . .[2]

Simpson then retraced his route to where Dease was camped. After returning the umiak to its owners, they started east. On 11 August near Demarcation Point (the Russian–British boundary) they met again with the same group of Mackenzie Eskimos they had seen in Camden Bay and who were returning from the trade rendezvous with the Indians and north Alaskan Eskimos. 'They knew at once that we had been among the far west Esquimaux from the boots we wore, which were of a wider and clumsier shape than their own.'[3] Dease and Simpson then retraced their route up the Mackenzie River. For the next two summers they carried out equally important explorations of the continental coast near Victoria and King William Islands.

In 1838, the year after Dease and Simpson's Alaskan explorations, the Russians reached Point Barrow. The impetus for their arrival was Baron Ferdinand von Wrangell, the former general manager of

[1] Simpson, 1843, p. 147.
[2] Simpson, 1843, p. 157.
[3] Simpson, 1843, p. 177.

the Russian–American Company. Knowing full well the territorial control that exploration for fur trading brought, he proposed to the company's general administration that an expedition should be sent to northern Alaska to close the unexplored gap between Beechey's and Franklin's surveys. Accordingly in 1837 preparations were begun for an expedition to be led by A. F. Kashevarov.

On 17 July 1838[1] the brig *Polyphem* reached Cape Lisburne and discharged Kashevarov's party into five three-hatch Aleutian kayaks and one large umiak. Among the crew was a capable interpreter, the first to accompany an expedition in northern Alaska. On 26 July the group passed Icy Cape, and two days later they reached the village of Ulrunig, the present site of the town of Wainwright. On 4 August they reached Point Barrow and entered waters that they supposed had never been visited by foreigners; they were unaware that Thomas Simpson had been there almost exactly a year before.

Kashevarov wrote:

As we rounded Point Barrow, 32 natives in two [umiaks] came out from the settlement (Nuvuk) toward us and were about to release a cloud of arrows at us, but their insolence ceased when they saw that we were ready to defend ourselves.[2]

The group pushed on and entered Elson Lagoon, charting the south coast. On 6 August they were close to Tangent Point, where they made camp near a group of Point Barrow Eskimos. The Eskimos soon began to try to steal from the Russians and then threatened to attack them in large numbers and kill them. Later 40 Eskimo men, all armed with bows, arrived and began to threaten the explorers. Kashevarov, outnumbered, sensibly decided that it was best to turn back. On 7 August they rounded Point Barrow again and headed south, reaching the *Polyphem* in Kotzebue Sound on 17 September.

At the same time the Hudson's Bay Company was continuing its expansion into Alaska from the east. In 1840 it made direct contact with the Mackenzie Eskimos by establishing a trading post (later called Fort McPherson) close to the Mackenzie delta on the Peel River. In 1845 it sent an exploratory party over the divide and into the Yukon drainage, and in 1847 Alexander Hunter Murray set up the Fort Yukon post at the confluence of the Yukon and Porcupine

---

[1] I have converted Kashevarov's dates from the Julian to the Gregorian calendar.
[2] VanStone, 1977, p. 36.

rivers – more than one hundred miles inside the border of Russian-America. This post supplied trade goods to the Kutchin Indians, who also traded with the Eskimos on the Arctic coast.

All of these events were, however, essentially a preamble to the large-scale invasion by the outside world, which began in 1848. Two unrelated phenomena caused these incursions.

In that year the search for Sir John Franklin's expedition began in the west with the cruise of H.M.S. *Herald* and the wintering of H.M.S. *Plover*. These ships were the van of a British presence that would remain for the next seven years and involve nine vessels and seven winterings.

Of even greater and more long-lasting significance for the western Arctic and its peoples was the arrival in 1848 of the first whaling vessel at Bering Strait. By 1852 more than 200 whaleships were cruising in those waters. The presence of the whaling fleet was constant in western Alaskan waters from then until the outbreak of the First World War, and in all, whaleships made more than 2,700 cruises there. The whaling fleet not only nearly exterminated the bowhead whale and walrus populations but they also soon developed a brisk trade with the natives.

After the purchase of Alaska in 1867, the United States government expanded its influence slowly. The year 1879 marked the first annual cruise of the U.S. revenue cutters north of Bering Strait – to curtail the trade in alcohol and other contraband. The second important year-round foreign presence at Point Barrow occurred from 1881 to 1883 when the U.S. Army's Signal Service manned a meteorological station there as part of the first International Polar Year. The station was deserted for one winter, but in 1884 it was leased to a whaling company, and foreigners have been living near Point Barrow ever since.

THE ESKIMOS OF POINT BARROW IN THE
MID-NINETEENTH CENTURY

When the *Plover* arrived at Point Barrow in 1852, her crew encountered an Eskimo society that had experienced relatively little direct contact with foreigners. Two miles west of the *Plover*'s anchorage was the village of Nuvuk, located at the very tip of the Point Barrow sandspit. The villagers were members of a larger Eskimo society, the Kakligmiut, that in the 1840s comprised several villages and occupied the territory from Point Belcher in the west to Point Christie in the east and inland for about 25 miles.

The Kakligmiut were one of twenty-five Eskimo societies that spoke the Inupiaq dialect and occupied northwestern Alaska.[1] Each of these societies had grown from a common ancestral population that had entered Alaska from northwestern Asia between about AD 500 and AD 800. In the following millennium these Eskimos spread into every unoccupied and habitable area from Norton Sound to the Colville River delta, exploiting the combination of food resources that were to be found in each.[2] As time passed the population increased and the territories of each group became clearly defined. It seems likely that one result of this increase was the development of conflicts among the various societies, conflicts which grew to such a level that warfare became a normal part of life.[3]

The anthropologist Ernest S. Burch, Jr, has written: 'Despite the conventional image of Eskimos as being peaceable friendly people, the traditional *Inupiat* of Northwest Alaska were aggressive fighters who had developed a relatively elaborate pattern of conducting warfare . . . The members of most societies considered themselves to be under constant threat of attack from their neighbours.'[4] There were, nevertheless, mechanisms by which safe passage would be allowed in another society's territory. This was established, on the one hand, by inter-personal alliances between members of different societies via the mechanisms of trading partnerships and co-marriages (often called 'spouse exchanges') and, on the other, during the general truce that existed in the height of summer to allow people to travel safely across territorial boundaries to the annual trade fairs at Nirliq in the Colville River delta, at Sheshalik on Kotzebue

[1] Burch, 1980 *passim*.   [2] Bockstoce, 1973, 1978b, pp. 93–5.
[3] Burch, 1980, p. 273.   [4] Burch, 1980, p. 272.

9

Sound, at Barter Island, and at other places as well.[1] Strangers who lacked the protection of these conventions were greeted with hostility;[2] hence the Eskimos' routine aggressiveness against foreign expeditions – which usually always increased in proportion to the Eskimos' relative numbers versus the foreign party's numbers.

At the village level, Eskimo life was organized into one or more extended local families, each of which included several pairs of husbands and wives, as well as parents, grandparents, and children, and often extending collaterally as far as second cousins. The members of this family unit inhabited two or more adjacent houses – wooden semi-subterranean structures covered by earth and sod. In the large communities, such as Point Hope and Point Barrow, there were several extended families, each with as many as 100 members. Each family was roughly equal in rank, and each had a leader, an *umialik*; the more effective the *umialik*, the more people who wished to benefit from his leadership, and hence the larger the extended family. Each family unit worked and hunted together, sharing food and other products. When they were not hunting or travelling, the men and boys spent much of their time working or relaxing in *qazgi* – the family's community house – where the women brought them food and joined them on ceremonial occasions.[3]

The village of Nuvuk was located at approximately 71°24'N,[4] a position where the sun is below or above the horizon continuously for 72 days. In this setting the average daily temperature for the year ranges between +15.9°F (−8.9°C) and +4.2°F (−15.4°C), with recorded extremes being +78°F (25.6°C) and −56°F (−49°C). There is only about 4 inches of precipitation per year.[5]

The village was surrounded by water: the Chukchi Sea to the west, the Arctic Ocean to the north, the Beaufort Sea to the east, and Elson Lagoon to the south. Although they exploited virtually every food resource that was available to them, it is not surprising that the livelihood of the Point Barrow Eskimos was heavily dependent upon marine resources and that sea ice played an important part in their lives.

The year, for the Point Barrow Eskimos, can be said to have begun in September, when most of them had returned to Nuvuk

[1] Burch, 1980, p. 274.   [2] Spencer, 1959, p. 72.   [3] Burch, 1980, *passim*.
[4] The sea has since almost totally eroded it away.
[5] *United States Coast Pilot, Alaska* (vol. 9), 7th edition, 1964, Washington, D.C., U.S. Government Printing Office.

from their summer's trading and hunting expeditions. They repaired their houses in preparation for the winter and then got ready for the autumn whaling season. By that time the bowhead whales (*Balaena mysticetus*) would be returning from their summer feeding grounds in the eastern Beaufort Sea and would be slowly moving past Point Barrow. The Eskimos paddled their 18-foot umiaks, skin boats, after them in the relatively ice-free waters of September. The largest bowheads are more than sixty feet long and can weigh more than sixty tons. If the Eskimos were lucky enough to harpoon and kill one or two, the meat and blubber – added to what they had caught in the spring whale hunt – would insure a winter without famine.

The ocean usually begins to freeze in early October at Point Barrow. Slush ice begins to form out from the shore while the pack ice, which can have retreated as many as 100 miles during the summer, begins its southerly advance. From then until later November or early December, the hunting conditions were particularly treacherous and unrewarding on the young sea ice – and the Eskimos enjoyed their only leisure time of the year. The men and boys spent most of the time in the *qazgi*, resting, working on tools, and telling stories.

By the beginning of December, the sea ice had usually increased enough in thickness to allow some seal (*Phoca hispida*) hunting at that time of year. The Eskimos took these animals both by spearing them through their breathing holes and by setting nets under the ice, which the seals were unable to see in the dark mid-winter nights.

As January wore on, the daylight increased; so also did the Eskimos' hunting activities. Their food stocks were usually low by then; consequently the pace of seal hunting was stepped up and time was devoted to jigging tomcod (*Boreogadus saida*) through holes in the ice. Other families moved inland for three months to hunt for caribou (*Rangifer tarandus*). Both caribou and seals were necessary, the former for their warm hide for clothing, the latter for their rich oil for light, heat, and food.

In April the caribou hunters returned to Nuvuk to begin preparations for the spring whale hunt. At the end of April a north–south lead usually opens between the shore-fast ice and the moving polar pack ice, and it is in this narrow waterway that the bowhead whales migrate northward toward the Beaufort Sea. The Eskimo whaling crews dragged their umiaks to the lead edge to wait for the whales to pass. If they caught a dozen or more, there was cause for rejoicing because famine would be unlikely for a year.

Most of the bowheads had pased Point Barrow by the end of June, by which time the ice was in such a state of disintegration that the crews returned to shore to prepare for the annual whaling festival, a social ceremony in which the family groups that had been successful in the whale hunt distributed the whale products among others in their own and nearby villages. At the same time hunters would paddle among the broken ice floes, hunting for bearded seals (*Erignathus barbatus*). These large seals were sought primarily for their skins to use as boat coverings and boot soles.

As soon as the whaling feast was over, the Point Barrow Eskimos dispersed to take advantage of the several food resources that were available in the Arctic summer. Some merely moved a few miles south on the sandspit to the site of Pirginik, a point where millions of eider ducks cross the spit on their southward migration. There the hunters could take vast quantities of ducks with their bolas. Some Eskimos chose to remain all summer at Nuvuk, hunting the basking walruses and seals on the ice floes that drifted past the point. Other Eskimos moved inland to the rivers south of Point Barrow for a combination of gill net fishing, catching moulting ducks, and caribou hunting. Still others moved east, laden with goods, to the trade rendezvous at Nirliq in the Colville River delta to meet natives who lived for the greater part of the year in the interior. The Point Barrow Eskimos usually traded their sea mammal oil and products in return for caribou skins and Russian trade goods. The interior Eskimos would have obtained these manufactured goods the previous summer at the trade rendezvous at Sheshalik on Kotzebue Sound, where they met Bering Strait Eskimos and, occasionally, Asian natives.

After the Nirliq fair was over, some of the Point Barrow Eskimos moved even farther east to Barter Island, where they encountered the Mackenzie Eskimos, and even some Indians, to trade their sea mammal products and Russian goods in return for wolverine skins and other furs – as well as for English manufactured goods, and stone lamps. The English goods were obtained from the Hudson's Bay Company's trading posts, and the stone lamps from the Copper Eskimos who quarried the stone south of Victoria Island.

By the middle of September most of the families had returned to Nuvuk to prepare for the autumn whale hunt. A few families remained inland, however, to continue fishing and caribou hunting until returning to Nuvuk in late November for the communal ceremonies that took place during the darkest days of the year. At this time of the year there was often a Messenger Feast, a ceremony in which an individual of wealth and power invited another, with his entourage, from a distant community for a celebration of gift giving – in the full expectation of a reciprocal invitation and equal largesse.[1]

Many of the food resources upon which the Eskimos depended could vary widely in availability from year to year, and consequently the Eskimos were very flexible in switching to another food source when a particular one was not abundant. It is often maintained that famine became a problem for the Alaskan Eskimos only after foreigners entered the region and depleted its natural resources, but in fact barren times were well known before the beginning of foreign contact. Caribou populations, for instance, experience steep cyclical rises and falls in their numbers. Similarly, weather and ice conditions can also play a role in the Eskimos' ability to hunt sea mammals: the famine of 1853–4 (recorded by Maguire) is proof of this. Thus it seems likely that, as Ernest S. Burch, Jr, contends, the Point Barrow Eskimos' nearest neighbouring society, the people who inhabited the Meade and Chipp river drainages, was dispersed by a famine in the 1840s. The survivors fled in three directions: north to the villages of the Kakligmiut; west to the Silalinarmiut and to the society that inhabited the lower and middle drainages of the Colville River.[2] It seems logical that the uninhabited lands were absorbed by these three societies – as well as, possibly, by the Nuatarmiut of the upper Noatak River drainage.

Thus the *Plover*'s crew at Point Barrow encountered an Eskimo society that was at once isolated and cosmopolitan, aggressive and vulnerable.

---

[1] Sonnenfeld, 1957, *passim*; P. H. Ray, 1885, *passim*; Spencer, 1959, *passim*.
[2] Burch, 1980, p. 285.

THE SEARCH FOR SIR JOHN FRANKLIN IN ALASKA

In January 1848 H.M.S. *Plover* sailed from England on a seven-year voyage to Bering Strait and the western Arctic. She was sent in search of Sir John Franklin's expedition which nearly three years before had vanished into the Arctic while searching for a Northwest Passage. The *Plover's* was the first of a long series of sea and land expeditions that took part in the search. Although more than three quarters of a million pounds were spent on the effort, at the beginning no one knew where Franklin had gone and at the end only one essential fact was confirmed: that Franklin and all his men had perished.[1]

Since the *Plover's* departure a number of writers have addressed the subject of the search for Franklin and most of these writers have understandably focused on the activities that occurred in the eastern Arctic. In fact, for two reasons the *Plover's* voyage – as well as the entire search for Franklin in Alaska – has received comparatively little attention. Although the fleet that operated via Bering Strait consisted of eight ships that made seven winterings, this was only about a fourth the size of the eastern fleet. And although the operations in the eastern Arctic were mostly too far north and west of where Franklin's men were lost, they were at least nearer than the Alaskan searches which took place between one and two thousand miles from the last position of Franklin's ships. Nevertheless, the Alaskan searches had a sound basis in logic and they were carried out efficiently with a minimum of fuss – against the dual impediments of being 17,000 miles by sea from England and with communications arriving only once a year.

When Franklin departed from England in 1845 he headed a superbly outfitted expedition. He had an excellent staff of nearly 150 men and two strong ships. His provisions were ample for three years with a year's leeway; hence there was little concern for the men's safety until two years had passed without word from the expedition. At that point, with anxiety rising, the Lords Commissioners of the Admiralty began planning expeditions to meet Franklin the following year, but his orders had been drafted so loosely that it was impossible to know where he might have gone. Depending on how successful he had been in traversing a Northwest Passage, Franklin's

---

[1] Gibson, 1937, p. 53.

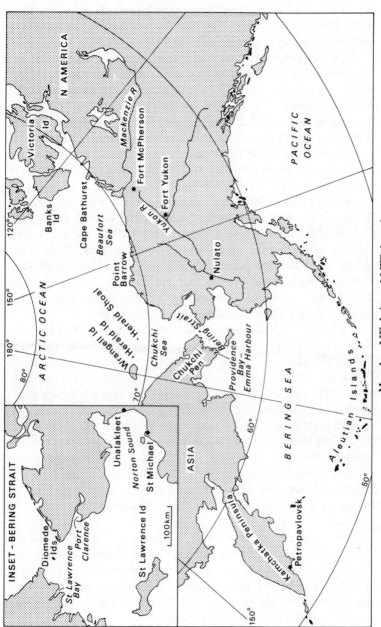

Map 1. NE Asia and NW America.

15

expedition could have been found anywhere in the vast area from Baffin Bay to Bering Strait. To cover the possibilities, the Admiralty sent out three separate expeditions in 1848.

The eastern expedition was led by Sir James Clark Ross who was given two ships, H.M.S. *Enterprise* and H.M.S. *Investigator*. He was to follow Franklin's presumed route, entering the Arctic via Baffin Bay and Lancaster Sound. The second expedition, led by Sir John Richardson and assisted by Dr John Rae of the Hudson's Bay Company, was to concentrate on the central area. They were to descend the Mackenzie River and travel east along the continental coast as far as Coppermine River. If Franklin had completed part of a northwest passage, he might be found on this stretch of coast.

The third expedition was to enter the Arctic from the west via Bering Strait. Two ships were chosen for the western expedition. One, H.M.S. *Herald*, under Captain Henry Kellett, was at that time engaged in charting the west coast of Central America. To assist the *Herald* the Admiralty planned to send out from England H.M.S. *Plover*, a sturdy, beamy vessel that had formerly been in the East India Company service. The *Plover*, laden with supplies, was to winter at Bering Strait as a depot ship for Franklin.

The Lords Commissioners of the Admiralty planned to have the *Plover* meet the *Herald* at Panama in the spring of 1848. The ships were to sail together to the town of Petropavlovsk on the Kamchatka Peninsula. There they were to take aboard interpreters for their work in the north. The ships were supposed to reach Bering Strait about 1 July 1848 and then to send four whaleboats north along the Alaskan coast to search for a good winter harbour for the *Plover*. The *Herald* was then to transfer additional supplies to the *Plover* before heading south for the winter. The Lords of the Admiralty also decided to send Lieutenant W. J. S. Pullen to join the *Plover* at Panama. He was to lead a boat expedition along the north coast of Alaska as far as the Mackenzie River, searching for evidence of Franklin.

These expeditions thus were intended to cover the entire continental coast of North America from Bering Strait to the Coppermine River in the summer of 1848. But the western division of the search started badly. Almost immediately the plans were changed – and for the next six years the expeditions in the west had to improvise to accomplish their mission.

The *Plover*'s orders were changed at once – possibly in recognition

16

that only one vessel would be needed to procure intelligence and interpreters while the other's time could be more profitably spent at Bering Strait. The *Plover* was ordered to bypass Petropavlovsk and to go directly to Bering Strait from Panama. The *Herald* alone would now stop at Petropavlovsk.

Other complications set in. The *Herald*'s captain, Henry Kellett, found that there were not enough fresh provisions available at Panama for both the *Herald* and the *Plover*. Furthermore, by the end of March 1848 Rear Admiral G. F. Seymour, Commander-in-Chief of the Royal Navy's Pacific Station at Valparaiso, Chile, realized that time was getting very short for the expedition to reach Bering Strait during the brief season of open water. He sent a steamer to Panama to tow the *Herald* west, out of the calms of the Gulf of Panama, so she could sail to Honolulu quickly. There she could take on provisions in a port accustomed to providing vast quantities of stores for the American whaling fleet. At Honolulu the *Herald* could also wait for the the *Plover*. The *Plover* was already at sea, but it was likely that she would touch at one of the ports on the west coast of South America. Seymour intended to instruct her captain, Commander T. E. L. Moore, to go directly to Hawaii.[1]

This change of plans meant that Lieutenant Pullen arrived in Panama only to find that the *Plover* would not touch there. With no way to join the *Plover* until the following summer, Pullen served aboard H.M.S. *Asia*, the flagship of the Pacific fleet, until 1849, when he was taken aboard the *Herald* for her return to Bering Strait.[2]

The *Plover* herself was forcing a change in the already much-changed plans. Although she proved to be sea-kindly, the *Plover* was slow – even in gale-force winds and under a press of sail. By May, when she should have been near Hawaii, she had only reached the Falkland Islands.

Also in May the *Herald* left Panama under tow. Apparently Kellett had been able to obtain his provisions in Central America after all because he sent his companion surveying vessel, H.M.S. *Pandora*, to Honolulu to wait for the *Plover* while he headed for Kamchatka. But the *Plover* was moving so slowly that not until 4 July did she reach Callao, Lima's seaport. By then the *Herald* was nearly 6,000 miles ahead of her.

---

[1] Great Britain, 1848, pp, 1, 74–81; Great Britain, 1849a, pp. 11–20.
[2] Pullen, 1979, pp. 27–30.

The *Herald* was also moving slowly. On 8 August, a month after she was due in Bering Strait according to instructions, she reached Petropavlovsk, the last remotely civilized outpost on the way to Bering Strait. Kellett remained there a week, learning what he could of the lands and seas before him and hoping in vain that the *Plover* might overtake him. Kellett knew, however, that the autumn weather in Bering Strait was brutal; if he were to have any time for searching for Franklin in 1848, he had to push on at once.[1]

The *Herald* arrived at St Michael, a Russian–American Company trading post on Norton Sound near the mouth of the Yukon River, at the beginning of September. There Kellett took aboard an interpreter, Pavil Aglayuk. Bosky, as the British called him, was a half-breed native from Kodiak who had spent some time in Bodega Bay, California, at the Russian–American Company's southernmost post, Fort Ross. Although he spoke no English and the British spoke no Russian, they could communicate in Spanish.[2]

On 14 September the *Herald* reached Chamisso Island in Kotzebue Sound, north of Bering Strait. The men climbed to the top of the island and found a monument pole with carved records of Kotzebue's discovery of the Sound in 1816, of subsequent visits by Russian vessels, and of Frederick William Beechey's visit in 1826. There was, however, no record of Franklin having visited the island. The *Herald* was the first British vessel to pass north of Bering Strait in twenty-one years.[3]

Mid-September is late in the Arctic autumn. Most of the natives who had camped at Chamisso in the summer had already moved up the rivers to their winter quarters. The sailors found only four natives and they were too frightened to be of much use as informants. One, however, told Bosky an odd tale, recounted by one of the *Herald*'s crew:

Our Russian interpreter was here informed by an old man, that he had heard from a person who had just arrived from the head of the Buckland river, that 'he had *seen* a party of men dressed like sailors, with an officer, having a gold band on his cap and brass buttons. They had come from a main body, who were further inland, and had bought up all the venison; they could not speak, nor make themselves understood to any of the natives; the spot where they are is ten days' journey from this overland, but a boat could reach it in a very short time.'[4]

[1] Seemann, 1853, II, pp. 5–9.
[2] Great Britain, 1849a, p. 16; Seemann, 1853, II, p. 8.
[3] Ray, 1983, pp. 95–102. [4] [Euryalus], 1860, pp. 228–9.

'A piece of information which,' according to Bertold Seemann, the naturalist aboard the *Herald*, 'opened a field for various but fruitless endeavours.'

The *Herald*'s men made a brief reconnaissance of Eschscholtz Bay to check on the rumour, but the weather quickly turned so cold that Kellett feared that he might be frozen in for the winter. They hoisted anchor on 29 September and passed through Bering Strait on 2 October.

Heavy weather forced them to pass by St Michael on their way south. Shortening the trip to the tropics no doubt cheered the sailors, but Bosky could hardly have been pleased; the *Herald*'s next port of call was Petropavlovsk, where Kellett put the interpreter ashore to spend the winter. It was a year before Bosky was able to return to his home in St Michael. He was paid off at the rate of a dollar a day for his summer's work, plus some winter clothing from the ship's stores. The *Herald* then headed for Mazatlan, Mexico, to resume her surveying duties until her return to Bering Strait the following summer.[1]

In the meantime, no one knew where the *Plover* was. After the *Plover* had left Hawaii on 25 August it had taken her a month to reach the Aleutian Islands. Moore then sailed her toward Bering Strait via the safest but longest route, going west, around the Aleutians, a detour which added a thousand miles to the voyage. The *Plover* reached Saint Lawrence Island near Bering Strait in the middle of October, having unknowingly passed the southbound *Herald* about a week before. The island was covered with snow and the men knew that winter was not far away.

Moore pressed on, but he was under a severe handicap. He had not received the charts of the area that the Admiralty had sent him. He sailed northward cautiously, sounding frequently as he worked his way around the west end of Saint Lawrence Island. Three days later he saw that the *Plover* was not only making no progress against the northeast wind and current, but had slipped back thirty miles on her previous day's position. He took the most sensible course of action. Closing with the shore of the Chukchi Peninsula, he began searching for a sheltered winter anchorage.[2]

He was lucky. Almost at once the men spotted a cleft in the high

[1] *Herald*, logbook; Seemann, 1853, II, p. 70.
[2] Great Britain, 1850, p. 35; *Plover*, logbook.

19

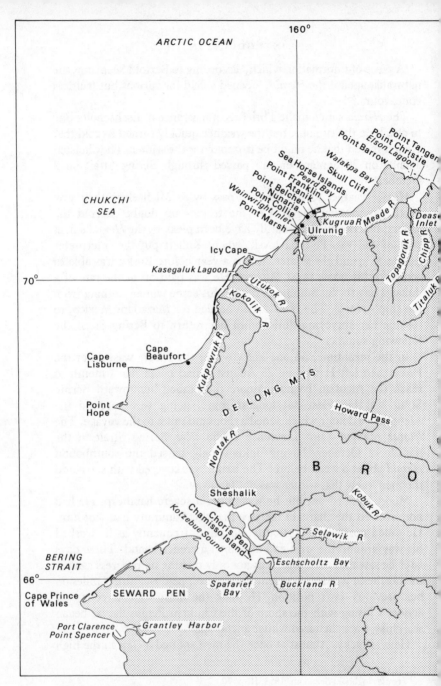

Map 2.   Northern Alaska.

20

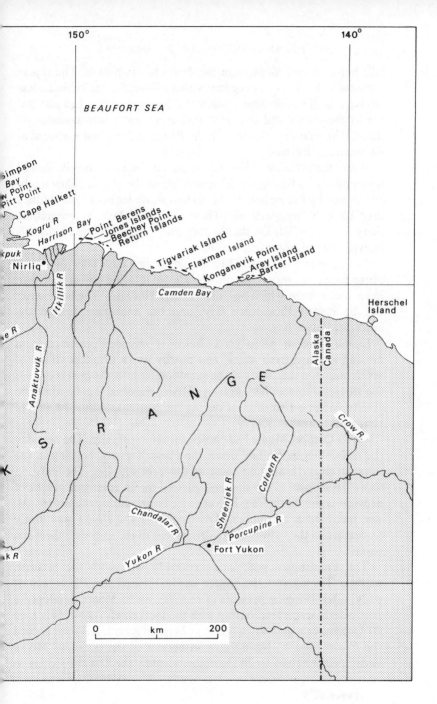

BEAUFORT SEA

Simpson Bay
W Point
Pitt Point
Cape Halkett
Kogru R
Harrison Bay
Point Berens
Jones Islands
Beechey Point
Return Islands
kpuk
Nirliq
Itkillik R
Anaktuvuk R
e R
K
k R
Tigvariak Island
Flaxman Island
Konganevik Point
Arey Island
Barter Island
Camden Bay
Herschel Island
Alaska
Canada
Crow R
Coleen R
Sheenjek R
Chandalar R
Porcupine R
Fort Yukon
Yukon R

S   R   A   N   G   E

0   km   200

150°   140°

hills before them. Moore sent two boats to examine it. The report came back that it was a deep bay with a safe anchorage behind a low sandspit. In the meantime a number of the local natives had paddled out to the *Plover* and indicated that fresh water was available on shore. The next day Moore took the *Plover* inshore and anchored at the mouth of the bay.[1]

Moore then canvassed his officers on how best to proceed. Should they push on to Bering Strait? It was late in the season. They might be trapped by the ice and unable to find a safe harbour. Should they drop back to Petropavlovsk? There their usefulness as a searching party would be nil. Or should they stay where they were, in this unexplored but promising harbour?

The answer was clear. They stayed. A few days later the water began to freeze. Moore moved the *Plover* into the bay and into an inner embayment which he called Emma Harbour. The large outer bay he named Providence Bay, and the anchorage behind the sandspit, Plover Bay.

Emma Harbour was a good choice. It was well protected from moving ice, had fresh water, and nearby was a Chukchi village of seven huts. On the slopes of the surrounding hills the men could see the village's reindeer herd grazing. Moore reasoned that he would be able to barter for fresh meat during the winter and thus be able to combat the onset of scurvy.

On 28 October Moore had chosen the wintering site. The next day the sailors began sending down the *Plover*'s yards, housing-in the upper deck and building a house on shore for supplies. The house on shore freed space in the ship and allowed for an emergency cache of provisions should the ship be lost to ice or fire during the winter. All was ready on 8 November. Ten days later the *Plover* was firmly frozen in and the natives began driving out to the ship with their dog teams.

The Englishmen got along extremely well with the Siberian natives. Throughout the winter natives visited the *Plover* almost daily, often bringing presents of reindeer meat. Moore developed a particularly warm relationship with the local chief, Akool. When on 20 December a granddaughter was born to Akool, the men aboard the *Plover* fired a 21-gun salute in honour of the occasion. Moore christened the child on 28 December – surely the first christening to

[1] Hooper, 1853, p. 12.

take place on the Chukchi Peninsula. In celebration they fired rockets from the ship.

A by-product of the sailors' association with the Chukchi was the natives' acquisition of a taste for alcoholic spirits, which they called *Tanuk*. The word '*tanuk*' was attributed to Moore. It was said that when Moore was on the trail he would occasionally stop for a drink of rum, saying to his guide, 'Come, Joe, let's take our tonic.'

Whenever the natives visited the ship the sailors quizzed them for information about any white men that might have been reported in the country. And as soon as the men had learned a bit of the native language Moore sent out travelling parties to search for Franklin's men.

One of these parties, led by the mate, William Hulme Hooper, reached as far as East Cape, Siberia, to check on the report of a shipwreck near there. The rumour may well have been a garbled account of the sighting of the American whaling bark *Superior*. In the summer of 1848 the *Superior*'s captain, Thomas Roys, had sailed her a thousand miles beyond the rest of the whaling fleet to explore for whales in the Bering Strait region. He spent a month cruising there, and the *Superior* and the *Herald* were probably the only foreign vessels to pass through Bering Strait that summer.

Despite the efforts of the *Herald*'s and *Plover*'s men, by the spring of 1849 the sum of their efforts had revealed only that Franklin's men were not near Kotzebue Sound, nor were they on the Chukchi Peninsula. Perhaps the only useful product was that the crews of both vessels had honed their skills in polar navigation and the *Herald*'s men had developed skills for living through the Arctic winter in the comparatively benign environment of the Chukchi Peninsula.

At the beginning of April 1849 the edge of the shore-fast ice at the mouth of Providence Bay began to break up, signalling to the *Plover*'s men that spring was approaching. Moore set the crew to rerigging the ship for sea. While the margin of open water moved farther into Providence Bay toward the ship, the sailors began sawing a trench out of Emma Harbour. On 13 June the *Plover* was afloat in relatively clear water although loose floating ice still hemmed the ship in.

Almost at once Moore received word that the natives had sighted two ships not far away. He sent Henry Martin, the second master of the *Plover*, to investigate. A few days later Martin boarded the

H.M.S. *Herald* and H.M.S. *Plover* in Bering Strait, 1849.

BOATS PROCEEDING TO THE MACKENZIE RIVER

Lt Pullen's boat expedition at Wainwright Inlet leaving for the Mackenzie River, 25 July 1849. Left to right, H.M.S. *Herald*, Pullen's four boats, H.M.S. *Plover*, yacht *Nancy Dawson*.

American whaleship *Tiger* of Stonington, Connecticut, and the
British sailors found that they would have plenty of company in the
Arctic. Reports of the *Superior*'s whaling success in 1848 drew fifty
whaleships to Bering Strait in 1849. By 1852 the number had grown
to more than two hundred.[1]

The *Plover* finally reached her designated rendezvous at Chamisso
Island on 13 July 1849 – a year and a half after she had sailed from
England. Moore climbed to the top of the island and found the post
with the names of the ships that had been there before. He thus
learned for the first time that the *Herald* had been in Kotzebue
Sound in 1848.

But the *Plover* was still out of touch with the rest of the world and,
more important, the Lords of the Admiralty had not heard from any
of the search expeditions. No one knew where Franklin was. In the
winter of 1848–9 no word had been received in England from either
Sir James Clark Ross's expedition to the eastern Arctic or from
Richardson's and Rae's on the continental coast of the central Arctic.
As the navigation season of 1849 approached, the Lords of the
Admiralty, no better off than they had been in 1848, had to plan for
any number of contingencies.

The Lords Commissioners sent instructions to Captain Henry
Kellett, who was again surveying with the *Herald* at Panama, to
return north with a year's provisions for the *Plover*. To gain enough
room for the *Plover*'s stores he was to load the *Herald*'s guns and
equipment aboard the *Pandora*. Kellett was ordered to stop at
Honolulu and Petropavlovsk in case the *Plover* had wintered at
either place, and then to go to Kotzebue Sound. Should he not find
the *Plover* at Chamisso Island he was to search north along the
Alaskan coast as far as Point Barrow.

Should he not find the *Plover* anywhere, Kellett was to put the
Herald into winter quarters at Chamisso. If, however, Kellett should
find the *Plover*, he was to help her establish herself in a suitable
wintering site and then to leave for the south before the foul weather
of autumn set in. In that case the *Herald* was to go no farther south
than Honolulu in the winter of 1849–50 to be able to return quickly
to Bering Strait in the summer of 1850.

When Kellett received these orders in the spring of 1849, an

<hr/>

[1] Great Britain, 1850, pp. 35–7; Hooper, 1853, pp. 61–3; *Plover*, logbook;
Bockstoce, 1986.

epidemic of cholera was sweeping Central America and few supplies were available. Kellett took the *Herald* to Honolulu, where he took aboard not only fresh provisions but also Lieutenant W. J. S. Pullen, who had missed going aboard the *Plover* a year before. The *Herald* reached Petropavlovsk on 23 June. Kellett learned that the *Plover* had not been there but he heard a rumour that she had wintered somewhere to the north. To the Englishman's amazement, amid several American whaleships in the harbour was an English yacht, the schooner *Nancy Dawson* of the Royal Thames Yacht Club. Her owner, Robert Shedden, had brought her north from Hong Kong to help in the search for Franklin. The two vessels left the harbour together.

At 9 a.m. on 15 July, the day after the *Plover* reached Chamisso, the *Herald* stood in toward that anchorage. Only a few hours earlier Moore had sent out two boats under the command of Lieutenant W. A. R. Lee to survey the coast to the north. As soon as Moore saw the *Herald* he had the *Plover*'s guns fired, signalling Lee to bring the boats back.

The crews immediately began transferring supplies from the *Herald* to the *Plover*. A few men were exchanged as well, and principal among them was Lieutenant Pullen, who replaced Lee, and thus joined his ship fourteen months after he had left England.[1]

Kellett was the officer in charge. He examined the anchorage near Chamisso Island and judged it to be an acceptable place for the *Plover* to spend the coming winter. Then he and Moore went ashore and supervised a crew digging up a cask of flour and beads that Frederick William Beechey had buried for Franklin (who had then been on his second expedition to the American Arctic) more than twenty years before. Half the flour was found to be in good condition and Kellett entertained his officers with pies and puddings made from it.[2]

A few days later the *Herald* and *Plover* stood out of Kotzebue Sound together and almost at once saw the *Nancy Dawson* approaching. By 19 July the three ships were off Point Hope with bowhead whales spouting all around them and American whaleships in sight. Using boats to scout close to shore, the ships worked their way north through shoals of birds and seals and whales and the 'continual bellowing' of vast herds of walruses. They were frequently

[1] Great Britain, 1849a.   [2] Ritchie, 1967, pp. 258–9

boarded by Eskimos who, Kellett reported, came 'alongside fearlessly, and disposed of every article they had, the women selling their fur dresses, even to their second pair of breeches, for tobacco and beads'.

On 25 July they reached Wainwright Inlet. Kellett sent parties in to see whether the inlet could be used as a wintering site for the *Plover*. The men found, however, that the bar at the mouth of the inlet was too shallow for the ships.

Kellett pressed on with his fleet. Time was of the essence. Franklin's expedition had been out of touch by then for four years. Presumably the men were at the end of their supplies and possibly they were somewhere between Wainwright Inlet and the Mackenzie River. But it was considered dangerous for ships to proceed farther up this coast where no ships had ever been. Kellett also knew from Beechey's, Franklin's, and Dease and Simpson's explorations that the water was very shallow along shore as far as the Mackenzie. Kellett consequently ordered Pullen to begin his boat expedition to the Mackenzie.[1]

While the ships waited off Wainwright Inlet the men loaded four boats. The largest of the boats was the *Owen*, the *Herald*'s pinnace, a thirty-foot decked schooner. The *Plover*'s yawl-rigged pinnace was also to go. It was only half decked. Two partially covered 27-foot whaleboats made up the rest of the party. They were outfitted with more than seventy day's provisions for the twenty-five men as well as with extra rations for Franklin's men.

Pullen was instructed to try to go as far as the head of the Mackenzie delta and return to the *Plover* that summer – a total distance of 2,000 miles. This was clearly impossible. If he found himself unable to return, Pullen was to go up the Mackenzie to a trading post from which he could send messages overland to the Admiralty.

Pullen's expedition started out at Wainwright Inlet on the night of 25 July 1849.[2] In four days the boats were within ten miles of Point Barrow but there the men found themselves completely blocked by the ice. They tied up to a large grounded piece of ice to wait for a change in the pack and, to their surprise and comfort, the *Nancy Dawson* arrived to wait with them. The boats worked their way to Point Barrow on 1 August, but there they were again stopped by the pack which was hard on the land.

[1] Great Britain, 1850, p. 13.
[2] Pullen's account of his boat expedition (Great Britain, 1852a, pp. 23–33) is reprinted as Appendix One, pp. 445–58 below.

Pullen used the time to go ashore and trade with the natives. He bartered for an umiak to carry some of the supplies. After a wait of several hours, the ice began to lift and just as they were getting underway, the *Nancy Dawson* came into sight once again. Unsure whether or not the Eskimos were hostile, Shedden was doing his best to keep an eye on the boat expedition. The *Nancy Dawson* rounded the point and became the first ship to enter the Beaufort Sea.

Here Shedden turned back. Pullen pushed on and was at Cape Simpson two days later. There Pullen decided that the two larger boats would be a handicap in the shallow waters. He appointed Henry Martin to lead the *Owen* and the *Plover*'s pinnace back to the ships southwest of Point Barrow and continued eastward with 13 men in the two whaleboats and the umiak, heavily laden with provisions.

As they made their way across Harrison Bay two strong gales threatened to swamp Pullen's overloaded little boats. The men were soaked to the skin with the flying spray. At Point Berens on the east side of the bay they stopped to dry out and to bury a cache of provisions. They were met by a group of Eskimos who appeared to be friendly. While some of the men surreptitiously buried the cache, Pullen engaged the Eskimos' attention by handing out presents. But still uncertain about the Eskimos' intentions and hardly reassured when one Eskimo attempted to steal a shovel, Pullen got his men underway as soon as possible. They moved on a few miles before stopping to cook dinner. The Eskimos followed, their number increasing.

Pullen and his men pushed off again and passed several Eskimo camps, reaching Beechey Point early on the morning of 12 August. The point had been named by Franklin at his farthest westward penetration in 1826. They landed and were soon surrounded by a group of Eskimos that Pullen estimated to number at least eighty. To Pullen's surprise one of the Eskimos had a musket. No firearms were thought to have reached this region. The man with the musket approached the sailors and demanded gunpowder. Pullen refused. The Eskimo went back to his group but returned with a large number of men, all armed with bows and arrows. The sailors immediately launched their boats and after some tense moments, moved on.

The Eskimos shadowed the small group for several days, apparently waiting for a chance to catch the sailors off their guard and overpower them. At one point, when Pullen's party had gone ashore to cook a meal, two large umiaks, carrying some forty men, beached close to them and fired several arrows. The British returned fire with their muskets while the Eskimos were still out of range. Evidently frightened, the Eskimos dropped to the ground and the British safely set sail.

Pullen's men finally outdistanced the Eskimos and on 18 August, near Barter Island, they buried another cache of provisions and set up a signal pole for Franklin. They passed the 141st meridian, the treaty line between the Russian and British possessions in North America, and on 21 August they were at Herschel Island, reaching the Hudson's Bay Company post, Fort McPherson, on the Peel River, a tributary of the Mackenzie, on 5 September.

Pullen's group thus finished a significant open boat voyage without serious incident – but they had discovered only that there were no signs of Franklin on the coast west of the Mackenzie River.[1]

Once Pullen's party had pulled away from the fleet at Wainwright Inlet in July, Kellett returned to his own searches. He ordered Moore to take the *Plover* to find suitable wintering sites while he took the *Herald* west, searching along the ice edge in waters where no ships had ever been.

On 9 August in the northern Chukchi Sea the *Herald* overhauled the carcass of a dead whale. The creature had been killed by whalemen some time before. No doubt they had stripped it of its blubber and baleen and set it adrift. In any case it would have been bloated, gaseous, and fetid and would have had masses of sea birds wheeling around it and feeding on it. Kellett then devised a novel method of communication. He ordered the men to set a flag up on the carcass and to bury a bottle containing a message in the putrefying mess. The message notified the *Plover* of the *Herald*'s whereabouts. There is no record of its receipt.

Sounding carefully, Kellett pushed on. Suddenly, when they were more than 150 miles from the nearest point of land in Alaska the soundings jumped from about twenty fathoms to about seven fathoms. There was no land in sight; Kellett named the feature Herald Shoal. Kellett kept on to the northwest and on 17 August as the lowering clouds parted ahead of the vessel the tiny granite bastion of Herald Island loomed ahead, rising nearly vertically to a

---

[1] Great Britain, 1852a, pp. 23–30.

height of 1,200 feet. They were the first men since the Ice Age to see the island. Kellett went ashore and took possession of the island in the name of Queen Victoria.

Almost at once the men spied another land mass to the west. It seemed to be about forty miles away at the nearest and was apparently vast, running far to the north. There were a few small islands to the east of it. Kellett headed west toward this new land but the pack ice blocked his way. These islands were, in fact, the eastern headlands of Wrangell Island (in Russian Ostrov Vrangelya). The vast landmass beyond was cloud. Kellett had been deceived – as have many arctic mariners – by the peculiar atmospheric conditions which produce the appearance of land at a great distance. Kellet named one of the islands after the *Plover*. Not until 1867 was Wrangell Island's southern shore delineated. Captain Thomas Long coasted along it in the New London whaling bark *Nile* and named the entire island after Baron Ferdinand von Wrangell, who had reported the loom of this land during a journey on the Siberian mainland nearly fifty years before.[1]

When the ice stopped him east of Wrangell Island, Kellett turned the *Herald* southeast. Near Point Hope she fell in with the *Nancy Dawson*, which was escorting the boats back from Point Barrow. These vessels kept on for Kotzebue Sound while the *Herald* returned briefly northward to Icy Cape and then returned, rejoining the *Plover* and the *Nancy Dawson* at Chamisso Island on 1 September. The *Owen*, with Moore aboard, was at that time surveying up the Buckland River.

When Moore returned, Kellett took several boats back up the river and enjoyed excellent relations with the natives there. Kellett was puzzled by the fact that these river natives were so friendly: two decades before they had been actively hostile to the crew of H.M.S. *Blossom*. Kellett believed that the change in the natives' attitude was due to the presence of Bosky, the interpreter who had been taken aboard after his winter in Petropavlovsk. Kellett assumed that he was able to tell the Eskimos that the British were there for peaceful reasons. It is more likely that the presence of three ships at Chamisso Island and a large number of well-armed men kept the Eskimos quiet.

On 26 September the carpenters from both the *Herald* and *Plover*

---

[1] *Herald*, logbook; Great Britain, 1850, pp. 16–17.

had finished building a supply house on shore and had completed the initial winter preparations for the *Plover*. She would winter on the east side of the Choris Peninsula near Chamisso Island.

One task remained. Robert Shedden lay mortally ill aboard the *Nancy Dawson*. To make matters worse his crew had refused duty on the way back from Point Barrow. Moore had been forced to put three of the men in irons and to station a corporal and two marines on board the yacht.

The men aboard the *Herald* and *Plover* were genuinely grateful for Shedden's assistance. He had put his vessel at risk to help Pullen; he had freely given his stores to the expedition; and he had cached provisions for Franklin as well. Kellett consequently sent the second master of the *Herald*, W. F. Parsons, aboard the yacht to navigate her to Mazatlan, Mexico, where he would rejoin the *Herald*. Kellett weighed anchor on 29 September and reached Mazatlan on 14 November. In the harbour, amid a gaggle of stampeders heading to the California gold fields, he found the *Nancy Dawson* which had arrived only a few days before. There Robert Shedden died. He was buried in Mazatlan's Protestant graveyard. His last wish was that the *Nancy Dawson* be returned to her builder in England. She was – and she thus became the first yacht to circumnavigate the world.[1]

After the *Herald* left for the south the *Plover*'s crew prepared their ship for the Arctic winter. They dismantled the *Plover*'s upper masts and carried most of her provisions ashore for storage in the house. Without her provisions the ship was much lighter and Moore moved her into her winter quarters near the shore in 12 feet of water.

All winter Moore sent out travelling parties to search for news of Franklin. One of the most interesting journeys was undertaken by Lieutenant Bedford Pim. In 1848, when the *Herald* visited Kotzebue Sound, the Eskimos had told the sailors that there was a report of whitemen travelling in the interior. In November 1849 Moore heard another vague rumour about two ships being east of Point Barrow. It seemed possible that the two stories might refer to Franklin's men. Pim offered to go overland to St Michael, the Russian–American Company trading post at the mouth of the Yukon River, to learn whether any such news had filtered down the river to the traders.[2]

He set out in March 1850 with Bosky, the native interpreter, and

---

[1] Great Britain, 1850, pp. 9–22; [Euryalus], 1860, pp. 260–1.
[2] Great Britain, 1850, pp. 29 ff.

reached St Michael in early April. Pim talked at length with the chief factor there. At first he concluded that the report of white men in the interior referred to a party of Hudson's Bay Company men. It probably did – Alexander Hunter Murray had set up a trading post at the confluence of the Yukon and Porcupine Rivers in 1847. Later Pim changed his mind and concluded that in all likelihood the story was a report of a small starving group of Franklin's men.

Pim returned to the *Plover* at the end of April and summarized his investigations for Moore, reinforcing the idea that Franklin's men were somewhere in Alaska.

The middle of June brought terror to the *Plover*'s crew. By then the spring melt had progressed far enough to begin breaking up the ice in the bay. As the rivers began to run hard the masses of water flushed the ice across Eschscholtz Bay and fast against the east shore of the Choris Peninsula where the *Plover* lay. For nearly three weeks the crew watched in horror as the ice floes pushed the ship toward shore, time and again nearly crushing her. Then, as the force eased through a change of wind or tide, the men had slowly and laboriously to kedge the *Plover* back into deeper water – only to have the whole process repeated again and again.

While the *Plover*'s men were coping with the winter of 1849–50 in Kotzebue Sound, in England it was becoming increasingly clear that nothing whatever was known of Franklin's whereabouts. His expedition had been provisioned for three years and by then had been gone for four-and-a-half. Neither Sir James Clark Ross's expedition nor Richardson's and Rae's expedition had turned up anything. Completely baffled, the Lords Commissioners of the Admiralty canvassed a group of polar experts for their views on where Franklin might be. In general the consensus was that he had pushed west from Lancaster Sound and that he was somewhere near Banks or Melville Islands – or farther to the west.[1]

Sir James Clark Ross's expedition had recently returned to England and the Admiralty ordered his two ships, the *Enterprise* and *Investigator*, to return to the Arctic, this time via Bering Strait, under the command of Richard Collinson. Five other expeditions would enter the Arctic via Baffin Bay. The *Plover*, no longer in the van, became a depot ship, a back-up for the searching expeditions.

There was still a large body of ice in Kotzebue Sound on 15 July

[1] Great Britain, 1850, pp. 74–9.

1850 when the *Herald* returned from the south with new supplies for the *Plover* at Chamisso Island. While the men transferred supplies to the *Plover*, Moore told Kellett of the rumours about white men in Alaska. Kellett had not yet heard reports of the progress of Pullen's expedition the previous summer and he thought that the stories of ships east of Point Barrow might refer to Pullen's group. He ordered Moore to take the *Plover* north along the coast to investigate.

The *Plover* reached Icy Cape on 23 July. Moore immediately set off with 13 men in two boats, hoping to run up to Point Barrow in a lead of open water between the pack ice and the shore. He reached Wainwright Inlet the same evening and although he found a large group of Eskimos camped there, he learned nothing of interest from them. He kept on and the next day, near Point Franklin, buried a cache of provisions for search parties – or for Franklin.

On the 27th the boats arrived at Point Barrow. Moore estimated that 300 Eskimos were living in the settlement on shore. One of the natives told Moore that a party of white men had recently been killed far to the east of Point Barrow. The story might have been an exaggerated account of Pullen's encounter with the hostile Eskimos near Beechey Point. Moore correctly discounted it as rumour; nevertheless he offered the highest price possible – a musket and powder – to anyone who would lead him to the spot. No one took up his offer.

Moore then took the boats around Point Barrow and ran east nearly fifty miles, closely charting the coast as he went. He turned back at Cape Simpson and returned to Point Barrow on 2 August. During the trip in the Beaufort Sea he examined Elson Lagoon and found that although most of it was very shallow, one small area was deep enough to harbour the *Plover* for the winter. A week later the party rejoined the *Plover* off Wainwright Inlet.

While Moore was underway on the boat survey, Kellett took the *Herald* to Cape Lisburne to bury a bottle with information for Captain Richard Collinson, commander of the *Enterprise* and *Investigator* expedition to the waters near Banks and Melville Islands. Then Kellett headed north for the ice. He found it quickly – fifty miles south of where the ice edge had been in 1849.

Kellett turned back and, when he was fifty miles from Cape Lisburne, was amazed to sight the *Investigator*. She had left Hawaii after the *Enterprise*, but her captain, Robert M'Clure, had made an unusually fast passage of only 26 days from Honolulu. Boldly striking straight north, he had sailed through the Aleutian chain rather than taking the more circuitous route around the west end of the islands. The short cut had saved the *Investigator* a thousand miles and M'Clure had passed Collinson's ship, the *Enterprise*.

In view of the fact that Collinson was commander of the expedition, Kellett suggested that M'Clure wait for the *Enterprise*. But M'Clure was apparently motivated primarily by a desire for personal glory. He hoped to be the first to traverse a northwest passage. He refused to wait and pushed on in a strong northeast wind 'under every stitch he could carry'.

The *Investigator* was seen by the *Plover*, but not spoken to, on 5 August. The ship rounded Point Barrow and on 11 August reached the Jones Islands, near where Pullen had had his tense encounter with the Eskimos the year before. Two umiaks full of Eskimos came out to the ship. Although they appeared friendly, one of the men carried a musket – probably the same men who had threatened Pullen.[1]

Ten days after seeing the *Investigator*, the *Plover* met the *Herald* at Cape Lisburne. Moore told Kellett that Elson Lagoon at Point Barrow could be used as a wintering site. He wanted to winter the *Plover* there for two years and to send another boat expedition along the coast. Kellett, however, vetoed the idea. M'Clure had told him of Pullen's safe arrival on the Mackenzie, and he believed the story about the killings to be a fabrication. Furthermore, he thought that in the event of heavy summer ice at Point Barrow, the *Plover* might not be able to work out of Elson Lagoon to meet her supply ship. Grantley Harbor, the inner embayment of Point Clarence, seemed to be the only safe choice for a wintering site: it was impossible to get into Wainwright Inlet, and Kotzebue Sound had proved dangerous. Grantley Harbor was spacious and well protected from moving ice.

Moore, therefore, took the *Plover* south toward Port Clarence on 15 August. Along the way he searched for the *Enterprise*, which was by then two weeks overdue. After a stop at Chamisso Island to bury emergency provisions, he arrived in Port Clarence on 30 August without having seen the *Enterprise*.

Meanwhile Kellett waited for the *Enterprise* for a few more days at Cape Lisburne, then took the *Herald* to St Michael to check on the

---

[1] Seemann, 1853, II, p. 179; Great Britain, 1851, p. 21; M'Clure, 1856, p. 73; Great Britain, 1854, p. 26; Moore's report of his boat voyage to Point Barrow, is reprinted as Appendix Two, pp. 459–68 below.

rumours that Bedford Pim had reported during the winter. To Kellett's disappointment he found that Pim's sources, the chief factor and his assistant, had been transferred to Sitka. Nevertheless it seemed to him that the Russian–American Company's trading post at Nulato on the Yukon River would be an excellent place to get first-hand information about the whitemen that had been reported in the interior.[1]

Kellett returned to Port Clarence to check on the *Plover*'s preparations for the winter and was surprised to find the *Enterprise* in the harbour. Kellett had assumed that the *Enterprise* had passed him unseen and gone into the Arctic. Collinson had, in fact, passed Kellett about 13 August, but when the *Enterprise* reached the ice edge, Collinson had found no passage open to the east into the Beaufort Sea. He had turned south on 30 August, stopping at Point Hope, where he had discovered the buried bottle with a message from the *Herald*. He thus learned that his subordinate, M'Clure, had passed him and had gone on into the Beaufort Sea.[2]

Collinson intended to have the *Enterprise* take the *Plover*'s place: The *Plover*'s men already had put in two northern winters and Collinson wanted to allow them to spend the winter in the south. But as he began warping the *Enterprise* through the narrow channel into Grantley Harbor, the wind changed and forced the ship aground. Only when 100 tons of the *Enterprise*'s supplies had been unloaded, was she floated free of the strand. Collinson considered wintering north at some other site, but he concluded correctly that in the following spring he would be able to get into the Arctic earlier if he arrived from the south; the Bering Strait region is usually ice free when most of its harbours are still frozen. The *Plover* was already anchored in Grantley Harbor and Collinson decided to leave her there. He planned to winter the *Enterprise* in Hong Kong, bringing fresh supplies in the spring.[3]

The *Herald* left Port Clarence at the end of September, bound back to England via Hong Kong and Singapore. The *Enterprise*, after another journey north to the ice edge and an inspection of the coast, sailed from Port Clarence on 7 October. Collinson first went to St Michael and put ashore a party of three: Lieutenant John Barnard, Assistant Surgeon Edward Adams, and one sailor. They were to

[1] Great Britain, 1851, p. 22. [2] Collinson, 1889, pp. 59–69.
[3] Great Britain, 1851, pp. 14–16, 42.

spend the winter and to try to get to the Russian–American Company's post at Nulato (then called Darabin) to check on the rumours that Pim had reported.[1]

The *Enterprise* then sailed to Sitka, arriving there on 1 November. Collinson stopped long enough to tell the Governor of Russian America about the progress of the search for Franklin. The Governor supplied the *Enterprise* with fresh provisions *gratis*. Collinson also met the great Russian explorer and geographer M. D. Tebenkov. Tebenkov had carried out explorations of the Bering Sea and had recently completed work on an atlas of the area. He readily shared his knowledge with Collinson. The Russians also offered to send 18 Aleuts and 20 Kayaks north to assist in the search in 1851. The *Enterprise* left Sitka in mid-November, touched at Hawaii, and reached Hong Kong in February.

Meanwhile the *Plover*'s men settled in at Grantley Harbor for their third northern winter. Apart from an outbreak of scurvy, the winter passed without significant problems, thanks in part to the good relations that the British enjoyed with the Eskimos of the region.[2]

In February Moore sent a party to St Michael to check on Lieutenant Barnard's group. It was not until 6 April 1851, when the *Plover*'s second master, Thomas Bourchier returned to the ship, that Moore had his report. The news was deeply saddening. At first the winter had gone fairly well for the three at St Michael. Bosky, the interpreter, was also living at St Michael that winter, and he helped the sailors to question the native travellers that visited the site.

Initially the British heard only repetitions of the rumours that white men had been murdered on the north coast of Alaska. But on 23 December 1850 Vasili Maksimovich Deriabin ('Wassele Maxemoff'), the factor in charge of the post at Nulato, arrived at St Michael. Deriabin confirmed the stories of white men to the east, but he believed – correctly, as it turned out – that the men were traders rather than the lost Franklin party.

In the summer of 1849 Deriabin had been on a trading trip upriver from Nulato. There he met Indians who were well supplied with trade goods: 'muskets, powder and shot, English knives, beads, tobacco, and a few preserved meat tins'. With the exception of the

---

[1] Great Britain, 1852a, p. 66; Collinson, 1889, pp. 80–1.
[2] Great Britain, 1852a, pp. 201–3; John Matthews' journal, H.M.S. *Plover*; Collinson, 1889, p. 131.

meat tins, the manufactures all appeared to be the types that the Hudson's Bay Company sold. The Indians said that the white men who sold them the goods had been living on the river for two years. The following year Deriabin had received a letter from Alexander Hunter Murray of the Hudson's Bay Company stating that in 1847 he had established a trading post on the upper Yukon – more than one hundred miles inside the borders of Russian America – at the point where the Porcupine River joins the Yukon.

Nevertheless, when Deriabin returned to Nulato Lieutenant Barnard decided to go with him to explore the area. He left Adams and the sailor at St Michael to interrogate any natives who might visit the post. Barnard hired Bosky to accompany him as interpreter. They set off at the end of December.[1]

Adams had no word from Barnard until 24 February when a native appeared at the fort with a shocking letter:

Dear Adams

I am dreadfully wounded in the abdomen, my entrails are hanging out. I do not suppose I shall live long enough to see you. The Cu-u-chuk Indians made the attack whilst we were in our beds. Boskey is badly wounded, and Darabin dead.

I think my wound would have been trifling had I medical advice. I am in great pain; nearly all the natives of the village are murdered. Set out for this with all haste.

(Signed) JOHN BARNARD[2]

Adams immediately asked the Russian factor for a dog team and men. It took several days to round up the outfit, and Adams did not reach Unalakleet until 1 March. There, he was held up for a couple of days by the thawing river. By chance, while he was at Unalakleet the party from the *Plover* arrived. Adams pushed on with the *Plover*'s interpreter and four Nulato Indians who were visiting Unalakleet.

When Adams reached Nulato he pieced the story together. Barnard had arrived there on 16 January and stayed in the trading post. On 15 February at about five o'clock in the morning Deriabin happened to go outside his log cabin and found about eighty armed Koyukon Indians there. They grabbed him and stabbed him with a knife, but he managed to break free and stagger mortally wounded

---

[1] Great Britain, 1852a, pp. 73–8; Edward Adams journal.
[2] Great Britain, 1852a, p. 208.

into his room just in time for his native wife to bar the door. The Indians then burst into Barnard's room.[1] To quote Adams's own words:

It appears that Mr. Barnard was awoke by the noise of their approach, and asked what it was? Pavil [Bosky] answered, 'The Indians are come; take your gun and shoot them.' Both barrels of his gun had been left loaded with small shot; these were fired; but from the direction of the shot-marks on the wall, I think they must have gone off whilst he was struggling with the Indians. He then appears to have struck with the butt until the stock broke, and he fell dreadfully wounded. Before Pavil had time to get out of bed, an attempt was made to stab him; but the knife, badly aimed in the dark, passed between his arm and side. Being without a gun or other weapon, he warded off the spears with a blanket, and took five of them away, with one of which he wounded some of the Indians, and ultimately cleared the room, although badly wounded with three arrows which were sticking in his body. The Indians then left the house, and congregated on the bank of the river, planting their shields in a row so as to form a wall, as if intending to attack the other building. At the time of the arrival of the Indians, a woman was in the cooking house, boiling her kettle; she saw them, but dared not go out until they were in Maxemoff's house, when she ran to the barracks, and alarmed the men, who were all asleep. By this time the Indians had collected outside, and one of the men fired from a window and killed one of them, when the rest immediately snatched up their shields, and made off for the woods.

They then went down to the village, and finding the unsuspecting inhabitants asleep succeeded in murdering all but four; one man, who made his escape, and three women, whom they took away captives. They killed men, women, and children, fifty-three in number; and after eating part of one of the men, set fire to the houses, and took their departure, carrying one man, who had been wounded by Pavil, on a sledge. The Indian who was killed they left behind; he was pitched down upon the river, and afterwards eaten by the dogs . . .

Mr. Barnard lived till the morning of the following day, but was too severely wounded to be able to write any account of the affair . . .

I found upon my arrival at Darabin [Nulato] that they had buried neither Maxemoff nor Mr. Barnard; and upon examining the bodies I found that the former had one wound about two inches in length, under the left clavicle; the latter had received nine wounds in all; one large one in the left side, below the ribs, from which a large bunch of intestines had protruded and become strangulated, evidently the cause of death; two in the back, 1½ inches in length, from spears; four in the right side of the chest, one from a

[1] Great Britain, 1852a, pp. 74–5.

39

spear, and three from arrows; one slight cut under the chin, and another across the back of the right hand. The bodies having been kept in the uninhabited house were so firmly frozen that there was not time during my short stay to make a more minute examination.

I buried Mr. Barnard on the 16th March, in the burial ground at Darabin, some of the Russians, at my request, firing a volley over his grave, at the head of which I placed a board, inscribed with his name, the cause of his death, &c.

Adams was at a loss to explain why the Indians had attacked Nulato. In all, the Koyukons killed 56 people in the village; more than fifty of them were Indians. In the light of recent research it appears that Barnard had stumbled into an internecine feud and he and the other foreigners were merely killed along with the local Indians.

Adams left Nulato on 18 March, carrying Bosky, whose wounds had healed enough to allow him to ride on the sled. Ten days later they reached St Michael, but Bosky's health began to deteriorate and on 20 April 1851 Bosky, a faithful assistant in the Franklin Search, died at St Michael.[1]

During the same winter the Lords Commissioners of the Admiralty were at work deciding the future of the search. By then Franklin's expedition had been gone for more than six years. They convened a group of Arctic explorers and experts, called the 'Arctic Council' to give advice on how to proceed. Kellett had just returned to England in the *Herald* and offered his opinion that Franklin was alive somewhere south and west of Melville and Banks Islands in a land mass that might be part of the Islands he, Kellett, had discovered in the Chukchi Sea.[2]

The Admiralty decided that Collinson should take the *Enterprise* into the Arctic, searching for the *Investigator* so that the two vessels could explore the possibility that Franklin was west of Melville Island.

The *Plover* was ordered to remain as a depot ship in case any of the ships had to fall back. The *Plover* needed to be supplied for another year, and the new Commander-in-chief of the Pacific Station, Rear Admiral Fairfax Moresby chose H.M.S. *Daedalus* to go north carrying twenty months' provisions for herself as well as twelve

[1] Great Britain, 1852a, pp. 76–7 ff; McFayden-Clark, personal communication.
[2] Great Britain, 1852c, p. 168.

months' provisions for the *Plover*. Moresby ordered that if Captain George Greville Wellesley of the *Daedalus* should find the *Plover* wrecked, then the *Daedalus* was to stay north for the winter of 1851–2.[1]

Collinson reached Port Clarence from Hong Kong on 3 July 1851. The next day the British ships were joined by three whaleships, the *Lagoda* of New Bedford, the *Nancy* of Havre, and the *Sheffield* of Sag Harbor. The latter was under the command of Captain Thomas Roys, who had discovered the Bering Strait whaling grounds only three years earlier and who was now accompanied by nearly two hundred whaleships. He and a number of other whaling captains had offered to search for Franklin along the ice edge in the Arctic Ocean.

Collinson ordered Moore to take the *Plover* to St Michael to collect the Aleuts that the Russians had offered to send north. (It turned out that the Russians had been unable to procure them.) He was then to go to Saint Lawrence Bay on the Asian side of Bering Strait. There he was to pass dispatches to the whaling ships that usually congregated there. They in turn would deliver them to the British consul in Honolulu.

The *Enterprise* sailed from Port Clarence on 10 July, rounded Point Barrow before the end of the month, and passed Barter Island on 8 August. Then she vanished for three years.[2]

The *Plover* returned to Port Clarence from her trip to St Michael at the end of July. There she found the *Daedalus* at anchor, having had a hair-raising experience on her way north. Wellesley had taken her around the east end of Saint Lawrence Island and was trapped by the pack ice. His ship was badly squeezed by the ice before she got free. Had he gone around the west end of the island, he probably would have avoided the problem by sailing in more ice-free waters.[3]

Wellesley's carpenters surveyed the *Plover* and found her fit for another year in the north, then the two vessels went to Saint Lawrence Bay briefly. After a short cruise to the north and to Kotzebue Sound the *Plover* returned to Port Clarence where the carpenters from the *Daedalus* caulked her while men from both of the ships transferred provisions. Because the entire crew of the *Plover* had either been aboard her since she left England in 1848, or had started out aboard the *Herald* in 1845, twenty-seven new men

[1] Great Britain, 1852a, pp. 79–80.
[2] Collinson, 1889, pp. 132–3, 135–40.
[3] Great Britain, 1852b, pp. 89–91.

were transferred to the *Plover* to allow others to return home. On 1 October the *Daedalus* left for San Francisco, leaving the *Plover* at Port Clarence for her fourth northern winter.[1]

The winter passed uneventfully for the crew of the *Plover*. Nothing was accomplished in regard to finding Franklin's expedition, but in one respect it was a good winter: none of the men suffered from scurvy. The crew's better health was thought to be accounted for by the high quality of the fresh provisions that the *Daedalus* had brought north.

In England, however, 1852 brought only gloom. Franklin had been missing for nearly seven years and there remained little hope for his survival. In the west, the *Plover* had now become the fall-back supply ship for the *Enterprise* and *Investigator*. It was up to Admiral Moresby to supply the *Plover*. He chose H.M.S. *Amphitrite* for the northern cruise.[2]

Aboard the *Amphitrite* was Commander Rochfort Maguire. Maguire had been first officer of the *Herald* and was returning to the Arctic to take command of the *Plover*, relieving T. E. L. Moore, who by then had spent four winters in the north and who had been promoted to Captain. Maguire was to put the *Plover* into winter quarters at Point Barrow in the harbour that Moore had discovered on his boat expedition in 1850. If Maguire heard no word from the *Enterprise* or *Investigator* in the winter of 1852–3, he was to remain north for another winter as well.[3]

The *Amphitrite* reached Port Clarence on 30 June 1852. The commanding officer, Captain Charles Frederick, quickly ordered a survey of the condition of the *Plover*'s stores of canned meat. Word had come from England that Franklin's first wintering site (1845–6) had been located and that a great number of meat tins had been found on shore there. The number of tins led to the suspicion that Franklin's men had found them spoiled. It was thought that the supplier, Stephen Goldner, might have sold inferior stores to the Admiralty. The survey of the *Plover*'s stores revealed that all of the 10,000 pounds of canned meat were unfit for consumption, reinforcing the belief that Franklin may have starved from a lack of proper provisions. This charge has been effectively rebutted in recent years.[4]

[1] Great Britain, 1852b, pp. 42–3.   [2] Great Britain, 1852a, p. 147.
[3] Great Britain, 1852a, p. 187.
[4] Great Britain, 1852b, pp. 60–2; Cyriax, 1939, pp. 109–18.

The *Amphitrite*'s surgeon then examined the *Plover*'s crew. Those that he found unfit and those who did not want to spend another northern winter were transferred to the *Amphitrite* and fifteen volunteers left her to join the *Plover*. One notable arrival aboard the *Plover* was Dr John Simpson, the surgeon. He had been aboard the *Plover* for her first three northern winters but had left for England in 1850 aboard the *Herald*. His fluency in Inupiaq, the Eskimo language, made relations with the natives go much more smoothly in the next two years.

While the men transferred a year's provisions to the *Plover*, the carpenters surveyed the *Plover*'s hull and made her ready for sea and for the coming winter. Frederick wanted to head north as soon as possible to check on native rumours that the *Enterprise* had wintered at Point Barrow. Maguire also wanted to survey the coast by boat before taking the *Plover* into her winter quarters.

The *Plover* reached the pack ice at Icy Cape on 19 July, and Maguire started out with fifteen men in a gig and the *Plover*'s pinnace, a small yawl. He headed north in the lead of water between the pack ice and the shore and arrived at Point Barrow four days later. He found no evidence that either the *Enterprise* or *Investigator* had been there during the winter, but he examined Elson Lagoon, as T. E. L. Moore had in 1850, and confirmed its suitability as a winter anchorage for the *Plover*. Maguire then took his boats south to Wainwright Inlet to wait for the *Plover*. The *Plover*, however, because of some confusion on the part of Lieutenant Charles Vernon, the acting commander, had gone south. With provisions running low, Maguire sailed to Cape Lisburne, where the *Plover* and *Amphitrite* were supposed to rendezvous. Maguire and his men, weak and weather-beaten, boarded the *Amphitrite* on 12 August, and six days later they found the *Plover* at Port Clarence.[1]

The *Plover*'s men made a cache of provisions on shore in Grantley Harbor and left for the north on 21 August. The *Amphitrite* sailed for San Francisco Bay on 6 September.

At Point Barrow the *Plover*'s men settled in to an unpleasant winter. Scurvy broke out and the Eskimos proved to be aggressive and overbearing. Their winter searching operation had to be curtailed as well. To make matters worse, during the winter the men

---

[1] Great Britain, 1852b, pp. 48–59. Maguire's report of his boat expedition to Point Barrow is reprinted as Appendix Three, pp. 469–92 below.

often found a wide lead of open water running east–west across the horizon. Maguire had planned to explore northward over the ice toward Kellett's hypothetical landmass where the *Enterprise* or *Investigator* might be wintering. He sensibly cancelled these quixotic adventures and, in the spring, did not fare much better. He tried to probe along the coast to the east, but his sledges were weak and overloaded. They broke down frequently and Maguire never got very far. Furthermore, he learned nothing of importance about Franklin's or Collinson's squadrons.[1]

The only intelligence that the *Plover* gathered that winter was from an Eskimo who visited the ship from about seventy-five miles to the east. He carried a letter from M'Clure, who had given it to him nearly three years before, when the *Investigator* had sailed into the eastern Beaufort Sea.

In July, while the *Plover* was still frozen in, Maguire sent two boats south to meet his supply ship. This expedition, too, ended in failure.[2] Both boats were crushed in the ice within fifty miles of Point Barrow and the men straggled back to the *Plover* on foot. The *Plover* finally broke out of Elson Lagoon on 9 August 1853. The next day she met the *Amphitrite* south of Icy Cape. The two ships reached Port Clarence on 15 August and the usual surveys, caulking, and transfers of men and supplies got underway.

On 22 August 1853 just as the *Plover* was heading seaward to return to Point Barrow, she met H.M.S. *Rattlesnake* at the entrance to Port Clarence. The *Rattlesnake* was under the command of Henry Trollope, Maguire's old shipmate, a lieutenant aboard the *Herald* from 1845 to 1851. The *Rattlesnake* had been sent north to serve as a depot ship for the winter at Port Clarence. The *Plover* was to return to Point Barrow as an advance fall-back position for the crews of the *Enterprise* and *Investigator*, while the *Rattlesnake* was to serve as a fall-back position for the crews of all three ships in case the *Plover* might be lost. Trollope was to build a large house on shore at Grantley Harbor – large enough to house seventy men. Thus, by 1853, the British naval activities near Bering Strait had become a watch for the *Enterprise*, now gone two years, and the *Investigator*, now gone three. There was little hope for Franklin.[3]

---

[1] John Matthews journal; Rochfort Maguire journal; Great Britain, 1854a, pp. 160–85.

[2] Vernon's report of his boat expedition is reprinted as Appendix Five, pp. 495–7 below.

[3] Great Britain, 1854a, pp, 147–8, 156–8; Great Britain, 1853, p. 1.

After taking on fresh provisions from the *Rattlesnake* the *Plover* went back to Point Barrow, the *Amphitrite* to Hawaii, and the *Rattlesnake* moved into Grantley Harbor. The *Plover* was warped into her anchorage in Elson Lagoon and the ship began her sixth northern winter.[1]

As soon as the ice was thick enough Maguire set out to the east with a sledge party in search of the *Enterprise* and *Investigator*. He learned nothing on this trip. The winter proceeded without incident and he set out again in April. This time he had to turn back near the Colville River delta because his party met a group of armed Indians who began following his sled with, thought Maguire, every intention of trying to kill the sailors.

At Grantley Harbor things were also relatively uneventful. Trollope sent travelling parties out from the *Rattlesnake* all over the western Seward Peninsula but, of course, learned nothing. On 25 June 1854 the *Rattlesnake*'s men saw H.M.S. *Trincomalee* sail into Port Clarence. She was arriving from Honolulu with orders and supplies, including four cattle and twenty pigs.

Most important, however, she brought news of the *Investigator*. The *Investigator* had spent two winters frozen in Mercy Bay on the north side of Banks Island. The crew was on the verge of starvation when they were discovered by Lieutenant Bedford Pim. Pim had formerly been aboard both the *Herald* and the *Plover* and was at that time serving on H.M.S. *Resolute*, which had entered the Arctic via Baffin Bay. After this encounter M'Clure ordered his crew to abandon the *Investigator* and his men had walked out to the eastern Arctic, thereby becoming the first people to traverse a Northwest Passage.[2]

Now only the *Enterprise* remained to be accounted for – apart, of course, from Franklin's ships. The *Enterprise* was the only reason for the *Rattlesnake* and *Plover* to remain north for the winter of 1854–5, and it seemed likely that by 1855 Collinson and his crew would appear somewhere, with or without the *Enterprise*. If no word had been received from the *Enterprise* by the end of that winter, then both the *Plover* and the *Rattlesnake* were to leave the Arctic – for no supply ship would be sent north in 1855. Thus the Admiralty appeared to be preparing to abandon hope of Collinson, as it had of Franklin.

[1] Great Britain, 1855, pp. 905–13.   [2] Great Britain, 1854b, p. 2.

The orders continued that if the *Plover* should be unable to reach a safe winter harbour north of Bering Strait in 1854, she was to put her spare supplies aboard the *Rattlesnake* and head for the south. The *Rattlesnake* would then remain at Grantley Harbor. If the *Plover* should be able to work into Elson Lagoon again for the winter of 1854–5, but should be found unfit for an ocean passage the following spring, she was to be placed in a safe harbour and her crew was to go south aboard the *Rattlesnake*.

The orders went on, ominously:

In the event of England being at any time involved in hostilities with any other power during your employment on the above service, you are clearly to understand that you are not to commit any hostile act whatever, the ship under your command being fitted out for the sole purpose of aiding those engaged in scientific discoveries, and it being the established practice of all civilised nations to consider vessels so employed as exempt from the operations of war.

On 15 July 1854 the *Rattlesnake* sailed north from Port Clarence in search of the *Plover*. She arrived at Point Barrow on 30 July to find no sign of the ship. Trollope then took the *Rattlesnake* south and landed at Wainwright Inlet on 7 August. There he was 'overwhelmed' by printed notices that the *Plover*'s men had distributed to the natives. The *Plover* had passed there, bound to Port Clarence, two weeks before. The *Rattlesnake* sailed into Port Clarence four days later to find the *Plover* and *Trincomalee* at anchor.[1]

The usual surveys and transfers of supplies went on, and the *Plover*, although slightly leaky, was declared fit for another northern winter. The *Plover* left for her winter quarters at Point Barrow on 19 August, and the *Trincomalee* sailed for San Francisco two days later.

The *Plover* reached Point Barrow on 28 August. If things had gone as expected, the crew would have begun preparations for her seventh northern winter, but to the surprise of all, the Eskimos came aboard the ship and reported that four days after the *Plover* had left Point Barrow, a boat from the *Enterprise* had reached the point from the east. As it happened, five American whaleships were then cruising near the point, and they confirmed the story; in fact, one of them had spoken with the *Enterprise* on her way to Port Clarence – and just then the *Enterprise* herself hove into sight.[2]

[1] Great Britain, 1855, pp. 859–60, 900–1.
[2] John Matthews journal.

Collinson had spent two winters on the coast of Victoria Island, one of them in Cambridge Bay, not far, as it turned out, from where Franklin's ships had been abandoned. Theirs was the farthest eastward penetration by the Bering Strait fleet. On the way back toward Point Barrow the *Enterprise* was caught by the ice and forced to spend a third winter, this time in Camden Bay, Alaska, only 350 nautical miles east of Point Barrow. On 2 July 1854 natives brought a notice to Collinson that had been printed on the *Plover* a year before. On 10 July, when there was enough open water, Collinson sent Lieutenant C. J. Jago in a boat to Point Barrow where he arrived only four days after the *Plover* had sailed.

By the time that the *Enterprise* had met the *Plover* at Point Barrow, Collinson had already been to Port Clarence, and as senior officer, he had sent the *Rattlesnake* south. The *Plover* and *Enterprise* then sailed back to Port Clarence and exchanged provisions before sailing south. The *Rattlesnake*'s storehouse at Grantley Harbor was given to an Eskimo headman there. The *Enterprise* then headed for Hong Kong and England, the *Plover* for San Francisco. Thus ended the search for Sir John Franklin in the west.

The *Plover* entered San Francisco Bay on 28 October and anchored in Sausalito Bay. The *Plover*'s men then heard the news of the outbreak of the Crimean War and of that year's disastrous Anglo-French assault on Petropavlovsk, in which the *Amphitrite* and *Trincomalee* had taken part, and in which 190 of the allied troops had been killed before the landing force was repulsed by the Russians.

A few days after the *Plover*'s arrival officers from other British ships held a survey of the *Plover* and found her unfit for further service. On 20 November the ice-scarred *Plover* was taken across the bay to San Francisco to be sold at auction. The firm of Moore and Folger, ship breakers, bought her for £1,350.

The *Plover*'s crew then moved aboard the Russian bark *Sitka* which had been taken as a prize in the abortive siege of Petropavlovsk. The *Sitka* belonged to the Russian–American Company. The *Plover*'s crew sailed her back to England. Shortly before they left San Francisco the *Plover*'s men learned from an American newspaper that near King William Island, more than 1,000 miles from Point Barrow, Dr John Rae had found the remains of some of Franklin's men.[1]

[1] Rochfort Maguire journal; John Matthews journal.

SUMMARY OF EVENTS IN THE SEARCH FOR
SIR JOHN FRANKLIN IN ALASKA

1845

Sir John Franklin's expedition departs from England in search of a Northwest Passage.

1848

H.M.S. *Herald* reaches Kotzebue Sound in September and returns south, having failed to meet H.M.S. *Plover*.

H.M.S. *Plover* reaches the Bering Strait region only in mid-October and winters in Plover Bay on the Chukchi Peninsula.

1849

Herald, with supplies, meets *Plover* at Chamisso Island in Kotzebue Sound. The yacht *Nancy Dawson* joins them there. The three proceed north along the Alaskan coast. At Wainwright Inlet Pullen's boat expedition sets off for the Mackenzie River. Herald Island and the eastern tip of Wrangell Island are seen by the crew of the *Herald*.

Plover winters in Kotzebue Sound, near the Choris Peninsula.

1850

Herald resupplies *Plover* in Kotzebue Sound.

H.M.S. *Investigator* rounds Point Barrow and goes into the Beaufort Sea.

H.M.S. *Enterprise* reaches Point Barrow too late in the season to enter the Beaufort Sea and returns south for the winter.

Plover winters in Port Clarence.

1851

H.M.S. *Daedalus* resupplies the *Plover* at Port Clarence.

Enterprise rounds Point Barrow and enters the Beaufort Sea.

Plover winters in Port Clarence.

1852

H.M.S. *Amphitrite* resupplies the *Plover* at Port Clarence. Rochfort Maguire replaces T. E. L. Moore in command of the *Plover*.

Plover winters at Point Barrow.

1853

Amphitrite resupplies *Plover* at Port Clarence.

Plover winters at Point Barrow.

H.M.S. *Rattlesnake* winters in Port Clarence.

Enterprise winters in Camden Bay.

1854

H.M.S. *Trincomalee* resupplies *Plover* at Port Clarence, and *Plover* returns to Point Barrow to winter as a depot ship for the *Enterprise*. The *Plover* reaches Point Barrow, and her crew learns that, unknown to them, the *Enterprise* had wintered in Camden Bay, Alaska, and had recently passed Point Barrow, bound south.

All British ships leave the western Arctic.

Plover is sold at San Francisco, and her crew sail the bark *Sitka*, a Crimean War prize, back to England.

THE *PLOVER*, MAGUIRE, AND THE MANUSCRIPT

H.M.S. *Plover* began her naval career at Canton, China, in 1841, when the East India Company sold their pilot brig *Bentinck* to the Royal Navy for £5,951. She had probably been built in Bombay, but the date of her launch is unknown. The *Plover* was a sturdy, beamy vessel. Copper fastened and double planked of teak, she was 82 feet long on the deck with a beam of 25 feet. Her weight and dimensions made her a slow sailer. To her first naval commander, Richard Collinson, who would use her as a survey vessel during operations against the Chinese – and who would also see a good deal of her during the Franklin search – she was just about the ugliest vessel he had ever seen, but one, nevertheless, that was very roomy. She was rated for 50 men and carried four eighteen-pounders and ten hundred-weight carronades.

After her service in the Far East the *Plover* returned to England in 1846 and served as a receiving hulk at Woolwich, but after only a year she was recalled to active duty. As the summer of 1847 wore on, the nation became confronted with the fact that the Franklin expedition had been gone for more than two years and that no word had been received of its whereabouts. With anxiety rising and the plans for relief expeditions forming, no doubt the *Plover* was chosen for the search because of her strength, relatively light draft (an asset in the shallow waters of the western Arctic), and ability to carry large quantities of supplies.

In October 1847 the *Plover* was taken to Sheerness dockyard for a refit that cost more than £10,000. She was resheathed and coppered, re-rigged as a bark; most of her gun ports were closed and she was internally fitted for arctic work and to house a crew of 41. She spent most of the month of January 1848 at Devonport, preparing for her voyage, and sailed for the western Arctic at the beginning of February. After seven years in the north she was taken to San Francisco Bay, where on 22 November 1854, worn and leaky, she was sold to the firm of Moore and Folger for £1,395. She was later broken up by Charles Hare. Some of her timbers no doubt lie today under downtown San Francisco.[1]

---

[1] D. J. Lyon, personal communication; A. C. F. David, personal communication; *Alta California* (San Francisco), 5 June 1882; Progress book (copy), Department of Ships, National Maritime Museum, Greenwich, U.K.

H.M.S. *Plover* – drawn by Condy. From *The Illustrated London News*, January 1848, p. 39.

Rochfort Maguire took command of the *Plover* on 1 July 1852 at Port Clarence, Alaska, replacing T. E. L. Moore, who had been in command since her departure from England more than four years earlier. Judging from his journal, Maguire appears to have been an able, if somewhat unimaginative, officer; thorough, kind, and steady.

Maguire was born on 18 June 1815 (Waterloo Day) and was baptized three months later at St George's Church, Dublin. His parents were Bernard and Eleanor Maguire, minor gentry of Belmont, County Westmeath. He adopted a course often taken by such families and began his career in the Navy via the Royal Naval College, Portsmouth, which he entered in 1829. There he was reported as being good at mathematics but not as skilful at other subjects.[1]

He passed his examinations after two years and was posted aboard ships on the South African station. In 1835 he passed his examinations for lieutenant and began his service in the Mediterranean. He was aboard several vessels there, and in 1840 in the Syrian campaign, on H.M.S. *Wasp*, he distinguished himself at Sidon and was severely wounded. He was promoted for his actions and posted aboard H.M.S. *Vernon*, one of the finest frigates of the time. He then served three short assignments on other ships before being appointed senior lieutenant aboard H.M.S. *Herald* in February 1845.[2]

All of Maguire's previous assignments had been aboard general service ships, but the *Herald*, under Captain Henry Kellett, was bound on a surveying voyage to the Pacific. Maguire had had little experience in surveying, hence it is likely that he was given his position to run the ship while the captain and the rest of the officers carried out the surveys.[3]

The *Herald* left Plymouth on 26 June 1845. She rounded Cape Horn and worked up the west coast of the Americas as far as Vancouver Island, then returned for survey work in Central and South America. In 1848 she was ordered to Bering Strait, to work with the *Plover* in searching for Franklin's expedition. As we have seen, the *Herald* operated north of Bering Strait in 1848, 1849, 1850. In September 1850 she sailed for home via Honolulu, Hong

---

[1] A. W. H. Pearsall, personal communication; ADM 1/3516, ADM 1/3517–8, Public Record Office (PRO), Kew, U.K.

[2] ADM 37/8406, ADM 11/22, ADM 107/75, ADM 11/27, ADM 37/8694, ADM 37/10083, Public Record Office (PRO), Kew, U.K.; Lean's Royal Navy List.

[3] A. W. H. Pearsall, personal communication.

Kong, and Singapore, and reached England in June 1851.[1]

Maguire must have served well aboard the *Herald* and impressed Kellett, because he was promoted to commander in July 1851. After his leave he was stationed briefly at the Royal Naval College, Portsmouth. It was from there that on 29 November 1851 he wrote to the Lords Commissioners of the Admiralty, echoing a proposal that Kellett had made a year earlier. Maguire offered his services to command a propeller steamer in going east of Point Barrow to communicate with the *Enterprise* and *Investigator*, then to explore whether Herald Island might be part of a land mass that was in some way connected with Melville Island in the Arctic Archipelago.[2]

On 3 January 1852 Maguire met with the First Lord of the Admiralty, Sir Francis Baring, who accepted his offer of service, but not his plans for exploration. Maguire would take command of the *Plover*, and the *Plover* would remain as a depot ship. T. E. L. Moore's boat survey of Point Barrow in 1850 had shown Elson Lagoon to be a secure enough harbour. Maguire was to put the *Plover* into winter quarters there. She would be an advance base in case the crews of the *Enterprise* or *Investigator* might have to fall back to her. If there was no word from Collinson by the summer of 1853, Maguire was to wait for another winter.[3]

The *Plover* was warped into her anchorage in Elson Lagoon on 3 September 1852. At first the relations between the British and Eskimos were uneasy, at best. Gradually, however, the two groups grew to tolerate and then to begin to understand one another. The Eskimos, contrary to their reputation for pugnacity, carried out a number of generous acts for the British, and many of the sailors found themselves becoming genuinely fond of these people. This growth of mutual acceptance was measurably aided by the presence of Dr John Simpson.

Simpson had sailed from England aboard the *Plover* in 1848 and had been aboard her for her first three winters at, respectively, Plover Bay, Kotzebue Sound, and Port Clarence. He was sent home to England, ill, in 1851, but he returned with Maguire in 1852.

---

[1] Seemann, 1853, *passim*.
[2] A. W. H. Pearsall, personal communication; Lean's Royal Navy List; ADM 196/1, ADM 11/73, Public Record Office (PRO), Kew, U.K.; Great Britain, 1851, p. 41; Maguire to Lords Commissioners, file 3.13b, Hydrographic Department, Ministry of Defence (N), Taunton, U.K.
[3] Great Britain, 1852a, p. 187.

During his winters in Alaska he had learned to speak some of the Eskimo's language and he thus became the *de facto* interlocutor between the ship and the Eskimos. As a gifted observer of events he also became a skilled ethnographer, and thus was able to explain the seemingly peculiar behaviour of each group to the other. On his return to England he wrote a monograph on these 'Western Eskimos' which, to this day, remains at once an extremely perceptive study of the Eskimos' aboriginal life ways and the basis for all subsequent ethnographical work in the region. His monograph has been reprinted in this volume as Appendix Seven.

Of the friendships that developed between the Eskimos and the British one of the closest and most interesting was that of Maguire and 'Erksinra'. Maguire's journal is a study in the gradual shedding of racial preconceptions and the growth of tolerance – and 'Erksinra's' feelings must have run the same course. After a year at Point Barrow Maguire came to the conclusion that 'It is no use judging [the Eskimos'] feelings by our own standard.' Later, when seeing the helpless despair of a wife for the loss of her husband on the drifting sea ice, he recognized in her situation the same inability to control events as in the Admiralty's fruitless search for Franklin's expedition. He also grew to understand implicitly the territoriality and hostility between native societies in Alaska and thus to accept the Eskimos' aggressive reception of foreigners.

On the day the *Plover* sailed from Point Barrow for the last time, Maguire was genuinely sad at leaving his friends behind. He left them his winter supplies and the Eskimos promised to spread the word to all their neighbours about the friendly dispositions of the British. Maguire wrote of 'Erk-sing-era': 'a man of considerable influence at the settlement who had bourne a uniformly good character throughout the years of our intercourse, and who by the steadiness of his conduct and friendly disposition had the good fortune to acquire the favourable opinion of everyone on board the ship'.

These feelings were reciprocated by the Eskimos – and particularly by 'Erksinra' – who thirty years later told the ethnographer John Murdoch about their friend, 'Magwa'.[1]

Maguire returned to England in April 1855 and was immediately promoted to captain. He spent the next two years at the Royal Naval College and then was given several important commands and served

[1] Murdoch, 1892, p. 52.

in the war on the China coast. In 1866 he was put in charge of the Australian squadron, and his future naval career looked promising indeed. A year later, however, he became ill and was sent home. He died at Haslar Royal Naval Hospital on 29 June 1867.[1]

Maguire's journal was given to the National Library of Ireland in 1931 by Dr Katharine Maguire. Judging from internal evidence and from the remarkable consistency of the handwriting, Maguire copied this version from a rougher journal that he kept aboard the *Plover*. The manuscript comprises approximately 240,000 words – a very thorough daily account of everything that happened to Maguire from January 1852 until his return to England in 1855. Approximately 30 percent of the manuscript has been removed in this editing: principally Maguire's account of his voyages to and from the Arctic and his meteorological and auroral observations. The method of transcription conforms to the Hakluyt Society's guidelines.[2]

[1] Lean's Royal Navy List; ADM 196/1, ADM 11/73, Public Record Office (PRO), Kew, U.K.
[2] Hakluyt Society, 1975.

THE JOURNAL

JOURNAL
OF ROCHFORT MAGUIRE

<u>Saturday Jan'y 3^d</u> [1852] I left my house . . . for London in
consequence of having received an intimation from Captain W. A. B.
Hamilton, Secretary of the Admiralty, that it was the intention of the
House of Lords to appoint me to the Command of the Plover. I
presented myself at the Admiralty on the Monday morning following,
where I endeavoured by all the argument I was master of, to persuade
their Lordships to send out to Bherings Straits, an efficient aid in
steam for the purpose of advancing assistance to the ships already
gone on[1] And also more thoroughly examining the Northern portions
of that sea, with the hope of finding traces of Sir John Franklin's
expedition. All my endeavours[,] assisted by many well wishers to the
cause, were unable to move Sir Francis Baring[2] with whom I had a
private interview, and on my mentioning a wish to explore the space
Eastward of the land[3] discovered by H. M. S. Herald, in the direction
of Melville Island, he answered all, by 'that's discovery! that's
discovery!' from which I presumed that any further representation on
my part would be useless. I accordingly made up my mind to make the
most of the means I had offered me, viz. the Command of the Plover as
she stood, without any alteration, thinking at the same time, that my
suggestions relative to steam, would become necessary next year,
when being on the spot, my local knowledge would I hoped be taken
advantage of –

I had the good fortune at this time to meet with Mr John Simpson,
Surgeon R. N. who had just arrived home from the Plover, having
been superceded on promotion – but wishing to continue his service in
Arctic search, he applied for, and received his appointment as

[1] H.M.S. *Investigator* and H.M.S. *Enterprise*, vessels which had rounded Point
Barrow and entered the Arctic, respectively, in 1850 and 1851.

[2] First Lord of the Admiralty.

[3] Landforms which are today designated as Herald and Wrangell islands and which
were reported by Captain Henry Kellett in 1849.

Surgeon to the Plover – from this gentleman who I had been previously acquainted with,[1] and with whom I now located myself in lodgings, I received many valuable hints, as to our probable wants on joining the Plover . . .

January 10th I received my Commission for the Plover, and a few days afterwards had the satisfaction to have M[r] T. A. Hull[2] appointed as 2nd Master & M[r] Edwin Jago[3] Clerk in Charge both of whom had served with me for six years in H. M. S. Herald. Making up our party to four. Our time was now passed in making our arrangements for leaving Southampton by the West Indian steamer Orinoco on the 2nd of February – by which route we had been ordered to take passage. During these arrangements I received much kind assistance from M[r] John Barrow[4] of the Admiralty and Sir Francis Beaufort the Hydrographer, under whose department I had served six years in the H. M. S. Herald . . .

Saturday evening January 31st I received my Instructions from the Admiralty, containing at my requisition permission for the Plover to be advanced to Point Barrow, if it should be found available as a winter Station . . .

Sunday February 1st Our friend M[r] Barrow called at our lodgings early this morning & (found us all in our shirt sleeves busily packing) to inquire if we wanted any thing, that he could do for us, but as we had been daily taxing his good nature for the month past, we replied to his offer with the most heartfelt thanks for his past kindness without drawing any further on his good nature. At 5 P.M. we left London from the Waterloo Station for Southampton and embarked on board the Orinoco at noon on Monday February 2nd . . .[5]

Wednesday June 30th by 1 Am we made out the Plover lying in the

---

[1] Maguire had been first lieutenant aboard H.M.S. *Herald* from 1845 to 1851, and Simpson had been assistant surgeon aboard the *Plover* from 1848 to 1851. No doubt they were acquainted from their service in the western Arctic.

[2] Thomas A. Hull had served aboard the *Herald* as master's assistant from 1845 to 1851.

[3] Edwin Jago had been clerk aboard the *Herald* from 1845 to 1851. He should not be confused with C. J. Jago, who was third lieutenant aboard the *Enterprise* from 1850 to 1854.

[4] This is the son of Sir John Barrow. When he retired in 1845 Sir John Barrow had served for four decades as second secretary of the Admiralty. It was he who had drafted Sir John Franklin's orders for the 1845 expedition. Since 1844 the younger John Barrow had been head of the Record Office of the Admiralty.

[5] Maguire and his party reached Panama, crossed the isthmus, and then sailed to Honolulu. There they boarded H.M.S. *Amphitrite* and departed for the North on 30 May. They reached Port Clarence on 30 June.

fair way between Grantley Harbour and Port Clarence. at 4 Am anchored. Captain Moore[1] came on board during the forenoon. I accompanied him to the Plover. Captain Frederick,[2] Captain M & myself held a survey assisted by the Medical officers of the two ships, on the Plovers officers and Crew, to ascertain their fitness for further Arctic service. Fourteen were found either unfit or unwilling, and were removed. They were replaced by Captain Frederick by others, selected from the list of his crew.

Thursday. July 1st 1852 I took command of the Plover this morning and commenced making arrangements for our departure to the North. In my orders from the Admiralty I was directed to place a supply of provisions at the Russian post Michaelowskoi[3] in Norton Sound. As the Plover had left a supply there the year previous I considered that part of my orders complied with, having nothing to prevent my proceeding North from this place. In the afternoon we weighed in order to work out over the bar, to be ready for receiving stores and provisions. The winds and tide both proving unfavourable, we had to Anchor, without having gained anything.

Friday. [July] 2nd A slant of wind this morning enabled the Plover to be brought out of the Channel leading from Grantley Harbour to Port Clarence. And Anchored alongside of the Amphitrite. When we commenced our labours provisioning, surveying stores and provisions and getting the hull of the vessel caulked and refitted – rainy weather for two days. Kept our work a little backward. The promptness of Captain Frederick, who assisted us with all the means at his command, got us forward with all our preparations.

[July] 3d 4th 5th 6th 7th 8th 9th 10th 11th By the evening of the 8th we had all our provisions on board, and ready for sea. I deferred my departure for Monday 11th to allow time for the ice to clear away to the North so as to enable me to pass Point Barrow in the boat.

Sunday [July] 11th I went on board the Amphitrite this morning to make arrangements with Captain Frederick for our meeting in Bherings Sea, and settled the 2nd of August to rendezvous off C. Lisburne on inspection –

Monday [July] 12th My first day at sea in command of a ship. The

---

[1] Maguire was sent to replace T. E. L. Moore, who had commanded the *Plover* since 1848.

[2] Charles Frederick was in command of the *Amphitrite* and was senior officer.

[3] The Russian–American Company trading post near the mouth of the Yukon River; today, Saint Michael, Alaska.

morning was beautifully fine, without wind – at 6.30 a breeze springing up from the S.W., we weighed and made sail on the Port tack and stood out of Port Clarence; the wind remaining favourable until noon – when it came from the West, obliging us to tack to the South, to increase our distance from Cape York, we did little more than drift to the North and West obliging us to tack to the South to increase our distance from Cape York. We did little more than drift to the North & West with the current, until 8 P.M., when favoured with a light breeze from the South, we shaped our Course through Bherings Strait, a place seldom passed until the search for Sir John Franklin brought vessels into these seas. About the same time the American Whale Ships have extended their cruising to the Ice. I imagine that a few years will see these regions as seldom visited as of old. The country is so desolate that it affords little inducement to adventurers. The small supply of Furs and Ivory 'Walrus Tusks', possessed by the Native Esquimaux, offers for the present an advantage to the Whale Ships to barter with Rum & Tobacco. The supply will in a short time fall short of the demand and the dangers of the Navigation render it so hazardous, that a few years will see this sea left as solitary as it was at the time of Cook & Beechy[1] [sic] & whale Ships are properly strengthened to contend with the Ice When the Whale fishery will no doubt be found profitable for a limited number of vessels . . .

<u>Wednesday July 14th</u> . . . Since leaving Port Clarence I have been engaged arranging our boat expedition for Point Barrow. I am now quite ready for a start. If the winds would keep pace with our wishes for getting forward, we should be nearer to the Ice than we are at present.

P.M. a heavy swell from the North indicated the approach of a strong breeze from that quarter that we had to contend with during the night, accompanied by a heavy cross Sea. At 3 P.M. as I was sitting down to dinner with Captain Moore, who has very Kindly volunteered to remain in the vessel as an Amateur, during the time I am to be away in the boats at Point Barrow, our attention was called by hearing water trickling into the cabin & in looking around we

---

[1] Captain James Cook's vessels, H.M.S. *Resolution* and H.M.S. *Discovery*, had operated in the Bering Strait region in 1778 and 1779. Frederick William Beechey commanded H.M.S. *Blossom* in the same waters in 1826 and 1827. Beechey had been sent to meet John Franklin, then in command of his second Arctic expedition, who was trying to traverse the northern Alaskan coast by boat from the Mackenzie River.

found it getting out of a small hole, about a foot from the deck in one of the side lockers. It was soon ascertained to be pure salt water, and as it was coming in at a good rate, we were puzzled to account for it. We fancied all sorts of causes, amongst others, that the Carpenters of the Amphitrite might have left a hole through her when boring for survey. However, in that case, the water would not show itself on the inside, but would run down between the lining into the well. Altogether the circumstance was an unpleasant one. The Ship was already making a great deal of water from her heavy load of provisions. And the Cabin through which this salt leak was passing, was more than half full of slops & underneath it, almost all our dry provisions were stored. After clearing out one or two of the lockers, the water was found to enter the Ship through the Port after round house scupper pipe. It had been broken during the winter and had escaped the notice of the carpenters. Now all that remained to be done was to block it from the outside, a difficult task in cold weather when . . . it was awash with the water and a heavy sea running. We succeeded in getting it done, glad that it was no worse . . .

Sunday July 18th I had not left the deck more than five minutes and had got partly undressed when we made what was at first thought to be the pack. On coming closer it was found to be sailing Ice[1] which we entered and continued our course to the North for ten miles passing on both sides heavy Ice. At 6.30 Am the Ice became so heavy in the line of our course that I was obliged to haul to the East hoping to be able to get in shore and be enabled to start in the boats. On this course the Ice was very little better. In an hour finding the leads no better, and the appearance of the weather very unfavourable, the wind backing from West to the South with a falling Barometer, At 7 Am I resolved to haul out the way we had come in to wait the result of the weather. We had no difficulty in threading our way out, and at Noon found ourselves in comparatively open Water with three American Whale ships in sight. They were Cruising off the edge of the loose Ice, without any success. We spoke the Ship 'Sea' of Wareham, New Jersey.[2] A large fine ship. the Captain Kindly offered us any assistance. I declined detaining him as we were on the weather side of the floe, or we might have provided ourselves with a few extras for our Messes. At 1 P.M. Having fixed the ships position

---

[1] Small pieces of ice that had been driven away from the pack ice by wind or current.

[2] The *Sea*'s home port was Warren, Rhode Island.

accurately, we put her head again to the North, and at 4 P.M. got amongst heavy sailing Ice. The weather looking better, I shaped a direct course for Icy Cape, intending to run within thirty miles of it, and there leave in the boats for Point Barrow. We pursued our course as near N.E. by N as the Ice would allow. The ship sustaining some unavoidable contacts with the Ice. I was obliged to take this means of getting in shore, as our time would not admit of waiting until the Ice cleared away. By 9 P.M. we reached the open water in shore and made preparations for hoisting out the boats the moment we had run our distance . . .

Monday July 19th We had run to our intended distance from Icy Cape by 3.20 Am when the Ship was rounded to in 15 fms and Anchored . . . The wind for the last two or three hours, had been gradually increasing and drawing to the South and the barometer falling rapidly. By the time the ship was rounded to, it was blowing fresh with a good deal of sea on, but not to the extent to prevent the boats being hoisted out & provisioned for their Voyage to Point Barrow . . . By 5 Am everything being in readiness for the boat expedition to Point Barrow, I shoved off, just as the Cable parted from the ship pitching so heavily.

Vide Journal of boat expedition to Point Barrow from the 19th of July to the 11th of August.[1]

When the boats shoved off the Cable was hove in to where it was found to have parted at the Anchor Schackle [sic] and the Ship put under sail & stood to the West. She was ordered [to] be at the rendezvous seven miles off the North end of the Shoals off Icy Cape by the 28th of July to pick us up on our return, then to meet the Amphitrite on the 2nd [of August] off Cape Lisburne, and to complete our provisions from her, previous to our departure for winter Quarters at Point Barrow. It will be seen by my boats Journal, that the Plover never came within ten miles of the rendezvous but came in to the South of the Cape on the 3[d] of August, & not seeing us, an impossibility from their distance from the rendezvous, they made sail to the South without remaining an hour. The ship in standing to the West[d] soon got amongst the Ice, in smooth water, in the afternoon, the wind shifting to West, she was tacked to the South and reached open water by midnight . . .

---

[1] Maguire's journal of his boat and sledge expeditions has apparently not survived. His account of this boat expedition appeared in the Parliamentary reports (Great Britain 1852b, pp. 48–59) of the Franklin Search. It is reprinted as Appendix Three, pp. 469–92 below.

Thursday August 5^{th1} Steering S by W for Cape Lisburne at 7 P.M. signalised with H. M. S. Amphitrite in the rendezvous off D[itt]o at 9 received from her two officers, a twenty three foot Cutter, and boats crew, to search for the boat party they did not reach within ten miles of when they went to Icy Cape for the purpose of picking them up. Sent twenty-one cask to the Amphitrite to lighten the deck load . . .

Saturday [August] 7th at 1 Am a sail on the Port quarter. At 3 H. M. S. Amphitrite signalised that boats were safe at Icy Cape and finding that the Plover sailed so slowly, Captain Frederick determined to take his own ship to Icy Cape, to pick up the boats. It will be seen by reference to the boat journal, that we had left for Cape Lisburne, before she could reach, to which place he returned with all dispatch and fortunately for us in the boats, succeeded in overtaking us there and received us on board . . .

Tuesday August 10th Hove to at rendezvous waiting for the Amphitrites return from Icy Cape. During the forenoon fired 7 guns in answer to his approaching in a thick fog. Communicated with her at 11 Am and made sail to the S.W. . . .

Wednesday [August] 11th Steering S by W. Light airs. At noon boarded the American Whaler[,] ship Washington of New Bedford . . .

Sunday [August] 15 Standing to the S.W. and S.E. Communicated with two American Whalers . . .

Tuesday [August] 17th Running for the Eastern passage of Bherings Strait. At 2.25 obs[erved] the Diomede Islands on the lee bow. Bore up and came through the strait . . .

Wednesday August 18th at 0.10 Am came to in 13 fms. Under high land about Cape York. At 4.30 Weighed and ran for Port Clarence. At 9 came to in 5 fms. Cape Riley S 16°W South – Bluff of Grantley Harbour S 79°E. At 9:30 P.M. arrived H. M. S. Amphitrite in which ship I was a passanger for the second time. With my companions in the boat expedition to Point Barrow. Our own ship having in two instances run away from us, it was fortunate that we had a fall back as the Amphitrite proved . . .

Thursday [August) 19th At 6 Am I took my leave of the Amphitrite a second time to join the Plover, much vexed at her being brought

---

[1] Maguire's entries of 5 August to 18 August 1852 describe the *Plover*'s activities during the period of time that he was away from the ship on his boat expedition. The information was presumably extracted from another officer's journal.

back to Port Clarence as it did away with the benefit of the Amphitrites trip to the North. It was intended to fill the Plover up with Provisions off Cape Lisburne, where she had proceeded for that purpose. By that means it was hoped, a week would be gained by the Plover in getting to Point Barrow. However as we had to get there, I commenced our preparations for departure without delay. My first precaution was to see all the sails well bent and the storm gear all in its place, and mast & rigging well overhauled. Through the assistance of Capt[ain] Frederick, who sent his carpenters for the purpose, our spare bower anchor was wooden stocked. The iron one having been broken on a former occasion. We now repaired it to take the place of the Anchor lost off Icy Cape. Mr. Bourchier,[1] addit[ional] 2[d] Master, and Mr. Forster, assist[ant] Surgeon, going home from the Plover, had remained to do duty in the absence of Doctor Simpson and Mr. Hull, who accompanied me in the boat expedition to Point Barrow. They were now discharged and in the vacancy of Mr. B., on my requisition, Captain Frederick discharged Mr. Wright,[2] midshipman, from his ship to the Plover, A young officer highly recommended, who will be very useful in assisting at our Magnetic observations during the winter. This made our compliment forty-one in all, a small number considering the service we were going on, having to winter in the neighbourhood of a numerous tribe of Esquimaux, with the character of not being very friendly. The small number had one advantage only. it enabled one to complete provisions for two years in the event of any unlooked for detention at Point Barrow by the Ice; this we could not have done for a large Number . . .

Friday August 20th As I was not desirous of working against the prejudices of sailors, not liking to sail on a Friday, particularly in a case where we were likely to have some difficulties to contend with, I did not hurry our departure to be today, as I might have done, preferring to occupy it in making every preparation that suggested itself. As our masts, yards, sails, and rigging had been thoroughly overhauled the previous day, we had today for completing stores, provisions, fuel and water from H. M. S. Amphitrite and hoisting in our boats. This we had completed by 4 P.M. The anchor stock was

---

[1] Thomas Bourchier became master of H.M.S. *Rattlesnake* and wintered at Port Clarence in 1853–4.

[2] T. D. Wright spent the winter of 1852–3 aboard the *Plover* and then was invalided and sent home.

worked hard upon during the same time, and got to the bows by 6 P.M. Completed, considering it makeshift, in a very perfect way.

I had now nothing left undone except to close my letters, both public and private, unfortunately much behind the rest of our work, from the shortness of our stay. Through the industry of Mr. Jago, this difficulty was also conquered. By 8 P.M. seeing everything in a fair train to be finished by midnight, I went on board the Amphitrite, to take leave of my kind senior officer Captain Frederick, to whom I had been much indebted, for many acts of kindness during my passage with him from the Sandwich Islands And subsequently when taken on board his ship in our boat expedition from Point Barrow. On parting I received many good wishes from him, & his officers, and I felt as one does on leaving kind friends. On Returning on board I found all my public letters finished and by Midnight I was enabled to take a few hours rest, previous to sailing at 4 Am on our anxious & uncertain voyage to Point Barrow – With an inward wish for a prosperous passage . . .

Saturday August 21st At 4 Am. I was informed that a light breeze had set in from the East, fair out of the harbour. On going on deck I found it very light and variable. As the tide was ebbing strong, I saw if we could clear the Amphitrite, it would drift us a few miles before the breeze made steady. I accordingly weighed with the first catspaw, and passing close to the Amphitrite, got fairly off. Port Clarence is a fine sheet of water, easily entered with all winds. The distance from the entrance, to where our ships have usually laid near Grantley Harbour, is about seven Miles. This is rather against it, when time is an object, in a dull sailing ship, as it takes the best part of a day, unless favoured by the wind. This proved to be our case on the present occasion, as we lost our favourable breeze soon after weighing and had to try, against a contrary one from the West all day making but little progress as it occupied us until the P.M. to get to the Entrance, when it fell calm, obliging us to Anchor, to avoid being set on the spit of Cape Spencer, as the ship was drifting towards it with the Current . . .

Sunday [August] 22nd At 3 AM a light breeze from the S.E. enabled us to weigh and shape a course along the land by Cape York for Bherings Strait. At 8 Am the fair way rock of the Diomede group was made out from the deck, and steered for to open the Eastern passage. In the forenoon several Whalers heaving in sight, I determined to chase them, although at the sacrifice of time, to increase our store of tobacco for bartering as we were very short of that article, and its value in our case, was greater than gold. By 11 Am, after divine services, we succeeded in cutting off the sternmost of the group of four vessels. The Captain was so little used to seeing National Flags, that he mistook our blue Ensign for the Russian Flag, and when we hailed him the first time, shook his head most forlornly, as much as to say, its no use, I don't understand your language. On my second attempt to induce him to understand English, his ears appeared to bristle up and at last he understood that we were speaking his own language and wanted to be supplied with some tobacco, which he very kindly supplied us with. And also gave us a barrel of potatoes as a present. His ship proved to be the Julian of New Bedford, Capt[ain] J. L. Cleveland. I purchased from him 466 lbs of Tobacco, giving him an order on General Miller our Consul General at the Sandwich Islands for 140 Dollars, the Amount of his charge.

At Noon we parted company from the Julian in the centre of the channel, and shaped a course true North to pass thirty Miles West of point Hope. At 8 P.M. we came again upon a cluster of Whalers, and procured from the ship Liverpool of New Bedford 73 lbs of Tobacco & 50 lbs of shot for Ninety Two Dollars. At 10 Continued to the North on our Course. at Noon left tangent of the fair way rock S18°30′ W. D° and Cape Prince of Wales . . .

Monday. August 23^d A favourable breeze during the night enabled us to make good way to the North. At noon, I found a North course was taking us more to the West than I wished, and hauled to the East two points, the winds soon afterwards headed us from N.E. to which we braced up. We passed several Whalers during the forenoon all anxiously on the look out for their game. Some of the ships had their boats away on the look out also. We were favoured with very fine weather, which was taken advantage of, in making preparations for contending with the reverse. A Casualty to be expected from the lateness of the season. After the 10th of August usually the winds set in from the West, increasing in strength as the season closes. Which makes the whole American Coast a dead lee shore, for this reason, I was desirous of keeping a good distance from the land, the Plovers lewardly [sic] qualities making that precaution necessary . . .

Friday September 3rd [1852] The wind veering to the Southard as was anticipated, we made good way on our course, the water remaining smooth with an increasing breeze. Soundings were obtained every hour in from 30 to 35 fathoms over an even bottom of sand. At 6 AM the low coast about Refuge Inlet[1] was observed from our mast heads, agreeing very well with our reckonings. As we advanced in shore Cape Smyth was distinguished and a course shaped for it, which would bring us in with the spit of Point Barrow.

By 9 Am we were abreast of Cape Smyth & soon afterwards made out the top of the fishing stakes at Point Barrow.[2] Our course now lay close along the land, and with a pleasant breeze and smooth water our advance was rapid. All hands looking with interest upon a shore that had not been passed to our knowledge under such circumstances previously. Three oomiaks[3] full of men put off to us from Cape Smyth where there is a larger Esquimaux settlement,[4] with the hope of getting on board, but, I was too anxious to get the Ship in security previous to bad weather coming on, to heave to for them. On nearing Point Barrow the water shoaled suddenly to five fms, and as we were ignorant of the Soundings in shore to the East[war]d of it, we hauled out until they again increased.

At 10.30 we were enabled to see into Elson bay[5] over the low land of the spit, and were rejoiced to find it perfectly free of Ice. Making it almost a certainty our being able to winter there, previous to knowing this, our success was uncertain. At noon we rounded Point Barrow under all sail distant about two miles, in five fms. We had now to haul sharp to the Eastwd, along the spit East of the point to Moores Channel[6] leading into the bay, the wind now at South, blowing straight out of it.

At 30 minutes past noon, we tacked to close the spit, intending to work along it. Mr Gordon[,] Mate[,] had been previously dispatched to sound the approach to the channel, in standing in the water shoaled gradually to three fms & two and a half, the Natives who had got round us in crowds pointed towards the spit, as the direction of the deep water, but finding that our soundings did not increase, I let go an

---

[1] Now Walakpa Bay, about 19 nautical miles southwest of Point Barrow.

[2] These 'fishing stakes' were presumably the racks which stood above each house for drying skins and for storing equipment out of reach of the dogs. The settlement at the tip of Point Barrow was called Nuvuk.

[3] An umiak is a large open skin boat, similar in shape to a dory, with a skin covering stretched over a wooden frame.

[4] The settlement at Cape Smyth was called Utqiarvik. It is the site of the present town of Barrow.

[5] Today, Elson Lagoon.

[6] Today, Eluitkak Pass.

Anchor until we could ascertain where the deepest channel laid.

I now sent M[r] Hull the 2nd Master in the gig to sound out the channel, and recalled M[r] Gordon, in whose boat I went myself to find out our best course. In pulling directly in I found we had to cross a bank with little more than 16 feet water on it. From this it increased gradually to 4 fms. M[r] Hull who I communicated with informed me that in pulling for the spit, he had found 16 feet.

Seeing the necessity for dispatch with night and bad weather coming on, I hurried on board, got the Ship underweigh, and stood for the spit, passing over very shoal water, certainly within 6 inches of our draft, and tacked almost touching the Spit, I now worked in short tacks along the beach, with a boat ahead calling the Soundings, until close off the passage, when standing over for Martins Isl[an]d,[1] the helm was put down in five fms, and as the ship came head to wind, she took the ground, and hung for a few minutes. Fortunately she was sufficiently round to take the head sails aback, which forced her off and astern just as [I] was meditating about laying out an anchor to heave her off. When making a board back in the same direction, we grounded again and got off under similar circumstances. But not wishing for a repetition of it, I gave up the idea of beating any farther in such narrow water and Anchored in Mid channel, Intending to warp in without delay, under shelter of the spit. In sounding round the ship, we had no more than 5 feet [of] water, at a ¼ cable[2] length astern.

The launch was now hoisted out and preparations made for warping in. which was commenced as soon as possible, in laying out the warps a second time, the wind had so much increased, that our three boats, could scarcely get an end with them and by the time they had returned, it was blowing so hard, that I feared to trip the Anchor. Notwithstanding the unsafe position of the Ship. Whilst the boats were hoisting up, a strong weather current made, that brought the Ship to swing broad side to the wind, this induced me to trip the anchor, and in working in we were swung so as almost to scrape the Point of Martins Island with our stern, the drift of the hawsers allowing great scope.

[1] The low sand islets that enclose Elson Lagoon have undergone considerable change since the 1850s. See Map 4, p. 84 below for the situation then. On the British charts Martin's Island was the first island east of the Point Barrow sandspit. Many of the British names for the islands near Point Barrow were rearranged by Ernest de Koven Leffingwell during his surveys in the first years of the twentieth century (Leffingwell, 1919, pp. 93–100).

[2] A cable is 100 fathoms, or 200 yards.

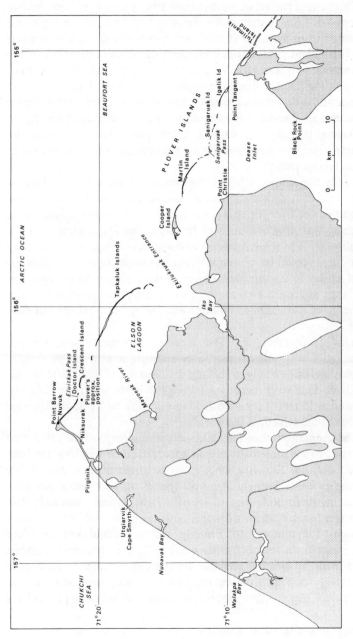

Map 3. Point Barrow and vicinity today.

This danger passed we were comparatively secure and our Anchor dropped in 5 fms. rather within the points of the Island and spit, and sheltered from the wind at West, we now made all snug by sending the Top gallant yards down & pointing the yards to the wind. When this was done it was 11 P.M. and so constantly had every one been on deck for the day that the people had not been able to have any supper and a very limited time to their dinners. I now ordered them to receive an allowance of grog, their long exposure requiring it.

During the night it blew a heavy gale from the South[a]rd (Mag[neti]c).[1] a strong weather current caused us to ride with little strain on one cable . . .

Saturday September 4th The appearance of the offing at daylight was cause of congratulation to us on being inside. The shoal water we had passed over yesterday, and the position where the Ship was at Anchor, was now one mass of breakers, the Ice coming over the whole of it. Whilst we lay in smooth water, although not in so safe a position, as could have been selected had we more time. It blew too hard all day to attempt moving into a more secure Anchorage. The sea in the afternoon we were sorry to observe, broke completely over the spit, we had intended building a house upon, to receive our deck load . . .

Sunday [September] 5th The weather becoming moderate this morning. I was obliged instead of allowing it as a day of rest, to employ all hands busily in shifting the Ship to a place of safety inside the bay. This work occupied us until 2 P.M. when the ship was moored in 15 feet of water with 60 fms of cable to the South[a]rd and 50 fms to the N[orth]W[estwar]d.

The evening proving fine, I landed with a party of the officers on the spit, to see some natives who appeared to be watching the Ship Anxiously, not Knowing whether to be afraid of us or not. A few trifling presents brought them all round us, and seeing our Men collecting driftwood, they all set off to assist them, returning after each trip to the boat for a reward . . .

Monday [September] 6th Finding that we could not land our provisions from seeing the sea break over the spit. Arrangements were made by clearing away all the spare spars from amidships, to stow the provisions at present on the lower deck, there, and leave the lower deck clear for the people – A comfort they had not known for

---

[1] Approximately south-southwest true.

some time. By the same means we were enabled to open the main H[atch] way, previously stowed full of flour which gave us another ladder to go below. Several other alterations were made, to the same end, clearing the decks as much as possible for room, but as yet nothing could go out of the Ship.

I sent Lieut. Vernon in the launch to collect fire wood on Martin's Island and to get a general idea of what quantity of that useful article we were likely to obtain. Mr Hull was dispatched to sound out the channel we had entered. And Mr Gordon Mate and Mr Jago Clerk in Charge proceeded in the gig to the opposite side of the bay (South) to look for fire wood.

At 1 P.M. The weather becoming very unsettled with thick fog, our different boats returned in board, without have been able to effect anything. We had two oomiaks along side full of natives but as yet they had not commenced giving us much trouble.

Tuesday September 7th A gale from the N.E. prevented any of our parties leaving the ship. We were busied on board restowing the provisions on our decks, And transporting our spare Anchor to the Cathead to be available if necessary, in which purpose three lengths were taken off the Port hawse Cable, and bent to it.

Wednesday [September] 8th The weather was sufficiently moderate today to send Lieut. Vernon & a party of hands in the launch to stack wood on the 1st Island from the Ship – Called by us Martins Isl[an]d. The Carpenter and his mate accompanied him to select some pieces for sawing down into rafters for the housing. The Natives along side the Ship, in their oomiaks, give a great deal of trouble to prevent their coming on board and stealing everything they can lay their hands upon. In fact it would take us all our peoples time, supposing we had not got ample employment for them, looking after them to prevent their thieving.

Saturday [September] 9th As I was anxious to keep up our stock of water, I sent Lieut Vernon in the launch this morning to the village to try whether the Natives would be troublesome or not. Two of the officers walked up carrying their guns, to shoot small birds 'Phalaropes'[1] found in great numbers along the spits. The guns had a very good effect on the Natives who are very troublesome to our parties away from the Ship And although it has been my wish to

---

[1] These may have been both northern phalaropes (*Phalaropus lobatus*) and red phalaropes (*P. fulicarius*).

keep our fire arms as much out of sight as possible, the show of them on two or three occasions, has been already found necessary. Our boat succeeded in getting three tierces of water, without being much interfered with. We have been enabled to procure a good supply of driftwood, for rafters and the Carpenters have commenced sawing it down. Mr Hull has been employed with one boat, taking soundings in the offing.

<u>Friday September 10th</u> Mr Gordon was employed in the launch watering. Mr Hull and Wright with one boat continued their work sounding out the bay. In the afternoon I took a passage in the launch to the Village taking Doctor Simpson and Mr Seath the Carpenter with me, to get an idea for building our storehouse from the Native dancing houses at the Village, as they seemed to me large & roomy & would answer our purpose very well.

Whilst we were engaged examining their construction, some of the Natives, endeavoured by going from one to the other, to prevent our men taking the water. Without success as not more than four or five joined in it. One old man in particular was very energetic, he had been, it appeared refused admittance into the Ship, in consequence of some thefts had been committed, and now retaliated, by saying that we stole the water,¹ he commenced by capsizing several full breakers,¹ and then put the Anchor into the boat & shoved her off.

The officer of the boat referred him to me, as I was seen advancing toward them, seeing the old Man coming towards me, looking dreadfully out of humour, I remarked to Doctor Simpson, that I must appease his wrath with something in the way of a present, although I was not aware at that time that any thing had gone wrong. before he reached me I advanced with a needle in my hand for him & on my presenting it all his choler vanished as if by magic. He returned with me to the boat, almost appeased & sat down on the beach with his wife beside him, all the rest of the men women & children present followed their example, forming a ring in the centre of which, Doctor Simpson & myself found ourselves placed.

The old man then with the assistance of his wife, commenced relating his grievances, to the effect that they ought to be allowed on board to barter, if we came on shore for water, it appeared also that in keeping the old lady out of the ship, she had received a push on the head.

We endeavoured to explain that the numerous thefts, made it

---

¹ Small barrels for the storage of drinking water.

necessary to keep them out of the Ship and that our object in coming here was not bartering – but for good moccasins, coats, & gloves, tobacco and beads would be given in exchange, as well as for Reindeer flesh. And that they in particular would be allowed on board whenever they came. A little tobacco was now given round, when the boat being loaded, we shoved off, leaving them all perfectly satisfied. It was fortunate I happened to be present, when this misunderstanding occurred, otherwise it could not have been so easily explained away.

Saturday 11th September Hearing from Mr Hull who has been along at the Islands to the Eastward, and had discovered two more, on which there was [an] abundance of driftwood. I have determined to send a strong party under Lieut. Vernon in the launch, to raft a sufficient quantity to the ship to complete our housing, provisioned for four days. Mr Hull in the gig, who was continuing the survey in that direction, was also provisioned for the same time, in order to extend it to the end of the chain [the Plover Islands], and accompanied the launch, to point out the position of the Island, then to continue his operations.

They left the ship at 7.30 Am 18 hands in all. the remainder on board were employed unbending the storm gear, sawing down plank and protecting the ships stores from being stolen by the Natives. nothing can be compared to their propensity for thieving. They are so much accustomed to living by their own resources and consider-ing every thing that comes within their reach, in the light of fair game, in the same way they would a Reindeer or a seal, they make no scruple in committing the most bare faced thefts, in some cases resenting being stopped. No part of the ship outside, escaped them. our leaden scupper pipes, when not narrowly watched, were cut at with their knives. The rudder coat was hacked to pieces and it was almost impossible to keep a boat down, without losing something out of her so that with a very small ships company, and a great deal of work to be done, it took the attention of quite half to protect ourselves against their thieving.

At 10 P.M. previous to going to bed, I burned a blue light to ascertain if the launch was returning as Lt Vernon had ordered to get back the same day if possible, intending to give him a tow up with our remaining boat. He saw it from the Island, where he had bivouacked for the night & unluckily answered it, which made me imagine he was returning, and lowered the boat, and sent her towards him, thick weather coming on, they returned, when I sent them a second time, when they remained until an hour after midnight, in a fruitless search, causing us some anxiety on board from the thickening of the weather and expending many rounds of ball cartridges as well as three blue lights to guide their return.

Sunday September 12th At Daylight the launch was observed beating up for the Ship. At 8 Am Our boat was sent to give them a tow up. They arrived on board at 9.30 bringing a supply of wood, sufficient to complete our housing. In the afternoon I walked to the Village to observe the state of the Ice in the offing, and to commence a friendly intercourse with the Natives if possible. I was accompanied by Doctor Simpson & Mr. Jago, who carried their guns, being armed myself with a spy glass and compass. We observed the ice packed heavily on the shore to the South[a]rd about Cape Smyth and all along the Northern side of the spit, the offing sufficiently open to allow a ship to navigate without much difficulty.

The natives collected round us in great crowds, the guns having the effect of making them very civil. Doctor Simpson shot about twenty phalaropes at one discharge, for their amazement, which seemed to amaze them all beyond measure. We took great pains to explain to them by signs and speech the object of the Ship being there, to assist two others that were in the Ice and we were waiting for them.

On our return to the Ship, we met several u-mi-aks returning from fishing. They had killed two whales,[1] but did not seem disposed to barter the blubber. Mr Jago shot at a fine White owl[2] on the spit, but unfortunately missed him, for which I was sorry and as it would have been an excellent specimen.

At 6 P.M. Mr Hull returned from his surveying excursion, he extended his examination of the chain of Islands running E by S true from our position and named by Captain Moore the Plover group, to a distance of twenty miles, without coming to the termination of them, when he returned as the weather was unfavourable, and the natives he met with, all returning to Point Barrow, from their summers's excursions, all gave him a great deal of trouble and stole

---

[1] These Eskimos were returning from their autumn hunt for bowhead whales (*Balaena mysticetus*) in the relatively ice-free waters east of Point Barrow, where they tried to intercept the whales as they migrated west out of the Beaufort Sea. The spring hunt, on the other hand, was carried out at the narrow leads in the ice on the west side of Point Barrow and its sandspit to the south. Because the whales' movements were more restricted in the narrow leads, the spring hunt was usually more productive.

[2] The snowy owl (*Nyctea scandiaca*).

several articles from our party. He reported having seen some wild geese, which Doctor Simpson thought must have been either Eider, or King ducks.

The temperature has fallen to 24 degrees and the water to 30 degrees, some pieces of Ice that has been drifted inside will have the effect of reducing the latter lower . . .

Monday September 13th Lt. Vernon & Mr Gordon in the launch and whale boat, went along the Islands to collect fire wood. Mr. Hull and Mr. Wright continued the survey of the bay and coast line. The morning was calm, and there had been a light fall of snow during the night, sufficient to deaden every echo and produce that remarkable stillness which succeeds a heavy fall of snow. A few moderate sized floes have closed on the Northern shore, and a great quantity of smaller ice, some pieces finding their way into the bay through the narrow passage of the Island & spit. The boats did not bring any heavy wood today. On the last occasion, the layer pieces had to be dug out of the frozen ground, which would show a mean temperature here, below the freezing point.

In the afternoon we had a visit from a native Chief.[1] He came draped in a coat of the Martin or Sable skin,[2] evidently to excite our cupidity, but as Mr Hull had some trouble with his party to the Eastw[a]rd, one of whom stole our . . . boats crutches, I received him rather cooly, and endeavoured to have explained to him the cause, but it is hard to persuade them that thieving is an offence. After his being on board some little time, I took him down to the cabin, and made him a small present with a view of establishing a friendly intercourse with him. His coat was not taken notice of purposely, rather to his annoyance when he at last took it off and seemed anxious to dispose of it. As there is no fir, or beech trees in the neighborhood, where the martin would be found, we concluded he must have procured it to the East[war]d near the Colville River where their trees are found.

---

[1] The Eskimos of northern Alaska did not have chiefs, *per se*. Leadership within a community was generally invested in a number of men of power and wealth who, in whale hunting communities such as Nuvuk, were umiak owners and captains of whaling crews. Such a man was *umialik*.

[2] This man, 'Angunisua' or 'An-goon-iz-wa', is elsewhere referred to as 'Sable Coat', 'Sables', or 'the Black Chief'. His coat was probably of pine marten (*Mustela americana*) skins, animals which do not occur in Arctic Alaska, and which therefore must have been acquired in trade with the Indians. Such a garment was no doubt a sign of substantial wealth.

The Natives I am sorry to find appear Mischievously inclined towards us. Mr Hull finds great difficulty in Keeping up his surveying marks as he has no sooner left them, than they are thrown down . . . Tuesday September 14th We had two boats employed collecting and stacking wood, under Mr Gordon & Jago. Messrs Hull & Wright continued their surveying operations. As we had very few people left on board, I made a point of remaining on the ship myself. The number of natives around us at all hours of the day, making every precaution necessary, to prevent pillage and destruction to the ships hull outside.

In the forenoon I requested Lt Vernon, and Doctor Simpson, to walk up to the village and buy some logs of wood I had seen there that would answer our purpose for sawing down into planks. They found very few natives at home and amongst those remaining, there appeared some difference of feeling towards our officers. One man took them to his tent at once whilst others pushed the boat off, accompanied them, but the greater number remained indifferent. The Man with the sable coat of yesterday, had the largest tree to dispose of, but did not seem to care for tobacco. He also, took the officers into his tent and showed them three glutton[1] skins, of great value about Kotzebue sound and three large fine Wolf[2] Skins. He had several crudely forged, double edged Knives,[3] like spear heads, and expressed that he wanted something of that kind, with a longer blade. He did not want tobacco as he showed them a bunch of it weighing nearly 70 lbs. which he had procured to the South[a]rd, he did not open it, but they concluded it was Circassian[4] from seeing a

[1] Wolverine (*Gulo luscus*).

[2] Gray Wolf (*Canis lupus*).

[3] In the eighteenth century the source for these double-edged knives would have been the trading centres of eastern Siberia, from which points they would have passed through many hands. They were carried across Bering Strait and traded at the great trade rendezvous at Sheshalik on Kotzebue Sound. Then they would most likely have been carried north, over the mountains to another trade fair, at Nirliq on Colville River delta, where the Eskimos from Point Barrow would have acquired them (Spencer, 1959, pp. 198–9). By the 1850s, however, the Mackenzie Eskimos were beginning to acquire substantial quantities of metal which originated with the Hudson's Bay Company in the Mackenzie River valley.

[4] This could well have been the true Circassian tobacco, the yellow broad-leaf grown near the Black Sea and then carried across Siberia and Bering Strait to the trade rendezvous at Kotzebue Sound, for it is well known that such a trade existed in the early nineteenth century (Spencer, 1959, pp. 462–4). Virginia leaf tobacco is similar to Circassian, however. It is possible that the origin of some Virginia leaf was one of the 176 whaleships that were cruising near Bering Strait in the summer of 1851 (Bockstoce, 1986, appendix 3).

few leaves of that sort in use. They seemed anxious for Plug tobacco, but knives were the chief article in request.

We allowed a few natives on board in the evening who behaved themselves very well. They we[re] all young men, very good humoured, and seemed less disposed to steal than most.

Wednesday September 15th A Southerly wind this morning had cleared the Northern shore of a good deal of Ice, but the bay to the Westward was closely packed. Our friend with the sable coat from whom a log of wood has been bartered yesterday for tobacco, came on board today and left it, he evidently wishes to have something else and as I was anxious to keep up a system of getting them to barter with us, I took some trouble to satisfy him & by changing half the tobacco, for a preserved meat tin it seemed to have the effect.

The time appeared now to have arrived for the Natives to return to their winter huts at Point Barrow, from their summers excursions along the coast. And as the ship lay in their direct track, we have very much to our annoyance a visit from all of them. No less than nine U-mi-aks came up from the lee[war]d today, having their tents, sledges, dogs, and families in them. They were all perfect strangers, and looked in Amazement at us and the ship. They come from the mainland, near a river[1] where they procure fish and Reindeer. They appear to be met by another tribe of Esquimaux at the place for the purpose of exchanging their articles of produce. Those from the East[war]d supplying furs and skins, in exchange for oil & blubber from the Sea about Point Barrow. The Natives here speak of their celebrating their Annual Meetings, in grand dances, & singing.

The party today brought with him a quantity of venison, salmon, and deer & fawn skins, in one or two cases, sable skin coats were offered. They parted reluctantly with their venison,[2] but we succeeded in procuring enough fish (salmon)[3] for five days consumption for the whole crew which was issued on each Sunday whilst-it-

---

[1] These Eskimos were returning from their annual summer expedition eastward, during which time they visited the trade fairs at Nirliq and Barter Island and did some hunting and fishing as well. At Nirliq they met Eskimos who lived primarily in the interior, who sold them Russian trade goods (obtained the year before at the Sheshalik trade rendezvous on Kotzebue Sound) and caribou skins for their sea mammal products. At the Barter Island trade fair the Point Barrow Eskimos obtained furs and English trade goods from the Mackenzie Eskimos in return for Russian goods and sea mammal products.

[2] This was actually meat from caribou (*Rangifer tarandus*).

[3] Probably arctic char (*Salmo arcticus*).

lasted in addition to the usual ration of salt-beef for that day, as it is very old and does not contain sufficient nourishment to keep people in health, where there is no other resource.

We found this party good humoured, but like all the rest, bare faced thieves. In the evening as a number of them had pitched their tents on the spit, I landed accompanied by Doctor Simpson to pay them a Visit, and distribute a few small presents amongst them. On Landing one old lady who appeared to be a principal seized me by the Arm, and carried me off to her tent, where she offered me the best fare her larder afforded. It consisted of blubber, in various forms, contained in rough wooden bowls, the distant smell of which was quite sufficient for me, not being as yet quite broken in to such highly scented dishes. As a set off to my refusal of her hospitality I gave her a needle & a few small beads, and made my escape. Doctor Simpson had in the mean time to undergo a thorough overhaul of his dress, until he satisfied them by showing his shirt, & skin. When this was over we returned on board, leaving them in high good humour. In the Morning their tents had disappeared.

All our force was employed today collecting Fire wood. The launch brings one load a day from an Island distant about five miles from the Ship. This we have placed in a stack on the spit, so as to be under our protection. The Ice in the offing we observe to be generally on the Move, according to the wind. In our case it becomes clearly packed on the shore, & remains until a shift of wind again lets it off.

Thursday Septr 16th Our wooding party in the launch with Mr Gordon. And surveying in the gig with Mr Hull & Wright, were continued today, The Number of Natives about the Ship prevented my detaching any more men. Indeed from the Number of our crew out of [the] Ship already, I deemed it prudent to keep the Ship clear of natives today & in consequence of one or two parties, not being let on board, they went on shore & retaliated, by Commencing to pull down our wood stack, & remove some of it to a distance across the Spit & when this circumstance was reported [to] me, it gave me very little uneasiness, as I knew any labour was not to their taste and they would soon get tired of it. This proved to be the case, as they did not carry it on more than five minutes. It was also assisted by another party coming up, who had been promised leave to come into the Ship. Amongst these were our friend with the Sable coat, and the old man & his wife, who had opposed our getting the water.

When they came on board, it seemed impossible to limit the admittance any further. They had too many friends & followers. The consequence was our deck soon became crowded, And a strange sight it afforded. There was our party[,] some twelve at most on deck, with forty or fifty of these savages, all roving about, with covetous and greedy looks for everything around them, the value of which to us does not appear anything, but to them, must have had about the same effect it would have on a London mob, being allowed to range amongst the treasure of the bank of England. This party was good humoured & [it] went off very well. I took about six of the principals down to my cabin, and showed them what I thought would amuse, & made each a small present, on returning to the deck, it appeared necessary to have a native dance before they went away. When this was accomplished, they wished to see us dance & in order to fully please them, The Serjeant who plays the Violin, brought his instrument on deck, and played a few airs accompanied by a bugle and drum, which appeared to delight them exceedingly, and sent them away in excellent humour.

Mr Gordon with his party met a set of Natives, who had buttons and preserved meat tins, which led him to the supposition of their having met either the Enterprise, or Investigator,[1] but it seems a remote possibility, as yet we are unable to obtain little information from them, from the difficulty of making them understand our meaning . . .

Friday Sepr 17th The launch was employed today with Mr Gordon getting a tierce of firewood. Mr Hull having completed sounding out the bay, the gig was sent with Mr Wright to procure a tierce of water from the Village. He was assisted by some of the Natives, whilst others tried to prevent the crew from filling their breakers. The day has been cloudy with a S[outh]E[aster]ly breeze & a light fall of snow but the air is still very drying.

About 7 Am The Quarter Master of the watch came down to inform me that an U-mi-ak full of Natives had arrived alongside. As the few hands we had remaining on board were at that time employed on the lower deck, I desired him not to let them on board for the present. He soon returned to tell me that they would take no refusal, and had forced themselves on board. As this was not an

<hr>

[1] The *Investigator* passed east of Point Barrow in 1850, and the *Enterprise* in 1851. The crews of both ships had contact with the Eskimos in northern Alaska (Collinson, 1889; M'Clure, 1856).

uncommon occurrence, I did not think much of [it] when I found that Lieut Vernon was attending on deck. He came down to tell me, that the Head Man of the party was a Chief, and that he wanted to barter for gun powder with Venison as he had a gun. This I considered the worst piece of information amongst many unpleasant circumstances, that I had experienced relative to the Natives. As I felt that if they had fire arms, we could not remain amongst them.

As the Chief[1] expressed a wish to see me, I went up, and found a large, powerful, old man, with a very bad expression of countenance He had a Hudsons bay Musket, with the name of Barnett on the lock, it was a good deal worn, but fit for service.[2] He had a powder horn slung over his right-shoulder, & hanging hunter fashion under his left arm, he had neither ball or shot, for which he was very anxious, and would not part with any thing except for Ammunition. I saluted him with all friendship, Made his wife a present, and took him down to my Cabin. I offered him something to eat, and made him a present of tobacco. When after satisfying his curiosity about the Ship below, I took him on deck with the idea that he would go away, but nothing seemed farther from his thoughts, as he kept roving about the decks, and several times slipped down the hatchways on to the lower deck, a part kept as yet, sacred from the Natives.

During the forenoon, several U-mi-aks arrived along side the Ship, discharging their crews in swarms upon our deck, making it literally crowded for the day. They were allowed every freedom, consistent with their known propensity for stealing, but some bolder than others were very hard to deal with. One fellow became so bold as to attempt to force his way down the Companion ladder, I immediately stopped him, which brought about a small scuffle between us. This did not appear to satisfy him, as he came soon in contact with the Quarter Master of the Watch, a quiet, but rather

[1] Later identified as 'O-mi-ga-loon' and elsewhere referred to as the 'Old Chief'. Dr John Simpson (Appendix Seven of this volume) referred to him as 'the principal man at Point Barrow'.

[2] 'O-mi-ga-loon' was probably the first resident of Point Barrow to own a firearm. He was the man who threatened Pullen's boat party near the Colville River delta in 1849 (see Appendix One, p. 453 below) and who met a party from the *Investigator* near the Jones Islands in 1850 (M'Clure, 1856, pp. 72–3). Maguire noted (entry for 18 January 1853) that he had obtained his gun from the Indians. Maguire may have mis-identified the tribe – it seems likely that they were the Vunta Kutchin, not the Koyukon – but in any case the gun almost certainly was sold to the Indians at the Hudson's Bay Company trading post at Fort Yukon.

82

short tempered, powerful young man. Who gave him a lesson in the Art of Pugilism that he will not forget in a hurry. He dealt him fair blows in the face, each of which would have stunned one not very thick in the head, but the Esquimaux received them for some time, until it had the effect of taming him. When he was put over the side into his boat in the presence of at least Fifty of his Countrymen, only one of whom offered to interfere in the short combat. He was easily kept back, the others looked on quite unconcerned.

About noon at my particular desire, three parts of the crowd went away, the remainder remained and were evidently detained on board by the old Chief. Who there was no possibility of moving out of the Ship, without having recourse to force, which I had no intention of doing – preferring to wait patiently until he should tire of his Visit. This there seemed no hope of, as he hailed three U-mi-aks passing full of people from the Eastw[ar]d, to come on board. I heard the word tawac used very often, as an inducement, with I imagined other alluring hopes, and the children having been all quietly removed, I feared they meditated an attack to pillage the Ship. Then again it seemed hardly possible as they had no arms with them. However, on second thought, it occurred to me that my duty was plainly not to allow myself to be taken by surprise and Acting from this idea, I had twelve muskets loaded quietly on the lower deck, & the bayonets fixed ready for handing up at a moments notice. In the event of their making an attack upon us with their knives, each without exception being provided with a good one, and adept in the use of them, from their frequent practice in Killing Animals, should mischief be intended I thought this their only plan as they could from their numbers, have had four or five Knives to each one of our people on deck, if they made a simultaneous attack. With the same crew, I sent the few men I kept on deck, down one at a time to Arm themselves with pistols, concealing them under their clothes, in this way I succeeded in Arming our party, & waited the result, perfectly satisfied of our advantage. Quite a silence prevailed each party watching the other.

Whether they did not like our looks, or never meditated any mischief beyond stealing everything that came within their reach, they all left, boat after boat, as night came on leaving the old chief with only his own U-mi-ak. He had continued throughout the day to range about the Ship in the most insolent way, requiring all our exertion to keep him off the lower deck. This I was determined

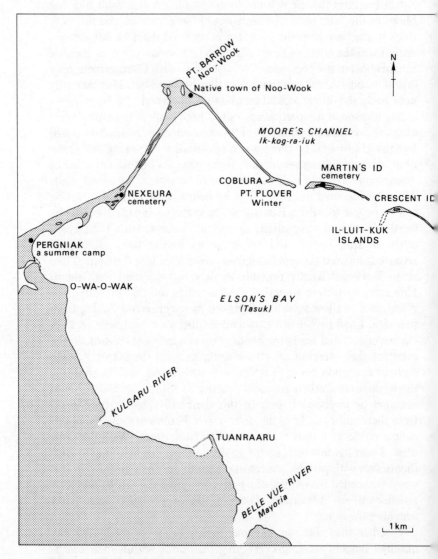

Map 4. Plan of Moore's Harbour, Point Barrow, after Thomas A. Hull, ca. 1853.

about, but I feel persuaded, it was only the fear of our two poor twenty four pound Carronades that kept him from Mischief. When left by himself, I took care to have him as much his own Master, as when he had twenty people at his back and left him quite to himself as to his leaving the Ship. He remained on board until 7 o'clock, a visit of twelve hours, & when gone I was so thoroughly tired out & provoked, that I made up my mind not to allow myself such another visitation, And in clearing up our decks, so many small articles were found stolen notwithstanding all our vigilance, that I arranged to stop all work for tomorrow, except that of keeping the ship & stores under our own control, and however they might take it, not to allow more than one U-mi-ak crew on board at one time . . .

Saturday Sept[r] 18th On going upon deck this morning, I was surprised to find the old chief, our plague of yesterday, sitting on the spit close to the Ship, and the Quarter Master informed me, he had been hailing for a boat. 'This I thought a better joke still.' He soon afterwards Came along side, dressed in a sable Skin coat, but to his surprise was refused admittance, on the plea, of the number of things that had been stolen the previous day. During the time he was standing on the gangway, our seamen were cleaning and discharging their arms. And examining the Carronades, at which he stared a good deal and went away. I was not quite satisfied with myself at the time for refusing him admittance, but felt that it was an Act of Necessity. And as I had commenced with him, I allowed no natives on board for the day, which appeared a great relief to every one, after the extreme Anxiety we had been in for several days, preventing the ship from being literally pillaged. The opportunity was taken to allow the crew to have the day to wash their clothes without any interruption. We had as usual six or seven U-mi-aks, fresh arrivals from the East[war]d alongside, and some bartering was carried on. They seemed hard bargainers, unwilling to part with anything except for large Knives, but some large blue Russian beads were highly esteemed & procured us several pounds of Venison, some fur mits & deer Skin Mocassins. After a steady refusal to allow them up the ships side, they remained about the Ship satisfied enough at staring at her. We had also a crowd of Kyaks[1] from the town, that remained until after 5 o'clock. The U-mi-ak remained along side later in which a young fellow behaved in a most indecent manner

---

[1] Kayaks.

offering his person, and was properly rewarded by one of the seamen throwing a bucket of cold water over him, which had the effect of turning the laughter of his companions against himself, particularly that of a woman who made one of the boats crew . . .

Sunday [September] 19th The day throughout has been gloomy with a wetting mist. We had an early visit from an U-mi-ak containing the old Chief, our friend with the Sable coat, and another man who had made himself very useful to us when we were here in the boats. They brought as a peace offering, all of the articles that had been stolen from the Ship during the several days past. I think it is reasonable to suppose that the display of our cleaning arms, before the old chief the day previous, led them to imagine we were intent on doing them mischief. This I considered a very satisfactory conclusion to our disagreement, and permitted them to come on board. And they remained the whole day, their tones very much altered for the better, the old Chief particularly, who was now content to remain on the Quarter deck, to which they were all restricted.

After Divine service, as they were expressing somewhat of surprise at our Carronades, I had one fired as if for their satisfaction, but in reality to intimade [intimidate] them, during the time the loading was going on, it was hard to distinguish whether fear or surprise predominated and when the gun was fired, they expressed themselves in a general shout.

They left the Ship in the evening, promising to bring back one or two trifling articles still missing. They were desirous of having music, & dancing but being Sunday, we could only indulge them with a tune from the Musical box, a piece of mechanism beyond their comprehension . . .

Monday Septr 20th . . . As the Natives begin to understand being kept out of the ship, the Launch with Mr Gordon was sent this morning for a tierce of fire wood. Two U-mi-aks full of Natives came off and hung about the Ship most of the day, but only our Sable Coated friend was allowed on board. Curiosity seemed to be the motive of his visits. he evidently admires and appreciates the skill of the Carpenter.

As I now considered that we were beginning to be understood by the Natives & thought I could leave the ship for two or three days without fear of a misunderstanding occurring during my absence, I turned my attention more to the object of our being here than I had been allowed to do, by the constant state of excitement we have been

kept in by the Natives since our arrival. And although now past the
time to be able to do much in boats, and just at the Equinox when
heavy gales might be expected, I could not at any time previously
have got-away from the Ship with any feeling of certainty that things
would go all smooth. and as we had not been able to place any
notices to the East[wa]rd, to point-out our position to any parties
falling back, besides which I was Anxious to take a line of Soundings
across Dease's Inlet, I arranged to leave the ship in the gig,
victualled for 14 days accompanied by Mr Hull on the morning of the
21st and with that double object in view, to get as far as we could, &
be guided by circumstances of weather etc. . . .

Tuesday Septemb^r 21st Weather gloomy & cold with the wind from
E.S.E. As all our arrangements for going away in the gig had been
made yesterday, we were ready to leave the ship at a little after seven
& shoved off. I have written a journal of the trip in a separate paper
to prevent confusion in this.[1] As more directly concerning the
movements of the Ship. I am indebted to Dr Simpson for the
remarks inserted here during my absence, and many others, that his
observations have pointed out to me. Numerous Natives alongside
but only our friend with the Sable Coat allowed on board.

Wednesday Septr 22nd Weather cold and clear. Five or six boarders
along side, but only the old Chief and others admitted. Their
curiosity and interest seems excited in the work going on in the Ship,
and from their manners it is likely they will be tractable enough in
the end. Our Sable coated friend missed his wife today, and thinking
she had gone astray, he kicked & beat her, holding over her his
drawn knife. Had she dared to resist his conjugal authority, it was
presumed he would in his fashion have used it. Fortunately these fits
of jealousy are very evanescent. The temperature of the Air has
fallen to $+20°$ [$-6.7°$C]. The water is at $29°$ [$-1.7°$C]. The Ice is
packed on the shore, but there is plenty of open water beyond, the
distant Ice being observed in motion to the Eastw[ar]d. The
apparent height of the pack is very variable owing to the light and
mirage.

Thursday, Septr 23rd We had the usual attendance of Natives along
side but none were admitted. Some of them on the spit lighted a fire
near one of our wood stacks, which took the flame, and a boat was

[1] Maguire's journal for this cruise has apparently not survived. His account, which
appeared in the Parliamentary reports of the Franklin Search (Great Britain, 1854a, p.
167) is reprinted as Appendix Four, pp. 493–4 below.

sent to put it out. Before she had returned to the Ship, the Natives could be seen collecting the timbers to make a small fire & then carrying brands to the stack, never dreaming that all their man-oeuvres could be seen with a glass. The boat soon after had occasion to be sent to the Island and as soon as she shoved off, all haste was made to scatter the brands again fearing some retaliation. There remained some smouldering fire on the shore but it was thought the Natives were hardly mischievous enough to be incendiaries. I returned in the gig at a little after noon . . .

Friday Septr 24th At an early hour this morning the ship was sur-rounded with sludge & cake Ice, driving rapidly with the current out of Moore's Channel. This continued throughout the day, the wind strong at North (Mag[neti]c) . . . which packed the Ice close in the offing. Our employment today has been cleaning and re-fixing the Sylvester stove. Was glad to have an opportunity of inspecting the construction of it. It is a close stove inside a large metal chamber. The smoke is made to pass downwards to its exit through the funnel. The space between the Chamber & the stove is open below, to allow the cold air to pass up freely, which becomes heated, and passes off into the hot-air pipes, led along the ships side. In its passage it comes in contact with an assemblage of hollow short cylinders which add very much to the extent of heating surface, and with a moderate fire must give heat to a considerable current.

Saturday Septr 25th The Ice becoming forward in the bay, I sent Mr Gordon to haul up the launch on Martins Isl[an]d, preferring it to the spit close to the Ship, because of its distance from the Natives. The gig with Mr Wright was sent to bring the crew on board. The launch met with some difficulty going on shore from the pancake ice, setting out with a strong Current through Moore's Channel, and was nearly carried out with it. They succeeded in hauling the boat up, and returning in the gig at noon, with a fresh wind directly in their favour, stuck fast in the sludge & pancake ice, the men used every exertion & means to separate it over the bows without avail, in this state, she was drifted by the current rapidly past the ship.

Seeing that she would have some difficulty in reaching us, a breaker & lead line was veered astern, which she picked up, but unfortunately when her cable that we were hauling on board, was within five fms of our stern, the line broke, and the boat drifted directly through the channel and to seaward. In this most distressing dilemma, I lowered our only remaining boat with Lieut Vernon who promptly volunteered his services, to run out a long line to her, after Veering 500 Fms the gig was reached, drifted in the mean time off the land. During this interval our anxiety on board was excepial [exceptional]. My own feelings seeing twenty-two people, out of a crew of forty-one in such jeopardy, cannot be described. I went to the mast head & could see the gig previous to her being reached by the line, carried off the land, notwithstanding all the efforts of the two crews to hold her against the set. Mr. Seath the Carpenter who was standing beside me, fancied the boat was full of water & the people standing on the thwarts. This was not the case. The drift of line was so great when it reached her, and from being very much fouled by the Ice, they could do very little with it for some time. From the Ship we were [in] worse circumstances, as a point intervened, round which they had been carried. After considerable delay the crews warped the boats back to the point, but round it they could not from the line being so foul, to make matters worse it parted in the attempt. Most fortunately a number of Natives had collected on the spit to witness the sight and the end of it being thrown amongst them, the boats were saved from being carried out a second time, when it would not have been in our power on board to have rendered them any assistance.

The Natives having hold of the line, hauled the boats up, & across the spit, ready for launching on the inshore side close to the Ship. When our people were seen to be landed safely on the spit, all hands on board seemed to have experienced a general relief. There they were obliged to be left for a time, whilst we cleared the hawse, as the Ship was riding with very strained cables, from the increased thickness of the Ice, and it being drifted fast by the current. To get our party off, a 4 Inch whale line was got on shore for that purpose, the increased thickness of the Ice making that size necessary, but with time we were reddy [sic], the Ice became firmly fixed, and all our efforts only made their position worse, as we dragged them half a cables length off the beach, (where they were safe), the crews getting back with difficulty on the Ice leaving the boats fixed.

Soon afterwards one of the Natives[1] succeeded in getting off to the Ship on the ice by using great caution. He crept along upon his hands & knees, carrying a light pole in each hand, so as not to bring his weight in any one point. As he advanced stealthily, picking his

---

[1] Later identified as 'Ne-pak-tok'.

way over the thickest parts of the ice, he looked from his bearskin dress, more like some animal of that species than a man. When he got on board, a present of tobacco induced him to take a light sledge on shore with him, with provisions, this he managed with great ease, travelling as before, and towing the sledge made fast round his waist. By this means our party were well provided with food. The boats sails made a very good screen to Keep the breeze off. And with a fire of driftwood, they got through the night, as well as people unprepared for such exposure could be expected to do . . .

Sunday Septemb^r 26th Early this morning the three officers, with their boats crews, walked on board without much difficulty, but not all escaping from wet feet. They passed a tolerable night, and the Natives behaved very well to them, especially some of the women, who pulled off our Mens Moccasins, and rubbed their feet, in some cases they put them under their skin dresses against their skins to restore their warmth. For this reason, and as they were now able to walk off, the Ship was crowded with Natives, but they refrained from theft, and did us good service by hauling the boats alongside, whilst our adventurers of the night had some sleep in their hammocks.

The ice near the ship has not moved today, although the channel along to the Village is clear & a Native boat passed us from the East[war]d along the Islands. Early in the afternoon we made a stir amongst the Natives, and made the excuse of hauling in our warps, to rid ourselves of them. We afterwards hoisted our boats up, considering ourselves fortunate in having them to do so . . .

Monday [September] 27th A clear bright sunny day. I thought the Ice was sufficiently fast to unmoor and get the Ship into her position for the winter. We had the greatest difficulty forcing her through the Ice, not of two days formation. It was four hours before we got one Anchor, in fact the day was spent in pulling it up & shortening in on the other Cable to where we left in the morning.

We had a great many natives about the ship, and a select few on board, but giving no trouble. Yesterday a coat belonging to the tribe of Indians called Ko-yu-kuk (the same who attacked the Russian post of Darabin,[1] when poor Lieut Barnard of the Enterprise was killed),[2] was offered for sale, but the price demanded a saw, was considered too much. Another of the same Kind was offered today. The tribe appears to be known to the Esquimaux of this place, but I

[1] Today, Nulato, Alaska.   [2] See above, p. 38.

90

fancy they easily communicate with each other. The old chief who has the Hudson's Bay gun, said he knew them, and that they lived a long way off. He explained that he had had a skirmish with them & showed us a cut that he had received on his head. He has a handsome little boy about 10 years old that we have all admired very much, & thought very good looking for an Esquimaux, who he tells us he stole from them. He is fonder of him, than any of his own children . . .[1]

Tuesday Septr 28th We had still open water in the channel outside the spit, and patches of water in the bay, where the current was strong. This day was spent in endeavouring to get the ship ahead to her anchor, much time being lost in getting rid of the Ice out of the Cuts, for the want of a space of open water to float it away. It was 6 P.M. before we got the cable shortened in to 13 fms. We had a numerous attendance of Natives round the ship, some of them not very well disposed.

Wednesday Septr 29th Finding that we lost so much time yesterday in the unavailing attempt to force the ship ahead through the Ice, I thought that a pool of open water at the beach would receive the Ice out of a canal cut from there to the Ship. This after about three hours of sawing was choked up, and left us no hope of success, in that way, so I commenced a cut from the ship, and tried Captain Parry's plan of sinking it under the floe on each side. This too was almost impossible, owing to both surfaces of the ice being so uneven from the pieces riding over each other whilst still in a sludgy state.

In the Mean time a strong breeze springing up from West, set the

---

[1] This boy is later identified as 'Passah' or 'Passak'. For a clearer account of the boy's story, see Maguire's entry for 2 July 1854.

Throughout his narrative, Maguire refers to the Indians by the term 'Ko-yu-kuk'. It is likely, however, that he inadvertently classifies more than one Indian group under this name. In the early nineteenth century, part of the upper drainages of the Colville and Koyokuk rivers was inhabited by a band of Kutchin Indians called the Dihai. This band was, as Ernest S. Burch, Jr (1980, pp. 280–1) has reported, 'harassed and driven progressively west, north, and east by the Koyukon [Indians], the Upper Kobuk [River] Eskimos, and the Upper Noatak [River] Eskimos, in turn. The reduced population finally was defeated and driven out . . . altogether by the members of the Colville River [Eskimo] Society, apparently around mid-century.' It would seem, therefore, that the boy 'Passak' was in fact a Dihai Kutchin, not a Koyukon, and that his flight and adoption may have occurred at the time of the final dispersal of this band.

In the spring of 1854, while on a sledge trip at Point Berens, Maguire met a group of four Indians who were armed with muskets (see his entry for 5 May 1854). It seems likely that they were Vunta Kutchin ('Rat Indians'), not Koyukon Indians. See footnote 2 for Maguire's entry of 28 August 1854.

Ice in Motion at 1.30 P.M. Causing a general rush Amongst the Natives for the Shore. We also hurried our people in off the Ice, with all their boats, and waited the result of the move, which was principally outside of us. It separated along our Starb[oar]d or outer side, & astern, leaving a large lane of open water. Along the Shores of the spit there seemed to have been great pressure, as the Ice was forced up to a considerable hight [sic] and separated in large cracks all along shore, from which I concluded, that it would all go out, if the strength of the wind remained the same. The Natives on board seemed to think it would remain. Along our Port or inshore side, it was driven up with some force but the way in which I observed it part at the cable, gave me the idea that we could hold on, whichever way it turned out. At 3 P.M. it appeared all stationary, leaving a large lane of open water astern, trending to the Eastward.

Thursday September 30th The wind had moderated today and the Sea remained perfectly stationary. Still after its sudden movement yesterday I felt uncertain about moving the Ship so close in shore and as I intended to place her for the winter. But at 9 Am, the weather was so fine, and the lane of open water to get rid of our Ice out of the Cuts, that we knew the value of from two days experience, looks so tempting, I made up my mind to turn to with a will, And cut her into her berth, without leaving off, if it took us the night as well as the day. The saws were set to work accordingly at the open water astern, and a canal marked out to take us 40 yards from the beach in 15 feet of water.

During the day we were unavoidably much mixed up with the Natives, and received a good deal of assistance from the well disposed part of them, who were rewarded with tobacco. Whilst with the troublesome, several slight scuffles had occurred with our seamen, from their playing their tricks, & endeavouring to trip them up. One occurred on board to Mr Hull, in endeavouring to get a hulking fellow out of the gang way, Another pulled out his Knife, and ordered the women & children to retire, I met them all starting off on the ice ahead of the Ship, and thought something must be wrong, but they told me they were going to dance. However I returned immediately to the Ship, & found out the cause, fortunately Doctor Simpson happened to be on deck at the time, and on the Man producing his Knife, he very quietly showed him a revolving pistol, and explained to him its seven charges, which alarmed them exceedingly, and had the effect of keeping them quiet all the rest of the day. Our sable coated friend happening to come down at the time, reassured the retreating party, and brought them all back, when we explained to him that if they used their Knives, we should use ours, but that otherwise we would be very good friends.

By 6 P.M. our Canal was complete, when we weighed our Anchor and forced the Ship into the Canal, bringing an exclamation of astonished [sic] from about eighty Natives standing bye – To whom we threw a hawser, by which they tracked us up to our winter Quarters, affording a strange sight, to see a ship walked along by a set of savages, who were it not, for fear of our Fire Arms, would not have left a bit of the ship together in twelve hours. At 7 we let go an Anchor under foot and secured the Ship in the direction we wished her to set fast – The Natives shortly afterwards leaving us.

Friday October 1st [1852] Our first arrangement for this morning was to fix upon a spot on the Spit to build a store house to receive our deck load of provisions to enable us to have clear decks for the people to take exercise, during the severity of the season. Whilst Lieut Vernon was carrying on with the arrangements, for unreeving the running rigging &c, I took Doctor Simpson, who is of a very mechanical turn, & Mr Seath the Carpenter on shore with me, to mark out the ground plan of the House. We were at first taking too low a position, with the view of being nearer to the Ship, but the Natives, standing bye, pointed to the highest part, as being dryer, which we saw and adopted.

The plan was made by the Carpenter and ingeniously contrived so that all our spare spars & rudder, were brought into requisition, and with the assistance of a few pieces of driftwood for rafters, completed the framing. The dimensions are thirty feet by fifteen. The hight [sic] will be about seven feet inside clear of the roof – it would have been a foot higher, but the floor could not be sunk more than two feet, without letting in water, as six inches more would be the sea level. Its direction is N.E. true the point of the prevailing wind, And end on to the Ships broadside, to afford as little cover as possible to the Natives. Mr. Simpson Kindly undertook the office of Superintending architect, and the Carpenter & a picked party of eight men, soon began to make a show.

As an additional security to the ship, we got the spare Anchor on shore in the afternoon, and bent the stream chain to it. We had some little cutting to do afterwards, so as to bring the house in fair view of our gangway when done. The Ship was allowed to freeze in with her head. N.W. by N (Magnetic).

<u>Saturday October 2nd</u> Our work was now before us, the house was getting on as fast as possible. The post[s] were all set up yesterday, and the gravel watered, but they were not sufficiently firm today to admit of the beams, and cross pieces being put-on them. So the ground tier of salt-provisions was stowed to steady them. Taking these out lightened the Ship ten inches, and cleared the upper deck a good deal.

We are as usual surrounded and tormented with Natives. There [is] now a joke got up between us! Whenever any thing is stolen, or a man is bad, they are certain on our enquiring, to Answer and point to Cape Smyth. Everything goes there. Of course we laugh and they follow our example. Mr Seath the Carpenter lost a valuable saw at the house today, as usual the thief belonged to Cape Smyth. But as I was determined to strive my utmost to check this propensity of theirs, I forbid all inter course with them, And allowed none onboard . . .

The forge has been got up for a short time, our fuel will not allow of much work being done with it. the present case is a necessity to make hinges for the door of our store house. Our Carpenters are kept in constant employment, sawing down drift wood to make rafters for the housing.

A large solitary gull[1] was observed today, skimming & hovering about in the vain search for water.

<u>Sunday Octob^r 3^d</u> The day has been remarkably fine with a light breeze from E.N.E. As usual from 40 to 50 Natives came about the ship, but none were admitted although the saw was brought back, as none of our friends were of the party. They keep us constantly on the alert, to prevent their ripping every thing in the shape of copper, or lead, off the Ships side – indeed so pertinacious are they after lead, that we have been obliged to cover the scuppers & parts that are leaded, with boards . . .

<u>Monday October 4th</u> A beautiful clear sunny day. The ice appears piled along the North side of the spit in broken pieces, to the hight [sic] of three and four feet, where the beach is steep and in shoal places, a good deal of pressure is observable, the whole offing is now covered with hummocky ice, becoming frozen in one heap. The ice near the Ship is cracked in several places, they open & close with the rise and fall of the tide, the ice having the appearance of a tough substance stretched across in rugged lines. There is a strong water

[1] This was probably a glaucous gull (*Larus hyperboreus*).

cloud hanging over the N.E. quarter, but we have no water in sight from our mast head.

We commenced this Morning clearing out the Fore hold, to get at the salt provisions in the ground tier to land in the house. The space made will be taken up with such things as will not bear freezing.

The Natives for the first time have come down with their dogs and sledges, several of them passing to the Eastw[ar]d along the Islands, for Whale blubber left from three Killed at the close of the open season. They continue to be very troublesome, pilfering every thing they can lay their hands upon, and they frequently draw their Knives on our Men, sometimes I think more from custom than with any idea of using them. This has been a cause of a good deal of anxiety with me, our men no doubt feel very much at their mercy, under such circumstances, from being unarmed. Their great forbearance is necessary, in the event of my arming them, and I am afraid many of them, from frequent provocations they have experienced would be found wanting in that way. However on giving the subject serious consideration, & considering it not a pleasant feeling to have a Knife pointed at you without the means of defence, I have ordered the Quarter Master of the Watch to be armed with a pistol, and two of the Petty officers of the party working at the house. These people being properly cautioned not to use them unless circumstances of necessity, I am in hopes the Mere show will be sufficient – of this we soon had one instance. One of them played off a practical joke on one of our men, by kicking him in the back of the knees when carrying a spar, for which he was rewarded with a blow in the face. He then drew his Knife, when the Corporal of Marines coming up, and Known to have a pistol put him to flight. None were allowed on board.

The room made in the Fore hold, has enabled us to clear the tanks in the neighbourhood of the Sylvester stove, and as the Ship had become very damp between decks, it was lighted and raised the temperature twenty degrees in two hours. As it had been taken to pieces last spring, it was now satisfactory to find that we had been able to replace it properly . . .

We had a calm fine night, with a very brilliant Aurora extending from West to N.E.

Tuesday Octob^r 5th There was a light fall of snow this morning, the particles of which were star shaped with six beautifully feathered points, our work on shore continues the same, getting on with our house, and landing the provisions as required. The Natives about in great numbers but moderately quiet. A great many of our people were attacked today with a sick headache, and griping, the cause is supposed to be eating the fried liver of Seals,[1] that have been brought by the Natives in great quantities. After this attack they will very likely fall into disuse.

Wednesday [October] 6<u>th</u> The weather at this time is very beautiful. The Ther[momete]r from all hands being a good deal exposed, is felt to be low. +10 [−12.2°C] . . .

We have commenced getting the rafters on for housing in the upper deck. Taking advantage of the experience gained by Captain Parry in wintering in the Arctic regions, where he says in the second winter of the 2nd voyage page 376, 'that each succeeding winter, had pointed out the expediency of leaving the Masts, yards, sails & rigging more and more in their places', I thought I could do no better than follow such an example and Kept everything aloft, the Fore Top gallant Mast was the only spar sent on deck. The Main was left up to afford a better mark for seeing the Ship at a distance, bearing in mind our being here in expectation of parties falling back on her for safety. And as the land here is very low in every direction, the ship is discernible at the distance of nine miles in clear weather.

In the arrangements for the safety & protection of our boats, we could not follow out Capt[ai]n P. recommendations, as our launch had been almost stript of her iron work from the Natives in the few days she was hauled up on Martins Island. Therefore, instead of hauling them up on shore & burying them in the snow the light boats were turned bottom up on the Quarter Davids (which were lowered square with the horizon) and then covered. The launch with the dingy turned bottom up on her thwarts, was covered and placed alongside the ship on the Ice so as to be out of reach of the Natives.

The night was very fine with a little snow drift. The Aurora appeared in regular bands or Arches. The Natives continue about us in numbers, some few remaining until Midnight.

Thursday Octr 7<u>th</u> Our work today continued the same, completing the house on shore, and preparing for housing in. I have been much occupied, bartering with the Natives for Walrus hides, to cover the roofing of our house. They bring them down on sledges and for the most part in small pieces, the old cover of their U-mi-aks, they seem

---

[1] It seems more likely that these headaches were caused by gases leaking from the Sylvester stove. For a detailed description of these stoves, see Alexander Armstrong's (1857, pp. 609–14) account.

to set a high value on them, from which I infer the Animal is not found in their neighbourhood,[1] as seal skins a[re] very abundant, and easily procured.

It is strange to observe how variable they are, as to the things they wish to have in exchange. On one day an individual asks for a preserved meat tin, (very much prized by them for cooking with,) then it matters not whether their article is worth one or not, they all ask for the same, and the rage lasts for a day or two, when something else comes in fashion. No bargain is ever concluded without a great deal of handing about from one to the other, and the women although perfect slaves to their men, in everything like labour, have, as in more civilized communities, a strong casting vote. They, poor things, generally ask for beads, of which they are passionately fond, but unfortunately for us, we have none that they place much value on. The Russians from their long experience with them, have provided themselves with the favourite colour, a sort of dull deep blue,[2] our English beads they accept in a present, but would give nothing for them.

They are a very difficult and unsatisfactory people to have any thing to do with, from their utter want of gratitude, and honesty. You may give them what you please, and they receive it graspingly, without any apparent feeling of thanks, and the only return you get, is to be importuned by those that you have already made presents to more than those who have got nothing, the same thing refers to their being let on board. When a man & his wife & children are allowed in, they never think of going away until they are told, or that they get hungry, And instead of these individuals being satisfied with eight or ten hours about the deck, and being content to remain at home for a day or so, or even quietly outside, and allow some one else a turn. We have the same parties, alongside the ship the first of any the

[1] In the 1850s the Pacific walrus (*Odobenus rosmarus*) population had not been substantially reduced by commercial hunting (Bockstoce and Botkin, 1982), and hence walruses would not have been scarce at Point Barrow. Although walrus hides could have been used for boat skins, they require more preparation and are less elastic than are bearded seal (*Erignathus barbatus*) skins. John Murdoch, who lived at Point Barrow in the early 1880s, reported (1892, p. 337) that bearded seal skins were preferred for boat coverings.

[2] These beads reached the Point Barrow Eskimos from Europe via the native trade link of Bering Strait. They were extremely valuable, but clear blue beads with a white core were even more highly regarded. The beads retained their value until American whalemen began selling large quantities of them, thus reducing their scarcity (Spencer, 1959, pp. 156–7; Bodfish, 1936, p. 212; Stefansson, 1914, pp. 388–9).

following morning, looking as if in compliance with the old invitation to come early, and bring your work. 'all ready for another day with you,['] and it takes with such, several days before they cease their demands for admittance. And so disheartening is it to our feelings of Kindness towards them, that those who have the least notice taken of them we generally find the most civil and obliging.

Friday Octob[r] 8th Our house was completed today, much to our satisfaction, as it allowed us to get the decks clear, the rafters for the housing are also in a forward state, and were it not for our constant plagues the Natives, we should be very content. They keep us in a constant state of watchfulness to prevent their stripping us of every thing. We are obliged to keep a look out man constantly on the ice outside of the Ship, to prevent their cutting her to pieces, and no sooner does he send a man away from under the bows than two or three get under the stern, and dodge about in such a way, as to be impossible to guard against- & commonly when sent away, threatening with their knives. To prevent this one look out man is armed with a cutlass, which I tell our men is a much longer Knife, than is opposed to them. I do not feel disposed to arm them indiscriminately, as some of them have become very exasperated against the Esquimaux from frequent acts of hostility & ill feeling, in return for the kind heartedness, Brittish [sic] Seamen have the character for, and of which ours are no exception.

Today I have carried out a plan that has occurred to me for some time, to keep the Natives clear of the Ships side, Posts have been driven in the Ice, at the distance of nine yards from the Ship, all round her, through these a chain has been rove and they are Kept outside, it appears to answer very well and will save us a great deal of trouble. The lower deck is very damp from the condensation on the beams over head. We had the Sylvester stove lit again today, it rose the temperature to 46 [7.8°C]. and dried up all the moisture . . .

Saturday Octob[r] 9th This being the last day of the week, pains were taken to get all the lumber off our decks carefully sorted, tallyed & stored in the house, the gun Room, and my cabin, both very full of stores of one kind or another, were enabled to be got clear, leaving what appeared a large and roomy ship – after having been so crowded.

We had a number of Natives on board all day, principally those who seemed to have control over the others. And when all our work was completed, I had the Carronade on the side next to the house, loaded before them, taking care to point out the merits of a bag of musket ball that formed a part of it and then laid for the house, which was explained also, and described as being intended for the 'Tiglig's' or thieves. As they have generally manifested a great fear of fire Arms, I thought the show of preparation before these people would have the effect of proclaiming it, amongst their country men, and save us from any interruption from them.

The night was fine, Aurora extending from East to W.N.W.

Sunday, Octr 10th We had a visit from the old Chief and his two wives, one of the latter brought a very good specimen of the great Northern Diver[1] & parted with it for a leaf or two of tobacco, but took it back again – it measured 33 inches from the tip of the beak to the tail, the plumage was complete and not much tossed.

Our storehouse looks curious along side of us, and appears almost like a companion, looming black against so much white, as our prospect at present displays.

In the evening I took a long walk with Doctor Simpson to the end of the second Island (Crescent) from the ship. The night was very fine, but the outward part of our trip was not very agreeable from a keen wind blowing in our face, the return was pleasant, and was beguiled by the company of a native & his wife, who were returning with a sledge load of blubber from the Eastward. This appears to be the best time for such business as travelling as every day or so brings its slight fall of snow, that remains at this early part of the winter unfrozen on the ice and in a months time will make travelling with sledges very heavy. Later it gets drifted away with the high winds of mid winter, & becomes frozen sufficiently hard to travel over without sinking in it.

Doctor Simpson drew my attention to a dark bank of clouds to the North, extending some distance to the East and West, he has remarked it stationary for several days, and he thinks it betokens open water in that direction, as we had not been able to see any from the Ships masthead for several days, we concluded the sea was frozen completely over.

Since our first visit from the old chief, with the Hudson's Bay gun, and his numerous applications for Gun powder for which he would give anything we proposed, & as they included valuable furs, their worth being well known to all our people, I was fearful that some one

[1] An arctic loon (*Gavia arctica*).

might be tempted with, by him. As a check [I] had called in all the Ammunition. Now finding the temper of the Natives such as to require us to be in a constant state of preparation, Each individual on board was served with three rounds of ball cartridge, & the Marines ten, the Arms of the latter being kept loaded.

Monday Octob^r 11th The ice being now permanently frozen, I considered the Anchor we had down under foot, would be safer at the bows, and had it weighed. I was surprised at the strength of the Ice, & supposed that our powerful windlass would have hove the Anchor through it without difficulty. On trial it was found to be powerless for that purpose. We had to saw a space sufficiently large to let it come up, the Windlass power being of little assistance. The ship was afterwards cut round to allow her to rise to her true draft. Since discharging our provisions, we found her to have lightened five inches, her mean draft being 12 feet 8 inches and the depth of water 15 feet.

Tuesday [October] 12th The first thing this morning, I received the unpleasant intelligence that our store house on the spit had been broken into during the night and three sails (The Main Top M[a]st stay s[ai]l, Main and Mizen try sails) stolen. A case of flour (contained in tins) belonging to the Gun Room officers, had been broken open, from the tin shining through the case attracting their notice – And finding its contents did not suit them it was left. It seems probable the Natives mistook it for their favourite (Ni-Ki-Moon)[1] as they term Cavendish[2] tobacco, and unwilling to depart empty handed, they took the sails. As nothing escapes their notice, they most likely remarked these cases landing, and had formed the idea that their contents were something valuable. Although I had taken particular pains all the time the landing was going forward, to explain to the principal men that there was nothing going on shore except salt provisions, which they cannot touch.

I was quite unprepared for this instance of theft, as I had been told by the officers here acquainted with their character, that they would never attempt any thing beyond trifling pilferings, for which I have been unable to find any remedy, except Keeping a vigilant look out, but now that they had commenced on such a large scale as breaking into our store – I had to consider seriously as to the best mode of

---

[1] Chewing tobacco.
[2] Cavendish is a process for preparing tobacco for chewing (rather than smoking) by sweetening it, then pressing it into cakes.

checking them, in all our former cases, a slight show of fire arms in the way of intimidation, had the effect of restoring to us our missing articles – And with a view to the same effect, I ordered one of our small brass three pounders to be prepared for mounting on a sledge, intending to threaten them with a visit to their settlement, if our sails were not returned.

A Native, who comes usually the first every morning, with food for our dogs came as before, and soon afterwards another, who if he was understood properly, told us that while they all slept, some people committed the robbery, making it evident that the affair was very well known at the town. About 9 AM our friend the old chief came down with a very determined air, with his musket slung across his back, to offer us his assistance to recover the things, but as he proposed leading us to Cape Smyth where he said they had been taken to, and not to Point Barrow, that story had been too often tried before, so his services were declined. After some hesitation he came on board, when it was explained to him, that the thieves had been traced along the snow on the spit half way up to P[oin]t Barrow and that we knew the sails were there, and if they were not restored, I should take the guns, which I showed him mounted on the sledges to the settlement to look for them. At the same time, I thought the opportunity of having his gun in my power ought not to be lost, and took possession of it, telling him when he brought back every thing that had been stolen from us, it would be returned quite safe. This appeared to place him in a serious difficulty. He endeavoured to persuade us they were not at Point Barrow. This was of no avail and we repeated our intention of going after them ourselves with the gun. After a great deal of talking, he took his departure, and we went on with our work of housing in, as usual, intending to await the result of his Mission.

He returned again in about two hours (unarmed) with some evasive story that they were going to bring the sails down. He remained about the ship apparently much disturbed, but not in any way distrustful. At this time there were also a few others, including women & children, round the Ship, and one sledge. We now observed with our glasses, an unusual stir at the settlement, in the first place some women and children were seen moving across the bay towards Cape Smyth. Afterwards the men were seen in single files, advancing down the spit, on getting closer, they were made out to be in three lines, and all armed with bows & arrows & quivers. I

101

fancied I saw at this time speers [sic] also, but did not observe them afterwards. The leading men were discharging their arrows ahead of them, as they advanced, & picking them up as they got there, Which satisfied me that their visit was not friendly.

A short time previous to this movement being apparent to us, I thought it necessary to call the officers and ships Co[mpany] to [sic] together, to express the necessity there existed of our keeping a watchful guard as one person, upon the chief and supplies entrusted to our care, and that any loss must be considered, & felt, by one, and all, as personal – and under such circumstances, our bearing towards the Natives, must be expressive of our displeasure at their thieving propensities.

About half an hour after noon, They had advanced sufficiently close to show me, that their intention was to carry the war into our quarters, and my mind was soon made up, that the higher course to pursue, was to keep them in check, at the distance of musket range, by firing over their heads. Wishing above all things, to avoid taking a life, unless under some urgent necessity. We went to quarters, and I distributed our small force, under the command of officers appointed to guard the Gangways, poop & Fore Castle.

Previous to their getting within Musket range, a blank charge was fired from one of our Carronades, and small boat guns off the Fore Castle, which had not the effect of dispersing them as I expected, they still moved forward steadily, and when within musket range, we commenced firing over their heads from the Fore Castle. This had the effect of dispersing them under cover of the spit.

Our friend with the sable Coat, made a rush down ahead of the ship, followed at first by others, but when he found the ball whistling over his head, he dropped on his face to avoid them and then running closer to the Ship, threw his bow and quiver containing seventeen arrows (four of them with iron heads saw shaped)[1] towards the Ship, and ran away. A few extended themselves under shelter of our Provision house, but as a constant fire was kept up over it, not many attempted to reach it. A carronade was also fired so as to graze it, which had the effect of dislodging them.

A false alarm was given at this time that they were breaking down the house, and carrying away boxes. I was on the Fore Castle, and on

---

[1] These arrows were probably made for hunting polar bears (Murdoch, 1892, p. 204).

hearing it, ordered the man next to me a Marine, to fire at a man crawling along on his hands and knees from it. When fired at, he fell flat, and kicked up his heels as I imagined Killed, immediately afterward the report was found to be incorrect, & no more shots were fired at them. And I had the satisfaction to find out that the man fired at (the only one instance) was not killed.

As the old Chief, who had been laying concealed under a Hummock of Ice close to the ship, now showed himself, and beckoned them back in a most energetic way, causing a general retreat, which we celebrated by firing a volley of small arm in the air, the people dispersed round the upper deck. As we had a commanding view from our Mast-Head, and could see that none remained on the field, I was glad to think that no lives had been sacrificed. Although this fact would give them (not appreciating our motives) a poor opinion of us as marks men, still I considered that many had heard the ball sufficiently close to their ears, not to wish for a nearer acquaintance.

As they retreated to the Village in parties, Doctor Simpson counted seventy-one men & allowing himself to have overlooked ten, he computed the number of fighting men at eighty,[1] a computation I consider as near as could be obtained.

Two had the curiosity to follow up the round shot & pick it up. The distance it had rolled over the Ice must have astonished them. It was returned on the following day with the other stolen articles.

The old Chiefs [sic] Neutrality seems strange, but I am inclined to the opinion, that he was content to watch the course of events, if we had allowed them to get within our range, so as to intimidate us by their Numbers, its hard to say what would have been the result, & he would no doubt have sided with his people. As it was, he appeared to have had sufficient Authority to disperce [sic] them. He remained about the ship for some time with another man unarmed. As I intended no compromise short of the return of our stolen stores, He was sent away to bring them. I now began to take my threat of visiting them at their settlement, into my most serious consideration, seeing that if we did not get the upperhand, there would be a difficulty in our future intercourse with them, my having the Chiefs gun, gave me an advantage I could have hardly expected as its value to him was greater than anything they had stolen of ours. Consequently [I] made up my

---

[1] These men would have been drawn from a total population of about 300 at Nuvuk; that is, virtually all the able-bodied men of the settlement.

mind to wait the result of his interference, before deciding upon any movement, not allowing any of them within gun shot, until every thing was returned.

During the night which was fine & clear, a Quarter Watch was kept on deck armed in the event of their attempting to surprise us. The House was also opened & inspected every half hour.

Wednesday October 13th The contrast this morning, not seeing a native, was remarkable, from the usual crowd about us. This I was determined should be the case for the present, considering that it would be an effectual means of bringing them to terms, knowing they would feel the loss of batering [sic] with the ship, more than they could gain by their theft. During the forenoon, one of our brass 3 P[ounde]r guns was mounted on the sledge, and placed on the Ice along side the Ship.

. . . At Noon two Natives were seen coming towards the Ship unarmed. Lt Vernon was dispatched to hear what they had to say, which was to the effect, that the men were all asleep, and our things would be brought down the next day. They had not left the place they advanced to, when I took a party away from the Ship, to try the range of the gun on the sledge, and to find how it Answered, in the event of further hostilities becoming necessary. I was rather glad they saw us maneuvering it, and after having done so, a musket was fired wide of them, as a hint to be off & report what they had seen which I hoped would have the effect of quickening their movements in returning our sails.

We have been unable as yet to get any snow sufficiently free of salt for thawing for use. Today by taking the surface of the recently fallen, it was found very good . . .

Thursday [October] 14th At 7.30 Am our friend the old chief made his appearance with seven Natives and a sledge, carrying our sails. I am told they were evidently in great trepidation. The sails had been cut into several pieces, adapted in size for a U-mi-aks' sail, and served out amongst those who assisted, before the old chief could bring them back. Their pieces had to be collected and were most ingeniously drawn together again by the women, they had been employed all the previous day about them. This accounted for the days delay in returning them. The Dingy Cover was all that was now missing of the robery [sic]. But as I was determined to strike while they were in a funk, No difference was made between the things stolen from the house, ship or boats. I caused a public enquiry to be made by the officers in charge of stores to find every article missing. And when the full extent was known, the old Chief was made acquainted, that everything must be returned, before his gun would be given him – or any of them allowed to come near the Ship. He soon afterwards returned to the town, promising to bring every thing down next day.

I was glad to have got the upper hand of them, without any further trouble on our part, as I felt that our duty was to conciliate as much as possible in the event of any of our missing parties, falling back amongst them. Our own travelling might also be made more difficult, from being at variance with them. Notwithstanding these considerations, it is most necessary for your preservation, with such a people as these Esquimaux – to establish respect from them, by a moderate show of displeasure at their tricks. Otherwise I feel we should not be able to hold our own. Had we not been employed on a Service essentially of peace, I should have most certainly taken a party up to their settlement, in the way of retaliation, on finding they had broken into our store. I am not certain that it would not have been the better plan in the present case, as Kindness and forbearance is lost upon them, indeed it is most deplorable to experience the total want of gratitude, for benefits conferred, they grasp at everything that is offered them, without appearing satisfied, or in any case showing a symptom of generosity. I cannot give a better instance of this than by stating that from the best information we could get, I found that the principals engaged in breaking into our house, and disturbing the sails were composed for the most part of the men we had been allowing aboard every day, making them presents to & treating with every kindness, with the hope of making friends of them in the event of requiring a Kindness in return. From my experience of them now, I consider they are incapable of such a feeling.

Friday October 15<u>th</u> The old chief came again this morning with the remainder of our Missing articles, when his gun was restored to him. I had the curiosity while it remained in my Keeping to examine the charge, & found it loaded with ball, as well as we could have done it ourselves. I made him a present of some tobacco for his trouble, and gave a knife to one of his wives, who it appeared had been very industrious sewing our sails together. The old man made us understand that he had been obliged to use his knife to make the thieves restore the property.

105

The housing in of the Ships upper deck is now finished, and considering it is the fifth year with the same tilt cloth, it is in wonderfully good preservation.

We are employed today shifting our spare Anchor higher up in the Spit, so as to make the stream chain attached to it, Answer for one side of an enclosure, of about an Acre, that includes the storehouse, and the site of our observatory about to be erected, a rope led through posts from the ship surrounds the other two sides within which no one is allowed to pass without leave, or he will be fired at. Our enclosing the Ship round before answered the purpose very well, this I hope will have the same effect, as it prevents their lurking about under cover of the house.

Whilst returning from a walk on the ice in the offing with two of the officers, two shots were fired by Mr Gordon at a mark close to the Ship, and on looking that way perceived a sledge and dogs between the Ship & the Island & two natives running away with all their speed. I endeavoured by making all the show of friendship I could, holding up my arms over my head to re-assure them, but it was all to no purpose, they seemed to run the faster from me. So I gave up the chase, to see that their sledge came to no harm.

On getting to the Ship I dispatched Lt Vernon alone after them, he succeeded in bringing them back, in company with another sledge returning with blubber from the Eastw[ar]^d.[1] They felt Mr Vernons breast for concealed weapons, but not finding any, became braver. They were however much surprised when he showed them a small pistol in each of his trowser pockets.

The men were armed with bows, which they handled ostentatiously, they were accompanied by two women. The men declared they ran away because the ball passed close to them, when in reallity [sic] they were fired in the opposite direction. To restore their confidence, and show them it was a mistake on their parts – I gave them a small present of tobacco and sent them away . . .

Our numbers for carrying out the usual theatrical Amusements for an Arctic winter, are I am afraid too limited to get up any thing passable in that way, And our Means in stage gear and dresses, is on the same scale. Notwithstanding these difficulties, we are having some talk about it, and no doubt an attempt will be made. As a small

[1] They were no doubt collecting blubber from the carcasses of the three whales that had been killed east of Point Barrow earlier in the autumn.

printing press formed a part of the liberal supply granted to us by their Lordships on leaving London – A weekly publication is likely to be undertaken by Doctor Simpson, but as it received its name and an accompanying set of illustrations, from a kind friend to all arctic adventurers at the Admiralty, its time has not yet come . . .

Saturday [October] 16<u>th</u> Our employment today consisted of getting up round shot and grape, for our Carronades, both being stowed rather out of their usual places in Her M. Ships – the former being under 120 fms of chain cable, and the latter in the pump well. Some of the officers have been Amusing themselves firing at a mark, and as the practice has been very good, I think it will have the effect of showing the Natives, that we can hit an object, when we wish to, and as some of them picked the bullets at a distance of 1200 yards, it will give them a good idea of fire arms, and enable them to grasp that they could *not* have been fired at the day they came down in such force.

Our friend with the Sable coat, who had thrown down his bow and quiver, in such a hurry on that occasion, came along side today demanding them to be returned. I had supposed, he would have been ashamed to acknowledge them, and would have lost cast amongst his people for his want of bravery, the reverse was the case, he appeared as bold as could be, and when told they would not be returned until a piece of bolt rope belonging to the sails had been brought back – he said he would steal again during the winter. when I told him if he did, we would shoot him . . .

Considering from the difficulty we had in purchasing our Anchor, that there was no likelihood of our wanting the Chain Cables, they were got below, and preparations made for covering in every crevice . . .

Sunday October 17<u>th</u> We had a visit from the old chief, his son and adopted son. After divine service – The officers took the old man down into the gun Room, and when asked his age, he said he did not Know, but he had many years. When asked the Age of his adopted boy,[1] he said he did not know, as he stole him from the Ko'-yu Kuk Indians in a fight – I gave him the bow and quiver, belonging to our friend Sable coat, as it appeared the piece of rope missing was unlaid and served out in the yarn – We had another Native and his wife on

---

[1] This is 'Passak'. See Maguire's entry for 2 July 1854 for a clearer description of his early life.

board, a very young couple, the woman is very near her confinement, he promised to call the baby (which we foretold him was to be a male) Lobver, the nearest approach his pronunciation could be brought to Plover. We explained to the old chief, that in the affair with his people, we had only fired over their heads, but if they stole again, we should fire at them. This he appeared to understand . . .

Monday October 18th Our employment today was getting a hole made in the Ice for the Double purpose, of the tide pole, and to be available in the event of fire. I made a days excursion today with Doctor Simpson, two men, and a light sledge with two dogs, to carry our guns. We got to the end of the fourth Island, from the Ship, called Doctors Island,[1] a distance of ten miles, the Ship at this point being barely visible to us, Knowing where to look for her. The day was beautifully clear & calm, but the temperature low. As we passed along the Islands we observed several Native Fox traps. They are simple and in some way injenious [sic] – A Moderate sized log of drift-wood, loaded about the Middle with a heavy block of ice, one end resting on the ground – the other supported on a thin stick about a foot long, in the same fashion, boys stick up a door in snowy weather, in our country, to catch sparrows. From the upright-stick another projects at right-Angles, to which the blubber used as bate [sic] is made fast, and the whole covered round with Ice & snow – so that Mr Reynard to get at the bate must come under the loaded log, which falls & crushes him, as soon as he pulls at the bate – They bring the skins along side the Ship for sale, but as they estimate them more highly than we do, few are bought. The distance of our walk was about twenty five miles, in all, we had native sledge tracks with us the whole way, and extending beyond our extreme, as marked as at the Ship, showing that they have taken some of the whale, a good distance to the East[wa]r^d . . .

Tuesday October 19th As I passed along the Islands yesterday, I observed that some more drift-wood might be collected, a[nd] so sent a party this morning under Mr Gordon, with a large sledge and dogs to bring a load[.] I tried it More as an experiment, than expecting any quantity . . .

We had a party of Natives along side the ship today from Cape Smyth, bringing some fish of the Salmon species[2] to barter. I was

---

[1] See above, p. 70, n. 1.
[2] These were probably chum or pink salmon (*Oncorhynchus keta* or *O. gorbuscha*).

much struck with the leader from his style in dress & manner, and invited him on board, when my favourable opinion soon vanished, on discovering him to be a man who had given us a great deal of trouble,[1] on one or two occasions, on our first arrival here, previous to our restricting their coming in. At that time he was dressed in a most conspicuous attire, made out of a White English Ensign, he must have stolen out of one of the boats, searching the coast – the Union Jack hung down in front & the fly made the back part of his upper Man – Their taste for large gaudy patterned, and shiny looking things is similar to what has been observed amongst all savages. But it has never been so much under my personal notice before, and is in some cases very Amusing. This individual on the former occasion alluded to, strutted about the deck the admiration of all his countrymen, merely from the contrast of the colours. And I suppose it was to make his conduct as conspicuous as his dress, that he gave us so much trouble.

The fish was all bought from the Cape Smyth people as I was anxious to encourage this coming to us, with any thing that could be of benefit to the Ships Co. I bought a very good sledge from our Union Jack friend, for our men to carry snow on for the ships use – a very inferior hand saw was the price. I imagined the labour to them of constructing one must be so great that they would be procured with difficulty . . .

Wednesday Octob^r 20th Mr Gordon having brought a fair turn of fire Wood, about three days Consumption, was dispatched for a similar turn today, the weather although very cold, was not too bad for travelling, as there was little wind. We have commenced building our observatory, the outer house is of ice cemented together with water, 12 feet square by 7 High; flat roofed, of the same material, within this, is a wooden frame work 7 feet square by 6 in Hight [sic], to be covered with Seal skins, having its entrance on a different side from that of the outer building, by this means we hope to avoid the snow drift, and maintain an even temperature–

We had a water sky today extending frm N.N.W. to South. The old chief Om-ig-a-lun was on board[.] He told us that the open water was close to the Village, and to the land both to the East and West. I engaged one of his sons to guide me in a trip over the ice to it tomorrow, as I am anxious to get as many soundings as possible to

---

[1] This man is later identified as 'Ne-lick-tua', 'Ne-lick-tuna', or 'Union Jack'.

seaward. Some of our gentlemen walking have been touched slightly
with frostbites today . . .

Thursday October 21st Our Wooding party were sent away under
Mr Wright. And the work of building the observatory continued. I
left the Ship at 9 accompanied by Messrs Simpson & Jago, one man
to carry a lead & line, and our native guide, to examine the Ice in the
offing, and the open water reported by the Natives. Our route was
nearly true North, through heavy hummocky Ice, for nearly five
miles – Close to the edge of the open water, we came to a large berg
23 feet in hight [sic], split near the Middle perpendicularly from the
top to the bottom, leaving a space of about 9 feet between the
severed parts caused apparently by grounding & pressure, the
perpendicular faces of ice had a beautiful bluish colour[1] . . .

We found one Native at the edge of the Ice, engaged watching for
seals, his implements were a speer, a net, a long slender pole to
which was fastened a noose, a skimming ladle, and containing a
wallet [of] other small articles, he had only commenced his
operations, by making a hole, through which we sounded in 7¼ fms.
the ice, being only four inches thick. The line of open water
extended nearly North & South Magnetic & probably leads along the
coast some distance to the East and West. Judging from the strongly
marked water sky. Our return was direct for the Ship arriving on
board a little before 3 P.M. . . .

Friday [October] 22nd Our wooding party left again this morning
under Mr Wright. And the observatory is getting into a forward
state. The temperature has taken a sudden rise of twenty degrees to
+4 [−15.6°C] caused by the sky becoming overcast, an effect I have
frequently observed, and have heard it simply accounted for, by
comparing the clouds to a covering, which retains, and adds to the
heat of the surface of the earth. And in contra distinction, in very
low temperatures the sky is most frequently cloudless.

Mr. Jago has been arranging our Printing press, and getting a
place established for it in the cabin. Doctor Simpson has also been
examining a parcel received from Mr Barrow at the Admiralty –
Containing illustrated books to be issued in winter quarters,
beginning the 5th of Nov[embe]r continuing weekly for three
months. They consist of humerous [sic] sketches, such as the comic

---

[1] Judging from the description of the colour of this ice, it must have been sea ice
that had formed one or more winters previously. Because of the passage of time it
would have lost almost all of its salt and its water would consequently now be potable.

history of Guy Fawkes, by Cruickshanks & others – Doctor S. purposes editing a small weekly paper, to accompany each of the illustrations, and to be included in one, under the title (as agreed upon before leaving London) of the – 'Weekly Guy' – As our Printing arrangements are on a very small scale, the paper must be in proportion, and the Editor purposes devoting its pages to articles not requiring much labour, from either the contributor or printer – such as puns, jokes, riddles & short humorous articles, adapted to the dullest capacities, a few copies are to be kept for the Kind originator, who has shown much kindness in everything connected with the Plover.

Screens are being carefully fitted round the Hatch way on the lower deck, to be triced up in the day, in the same way as fire screens on board Ships usually – the draft coming down having lowered the temperature while the men were in their hammocks, causing a good deal of condensation on the beams overhead. The after part of the deck in the Gun Room passage, from being colder, has been covered overhead with felt. The constant dripping from the beams Keeping the deck wet. These arrangements will I hope add a good deal to the comfort of the lower deck at night, without preventing due ventilation.

Saturday October 23rd Our wooding party went as usual this morning. The outer building of our observatory is complete. The frame work for the inner one is nearly so. A few days will I hope see our magnetical observations in progress. The Sylvester stove answered admirably today, raising the temperature of the lower deck to 62° [16.7°C] & thoroughly dried it– . . .

Monday [October] 25th Our wooding party continued their labours this morning. the temperature remaining at +24 [−4.4°C], is rather against them as it keeps the Snow very soft for travelling over. The tide pole was got into its place, and a commencement made with the observations. Our carpenters are busily employed building the frame work for the observatory. We have commenced building a thin wall of ice round the Ship, as a protection against the cold of the Atmosphere, with the hope that it will assist in maintaining a higher temp[erature]e on the lower deck – it is to be 'plumb' with the edge of the ice chock, leaving an interval of a foot or more between the wall and ships side, but not open to the external Atmosphere – The lower deck keeps at a temperature above fifty [10°C] but moist over head.

111

We have had an unusual number of Natives round the Ship today, amongst the Number our Sable Coated friend. They got up a dance opposite the entry port on the Ice, and seem very anxious to bring about a more cordial reconciliation, than at present exists between us, but they attracted no interest from our people. The Natives have in some way anticipated my intentions, for at the time they were dancing outside, Doctor Simpson & Mr Jago we[re] engaged in the Cabin printing a notice of a dance, I intended giving them on board on Thursday next. With the view of showing that we bore no ill will towards them, and wished to continue a friendly intercourse. The Notice headed 'Great Novelty' was turned out of hand by the Compositors in a very creditable form, but they regret that they have not four times the number of types . . .

Wednesday October 27th A wooding party was dispatched this morning under Mr Wright And our work about the ice wall, round the Ship & the observatory continued. The lower deck keeps at a temperature of 60° [15.6°C] without a fire. The prospectus of our weekly paper made its appearance today, and caused general satisfaction, both from the Matter, & Manner in which it was printed – We have had a number of Natives round the Ship today, they seem to understand about the dance for tomorrow, I expect we shall have a great crowd –

Thursday October 28th In the early part of the day our usual work went on – building the Ice wall and fitting the obser[vator]y. The afternoon was devoted to making arrangements for our visitors, who had in the mean time collected in great numbers, but the old chief was not amongst them – at 4 P.M. they were admitted on board to the Number of fifty, which was afterwards much increased by successive arrivals. After they were made to seat themselves round the deck, the entertainment commenced with serving each with a little tobacco, then our musical instruments – (a Fiddle, Carnopian [sic],[1] drum, & triangles) played up a lively air. Which from many of the Natives now hearing for the first time, caused a general exclamation of wonder and pleasure – This was followed by a request for them to dance, which they did willingly, then our seamen danced in their turn, and so the thing went alternately, in a little time the Natives entered fully into the spirit of the Amusement, stripping off their coats, and dancing naked to the waist, varying the dances a

---

[1] A cornopean is a cornet.

112

good deal & as the Men shout in a triumphant way who are dancing and all the lookers on join in a chorus, in this way they work themselves to a state of excitement little short of the performers, the whole taken at one view, makes a scene as savage as can be well imagined.

About the time I was thinking of breaking up the party – The Old Chief was announced as coming down on a sledge, as he was unable to walk from some lameness, accompanied by Sable Coat – or the Black chief, as he is now generally called. They got information I supposed that the affair was worth seeing, I was sorry they had not been on board sooner, but as all appeared to have had enough by 10 o'clock the party broke up, the whole company seemingly satisfied with their evenings enjoyment.

It will give a very good idea of these people that we have to deal with in such numbers – When we came to take down a few flags 'Ensigns' that had been hung for ornament, round the housing, we found several large pieces cut out with their knives, as if in hands full. This, after being treated with every kindness & consideration, is from all our experiences of them, what you may expect in return. The old chief, and the better disposed of those remaining, appeared very indignant, and promised the pieces should be returned, but they are of little use after the Flags have been destroyed.

The night was beautifully fine with a clear moon light. This Moon is called Shud-le-wik[1] the one in which the Natives are employed making their clothes – such was the account they gave tonight, and it would appear that the months or more properly, moons, which are only in their calender, the rest are included in one general term of summer – receive their names from the occupations they engage in successively through the winter.

Friday October 29th Our work continues the same. Parties away for wood, building the Ice wall round the ship, and preparing the observatory. The portions of Flags stolen last night were returned today. Now that we have got into a better understanding with the Natives, and have got an enclosure that is understood by them, which includes all our property outside of the Ship, and the admittance in board being kept in complete control, and confined to people who are known to be well disposed, & trusthworthy, I

---

[1] Simpson (Appendix Seven, p. 533 below) transcribes this moon as 'Shud-le-wing', meaning 'sewing'.

thought everything connected with our intercourse was in as fair a way of going on smoothly, as I could wish, And began to turn my attention to the means we might have of extending information along the coast to East^w[ard] through the Natives. As a preparation in this way. We had a Number of Notices[1] printed today, that I intend asking them here to distribute along the Coast. Unfortunately all their migrations take place in the summer, when they can be of very little use for our purpose.

With a view to make some enquiry on this subject, I walked up to the Village with Doctor Simpson accompanyed by the young lad the old Chief had stolen from the Indians – We were followed by several idlers from about the Ship, who as we neared the huts, spread the report of our arrival, which soon caused a great Number to gather round us, following to the old Chiefs House. The boy ran on in advance and gave the old Man Notice of our coming, we found him on his 'housetop' ready to receive us.

The winter huts are now covered with snow, the old chiefs does not stand more than five feet above the ground, having a square opening at one end, into which we followed the old man – Thence going through a low dark passage sloping downwards for five or six yards, we stood beneath the opening in the floor of the inhabited part of the hut, it is circular in form, just large enough for one person at a time. Passing through this we stood upon a smooth boarded floor about sixteen feet by ten. At the opposite end from the entrance was a sort of shelf, four feet from the floor, extending across the building & sufficient in breath [sic] to allow them to lay across it at full length, answering the purpose of a sleeping berth for part of the family. If we suppose them laying athwartships – The roof was about seven feet high, and in the centre of it, there was a small square Sky light – Covered over by thin transparent Whale Membrane, Kept up in an arched form, by two pieces of whale bone bent upwards from opposite corners, and crossing in the center –

The transition from the day light and glare, to the dark passage was sudden, and in some degree prepared your eyes for taking in at the first glance the appearance within. On each side was a large lamp or rather trough nearly three feet long, tapering towards each end, and divided into three compartments, of which the Middle was the

[1] These notices gave the location of the *Plover*, and it was hoped that the natives would pass them on until they reached the *Enterprise* or *Investigator*. One such notice did in fact reach the *Enterprise* in the spring of 1854 at Camden Bay.

largest. On the inside edges of the Middle compartments, were flames of a foot each in extent supplied by the melted blubber within, a sort of mop supplying the place of wick. Over the flame a piece of blubber is suspended and as it melts drops into the reservoir –

We were places [sic] in the centre of the tent, with our backs to the sleeping shelf described, I facing the hole of Entrance. The old Chief sat nearly opposite to us, supported on each side by his two wives, there was a young woman with a child on the right hand of Doctor Simpson, and beneath the shelf was a second whose child lay asleep beside her – Whilst on the shelf were four or five young men reclining, the whole party being naked to the waist, and the children in perfect nudity. On our entrance, whatever may have been their occupations, all was suspended.

The first breath of the interior Atmosphere was rather offensive but we soon got accustomed to it, and as the temperature was already high, being followed by a number of men whom it seemed impossible to accommodate in so small a space, there are [sic] appeared to be no limit to the company, whilst any room remained unoccupied. The first attempt to reduce the temperature was reducing the size of the lamps. This was found to be on too small a scale, when the old Chief got up with his Knife & cut a large hole in the skin sky light covering, which made an agreeable change in the air we were breathing, & a very necessary one in our crowded state.

Our arrival seemed to give great satisfaction, the first operation of course was a smoke. The remainder of our visit which lasted for an hour, I was engaged in endeavouring to get information as to where the nearest winter settlement of Natives is Eastward of us, with the view of communicating with them before the severity of the season set in. I also tried to get information of the Coast Eastw[ar]d, and Dease's Inlet (called by them Koone-a-lee). I always disclaim our purpose being for barter, which they have a difficulty in understanding, although they appear to be aware of the two Ships that are far away in the ice we are waiting for. The Chief's was the only house we visited, although invited to others.

We then took a turn round the point to the South[a]rd to observe the state of the Ice to Seaward, and returned across the bay direct to the Ship, accompanied by a young man and a boy,[1] who talked a

---

[1] This was 'Ke-o-wa', the adopted son of 'An-goon-iz-wa', or 'Sable Coat'.

great deal the most of which we could not understand. The former in endeavouring to describe the sort of tobacco he had been given on board a Ship (American twist Negroe Kind) led us in his description of the vessel to believe it might have been the Enterprise or Investigator, returning this summer, but we were unable to assure ourselves of the fact, and indeed afraid we were giving way to credulity in supposing it to be either of them.

As they willingly accompanied us on board, I was glad to avail myself of L[t] Vernon's knowledge of the language to sift their story thoroughly – He with the most exemplary patience, allowed them to describe in their own way, what they saw – and eventually ascertained that the ship they were on board of had *Diagonal decks*, and an *ice chock larger than the Plovers* & square luminators differing from ours which were circular. These marks were sufficient to show that she must have been either the Enterprise, or Investigator, but when the boy described the 'omelik'[,] Captain, as wearing a long hat, and spectacles, Captain Collinson was identified. The remaining point of importance was that she had gone to the Eastward, the *summer before last*, which also agrees with the time the Enterprise would be passing Point Barrow.[1] Thus a particular kind of tobacco with which we knew the Enterprise to be provided, led to a voluntary description of their having boarded a ship, affording us more information in a few minutes, than all the enquiries we could make of the chiefs and others in several months.

Near the large lagoon at Noowork[2] [the village at Point Barrow] were numerous slabs of ice about three inches in thickness laid together in separate heaps on their edges. These are evidently a store provided for melting in the huts & intended to last until the snow drift has become sufficiently thick to be unmixed with salt, an inconvenience we experience on board, so the drifted snow on the ice we find to contain more or less salt, the melted snow being often distinctly brackish. Doctor Simpson seems unable to account for this, but supposes that the saline particles are exuded on the surface from the sea water while in the process of freezing . . .

Saturday Octob[r] 30th Our ice wall round the ship is still in progress, the wood work of the observatory is complete & only requires to be

---

[1] Eskimos boarded the *Enterprise* off Wainwright Inlet on 19 July 1851, off Walakpa Bay on 21 July, and off Dease Inlet on 1 and 2 August (Collinson, 1889, pp. 137–45).

[2] The pond at Nuvuk.

covered with seal skin, when it will be ready to receive the instruments. The carpenters are employed fitting a door way and cover for the after hatch way, the volume of cold air rushing down it cools all the after part of the ship.

We have had a number of natives from the town today, who were admitted on board in consequence of a strong breeze and heavy drift. I endeavoured by drawing with chalk on the deck, the part of the coast that I knew in this neighbourhood to induce them to continue the coast line to Eastward, some of them gave a very good idea of the trending of it nearly as far as the River Colville, but the scale they went on was so large and irregular, it was not easy to recognise any of their points, in our chart. I was able to make out that none of them had ever been so far as the River Colville. One man said he had seen the Highland (the Pelly Mountains) and beyond them was a big river – Kok-pak.[1] It appears they meet a tribe called the Nuna-tag-mi[2] a distance of 70 or 80 miles to Eastward[3] of this place every summer for the purpose of bartering, and that seems to be the extent of their migrations. The Nuna-tag-mis must again barter with the Esquimaux East[w][ard] of the Colville[4] – & so on along the coast to the East[w][ard].

The people from this place seem to know the coast to the South[a][rd] as far as Icy Cape, but few of them have seen ships. The most that I ask say they have seen two ships, counting this as one. The other I suppose to be either the Nancy Dawson yatch [sic] or the Enterprise . . .

We fancy the Ice wall Keeps up the temperatures of the Ship after the stove goes out, By Keeping off the action of the strong winds against the Ships outside . . .

[1] The Mackenzie River. The Pelly Mountains, charted by Thomas Simpson (1843) near Harrison Bay, do not exist.

[2] Ernest S. Burch, Jr's ethnographical research has revealed that there were four Eskimo societies living between the Point Barrow Eskimos and the Nuatarmiut of the upper Noatak River drainage: on the Arctic coastal plain there were the Kuulugzuar-miut of the Meade River and the Ikpikpangmiut of the Ikpikpuk River, as well as two societies on the Colville River (Burch, 1980, and personal communication). Burch (personal communication) has written, 'At some point during the [early] 19th century (or possibly earlier) a terrible famine struck. Most of the population died and the survivors fled . . .' Some took up residence with the Nuatarmiut. All of the Ikpikangmiut apparently died in an influenza epidemic in 1900. The people of the Colville River apparently moved south into the mountains after the dispersal of the Dihai Kutchin band (see footnote 3 for 27 September 1852).

[3] The trade rendezvous at Nirliq in the Colville River delta.

[4] In fact the Eskimos from the interior and some from Point Barrow went east from Nirliq to Barter Island to trade with the Mackenzie Eskimos.

117

Sunday – October 31st The weather continues stormy from the N.E. with heavy snow drift. Notwithstanding which we had natives along side, but none on board until after Church Service . . .

Monday Novr 1st [1852] This month was ushered in with cold black weather accompanied with snow drift – our Ice wall is newly complete, we hope to gain a good deal in temperature by it. I dispatched Mr Hull to the Village to barter for some seal skins to cover the observatory, he succeeded in procuring sufficient, and was accompanied back to the Ship by some of the Natives.

I have commenced today making arrangements for a journey, I purpose making along the coast to the East[war]^d, to gain information of it, and place marks on the prominent head lands, for the guidance of any parties falling back on this place from their ships as it will take a day or two, to alter a tent, and prepare the most efficient equipment we can, against a very low temperature, that we must expect to encounter. I have fixed upon the 6th for starting, the 5th being looked upon as a Jubilee day in these Ships, where the smallest reason or Anniversary is brought up to have a merry making, as a set off against the general tedium of Arctic Sameness and I did not wish to deprive my companions of their share in it.

Our Gentlemen connected with the press have commenced their labours, preparing the first number of the 'Weekly Guy' for publication on its auspicious day the 5th . . .

Tuesday [November] 2nd The Notice of the Weekly Guy's approach was read by one of the Seamen on the lower Deck last night, amidst great applause and the Editor informs me that his box contains three contributions . . .

The snow drift on the Starboard or weather side of the ship is three feet high, at a distance of six yards from the ship, with a steep edge, caused by the Eddy wind off the side, laying broadside to the wind. This is a greater drift than we anticipated for the whole season, from the want of shelter in every direction round us.

We had sixty Natives along side today, mostly young people and children. I have been busy for an hour or so, getting alterations made in our travelling gear, according to the recommendation of the officers employed under Captain Austin. I have fixed upon Capt McClintock as a text, and only feel sorry, that I am such a poor imitator of his example . . .[1]

---

[1] Captain Horatio Austin was in command of H.M.S. *Resolute*, wintering in the

Wednesday. November 3ʳᵈ/52. The boy who had given part of the information relative to the Enterprise, was on board again today. He appears a very sharp intelligent lad, and catches at our meaning and words, quicker than any of the others. He spoke of having seen five ships, including this one, the Enterprise, a Whaler [probably meaning a whaleboat], the Nancy Dawson yatch [sic] & probably the Heralds decked boat, 'Owen'[1] – He mentioned also of a land to N.N.W. where they obtain their blue beads – he must have been wrong in the direction . . .

Thursday [November] 4ᵗʰ The praparations [sic] for our journey occupied all our attention today. I have been trying experiments as to the time snow will take melting in our Cooking apparatus & the quantity of spirits of wine, compared with the proportions allowed in Captain Austins Ship. I found by taking every means to retain the heat against the action of the Atmosphere, that we could not work with the same quantity. This I attributed to the Inferiority of our cooking apparatus which is only a make shift one, made on board the Amphitrite, and had to allow accordingly – One of the Natives today told us that the land where the blue beads they wear come from is a long way off, in the Westerly direction, which must be the coast of Asia. He has only heard of it from others who bring the traffic from Bherings Straits . . .

Friday Novʳ 5ᵗʰ 52. Lᵗ Vernon went to the main land to shoot deer this morning under the guidance of two Natives, who offered to show him a great many. He was also accompanied by two of our Men, who were considered good shots, in fact I had great hopes that at least one deer would be the result of their days work. They came back at 6 o'clock one at a time, one of the Men arriving first, saying that Lᵗ Vernon and the other man were coming, but they . . . were very tired & wanted a sledge to bring them in. I had previously hoisted lights as the night was dark and now hurried away a sledge with one of our men who had experience in such matters & two Natives. And I was gratified to find them all safely on board in less than an hour.

---

eastern Arctic in 1850–1. Leopold McClintock was one of the Arctic's greatest sledge travellers, having adopted a number of ideas from the Eskimos. His travelling procedures were employed by many Arctic explorers. Maguire is apparently drawing from their sledging reports that were reprinted in the Parliamentary reports (Great Britain, 1852c) of the Franklin Search.

[1] 'Ke-o-wa' was referring to the summer of 1849 when the *Herald*, *Plover*, and *Nancy Dawson* accompanied Pullen's boat expedition as far as Point Barrow.

As I mentioned before, the farce of Guy Faux [sic] is observed strictly. I allowed every thing to take its course, the men making all their own arrangements for the evening. I was some time on deck in the morning before I discovered the Effigy of Guy, hanging by the Neck to the Galley funnel under the housing, And could not help smiling at the figure, two young Natives who had not observed it either, and I am not certain they did not take it for a real figure, their Amazement seemed so great, when I pointed to the Lanthern & Matches, the use of which they understood, and explained by signs that he was hung for being a 'Big Thief' – 'Ange-zu-zik' – 'tig-lik', they both patted their breasts, looking in the most serious way & declared they were not thieves. I was so amused at their seriousness & simplicity, that I could hardly keep from laughing.

In the afternoon I took my party for a sharp of [sic] walk of three hours, to see if they had their clothes, all of Native construction, fitting properly, I found only one bad walker amongst them, And as he was a short, chubby fellow – with short legs, I consoled myself with the idea that when he was fast to the sledge, his draught was what was required, not his speed, & from his build I suspect he will be a match for the best at that fun.

At 7 the procession for the immolation of Guy Fawkes commenced on the deck, all hands marching round twice, preceded by a figure, meant to represent a Donkey carrying Guy Fawkes but which in reality might be taken for any Animal, between that and a Zebra. The procession then moved outboard towards a tar barrel, and gallows prepared on the ice and charged with a quantity of gun powder, and such fire works as our ingenuity could manufacture, the Natives did not know whether to be afraid or not, but they took an opportunity individually of protesting they were not thieves, which was very amusing, it almost seemed as if they expected their turn might come next to be served in the same way – As they were told he was a 'big thief' – The ceremony concluded by setting off a Rockett, on which they retired to a distance in dismay and were evidently much impressed with the whole proceeding – They were afterwards gratified with a dance on board which seemed to restore them to their usual confidence, our own people were also indulged with an extra allowance of spirits, which closed the days Amusements – . . .
Saturday November 6<u>th</u>/52 Our two sledges having been loaded on the deck the day previous. They were got out the first thing this morning and everything got ready for starting as soon as it was light

7 Am – my party consisted of Mr Wright in Ad[ditio]n 3 seamen and one marine, six dogs with two Native sledges, held together by a short piece of rope, heavily laden with tent, clothes, arms, ammunition &c and provisions for fourteen days.

The object of this journey, mentioned in my journal of it, was to trace more accurately than had been done before the chain of Islands lying off the coast to the E.S.E. (true), to communicate with the natives if any were to be found, and through them endeavour to circulate notices, on the principal points along the coast, for the guidance of any part of the expeditions which may come this way from the Enterprise or Investigator, or if it be possible Sir John Franklin's crews. It would also give me an opportunity of judging the state of the sea ice for an extended journey I purpose making if possible to the North[a]rd over it in the spring as well as giving us all experience in sledge travelling which we require and is very important, as it is only by experiment that any one can make his arrangement complete & know exactly what he may be able to perform with a limited number of hands –

I continue the journal of the Ship, Although not on board, from that of Doctor Simpson, who has again favoured me with the use of his for that purpose . . .[1]

Saturday Novr 7th After church service, the Natives to the number of eight were allowed on board, amongst the number sable coat and his wife. Messrs Simpson & Jago walked to the Village and half way up could see the open water from the recent breaking away of a large piece of ice caused no doubt by the fresh breeze of yesterday evening. When they entered the Chiefs hut, the place was very warm and had a strong smell which soon turned Mr Jago's stomach, and he was obliged to go out. Doctor Simpson soon joined him and they returned to the Ship.

One of the Natives who accompanied them going on arriving at the Village and being surrounded by a crowd of people made a flourish with his knife in imitation as he said of 'Magua Ennue' Maguires men, meaning our sentries, but as Doctor Simpson took no notice of it, it passed off as a joke that did not take. To avoid such displays it would be well always to go with someone to whose house one would pay a visit, which would look as if one were invited, and the companion would be a sort of guard of honour so to speak . . .

---

[1] Maguire's journal of this expedition has apparently not survived.

<u>Monday</u> [November] 8th Our Employment at present is necessarily confined to light work about the Ship, getting provisions off from the house, & such things . . . The first brew of spruce beer in progress . . .

<u>Tuesday November 9th</u> . . . Six or seven Natives on board and the usual Number round the Ship. The employment for today was cleaning and restowing the preserved meat lockers . . .

<u>Wednesday</u> [November] 10th As the Natives were found making free with our wood stocks on Martins Island,[1] our people were employed transporting it nearer to the Ship . . .

<u>Thursday</u> [November] 11th Continuing to transport the wood from Martin Island . . . Whilst several of the Natives were on board with their women, the crowd outside was more numerous than usual, and a party of our men being away, Some of the Native Men persisted in getting within the chain, in consequence of which one of them was knocked down by the Corporal of the Watch, Knives and Cutlasses were drawn on either side, and the Natives retired to a distance, those onboard also making a rush for the door but were prevented leaving the Ship by Lt Vernon and this affair soon subsided into a calm. Our friend sable coat was one of those on board, and did not attempt to move, though as an excuse to draw his Knife, and began to eat [sic] . . .

<u>Friday</u> [November] 12 The people were employed transporting the Fire Wood closer to Ship as before . . . In the Printing department a man named Daw[,] a Seaman, is making himself very useful. Not many natives about the Ship & none of our friends. In the evening a Man from Cape Smyth brought a few fish for barter – . . .

<u>Saturday</u> [November] 13th The Weekly Guy was received today with more eclat than was expected . . . Several Natives on board and anxious for the officers to Visit . . .

<u>Sunday Novr 14th</u> . . . Sable coats adopted son,[2] who spoke so clearly of having visited the Enterprise, was on board, and being invited to sleep on board, has acquiesced & is now lying on a locker quite comfortable. He talked a good deal today of the people of King-a-mute. Cape Prince of Wales – and named one of the Islands and Kok-leet (asiatic Tschuktschis) and described the coast as being mountainous. If we understood him he visited it with his father in an U-mi-ak . . .[3]

---

[1] This was the first island east of the *Plover*.   [2] 'Ke-o-wa.'

[3] This is unlikely. The knowledge of the Asiatic coast was more probably passed to the Point Barrow people by traders who had met Asiatic natives at the Sheshalik trade rendezvous at Kotzebue Sound.

<u>Tuesday Novr 16th</u> At 7.30 Am sent three men a days March to meet the travelling party – returned without meeting them. They went to the end of the fifth Island[1] & left some dogs food for the dogs . . . A good many natives about the Ship mostly women and children, who hung about until six o'clock, the old chief was also on board for a few hours.

<u>Wednesday Novr 17th</u> . . . The Anniversary of the Plovers Comm[issionin]g . . . a fatigue party left the ship to meet the travelling party, and returned without meeting them . . .

<u>Thursday Novr 18th</u> The travellers returned with the party sent out to meet them about 11 o'clock having gone as far as Point Drew – They had not suffered until yesterday when they made a long march thinking to reach the Ship. The Captain has a blister on his heel the size of half a crown, Mr Farland A.B. is laid up in both feet and Walton with one in both the members are a good deal inflamed and painful, otherwise excepting looking dirty as coal heavers, they are all well. Their garments especially the sleeping bags are frozen solid with condensed vapour. This is severe experience, but as I trust they will all soon recover, it will be most beneficial, and their leader will know to the full extent of what to guard against in his spring journey –

We had a large assemblage of Natives down and some of them took charge of the skin coats & Moccasins, to have them dried & rubbed soft.

The temperatures has been below −30 [−34.4°] all day & strange to say (at least as I little expected) without sun shine there was great mirage in the afternoon. Our friend the intelligent boy[2] I think I must call him. When I pointed it out to him, said it was nothing compared to what might be seen in the summer, and that it was [sic] a sign of fine weather. *'Cela Nook oo ruk'*[3]

The Captain says he never lost sight of the water sky, this I look upon as a bad sign of being able to make Northing in the Spring journey, besides the ice in Smith's bay was of new formation, rough, hummocky, thickly covered with snow and impassible with the sledges, I therefore think to travel over it in the spring might be dangerous, and I look upon the last formed ice as the most likely first

---

[1] This was probably the sand bar that the British called Rutland Island; today, the easternmost of the Tapkaluk Islands.

[2] Elsewhere, 'Ke-o-wa'.

[3] 'Good weather.'

to go. The only thing to be remarked were the tracks of wolves &
foxes, and some fresh water pools or lakes they crossed near the
Shores of Smiths Bay.

Friday [November] 19th The temperature was of that settled
description now below Zero, that you consider any rise unlikely.
And as protection to the lower deck from cold (the upper deck deck
[sic] being altogether too thin in substance for this vigorous climate)
we commenced covering it today with a thin layer of sand, previous
to putting down snow to the thickness of a foot. The sand is to
prevent the snow thawing, when in contact with the plank. Only a
few Natives about the ship today. The chiefs son[1] came along from
the Islands late in the evening. The mens feet a good deal inflamed
and blistered from the effects of the cold in the last journey.

Saturday Novr 20th The weather has become warmer and hazy. The
upper deck was covered with sand yesterday. The employment
today is covering it thickly with snow. Lt Vernon & Mr Hull went to
the Village today, and came back with two Natives, the intelligent
boy K-e-u-a, and another young man called by us – the Hard
Working lad from his willingness to assist in any work going forward
– Our 'Weekly Guy' made its appearance again today and was well
received –

Sunday [November] 21st After church service the weather being fair
Lt Vernon and Mr Simpson walked to the Village and visited Ang-u-
ni-sua's[2][,] sable coats[,] hut, after which they were invited to that of
an omelik[3] the man who in the Summer opposed our watering party,
and had in consequence received the soubriquet of the Water Chief[4]
– And then visited one of the men who returned a few days ago, after
having been adrift on a floe with two others for six days – It appears
that this small party went out to hunt the White bear, and the floe
became detached, floating them into the open water, and from this
perilous situation, they were only relieved by its coming again in
contact with the main ice – Although the weather was so severe, this
man was only slightly frostbitten about the nose and lips. As they
were without food, the description of their suffering would be one
of thrilling interest, if we could only understand their language
sufficiently.

[1] Probably 'Passak'.   [2] Elsewhere, his name is transcribed as 'An-goon-iz-wa'.
[3] An umialik; see footnote 1 for 13 September 1852.
[4] Elsewhere referred to as 'O-mig-u-a-a-rua' or 'O-mis-yu-a'-a-run'. See Maguire's
entry for 10 September 1852.

The officers describe all the huts as of the same construction, the seams between the boards of the floors are wonderfully close, and their surfaces scraped smooth. Some of the boards were nearly two feet wide, and brought from a long distance as they understood from the Eastw[ar]^d. Before the officers left the Ship a large Number of Natives, including the Chief,[1] his two wives, and the small boy, stolen from the Indians – Passah, who were admitted on board, had assembled round the ship, but choosing Ke-a-wuk[2] to conduct them to his Fathers Mansion, they were saved the Annoyance of a host of candidates for that honour – I have observed elsewhere on the sharpness of this lad, at 'repartee' with his countrymen, and now give Doctor Simpsons account of his proceedings as his guide – 'It was interesting to observe the conduct of this diplomatic lad in the Manner in which he treated the numerous parties we met coming this way, to some he was civil in explaining that we were going to his Fathers hut, to others his answers were short, some he ordered on to the Ship, when they offered to return with us, some he answered evasively & contemptuously, to others he was perfectly deaf, and to one Lt Vernon understood him to tell a direct falsehood' –

After the ship's Cr[ew] had had their dinner, I gave eight leave to go to the Village, as there had been a sort of invitation the day before from one of the Chiefs, for them to witness a dance, as I thought in return to those given on board. And fancying that an intercourse of this sort, would improve our acquaintance with them, instead of having the reverse effect, as it turned out – Some of the men had arrived before the officers left. The latter had been a little annoyed by a stammering fellow[3] (the same one who had been knocked down in attempting to force his way into the observatory – and who was known on board to be a bad character, for boldness and thieving) from his endeavouring to force them into his tent. The Quarter Master who had treated him in the way mentioned on his attempting the observatory, was one of those who had leave, and was one of the last to arrive – Until this all went well, but when the stammerer saw his enemy, he became furious and leaped upon him but was prevented by others from using his Knife – He afterwards tried to induce others to enter his hut, but perceiving that he had a weapon of some kind in his sleeve, they stopped outside, when several of the Esquimaux hustled, And tripped over some of our Men. After this,

---

[1] 'O-mi-ga-loon.'   [2] Elsewhere, 'Ke-o-wa'.   [3] Elsewhere, 'To-ko-la-rua'.

they found protectors who brought them in safety to the ship – The Carpenters Mate who by some means was left by his companions in the rear – was seized round the arms by two men (who had been treated well on board), Whilst the stuttering man picked his pockets, of some tobacco & beads, that he had taken with him for the Kind purpose – of giving away amongst them – My servant had been taken by Sable Coat to his hut, was treated very well, escaped the row, and did not return to the Ship for two hours after the others, his friend officiously accompanying him on board. The old Chief was very much put out by the affair, and endeavoured to get our people to go to his hut – His great aim throughout had been to get gun powder, so I presume after this show of feeling he will consider his chances of success in that way much lessened . . .

Monday Nov 22nd Completing the covering of our deck with snow, and bringing provisions from the house, gave us occupation for the day. The officers at the Village yesterday observed no water sky, or appearance of open water, today there is only a doubtful patch very distant. If they understood the Natives right, there will be no open water near Point Barrow for three Moons – that is until Feb[ruar]^y –

A Chief named Ang-oon-iz-wa his wife and boy came on board early today, and soon after another man who is a good deal about the Ship. I took the family down to my Cabin – they seem a good deal annoyed about yesterdays proceedings, and threw the blame on the stammering man – They also advise us to shoot him if he comes near the Ship – I got the man to draw the coast line to the Colville River, in which he pointed out the places they met other tribes of their own sort, – & the Koy-a-Kuk[1] Indians with whom they trade – . . .

Tuesday [November] 23rd Our work connected with the Ship is now all finished and a regular winter routine established after the Manner of Cap[tai]^n Parry, as near as our circumstances & means will admit And in following the same good example, the subject of a school has been for some time occupying my attention. As to the best time to be set apart for it – Our supper hour is ½ past 5 & I find that after that time, until the hammocks are piped down at 8 P.M. one of the Men is in the habit of reading aloud some entertaining & lively book, for the benefit of all listeners. And the Sergeant of Marine who is very fond of the Violin, generally gives them a treat in that way, during the same time – As it appeared that evenings were enjoyed rationally

[1] See above, p. 91, n. 1.

and without any feeling of tedium – I fixed the hours from 3 to 5 P. M., as those to be set apart for school each day. This allowed Ample time for the trifling duties about the decks. And gave have [sic] an hour to clear up the decks for Supper – After which time they were left to enjoy themselves in their own way – Lt Vernon undertook the Superintendance of the School, assisted by the Serg[ean]^t of Marines. A list having been previously taken by Mr Jago the Clerk in Charge – of all those who wished to take advantage of this opportunity to improve themselves. The number of applicants were twelve, & I found by their wishes & present acquirements, that learning to write was the grand aim of all – with that accomplishment they seemed to wish for nothing more. This day was fixed as the commencement, & copy books having been previously prepared, they were set to work according to their wishes –

The weather was disagreeable with a good deal of Snow drift, Not Many Natives about the Ship . . .

Wednesday [November] 24th We had the old chief on board today. I took him down to my cabin and as he happened to remain over my dinner hour 3 P. M., I gave him some preserved meat to eat which he appeared to relish uncommonly, and he gave me the benefit of his company much longer than I wished in consequence. Sable coat, his wife and a friend together with another family were on board, but left, the former seemingly disgusted at not being taken below. One man being left alone was allowed on the lower deck to wait for the Chief . . .

Thursday [November] 25th A strong East wind with heavy drift. Our employment about the preserved meats forward continued. The Carpenters from the state of the temperature being unable to work on deck, small jobs are taken in hand by them, between decks. They are at present making an alteration in the boatswains store room – from which I hope [to] derive a good deal of room. The sun is now no longer visible nor has it been seen since the 18th ins^t . . . very few Natives near the Ship and none admitted below . . .

Friday 26th of Novr A party were dispatched this morning for wood to Martins Isl[an]^d this [sic] & collecting snow afforded occupation for the day. The Carpenters still have employment about the Boatswains storeroom. We have a large assemblage of young people round the Ship today. And several allowed on board – It seems to be the general opinion that the lower deck shows more and more the benefits of the Ice wall round the Ship, and the covering on the deck of snow – in Keeping up an even temperature – . . .

Sunday Nov[r] 28th We had a numerous attendance of Natives. After Church service some of the officers took a walk across the ice astern of the Ship followed by two Natives. One of them seemed to say the 'Nunatagmutes' would come in this neighbourhood in two months. We have the Moon now throughout the twenty four hours – affording when not clouded a beautiful light – making up for the suns absence . . .

Tuesday [November] 30th Clearing away the Ice round the Ship within our enclosure formed our work for the day. The Carpenters fitting shelves in the store room for the travelling Cooking apparatus – We had several Natives on board. Sable Coat and his wife of the Number. They describe a party of their people having set out on a hunting & bartering Expedition to Point Hope[1] – (Query), which they consider near to the Asiatic Coast, as Cape Prince of Wales. The articles they receive are Kettles, tobacco, and beads, in exchange for glutton[2] & wolf[3] skins – Which appear to be held in high estimation by those people here – during the day the weather was calm & clear the therm[omete][r] standing at −30 [−34.4°C]. Since evening a breeze springing up from S.S.W. which raised the temp[eratu][r][e] to −8 [−22.2°C]. The effects of a magnet on iron was shown to some of the Natives on board today, much to their wonder. & two needles were magnetized and given for exhibition at the Village – There is now open water near the town, and the men are employed catching Seals in Nets . . .

Wednesday. Decemb[r] 1st [1852] As there was a doubt as to the quantity of bread on board, from its being stowed in bulk and on the present officers joining, there was not time to allow of its being weighed at that time. This day was devoted for the purpose and as it had all to pass through my cabin, I could do nothing in it except look

---

[1] The volume of trade with the Eskimos of Point Hope was smaller than that with the natives who were encountered at the Nirliq trade rendezvous. In both cases, however, most of the foreign trade goods had been obtained at the trade rendezvous at Sheshalik on Kotzebue Sound.

Inter-regional winter travel in northern Alaska could be dangerous. These Point Hope-bound traders would be passing through the territories of two other Eskimo societies, those of the Eskimos of the northwest coast of Alaska, the Silalinarmiut, and of the Point Hope Eskimos, the Tikirarmiut. Because 'strangers' were greeted with suspicion and hostility, these traders would have had kinship or partnership alliances with the people along the way and they, in turn, would have provided the traders with bona fides and safe conduct. By contrast, in the summer there were no such restrictions on travel to and from the trade meetings (Burch, 1971, 1980).

[2] Wolverine (*Gulo luscus*).   [3] Grey wolf (*Canis lupus*).

on – On clearing out the whole of it, we found ourselves one thousand pounds weight short, a very considerable quantity for our small vessel. The Shortness of our bread in comparison with the other provisions, previous to this discovery, made me think it would be necessary to go on reduced allowance – Now I decided upon doing so, but only in a slight degree for the present stopping 1 lb per man a week – until the Spring advances & we have an opportunity of picking up game of some sort or other.

The old chief was on board and stayed until 8 o'clock. Doctor Simpson got him to give him the names of the Months, or Moons of the Year,[1] ten in number leaving two or three of the same name which happen at the beginning of the Winter.

This was Doctor S[impson]'s birth day and with that good feeling which is so pleasant to fell [sic] on board a ship. The officers seem to have formed the plan of observing each of their birthdays with some little conviviality, I had the pleasure of being invited to be one of the party which made a very agreeable break in our usual monotony . . .

Thursday [December] 2nd In the forenoon we employed ourselves building a snow & ice embankment to fire at with musketry to exercise the crew as marks men. In the afternoon this was done, but the Number of ball picked up was very few in proportion to those fired – Our object in picking them up was to prevent their falling into the hands of the Natives, who are very sharp at finding them. And having a gun amongst them, I am anxious to provide them with as little ammunition for it as possible, for our own sakes.

Friday Dec.r 3d Employed clearing after bread room and restowing D[itt]o The Carpenters fitting a shelf on the lower deck to hold the seamens pouches. The old Chief and Sable coat were on board, I asked the latter below today, he appeared much rejoiced at the arrival of some men from the Westward[2] –

Saturday Dec.r. 4th . . . Filling the tanks near the Sylvester with snow, and levelling the snow on the upper deck, gave occupation for the forenoon – The afternoon was devoted to making & mending clothes – The old chief, sable coat, and several of the so called Noona-tag-Mutes[3]

---

[1] See Dr John Simpson's report, Appendix Seven, pp. 532–3 below.

[2] See Maguire's entry for 4 December 1852.

[3] These people appear to be a group of Eskimos from the Upper Noatak River who arrived for trading and conviviality via a travel route which led them to the coast southwest of Point Barrow (Burch, 1976, pp, 7–8, 1980, p. 294). See Dr John Simpson's report Appendix Seven below, p. 506.

were on board today, as well as Erk-sing-era[1] and his family, who we thought had left for the Westw[ar]^d on a very long journey with a party – These being met by the stranger or gone to them, returned with them. The chief object of the Visit – to the ship seemed to be the sale of a sledge skin, of six Reindeers Hides, The hair was short,[2] but otherwise they were well adapted for a travelling hunters equipment.

The Weekly Guy for this week seemed as it always does, to afford an agreeable surprise to the people on the lower deck . . .

Sunday Decr 5th Weather stormy & cold only 3 Natives about the ship. We were enabled to serve the crew with a fresh meal of Pork & potatoes out of our stock received from the Amphitrite. They were killed with the frost setting in, And now frozen so hard, as to require to kept [sic] by the Sylvester stove twenty four hours before they became sufficiently thawed for cutting up – The remaining four I purpose keeping to afford a fresh meal for Christmas and New Years day. the remainder will be kept to be at the disposition of the surgeon in the event of scurvy making its appearance . . .

Monday [December] 6th . . . It has been [a] matter of deep regret to me of late, to find that several of our men have been afflicted with gonarea gonorrhoa [sic] from their intercourse[3] with the Native women. I believe it to have originated in one of our seamen late of the Amphitrite, who although sound on coming here, appears to

---

[1] 'Erk-sing-era' became a close friend of Maguire. Maguire transcribed his name several different ways: 'Arksinera', 'Arksunra', 'Ak-sin-ra', 'Oxinera', 'Ak-son-ea', 'Erksinra', and other variations. John Murdoch met him thirty years later: 'Yuksiña, the so-called "chief" of Nuwuk, who was old enough to be a man of considerable influence at the time the *Plover* wintered at Point Barrow (1852–'54), was in 1881 a feeble, bowed, tottering old man, very deaf and almost blind, but with his mental faculties apparently unimpaired.'

[2] These may well have been caribou fawn skins, in which case they would have been of great use as underclothes.

[3] There had probably been sexual contacts between the Eskimos and the British sailors since 1849, when the ships first reached Point Barrow. Dr John Rae (1953, p. 75), the explorer, was told that there was a certain amount of sexual intercourse with the crews of Lieutenant Pullen's boats when his expedition was held up by the ice at Point Barrow. John Murdoch (1892, p. 53) learned during his research of the 1880s that there had been 'considerable intercourse' between the *Plover*'s men and Eskimo women. Although there were no clearly identifiable off-spring from these liaisons, 'one woman was suspected of being half English'. Charles Brower, for many years a resident whaler and trader at Point Barrow, believed that this woman was the daughter of one of Maguire's officers (Stefansson, 1914, p. 204). John Simpson lists thirteen cases of gonorrhoea aboard the *Plover* in the winter of 1852–3 (Public Record Office, Kew, U.K.: ADM 101/113/3).

have reproduced it on himself by excess. And from the source others have become tainted. It had now spread in the Ship to such an extent, that I thought it necessary to call the people together and interdict such intercourse – the more particularly as the Surgeon is totally unprovided with medicines for such an unlooked for contingency. In considering the case, the suffering of our Men, was the best consequence. I feared the contagion spreading amongst the Native population where from their pretty well known, promiscuous intercourse, the effects of it were to be the most dreaded and indeed not to be thought of except with a degree of horror – but strange to say, we have never heard of a case of it, amongst them. Aurora observed –

Tuesday Decr 7th Weather cold and clear. The old chief and some of his family paid us a visit today. The fith [sic] No of the Weekly Guy made its appearance today – Causing some good humoured criticism – The work of enlarging the observatory for the dipping instrument gave us employment for the day – . . .

Thursday [December] 9th . . . We had few Natives about us, one brought a small piece of Venison to barter, this was followed by two other pieces, they were all bought, but on thawing them, one piece was found to be walrus in disguise. & another although venison had been kept too long previously to being frozen for our palates leaving us only one piece about nine pounds good for Anything – which was reserved for the Surgeons disposition – The Natives report the water to be open near the Village – . . .

Friday [December] 10th . . . – I was sorry to find by the Surgeons report today that a tendency to sore gums, from scorbutic cause has been observed by him – in his usual examination of the crew twice a week . . .

Saturday Decr 11th Repairing the ice wall round the ship, and clearing round the guns in the forenoon – After dinner the people were allowed to amuse themselves preparing their dresses for a maquerade [sic] to be held in the evening – of which our Amateur printing press gave ample notice in a well executed, bill – Having given an invitation to a few Natives yesterday to it, a large number (70) assembled round the ship giving some annoyance, and trying to make a row, as they generally do when in large Numbers. The old chief however was very active in quelling their mutinous spirit, and got them all away by 7 o'clock – stealing before they went a thermomet[e]^r belonging to Doctor Simpson, and a small vial of quick silver, that he had attached to a post near the ship to try the temperatures of the freezing point of it – about twenty remained to see the masquerade, which quite surprised me in the number of very good characters that came forth. both amongst the officers & Men. After the 'Bal Maque' [sic] we had a round of some very good songs – which were interlarded with dances from our own people and the Natives, in this way the evening was passed pleasantly. I was sorry to observe some little irregularity afterwards amongst our own people, that ended in two of the Marines, a corporal & private, loosing a good conduct bage [sic] each – for their behaviour on the occasion –

Sunday Decr 12th At 1 – Am a Faint arch of the Aurora W.N.W. and E.N.E. after church service a few Natives were allowed on board, who reported that the Therm[omete]^r stolen yesterday had been buried in the snow. The intelligent boy Ki-o-wa was given some tobacco to buy it back. A strange sort of proceeding for the encouragement of theft but one we are obliged to have recourse to when a stolen article, is particularly wished for . . .

Monday December 13th Brilliant Aurora. Our employment in the forenoon was bringing in provisions from the house – And a game of foot ball after dinner. Until school time when the work for the day ceases. This is the first day that I have not seen Natives along side. In the evening cloudy & Misty with snow drift.

Tuesday Decr 14th I was sorry to [be] obliged to deprive one of the Marines of a good conduct badge. I mentioned the case on the occasion of our Masquerade – It appeared that several of the men had for some time saved their allowance of ½ a gill a day to enable them to exceed on that occasion – A custom unknown in Ships employed on this service, & introduced by the Men Volunteering from the frigate sent annually from the Pacific Squadron – As I looked upon this punishment, As taking the place of corporal punishment which the circumstance of the offence deserved. The warrant was read in presence of the officers & Ships C^o, to make it as effectual as possible.

The intelligent boy Ki-o-wa – brought back the tobacco today, provided to him to buy back the The[rmomete]^r saying his Father would get it bye & bye – Doctor Simpson made him a present of it for his trouble – It is the first time that the plan has not been successful. There was only one other man on board – whose wife has been lately confined. We had jested with him some time ago about calling the infant Plover, or as he called it Labba, and on enquiry today he declared that to be the babes name . . .

<u>Wednesday</u> [December] 15th Filling the tanks with snow, and drawing & knotting yarns, gave employment until school hour – the intelligent boy Kio-wa came on board today, & informed us that his Father was sick with a swelling in this thigh, and sleeps in a separate hut from his wife – who does not sew or do any work – The same custom of isolating the patient has been observed by Dr Simpson in Kotzbue [sic] Sound – . . .

<u>Thursday</u> [December] 16th The people had a little of what is called a midshipman's delight overhauling his chest. A portion of the crew were employed clearing out their clothes lockers, and seeing their clothes in good order – We had a number of Natives about the Ship, Sable Coat & his wife amongst them. We were surprised to find he had recovered so speedily, as his son Ki-o-wa had informed us yesterday that he was very ill. I took them down into the cabin and endeavoured to get the Names of the head lands to the South. The Names given in the Chart, being of no use, with reference to them. My success was very limited, and without any result, beyond finding out that it was off Icy Cape, and not Point Barrow that he had gone on board the Enterprise.[1] During our conversation he expressed a wish to go with us to Cape Prince of Wales – And when I offered him a passage he seemed delighted, and for the present seems determined to go . . .

<u>Friday December 17th</u> A strong gale from S.E. with very heavy drift temperature up to +23 [−5°C]. The Quarter Master having great difficulty to get to & from the store house, & observatory, from the force of wind and drift. The depth of water continually increasing – At Noon the gale seemed little abated, the depth of water had increased 2 feet above the average hight [sic].

Notwithstanding the strength of the gale, it was not sufficient to Keep the Natives from Visiting us. We had as many as nine or ten alongside, two were let on board – The intelligent boy Ki-o-wa – and the Father of the baby, Lub-ba – or Plover – Those outside soon went home, the two remaining on board being invited to take up their quarters for the night.

We had a strong water sky to the North and N.W. Magnetic, but no individual on board the ship can give a thought to the ice moving, for my own part I was quite unprepared to such an event, and had thought it was as likely for the ships bottom to fall out, as the ice to

---

[1] See above, p. 116, n. 1.

breakup – At 3 P.M. after it had become perfectly dark, it was reported to me that the Ice was breaking up in the passage and that the open water had extended to the observatory and was making its way inside the point – I walked out immediately and made my way with great difficulty across the spit, accompanied by Mr Hull the 2nd Master, and observed the ice to be entirely gone from the Northern shore of the spit, and in the channel as far as we could see. The water had also risen as high as the observatory – From this cursory observation two things presented themselves as necessary to be done at once. These were to remove the chronometer and Instruments out of the observatory, and to bend the Cables, an emergency, that no precaution had been taken for, An Ice wall of considerable thickness, besides tightly frozen hawse plugs had to be removed forward, and something similar was in the way of the pipes through the deck. But as I could see the water extending inside the bay towards the Ship, I could not imagine anything else that I could do – except to try and hold her on by the Anchors, and against such ice, three feet and a half thick, I feared their chance of holding on would be small. However I got on board & commenced at once – it seemed so odd under the housing, where every thing had been arranged as fixtures, to suppose there could be any chance of the Ship moving –

The cables were soon bent, and the Instruments through the energy of Mr Hull were got off safe – that was all we could do, in such a night of darkness & snow drift – I made an attempt about an hour afterwards to get on shore – but found the water welling up between the cracks & the shore. I was very anxious to get another look round at the water. As I could not help fancying that the water we saw, was merely an overflow on the Ice, carried by an unusual rise of three feet – I went out accompanied by a Quarter Master at 6 o'clock and succeeded in getting on shore when I soon found that the main Ice had been carried out, to within a short space of the Ship. the open water as seen before extending deep into the bay. At 8 P.M. we had the greatest hight [sic] of water, which was about 18 feet, it came quite out of the scale on our tide pole & had to be measured afterwards – this was fully three feet above the usual water level, and must be the cause of the Ice breaking up by lifting it bodily, and by that means freeing and giving it vent at the shores. otherwise in a bay so sheltered by land as this is, the ice could not have moved – The two Natives on board were asked their opinions, and they assured us at once. that no more ice would go out. And that the water would not reach us. The married one left the ship, at this time, as he said he wished to talk with his wife and child. The boy remained and seemed as happy as could be.

The night was clear over head, with a few appearances of Aurora. The wind blowing almost a hurricane in the squalls at S.W. (true), the margin of the Ice being within fifty yards of the Starb[oar]^d gangway. Fortunately the water has not risen since 8 o'clock and the wind seems inclined to veer more to the Westward I have therefore great hopes that we shall not be moved – though the swell is felt perceptibly on the Ice close to the Ship – should we be moved into open water, It is impossible to contemplate it, without a degree of great Anxiety. The chances of the Anchors holding us was very doubtful – And in the event of breaking adrift with the strong gale blowing we should have been either carried out of the channel & pounded on the shoals outside, or with the increased depth of water, perhaps have been taken clear of them into the open water in the offing, which would have been the most disastrous result that could occur[.] In the event of being grounded we had an increased depth of three feet of water – which would have placed the ship so high on the ground that on its receding would require to be cleared out to her ballast before she could be hove off. In any case we should have been removed from the protection of our provisions on shore which would have been immediately pillaged by the Eskimaux – & Although it contained only our Salt provisions & flour, they would have been a serious loss to us in the event of her being carried outside.

At midnight the water had fallen three inches and the wind perceptibly moderated – open water within 50 yards of the Starb[oar]^d gangway.

<u>Saturday Decr 18th</u> After Midnight although the wind moderated, the sea continued to encroach so far, as to break away a large piece of ice, between the ship and the shore on which two of the stakes of our boundary line were – the rope was strong enough to prevent its drifting out. This circumstance reminded me of Captain Backs thrilling description of his winter in the Pack in the Terror[1] – When his snow walls & terraces were separated from them, under circumstances incomparably worse than ours – And having no similarity except that of being exposed to being moved at a season –

[1] This incident took place in February 1837 when H.M.S. *Terror* was imprisoned in moving pack ice in the eastern Arctic (Back, 1838, pp. 223–45).

when four hours is the extent of day light with a temperature that renders it impossible for a man to remain exposed for any continuance – To this, in our case, must be added, that out of a crew of forty one in all, Nearly one half were actually under treatment of the Surgeon for scorbutic – frost bite – & other minor complaints – which would have rendered their services useless in the event of emergency –

At 6 Am The depth of water had fallen to 16 feet – Daylight showed that the whole of the Ice outside had cleared away, and the Gale had detached the floe inside the opening, so as to form a deep bight extending Southerly, a quarter of a Mile – When the character of the Ice in the offing which consisted of heavy hummocks, grounded hard on the shoals, for several days before the sea was frozen, is considered, it must have been no small force – of wind, rise in the water, & current that had completely cleared the sea of them in less than twenty four hours. I had with two of the officers walked to a distance of five miles from the land, two months previously, and considered it then as permanent as the Main land.

The weather being fine, I commenced making what arrangements, I thought prudent, to ensure the Ship holding on, or being driven on shore, as near to our house as possible – and for this purpose, the men were employed all day in transporting the shore Anchor, to a position ahead of the Ship, and bending a bower Chain to it, this I looked upon as the means of keeping us from being carried to any distance from our resources. I first intended cutting a hole through the Ice, and letting go a bower Anchor, but I found the work attended with so much labour & exposure – And in considering the circumstances, I thought the bower would be as available at the Cathead – as under foot, particularly as the water was shoal. Instead of the bower, to check the ship in the first move of the ice beaking [sic], before we could get an Anchor down – The stream chain was run out to its full extent, and secured by two ice anchors to the land floe, to the Westw[ar]d[.] This I considered would check the ship, until the Anchor was got down – between which, and that on shore, I hope we should hold on.

The Natives came down in large numbers, and from the hight [sic] of the snow drift accumulated, quite overlooked our deck and entry port – The old chief Omigaloon, came also and made the Natives assist in carrying the chain on shore, giving us great help. Then all assured us the ship was in a perfectly safe position and the old man seemed quite annoyed that we should so far overlook his opinion, as

136

to take precautions against being carried out. In the evening he again showed his authority, by sending his people home –

The night remained fine and clear, the reflection of the Aurora in the water has a beautiful appearance, and to us, a strange & unexpected one – In summer so much open water would be subject of rejoicing, but at the present unseasonable time, I think every one on board, wishes it farther off than fifty yards – & Brilliant Aurora S. E. & N. W. forming in circles to the East[wa]rd.

Sunday Decr 19th At 2 Am – a sledge with Natives passed the ship from the East[war]^{d1} going to the Village, they must have been out during the last break up – And will have experienced considerable difficulty in returning from the ice having been carried out from between the islands, by which they always travel –

The night continued calm, but the temperature we were sorry to observe did not fall very low and during the day rose again to +9 [−12.8°C] – with a breeze from S.S.E. – accompanied with snow and thick weather. The Barometer also falling – The depth of water has decreased two feet 5 inches – standing now at 15 feet 6 in. From the mast head a good extent of open water could be seen to the North[a]r^d, with floe ice sailing in it – After Church service, I sent Mr Hull to the Spit of Point Barrow to observe the state of the Ice, & open water, as far as he could discern along the coast to Cape Smyth – He reported the Ice to be packed up to the hight of 13 and 14 feet on the Shore between C. Smyth, & P^t Barrow, and a Lane of open water, extended from P^t Barrow to the Eastw[ar]^d. A dark water sky all around the North from West to East. Young ice forming in shore –

We have had a good many Natives round the Ship today . . .

Monday Decr 20th The weather was anything but settled yet and as a last measure of precaution, to Keep the Ship in her present place, in case of ice going out, an 8 inch hemp cable was lain out to the inshore beam, from the port quarter, making the third we had out for the same purpose. The temperature at this time, remained a week at +20 [−6.7°C], thawing everything under the housing, and

---

[1] These people may, in fact, have been returning from fishing at the small streams east of Point Barrow. After the rivers freeze, whitefish (*Corregonus* ssp) can be netted under the river ice and grayling (*Thymallus arcticus*) can be taken by jigging at the river mouths (Sonnenfeld, 1957, pp. 150–2). On the other hand, they may have been a group arriving to attend a messenger feast (see Maguire's entry for 29 December 1852).

making it almost impossible to move about the decks, from sinking nearly ankle deep at every step, in the snow covering. This temperature, and the proximity of the open water, together with the snow of the year made it anything but agreeable – And we sincerely wished for a return of the seasonable low temperature –

We had our friend Sable Coat and several others on board, but little notice was taken of them in consequence of all hands being busy laying out the hemp cable – The day was calm and clear, and presented to us the novel appearance of open water ending in a well defined line along shore, altering the view beyond description, making a strong contrast with what we had been accustomed to look upon since the end of September – and not the less striking, at is [sic] was unexpected – Indeed, with our constant watch upon the Natives, and an occasional disturbance with them together with this breaking up of the Ice, and A Ships Company with a general tendency to scurvy, It quite did away with the monotonous feeling of inactivity so generally spoken of in Arctic winters –

The moon today on rising was much distorted, presenting the appearance of a battered copper dish, or rather as described by Captain Parry, like a withered orange . . .

As The Surgeon attributes the appearance of scurvy to the badness of the provisions in use at present – Being as is customary the oldest – The flour, salt beef, and Pork, being certainly objectionable from age – I have considered it necessary, to cause the newest provisions of every Kind to be opened, and discontinued the issue of salt beef altogether, substituting in its Place preserved meats, until the health of the Ships C°, or a supply of Venison, or of other fresh food enables us,[1] to fall back upon the old stock.

Tuesday Decembe^r 21st . . . The Sergeant of marines has got into the way of brewing very excellent spruce beer – it seems to be much appreciated on the lower deck – it now becomes a matter of regret to me, that our supply of molasses for that purpose is so limited –

In the Midst of our uncertainty as to the Ice, preparations are going forward for Christmas – Which is to be ushered in, by the celebration of our first attempt at the drama – under the spirited management of Mr Gordon, who has kindly undertaken the thankless office of Manager – The cast of the Play, 'The queer subject', has

---

[1] Tinned meats would not have prevented scurvy. The lack of vitamin C, which produces scorbutic symptoms, would have been remedied by eating raw caribou meat.

been published today, with the Weekly Guy, and seemed to afford considerable Amusement for those it was intended for – This day being one of the Eras [sic] in an Arctic winter, it becomes a pleasant duty on my part, to express the satisfaction I feel, at the agreeable way the first and worst part of the winter has been passed – Which is owing altogether to the good conduct of the Men – And the excellent disposition of the officers, who have been at all times, & Seasons, Most ready, & forward – Either to perform a duty exposed to a severe temperature – or assist with their intellects and accomplishments, in making any time, that might be marked by tedium – one of Universal enjoyment, when if for a time, the usual etiquette and discipline was laid aside – respect for them under the circumstances was increased rather than diminished.

Wednesday – Decr 22nd Repairing the ice wall round the ship which has been much broken by the late gales, formed the occupation until school time – We had still no ice in sight from the masthead, from W by N. to the Eastward. The old Chief and several others were on board. The snow on deck still disagreeably soft for taking exercise. The woman with the young child, that I before mentioned as being called Lub-ba, their nearest approach to Plover, came on board today for the first time since her confinement, and received a present of some beads, a button, & a piece of tobacco. Faint Aurora above the clouds S.E. & S.W. Arch South – . . .

Friday [December] 24th Our Employment today was rigging the theatre, No ice in sight in the offing from the Masthead, horizon visible 3 miles water in shore freezing over – The old Chief & several other Natives on board, remaining to see the play of 'the queer subject', the preparations seeming to have great attractions for them – At 7 P.M. the performance commenced, and went off well, much to the Admiration of the Natives, Our friend sable coat, his wife, and about a dozen more were admitted when the performance commenced.

Saturday Decembe^r 25th Slight snow drift. Very few Natives round the Ship, and none on board. After Church service, preparations were made on the lower deck for all the Men to dine together, At one o'clock they all sat down to a comfortable dinner, of fresh pork, & potatoes, to which was added, An extra issue of preserved meats, to make two stupendous pies; plum & apple pudding & formed their second course, & each man had ½ bottle of porter, to which was added, a present of ale, to make half & half, that beverage being still in their memories from its strong recommendation in the play last

139

night – Speeches, toasts, and songs succeeded the good cheer – And was carried on with great propriety and good humour. I had the pleasure of dining in the Gun Room with the officers, as well as Mr Seath the Carpenter – Where we passed a very agreeable, and social evening . . .

Sunday – Decr 26th The sea frozen over as before, but presenting a continued level, instead of the hummocks formerly – water sky from N.W. to North – A great Many Natives about on the new formed fishing for seal. In the evening the wind came again from South, which was now become a point of anxiety with us – as it has the effect of raising the water – And blowing the Ice off the land. Faint Arch of the Aurora extending from East to N.W.

Monday Decembe^r 27th Bringing provisions from the house and repairing the ice wall the employments for the day – Few Natives about the Ship – The weather was clear in the Morning, but since Noon the temperature has risen to +19 [−7.2°C]. The Surgeons report of the state of the health of the Ships C^o, is very disheartening at present, no less than 21 out of 41 are under his treatment, but not more than half that number, are actually unable for duty, the scorbutic symptoms are those that are most to be feared. We have at present set every resource in our power at work, in the way of fresh meat, vegetables, and porter, with the hope of stopping it in those cases already attacked, and I hope the issuing of the New provisions, together with some regulations that have been made relative to the mens feet, and the general dryness and increased temperature of the lower deck, will prevent any new cases from occurring – At 4 P.M. We observed a water sky well defined from South to West, and from N.W. to East.

Tuesday Decr 28th It blew a heavy gale by 3 Am as the wind veered to S.S.W., it was not attended with the rise in the water, experienced in the last gale, this I attributed to the wind not being so much to the Southerd, And therefore did not expect any break up of the old floe the Ship is in – The wind continued to blow heavy all the forenoon veering gradually to S.W. Mag[neti]^c at Noon the young ice in the offing was observed to be breaking up and by 3 P.M. we had open water as before, within 50 yards of the Ship. As the water remained at an average hight [sic], we considered our floe pretty safe.

. . . No weather seems too severe for the Natives to visit the Ship, during the strength of this days gale, we had four or five outside, and three in board. I would have them all in, only that it would be a certain means of having their numbers doubled on a similar occasion in future, and as they know the state of the weather before setting out, they do not deserve the consideration of people caught in bad weather – . . .

Wednesday Dec[r] 29th Am. Obs[erved] a meteor in the North, falling to the N.E. The current was observed setting out of Moores Channel, apparently joining that outside the Islands, setting to the East[wa][rd] Moderate weather, at Daylight 10 Am. We had open water and far as the eye could reach, but the vaporation from the water, or as Cap[t] Parry quaintly calls it the barber, prevented our seeing very far. Our employment consisted of clearing our Provision house door of snow, and Keeping the ice wall round the Ship in repair – at Noon a water sky was observed from N.E. to S.W.

The Surgeons report I am glad to find becomes more favourable. A man named Fagan an A.B. who was severely attacked with inflammation in the lungs, & whose case was considered dangerous, has taken a favourable turn – And the Men afflicted with scurvy are all gradually improving – of our stock of pigs four in No 3 have been placed at the disposition of the Surgeon, the fourth will be expended, between our Christmas, and New Years day dinners, to all hands – There are also a quantity of potatoes brought from the Sandwich Islands, that are reserved for the Surgeons use – These and some preserved vegetables and other anti scorbutics, will I hope be effectual in eradicating the disease from Amongst us –

Since Christmas we have had fewer Natives about than usual, and none of the principal men – The old Chief told us on leaving the Ship the evening of the 24th, that he would be engaged dancing for four or five days,[1] and that we were not to expect him for that time. The others seemed to be similarly employed, celebrating some festival – Those on board to day, told us they had been dancing at the Village for several days, without taking any sleep – Now dancing was over, and they were walking round & round in a circle, talking, this is all we could make out of their description – And supposed it some

---

[1] This was no doubt to celebrate the messenger feast, a social event that was usually held near the first of the year. Its primary purpose was economic exchange, resembling in important ways the potlatch festival of the Indians of the northwest coast of North America. The feast was held reciprocally between men of power and wealth in different communities. The feast was celebrated by the exchange of food and by dancing, according to Robert Spencer (1959, pp. 210–28), and it served as an integrative vehicle, providing 'lasting contacts and a sense of cultural uniformity between the peoples of the Alaskan Arctic slope'.

superstitious ceremony, that concluded their festive season – It appears a coincidence worth Notice, that it should occur between Christmas day, and the New Year, and would be a strange fact, if it proved to be in any way connected with their religion – of which we have been unable, to get any insight – as yet. I believe Captain Parry, whose research amongst the Esquimaux has been very considerable, has not been able to come to any conclusion on that subject. The Native who gave us the above information, also gave us the Names of the Committers of the theft in our store house in the beginning of Winter, including in the list, our friend Sable Coat, & Oxinera,[1] our greatest apparent friends at present, & most constant Visitors – There were one or two others, who had been treated with greater Kindness if possible than these – who at first had not the boldness or brass to come near us, and have since been taken little notice of – Of course this Informers story, may be doubted, but it is not the less possibly true . . .

Thursday Dec[r] 30th Thick overcast weather, the young ice formed close to the Ship, is frozen sufficiently hard to bear the Natives passing over it to Martins Island. A Number of them are now about the young ice, catching seal, their method of taking them seems very simple, but requires an immensity of patience, which they seem to possess. The Seal Keeps an air hole open in the ice, by eating it away from underneath, which shows on the surface, in a slight projection or hummock, with a barely perceptible opening, one would hardly notice it, for the first time of seeing – Over these holes they take up their stations, standing on a small low stool, to keep their feet from constant contact with the ice, with their spears in hand, and remaining in that position like statues for hours, or the seal come up to blow, [sic] when they transfix him through the head, another break the ice round, and pull him out –[2]

Thursday has been usually a sort of holyday with us – we generally get the Guns, and Arms well overhauled, and kept ready for immediate use – today the Carronades had become so hard frozen, that it took sometime to get them free. When a shot was fired at a

---

[1] Elsewhere, 'Erk-sing-era'.

[2] This type of ringed seal (*Phoca hispida*) hunting took place in the late autumn and winter in areas which were completely covered by ice. The seals have to keep several small breathing holes open as they swim about in search of food. Later in the season, when cracks have opened in the ice, the seals prefer to use these larger openings for breathing.

mark, for the purpose of reminding the Natives that our guns were still on board – as there were a good Many of them about the Ship at the time – At Noon – there was no ice in sight from the Masthead in the offing – Inshore frozen over, In the afternoon we were employed heaving our springs taut [sic] in anticipation of Another Gale – And building an ice wall to protect the obs[ervator]y door from drift – open water from N.W. to North. Misty.

The Natives have not been very successful in their Sealing today. Several of them returned alongside, with their bows & arrows and geer [sic] – Two attempted fishing in the pools of open water in the Channel, for small fish with an apparatus something like what we term a jigg. It has one line with a piece of ivory shaped like a fish attached to it, from this three short lines are suspended with hooks turned towards each other, this when let down to the proper depth through a hole in the ice, jerked up brings with it the small fish[1] – which probably are attracted by the light – No success attended their operations today, much to our disappointment as we hoped to have procured some fish, for our New Years day feast – – – A large proportion of the Men are still occupied with their festivities at the Village . . .

Friday Decr 31st A fine clear morning to finish the old year, Some Natives were found lurking about the spit in the Middle Watch, and being observed by the watch on deck, were sent away. The old Chief with his two wives, and several others of the 'higher grades' of the Village were on board. The former has not been on board since Christmas eve, and now informed me that he will be engaged for four days more, before he can come again – his absence is a cause of pleasure to me, but as we find him useful, I receive him at all times civilly, at the same time, I have no opinion of his principles, as I fear if we were the weaker party, or in any way at his mercy, he would be about the worst enemy that we should have to contend with – . . .

Saturday January 1st 1853 . . . Glad of an opportunity for giving a change to our people – this has been observed the same as Christmas day – With the exception of a game of foot ball, which our Men were sent out for today, after Church Service, whilst the necessary preparation was making on the lower deck, for their dining together, as on the former occasion. At a little after 1 P.M. they had all assembled round the table, which was comfortably supplied with the

---

[1] They were jigging for tomcod (*Boreogadus saida*).

best provisions our Means afforded. It is an agreeable sight to see these rough sons of the sea, sitting round the social board, and as reasonable in their conduct as other people. This was particularly the case on the present occasion, a quiet round of Songs, toasts, and enlivening jokes, made the Middle portion of our most dull Season, pass over agreeably – indeed there exist[s] a necessity at present to Keep the Crew as Cheerful as possible – as a general tendency to scurvy (which we no doubt hear) is increased by peoples minds getting into a lethargic state – We had very few Natives about, and those chiefly young ones, some looking after seal with their usual apparatus, of three legged stool, spear & bow and quiver of arrows[1] . . .

Sunday Jan[y] 2nd Aurora in the north. A calm quiet day. a few Natives on board – From the masthead the offing was observed to be frozen over as far as could be seen – a few hummocks were observed off Point Barrow. To the East[war][d] the ice was perfectly smooth. It would be well to get into some method of classifying the Aurora's – Merely remarking that there has been an appearance of it, is not sufficient, and sounds very like the old song of Ditto weather – And a description of all that are worthy of it, would fill volumes. Between 3 & 4 P.M. We had a brilliant display of Aurora, extending from East to West, in a broad arch through the Zenith.

Monday [January] 3[d] The work of Keeping our enclosure round the Ship free of snow, after each successive gale, gives ample employment for our reduced working party, at present Amounting to only five when our different look outs against the Natives, are provided for – A continued fall in the barometer, & rise in the temperature, leads me to expect Another gale from the South[a]rd the wind continuing light from that quarter. Sable coat & his wife, with a few others were on board, but not a great many round the Ship. I took a few men & women to my cabin, & delighted the latter much by allowing them to paint their faces, with the printers ink, belonging to our Amateur printing establishment – They speak of the present as a fortunate time for catching seal, which are said to be abundant.

Tuesday [January] 4th Our employment today was cutting an outlet from our gang board, through a bank of drift-snow, eight-feet-high all along the port-side. The Barometer had fallen unusually low this

---

[1] The bow and arrows were probably carried in case they should meet a bear while seal hunting.

morning – 29.24, but the weather remained unaltered, Contrary to my expectations, and as the temperature is again falling, I hope it may pass off without a blow – open water in its proper season is hailed with pleasure, but when within 50 yards, no ice in sight in the offing, and only four hours of very dull light, with an average temperature of $-20°$ [$-28.9°C$], it has no very pleasant appearance to look upon. And we have had it – for some days – – – since the occasion of our Men being treated so badly, visiting the town, which I mentioned before – I considered that if the men could not go there, without ill treatment, out of justice to them, the officers ought not to do so either, although the latter might have done so with impunity – – – At the expiration of two months, finding no prospect of any understanding being come to with the Esquimaux and our Men, the latter in fact seeming to have no wish or inclination to renew their visit to the Village – I found if we pursued the system of holding back, a valuable opportunity would be lost of acquiring a knowledge of their habits and customs which it would be interesting to know. And as I am most anxious that Dr Simpson should turn his pen & talents to such a description – I have proposed to him, his going amongst them as much as necessary for that purpose – The only precaution that seems necessary in visiting the settlement, is to be under the guidance of some one native, who on being met by others, is to Answer for you, that you are going to such a persons hut, when their curiosity is satisfied, and you pass on without being teased – otherwise if you are unaccompanied by such an interpreter, you are followed by a crowd and bored to death, each hoping to make a prize of you & all expecting something –

With the above object in view, I encouraged the inclination of a party of four of the officers, to accept the invitation they were constantly receiving from one or other of our daily visitors, to go to the Village, the honoured person on this occasion was Sable Coat, or the black Chief, as the men call him – he has a boy who is very quick witted, & seems to understand & appreciate our ways, quicker than anybody else – Like other sharp boys, he seems to be well acquainted with human character, the officers describe him as being excellent as a guide, they are able to estimate the characters of the different people they meet, from the way the boy answers them – on a former occasion I gave Dr Simpsons account of a trip he accompanied him on to the Village, I now repeat this visit in his own words, as the best means of describing it –

'The boy Kiwoah[1] came up to escort us, evidently prepared for a refusal, as he had his fishing gear with the usual three legged stool & spear for catching seals – The old chief with his wives was on board, and told the boy he did not believe we should go – it was a sha-ga-look, (a lie). Nevertheless we went, taking a small sledge & were well received – Mess[rs] Vernon, Hull, Wright and myself – We stayed in the hut nearly two hours, entertained by Sables, his wife, and rheumatic Father – besides Kiowa and seven females – The greater number of the last, at least four were visitors, & as they came in were requested to undress, that is, take off their coats, whether as a complement to us, or to keep the crowded space cool, I know not, but most probably the latter, as their furs, when worn in the high temperature of their huts, become unpleasant to smell – they were all regaled with our tobacco, and M[r] Vernon gave a needle to each of the women, an old man, the oldest I have seen in the settlement, was presented, much to his delight, with a piece of Ni-Ki-Moon – or Cavendish cake tobacco. By this name I understand it to be chewing tobacco, like biscuit or other Nik-Ki (edible) We made a move to go, but were requested to stop, when some whale was brought in raw, and seals flesh boiled – I took a little of both for politeness sake, and found the only fault with the seal was that it was underdone – And the whale was edible, being the substance filling the intervals between the roots of the "baleine" and has a flavour something like cocoa Nut – Sables saw us clear of the Village, and the boy accompanied us to the Ship – It appears to me they were all a little surprised, but more pleased to see us, independent of all favours in the way of "Tawak" and needles – The boy coming towards the ship gave the Names of the different settlements, along the Coast towards Icy Cape, and we had him down in order to make a note of them, but unfortunately for this object, he saw the process of serving out tobacco to the crew, the quantity of which piled up in a heap excited his admiration so much, that his wits were adrift, so that we could get little of the information required' –

Faint Aurora in the North – The wind has been from the N.W. all day temp[eratur]e −15° [−26.1°C] with scattered clouds. The Native name of this wind is Ka-Niong-Na. the boys says that clouds usually accompany this wind –

<u>Wednesday. January 5th</u> Our employment today was building an

---

[1] Elsewhere, 'Ke-o-wa'.

additional snow wall round the starb[oar]^d round house, we have also been making an improvement in the Sylvester hot air pipes, by extending them a little farther forward on the Port side, so as to come out on the lower deck instead of ending in the foremost cabin. The preserved potato cases of thin sheet iron have been used for the pipe, and seem to answer the purpose – – – The sergeant of Marines continues to brew very excellent spruce beer. I am sorry our ingredients for it are so limited, as it makes an agreeable & wholesome beverage, the supply averaging three bottles each man weekly. The old man that Dr Simpson treated with some tobacco at the Village yesterday, came down today with a present of a pair of gloves for him. He was consequently taken below, and shown the 'Ig-lu' or interior, and given as well as his wife, a present in return. Dr S. tried as he had done with many others, to find out his age, which he supposed was not less than eighty – but could only learn that he was a great many years (a-mil-iak-tok) (many) – in proof of which he pointed to his grey hairs, and want of teeth, and almost of sight – His intellect is clear, and he seems to be held in some respect by his neighbours. Mr Hull reminded him of his activity, in the summer, in giving chase to his boat to beg tobacco, and the old fellow chuckled in describing to another native, how M^r H[ulls]^s boat – tacked & manovured [sic] to evade him – . . .

Thursday Janu^y 6th Our employment today might come under the head of exercising great guns & small arm men without firing – on Visiting the upper deck before breakfast this morning I was told that our friend Sable Coat, to whom the officers paid a visit the day before yesterday, was along side, and waiting to be admitted – Although much before our usual time of admittance, he was allowed on board, and the cold was so severe that I was obliged at a great sacrifice, to ask him below. The Misfortune is there is no getting rid of them – Nothing short of the plain fact, go away, does it – they will sit doing nothing for seven & eight hours without inconvenience or feeling tired – for them to understand that you suffer from loss time is quite out of the question. They made enquiries today as they often do about our Country, under the title of Englansa – and when it was described to them as being a large Island, Mrs Sables went off at once at a tangent – to describe a white woman, they had seen at (Noo-wook) P^t Barrow. She was with a party of Ko-Yu-Kuk Indians and she came from an Island, where there was a great Summer & no winter – but we could not make out the story very well.[1] Whether they had seen her here, or with the Ko-Yu-Kuks – It is not improbable that some Russian woman of Sitka, or half cast may have taken up with the Indians in the Neighbourhood of Derabin,[2] & may form the subject of the story.

Early in the forenoon, the old Chief with his two wives, & two boys, also came on board – As my occupation for the forenoon was already gone, with my present Visitors, I had the Old Chiefs party down also – – And instead of telling them to go away, I was so tired of the scene at Noon that I dressed in Native attire before them – thinking this would save me the trouble of telling them to go, as they know we never wear the skin dress on board – And must have known I was going out of the Ship. Finding they would not take the hint – I went away for a trip of two or three hours along the Islands on a sledge to observe the state of the ice, and left them to the tender Mercies of my servant, who as soon as I was gone, had less ceremony with them than I had, & soon cleared the cabin – – – . . .

Friday Janu^y 7th For several nights past, we have been visited by small parties of Natives with the Middle watch, generally females. At 3 Am this morning we had a party of five women along side the ship – And in being sent away, returned in two hours, with a number of females increased & two men – This latter party was sent away also, until our men had risen – On enquiry as to these untimely visits (as no doubt there is something of the character of spying about them, to see if we all went to sleep together) I was told, they came to search our dirt heaps for the tobacco stems, thrown out by our people, after making it up in the usual way for smoking – The time of issuing tobacco in these regions of Esquimaux, might be compared to a pay day, in civilized countries. As I find we have a very increased attendance of Natives on the occasion –

The very old man,[3] the patriarch of Noo-wook, was alongside before ten O'clock, and out of pity for his years, was admitted on board – I have mentioned before the unpleasantness of treating any of these people better than another, from their repeating their visits day after day, until you are obliged to cease your civilities towards them, whereas if they were to stop away, for a week or so, you would be glad of their return – So it was with the old man, who had not

---

[1] This may well have been a reference to a woman who was aboard the yacht *Nancy Dawson* at Point Barrow in 1849 (Foote, 1965, p. 160).

[2] Today, Nulato, Alaska.

[3] Later referred to as 'At-ka-na'.

been taken notice of until latterly, in the former state, we saw him
seldom, but now he had become a daily attendant –

This time his wife had a present of a good pair of deer skin Mitts
for Doctor Simpson who is their patron – It appears he asked a
young female what he should give in return, & was told that nothing
was expected, which he seems to think was the case as the old dame
neither begged, or looked wistfully at him as he walked the deck, a
practise common amongst them, as they make presents, hoping by
that means to get a larger return than by ordinary bartering – The
'ruse' is of course generally unsuccessful the first time practised,
Chiefly because it is politic to allow it to be so. but the ceremony of
interchanging gifts, if it be looked upon as of any weight among
them, either as an appearance of friendship or otherwise, does not
require frequent repetition – In the present case Dr Simpson whose
words I quote, did not like to feel himself outdone in generosity by
the old lady, so he gave her more than the equivalent in leaf tobacco,
as bargains go here – with which she seemed both surprised and
delighted, immediately calling the attention of the old man to it –

We had a great many Natives along side today, although the
weather was exceedingly cold −30 [−34.4°C] rising toward Noon to
−23 [−30.6°] and at 4 P.M. it had again fallen to −30. Although this
rise at mid-day cannot be accounted for by any heat received from
the Sun, as it is not visible – still it is remarkable that we experience a
daily rise in the temperature with the day light – Now of about four
hours duration – Our Fire Wood is now becoming scarce, And not at
the most favourable period, as the remaining part of the winter, will
no doubt be the most severe. we had a party away for some to the 2nd
Island[1] today, they brought enough to last for two days . . .

Saturday Jany 8th . . . The employment today was repairing the Ice
wall, and rigging our theatre, for the performance, intended for last
Saturday, but postponed from the illness of Mr Gordon.

At Noon, we had one of a number of disagreeable misunderstandings
with the Natives, that I am sorry to say we have become accustomed
to. The old Chief & his wives & several Natives were on board, Men,
Women & Children – all our best friends in fact. When the
Stammering Man, mentioned before on the occasion of our men
going to the Village, and getting ill used and robbed – He was
desired through the old Chief to go away – he had been down several

[1] Crescent Island in the British nomenclature.

149

times since that time, but had always gone away when desired by Lt Vernon, now, he evidently intended remaining, and if possible, to get a row. Another chief seeing this went out and made him a present of tobacco to go away. The title of chief given here is merely nominal, where every Man is his own providore [sic], the most industrious, bold, or successful hunter, becomes from the property he possesses, of more consideration amongst his countrymen, than others, but gives them no control beyond their own establishment – –

Seeing that the Stammering man intended braving us out, I made up my mind that he was to go, whether by fair means, or force – As in our Circumstances, it is necessary to secure respect, by showing that we have the power to enforce it when necessary – The objection to using force at once, is the difficulty to make those, who are well disposed, understand our motives & intentions, in separating one from the rest as bad – And so uncertain are they all, that this rascal, has on two occasions cried out for the women & children to retire, which they have always done without exception – Whilst the altercation with him was going on outside, those on board began to leave, notwithstanding many of them, had been daily on board and treated with every kindness – without its having the effect of giving them one particle of confidence in us – Our deck was soon completely cleared with the exception of a young female – who with perfect confidence in us, remained two or three minutes after the rest, and then left apparently from the feeling of not wishing to be alone – and not from any mistrust.

Lt Vernon then went out at my desire to tell the man to go once more, when the Natives, thinking that he was merely the first of a force to attack – two thirds of the Men and all the women and children walked straight off for the Village, leaving the objectionable character with a large Minority, these we were undecided in our opinions about, as to whether they were friends, or enemies, but the cause of the disturbance very soon went away – Saving us the trouble of making a show of force for that purpose – And confidence was again apparently restored – I took care that those who had been on board previously and had shown so little confidence in us, should not return, but either chose those who had been apparently indifferent spectators – The marines had been ordered to have their arms in hand on the lower deck, but as each individual on board seems to be alive to the necessity of being in Constant readiness for attack, as defence, the difficulty is to keep them in check – The old chief afterwards told me not to go to the Village, very impressively, a privation personally very little felt, the caution was worth considering, where no personal control is acknowledged.

In the afternoon I regaled a party of 6 or seven, besides children in my cabin, with Goldners[1] preserved Meats – they are rather strong for our tastes, but relished by the Esquimaux uncommonly. My party, with a few other select individuals witnessed the play afterwards – those on deck had some two hours to wait for the performance to commence – And seemed quite content, with gazing at a very inferior drop scene – in a temperature of −7 [−21.7°C] speaking little to each other or hardly removing their eyes from it – Usually they are very restless, moving from one sight to another.

Sunday Jany 9th Faint Aurora in the North. Fine clear cold weather. A number of Natives about from an early hour. After church service several were let on board, amongst others our friend the old Chief – O-Mi-ga-loon – who brought sixteen pounds of Venison to barter – for a Knife – As the quantity was not considered sufficient, he was offered & accepted two preserved meat tins – – – In this bargain, there is no doubt, that some diplomacy was used by both parties – We knew on board that he had Venison and was almost the only person who had sufficient to dispose of any – And had kept it for four months, thinking that we should be obliged to come into his terms, of giving gun powder for it – And finding we could live without his Venison, he had brought it, content to take what we chose to offer – Under these circumstances, I gave orders Lieut Vernon who is our barter Master, to be very indifferent about buying it, and not seem to care whether he did so or not – In reality the state of the Ships Co^s health, renders everything of the sort most acceptable, but I felt annoyed at this old savages pretended friendship for us, when in truth, I suspect he was looking with all anxiety for our running short of food – –

At Noon the stammering man who gave us so much trouble yesterday, came and sat down abreast of our entry port – this boldness on his part rather surprised me – And I concluded that he must not remain – I felt the circumstances connected with him, was doing us no good, at the same time it was necessary to control, and bring him to submission – determining to take the first favourable opportunity of forgiving him – This time he went away on being

[1] See Introduction, p. 42 above

151

told, more as it appeared afterwards, because he was going on a sealing excursion – than from a willingness to be obedient – There were 56 Natives round the ship and 18 inboard today, in sight of the Ship & outside 72 were counted making 90 in all. Men Women & Children . . .

Monday Jany 10th Brilliant Aurora in the South. Since I received the advice from the old chief, not to go to the Village, in consequence of sending the stammering man away from the ship. I have sent our wooding parties away armed, under an officer, although only to a short distance from the Ship. The mere fact of their going armed being sufficient to keep those in check who are inclined to be troublesome – Mr Wright was away with a party today & returned at Noon. That and bringing provisions on board gave us employment for the day.

The old chief brought down a part of a haunch of Venison weighing 32 pounds, and wanted a large Knife for it – but not getting the article he required, he took it away again – The increased length of day light is be coming very perceptible, having now quite five hours.

The rage for bows and arrows amongst our people does not seem to be yet satiated – And they continue to be parted with by the Natives Most willingly . . .

Tuesday Jany 11th Aurora visible above the clouds to the South[wa]^rd a wooding party under Mr Gordon at the 2nd Island. The temperature of the lower deck, has fallen below what it should be to keep the people in the best health. The recent change in the pipe was an alteration for the better . . . Two boys who are rather favourites on board came back after dark, in the hope of being allowed to sleep on board, but were disappointed. We have succeeded today, in getting the names of some of the head lands to the South[wa]^rd – – Point Hope seems to have been the extent of the farthest journey taken from this place. They had heard of Cape Prince of Wales people driving sledges, and one man seemed familiar with the diomede Islands . . .

Wednesday [January] 12th . . . I had a very laughable scene in my cabin today with the old chief – Omigaloon – & his two wives. After setting them all off in a sneezing match with some welsh snuff provided for the purpose of barter or presents, I showed them a little Ea-de [sic] cologne burning on my finger when the old chief must try the same thing & for the sake of some fun & to cure him his inquisitiveness, I poured plenty over his hand & when put to the candle, made a blaze that frightened the old fellow, to such a degree, that when it was out (which by the way took some trouble, & not before he was a little burnt) and found he was safe, he embraced me as if I had delivered him from something dreadful, then after looking round again to see that all was left – he joined my continued laugh at him, as well as his wives – afterwards we could understand the latter, telling each other of the wonderful appearance his hand made in the fire – Whilst the old fellow sat with his head down, looking at his hand – uncertain whether it was yet quite safe. We counted in board and found the Ship today eighty people – behaving very orderly, I begin to hope now, there is a chance of their understanding and appreciating us. The well disposed are the Most Numerous, And from the others, or bad ones, the only inconvenience they are – is our not being able to derive that Knowledge of their Customs, from a free intercourse with their houses – that our opportunity may lead people to expect from us . . .

Thursday 13th January Fine calm weather, the length of day light, perceptibly increasing – In the forenoon we fire six shots from our Carronades, at a Mark – to the astonishment of our neighbours – I have in this a double object, one, practice & employment for our own men. & I find it has the effect of Keeping the Natives very civil – When it is not done occasionally, the bad ones whenever a number sufficiently large are together, commence showing their tricks – . . .

We have had an unusually large assemblage of Natives today, our Men & Officers, seem to have a Mania at present for Esquimaux implements of chase, bows and arrows, [e]t^c [e]t^c And seem all surprised, at their supplying us with their weapons – perhaps on the whole it may show, they do not mistrust us. I purpose taking a fitting opportunity to describe all these different implements and uses, as well as a few general points of Esquimax [sic] character – although I much fear, that nothing new will be found or described by me – As Captain Parry, who was first in the field, and Capt[ai]ⁿ Beechy [sic] and Sir John Richardson & others have left very little untold of these people – whose 'characteristics', are very much the same, although spread over a large space, and without any intercourse with each other . . .

Friday Jany 14th A party away for firewood – and repairing the ice wall round the Ship, much broken by the firing yesterday, was the employment for the day – An unusually low temperature, keeps a Number of our visitors away . . .

<u>Saturday Jan^r 15th</u> . . . We have again had some trouble with the man mentioned before, as the stammering man[1] – he came today, and met me, when walking out on the ice, to look at our Anchors – I was rather surprised to see him – And for the first time, personally ordered him away. After making an uproar and endeavouring (As usual with him) to send away the women and children – who all came back immediately on my calling them and laughing at him – When he went away. While the disturbance was going on, I endeavoured to explain to the Multitude, that they were all good, and they had nothing to fear from us – But that this one man was an exception – he was bad, and must be sent away. About Noon. We had a cry that a bear was in sight from the Ship which cause a general rush of Natives in the direction, the officers ran down for their Rifles, unfortunately when every thing seemed in fair training for his destruction, it turned out to be only a dog on the first Island – which had caused such a sensation –

<u>Sunday Jany 16th</u> . . . The low temperature of −35½° [−37.5°C] was not sufficient to keep our usual attendance of natives away – No temperature seems to affect them – in the morning by 6 o'clock, 3 and 4 hours before daylight – they commence arriving. those not admitted in board, sit down on the snow – laughing, singing, & frisking about, as lighthearted, as a party of our own country people would be, on some green bank on a fine May Morning . . .

<u>Monday Jany 17th</u> Calm clear weather. Arch of Aurora from West to E.S.E. Bringing on board provisions from the house, and clearing away the gangway platform snow Employed us for the day. The lowest temperature we have yet experienced −40 [−40°C]. In my cabin it as low as +30 [−1.1°C] until after the fire is lighted. A good many Natives about the Ship. all quiet and orderly. I have several times invited the widow of a poor man who was drifted away on the Ice & lost, to come to the ship, and that I would make her a present – today I am told, that she is coming down tomorrow – The very old Patriarch – At-Ka-Na, was of the party on board, and as usual received much kindness from his friend Dr Simpson – who received some more information relative to the Neighbouring tribe called Nuna-tagmiut Ennui (Men) Mistaken by Simpson in 1837 for

---

[1] 'To-ko-la-rua.'

Russians[1] – They are a tribe of Esquimaux, who dwell on the rivers inland, and do not practice fishing in the sea – and have no boats.[2] It appears that they barter Russian Articles and produce of the land, for what the Coast tribes, can give them of the produce of the sea – . . .
Tuesday Jany 18th Calm clear & cold weather – Mr Gordon with a party made a trip to the 2^d Island for wood – The temperature −31° [−35°C] was lower than I wished to expose men to, but as the weather was calm, and we were in want of the article, they were sent – This & boiling down oil from seal blubber purchased along side – And cleaning out a tank, that had contained coal employed us for the day –

In the forenoon I had a visit from the old Chief and his two wives, they brought with them at my request the widow of the man who was drifted away on the ice,[3] a month or so back, I thought her a very fit object for our compassion, as we are sent here to assist people in a distress not altogether dissimilar – In making her a considerable present, I thought it would be a means (independent of the feeling of charity for the poor woman) to enlist their fellow feelings in our own cause, by drawing a comparison between our lost Ships and her lost husband. And if they are capable of gratitude, which I very much doubt, it must have a tendency to gain their assistance & friendship, in favour of any of our own or parties from the other ships, falling back along the coasts they frequent.

The widow was rather a nice looking woman, seemingly quiet and good tempered. She had a baby with her, about nine months old, and had left another child of three years at the huts – As Nature had not taught her to grieve for appearance sake, she appeared quite natural, although no doubt she feels her loss most acutely – She received her presents – Consisting of a large piece of tobacco, a preserved meat tin, some needles, and a few beads for the baby and seemed pleased with them, her manner was quiet & subdued, though she was observant of the Novelties around her in the cabin – Her baby soon afterwards became troublesome to her from crying, and she took her leave – being told to return to the Ship again in a month, when she would have another present made her –

[1] See Thomas Simpson's account (1843, p. 161) and see above, p. 117, n. 2.
[2] This was not true. The interior Eskimos used large umiaks for river travel and kayaks for hunting swimming caribou.
[3] See Maguire's entry for 4 May 1854.

With those remaining we had some conversation about their bartering pursuits, brought about by my remarking the same makers mark upon all their knives. I have observed the same upon every one amongst them, showing that they come from the same source – They of course knew nothing of it, and on being shown it were not conscious of its meaning, or Similarity – The mark [drawing of the mark] a Maltese cross over the letter I, we supposed to be Russian. They told us they got them from the Ko-Yu-Kuk Indians – A piece of information, I have not been able to get before – Upon enquiring if these people had guns, we were told they had, the old chief informing us, that he purchased his from them. We endeavoured to find if the Esquimaux here knew anything of the Russian posts in the country – or where the people they bartered with to the East[war]^d got their supplies. The only Answer we could get was they got them a long way off. And that the Ko-yu-Kuks had not much gun powder. The old chief noted particularly the things we had given to the widow, And we tried to make him understand that there were many like circumstances in our country – Ak-sin-nera[1] another Chief was present, and seemed to catch our meaning quicker than the others – he seems the most disinterested, and least selfish of our Visitors – He has evidently formed a high opinion of Piktoria as he calls the Queen – our great Ome-lik (Chief) to whom he has been told our ship, and almost everything in her belongs – A woman to have so much power and wealth, must of course amaze him, and it would be a matter of extraordinary interest to be able to give his impression of our great (Chief) 'Omelik' as he conveys it to his friends at the huts.

The water sky still hangs over the Village, though no open water can be seen from our Masthead. The weather has been cold, temp[eratur]^e −30 [−34.3°C] at 9 P.M. . . .

Wednesday – Jany 19th Brilliant Aurora from N.E. to S.W. passing through the Zenith, coruscating and changing colours. At Daylight we observed the tracks of three bears near our House on the Spit. The Natives it seems, seldom see them any distance from the open water, and told us the smell of the Ship had attracted them. They appear to think we ought not to have allowed them to escape, with our guns – Bringing snow to the Ship, and playing at Foot-ball were the occupations for the day.

We had a visit from the stammering Man again today. Lt Vernon

[1] 'Erk-sing-era.'

with great forbearance & kindness got him away from the Ship about
two hundred yards, and when left there, instead of returning to the
Village – he swaggered back leisurely towards the ship, when I was
informed of this, I saw there was no use trying any more mild
measures for them – And ordered two marines, loaded with ball, to
be placed on the Ice abreast of the gan[g]way, to prevent his coming
along side – When he saw them he threw off his skin coat and
seemed by his manner to challenge us to shoot at him. His wife and a
Man of some influence, who were with him, made him think better
of it, and he retired to the huts . . .

We had a good many Natives on board, and a few down below.
Amongst them the old patriarch[1] & his wife – I lent a man a picture
of the Ship drawn by the Carpenter, showing all the arrangements
for housing which they seemed to look upon as a wonder, and
wished to show to their associates at Noo-Wook – . . .

Friday [January] 21st A party under M[r] Gordon were dispatched for
fire wood this morning & returned at Noon – We have been unable
to prevent the accumulation of condensed vapour overhead on the
lower deck, from which it drops, either on the people sitting about
the deck or at night into their hammocks and in moving about in the
night, or getting in and out, the blankets wipe it off, and when taken
on deck become hard frozen – – – We have tried all sorts of
experiments in the way of funnels & tubes, for allowing some of the
heated air to escape, but all that we have tried have admitted more
cold, then allowed heated air to escape – As a radical cure for the
preservation of dry bedding, screens of canvas are making, to go
overhead to be rolled up in the day time, and placed along the
underside of the deck, ½ hour before the hammocks are piped
down.

The Surgeons report of the health of the Ships C[o] is more
favourable, but there is still a dormant sort of tendency to scurvy,
that I am at a loss to account for. No precaution towards warmth,
dryness & cleanliness is left untried – The provisions at present in
use, are better than we had for the six months previously, And it is
much hoped may make a change for the better –

The interest of the last two days at noon to see the sun was
damped today from the horizon being clouded to the South[wa]r[d]
The weather being cold and hazy, we were not so thickly attended

---

[1] 'At-ka-na.'

with Natives as usual, this we have learned from the first day of our arrival to be a pleasure rather than a privation – A day rarely passes however that I am not under the necessity of asking some Natives down to my cabin, where their dirt & smell is sufficient to make them a nuisance – And they never think of making a move until you plainly say go! & this word, unpleasant as it is to use, they sometimes oblige you to repeat, not wishing to understand you the first time – I had the old chief & his two wives down today for two hours, his constant attendance has become rather a task as I almost make a rule [sic] to ask him below – This with a character though a savage, so void of any feeling that can be construed into generosity, or a favourable quality of any Kind, makes it an unpleasant piece of courtesy treating him civilly – I sometimes wish they had a little of the generosity of the Savages described by the earlier Voyagers to the Pacific – An approach to anything like a feeling of gratitude is not to be found amongst these Esquimaux – a pair of gloves in value equal to a few leaves of tobacco are offered, with the hope of making a little bargain, in that way, calculating, on your present in return & when you refuse the gift, they seem to say then you reject the bargain – . . .

Saturday Jany 22^d . . . A woman from Cape Smyth brought above fifty fish[1] which were purchased with tobacco, and issued to the Ships C° a few being reserved for the sick. A few of the mens bedding that were wet have been Kept below to be dried at the Sylvester Stove – . . .

Sunday. Jany 23^d A strong wind from S.S.W. with snow drift, Ice [?] moving out of the Ship. The Natives about us as usual, no weather seems to prevent their going out, one is some time getting accustomed to their defence of cold which is accounted for by their dress of deer skin double. At 8 AM this morning when it was quite dark with a strong breeze and snow drift – there was a party of young people and children, playing about on the Ice alongside the ship, As lighthearted as if the sun was shining – – – During the morning part of a preserved potato case, of thin sheet iron, used outside of the Ship for placing the blocks of snow on for thawing, was found to be stolen. As we are getting over their propensity in that way – More stir was made by us, than its value deserved. And all admittance into the Ship stopped – The boy Kio-wa – called in my journal previously

---

[1] At this season, probably tomcod (*Boreogadus saida*).

the intelligent youth – when he came down mentioned the name of the thief without hesitation – Although he was one of his Fathers boat crew, and hastened back to the Village to inform Sable coat, who came down with the stolen article early in the afternoon, in great fear of losing a favour, from the delinquent being one of his followers.

As the weather was very bad for him to return to the Village, he was invited to sleep on board, to Keep company with another Chief, a great friend amongst the officers, invited also, and I was glad they accepted the invitation, as by sleeping on board, it would tend to give them confidence in us, which is still wanting, notwithstanding all our Kindness to them . . .

Monday. Jany 24th The weather had quite moderated this morning, showing no break up of the ice in the offing – Although a Native from Cape Smyth informed me, that the ice in the offing there, was very bad, and they had nothing to eat, from not being able to go out after Seal – In comparing their case with the people of (Noo-wook) Pt Barrow, It appears there must be something favourable in the position of the latter with regard to seals, as they have them in great abundance – – –

Of our three guests last night, two seem to have slept without any mistrust, but our friend Sable coat, More distrustful would appear to have slept with one eye open, as he fell asleep in an upright position several times in the morning and went away early to have his sleep out – We had a fair proportion of visitors alongside today, and an average number in board – Our enemy the stammering man came alongside and on being told to go away by Lt Vernon – seconded by the Quarter Master who had before given him an instance of his persuasive powers,[1] he retired without a question . . .

Tuesday [January] 25th . . . At 11 a.m. app. Time – we were gratified with a full view of the sun, after an absence of 65 days, the increased refraction from the low temperature, would have it visible three days sooner, had the state of the atmosphere been clearer – In order to add some sort of solemnity to the reappearance of the sun, we fired a gun and hoisted our Ensign on the occasion . . . 'As a great deal of blubber is used of late in the Silvester stove, the traffic in seal blubber has been considerable, but our stock on board being large, the sale is not now so brisk as it was. Two skins were brought

---

[1] See Maguire's entry for 21 November 1852.

alongside today, but not being purchased, the owners have left them standing on sticks about three feet high on the snow bank close to the Ship to be out of the way of the dogs. The circumstance is mentioned to show their trust in our right dealing with them'[1] We had a party of Natives along side from Cape Smyth all day, but as they brought nothing to barter, and as we have already a sufficient N° of the same sort of adventurers round us, they were not asked on board – – 'Some of the old chiefs party have gone away to look after deer, and he says they will not return for two Moons, although their station is not distant. I hope however we shall obtain some fresh meat for a change before that time elapses.'[2]

Wednesday. Jany 26th Am observed a halo round the Moon, Our fatigue duty today was repairing the ice wall round the ship, and 'sledging' away the blocks of ice removed from the tide hole. A Man who I know to be a chief from Cape Smyth (From his having been pointed out to me as a good man – possessing two wives 'as a female remarked to me on the deck about a month since') came along side. I invited them down to my cabin, and with the assistance of Doctor Simpson, entertained them with tobacco and the sights of the cabin for about an hour – but a more ungrateful, (of a generally ungrateful race) I never had to deal with, than this party – Which consisted of the Chief, his two wives, & Son – And his brother & wife – The first act of politeness on my part, was to offer the lady nearest to me some tobacco to smoke, having it on a small piece of board on the table – she was the brothers' wife and when she had helped herself, very cooly [sic] took out her own tobacco bag, and emptied the remainder into it – I had walked to the other side of the Cabin, and in turning saw her, much to my amusement, however I pretended she must pass the bag round – And replenished the board at the same time – When it was handed to one of the Chiefs wives who on being told by him to empty it also – was preparing her bag for its reception, when Dr Simpson quietly saved her the trouble – This did not prevent me making them all a present of some sort or other, But this step on the whole seemed rather to get me into trouble than favour – from the fault found by the Chiefs brother in his present, which was some leaf

[1] Maguire is probably quoting from John Simpson's journal.
[2] These people were probably going inland to hunt caribou, which, in the western Brooks Range, often begin to move northward from the mountains in late January or early February. These animals could be taken by herding them into a corral, driving them into a pitfall, snaring them, or stalking them (Sonnenfeld, 1957, pp. 122–6).

tobacco, which he wanted changed, and in fact seemed displeased, whereas the others whether pleased or not – Kept their feelings to themselves – And all I had of thanks was this mans evident disatisfaction on leaving my cabin –

The old Chief has completely tired me out with his visits which have now become daily, and feels, 'as he says' very cold on deck on taking advice on the subject as to the best means of informing him that his Visits come too often, I was informed that he was too deaf to understand anything he did not like, and that the best place with him would be, letting him remain on deck – then his visits would be less frequent & prolonged.

We have a good many natives round the Ship and about twenty in board. The night is perfectly cloudless with a bright moon – we got some Lunar distances but the cold −37 [−38.3°C] was intense.

Thursday January 27 . . . The old Chief appeared on board today, equipped for a sealing excursion. The first time I had ever observed him in any way industrious – he has a great difficulty in keeping away from the Ship, whatever the attraction is, certainly it is not my civility, or gifts, as he has quite worn his welcome out In Coming every day . . .

Friday [January] 28th Am Patches of Aurora in the West – The event of this morning was the Quarter Master of the watch, and one of the look out men, making an Esquimaux prisoner, he had been observed going into a tent erected over a Theodolite, for the purpose of observing the sun's refraction. The legs of the instrument were frozen too hard for him to move it, and he was coming out empty handed, when he was taken and as he had stolen nothing was beaten a little by the Men, and sent outside the boundary, but persisting in going in an opposite direction across our enclosure, was brought on board, and on its being reported to me, I ordered him to be kept on deck a prisoner, & in the mean time his companion supposed to be his wife who was looking out for him under the bows, made her escape –

This was what I had long wished for to catch one of these people in the fact and to give him a good flogging at any hazard, before any number of his country men outside of the Ship. Then let him go – however, on considering this case over, As he was found to have stolen nothing (which by the way was not attributable to any forbearance) – I thought it hardly strong enough to deserve the first mentioned punishment – And these people understand anything in the way of joke, or ridicule very easily, my next thought of a punishment, was dipping him in the tide pole hole and letting him go – This I was advised against, as it was so exposed that some of them might take an opportunity of pushing one of our men into it in retaliation – Our position amongst these people is so very peculiar, that it requires one to consider well every act connected with them. My plan under certain reservations, has been forbearance in its utmost limit, I believe myself it is a bad plan, that is as far as the Ship is concerned and I know it to be very unpopular Amongst the crew, whom nothing would please more than being ordered to fire amongst these people – But I expect & hope that whatever the inconvenience we may suffer, for not shooting & flogging some of these beauties – They will have no ill treatment, or loss of life to resent [?] upon any small detatched [sic] party of our own, and we are likely to have many so circumstances – And in the same way, none of our Countrymen following us here, let their party be small or great, will I hope receive any ill usage on our account –

It may be presumed after this long tirade, that the culprit in the present case got off very easily – In consequence of our having him a prisoner on board, only four or five women, & a few children came near the Ship – The old Chief I was glad to see came down, as I wished to have him, as a witness – about noon the stammering man & several detatched [sic] Natives, returning from sealing, Armed with their bows & spears, Kept dropping past the Ship, Just to observe as I suppose & what was going on – The stammerer being ordered away under these circumstances, went off without much persuasion – I then in the presence of the Chief and one or two others & most of the officers of the Ship assembled round – Explained to the prisoner about flogging with the Cat of Nine tails, and that the next person caught similarly circumstanced to himself, would have it – on his back and he was then shown out of the Ship – very much to the apparent disappointment of the Boatsw[ai]^{ns} Mate, who had evidently made up his mind, to have a sort of squaring up match, for a long score of remaining unsettled between him, and the scamp of the Esquimaux, connected with his work round the Ship outside – The chief and the others of course agreed that it was a just & proper mode of proceeding. But it seemed to me that both parties, wondered at the lightness of the punishment, I think most of the Esquimaux were quite indifferent as to whether, I had hung, or drown'd him, and skinning alive would not have appeared out of the way to the people on the lower deck. But the officers of the Ship, were without exception for lenient usage – from considering the case with regard to our lengthened stay here – and other circumstances – . . .

Saturday 29th January – . . . We had an average Number of Natives on board, one or two I invited to my cabin – Mr Hull accompanied one some way toward the Village, who informed him, that at present it would not be well his going to the Village, as the Men were talking, but that bye & bye it would be all right again . . .

Sunday [January] 30th The weather mild and gloomy The[rmomete]^r +7° [−13.9°C] to 10° [−12.2°C] – with a light fall of snow, which remains on the Masts & rigging from the dampness of the Atmosphere making it adhere – A good many Natives about the Ship and after church several were on board – In the afternoon a Number of our men Amused themselves shooting with their Native bows and Arrows at a mark – Several Natives were looking on, who of course looked upon our people as Novices and were ready to instruct them – One of the Chiefs Ak-sin-ea[1] – seeing the fun going on came out of the Ship, & showed his skill. He hit a mark about a foot square, at a distance of forty yards, once in ten times and once he cracked a piece of sheet Iron with a blunt arrow at the same distance – 'His accuracy of Aim was not so great as I expected and was not thought better, than a practised hand with a pistol could successfully compete with.'

In the Mean time I set out with Dr Simpson for a walk round Martins Island. Accompanied by the boy Ki-o-wa, we observed a remarkable pressure of the ice in Moores Channel, at a tide crack running across it . . . In passing over Martins Islands on the highest part of which there is a burial ground, we were curious to observe the effect of passing through it, on our guide and another boy who had joined us in our walk. They remarked that there was a dog eating their dead men, without seeming to think anything of it, and only showed a little delicacy in not treading over remains of their departed friends, lying exposed on the surface. We tried to find their ideas of the state of death by asking them whether the dead people could see – they evidently considered it an external sleep – . . .

In returning to the Ship, we passed two Esquimaux seated patiently on their three legged stools with their feet on a small piece of bear skin over seal holes – These holes mentioned before, are very small, just large enough for the Animal to breathe through, and require some

[1] 'Erk-sing-era.'

pains to discover – The boy Ke-o-wa – was allowed to sleep on board
at his own request – And appears to enjoy himself very much on the
lower deck – The weather remained thick throughout the night with
a little snow falling – . . .

Monday. January 31st Hazy mild weather. the temperature remaining above Zero – The Sylvester funnels requiring sweeping – They
were taken down & thoroughly cleaned, the temperature on the
lower deck was sufficiently high to dispense with the fire for several
hours – The boy Kio-wa seemed to have liked his quarters & feeding
last night, as he remained about the lower deck until the Afternoon.

We had several natives about the Ship, but not so many in board
today. The old Chief and his wives & Children, making up half the
Number. We had some more bow and arrow practice today & the
greatest distance any Native sent an Arrow was 150 yards & 'I should
think the best bow shot would not exceed 200 yards if so far –[']¹

As a precaution, in the event of the ship being moved out of her
present position by the ice & separated from our provision store,
I have brought on board a proportion of Salt Pork – And to make
the house and available retreat – All the launches gear, with the
boat have been placed at the house, to be available in case of any
disaster – . . .

Tuesday Feby 1st [1853] Am. Brilliant Aurora extending from East
to West through the Zenith – coruscating. The temp[erature]
remained during the night at −27 [−32.8°C] the Barom[ete]ʳ
continuing to rise –

Ana-tok-son-a a man in disrepute with us, was down early this
morning with a tale of people having been to Point Hope – (Tik-ki-
rame)² where they had seen a Ship. Ak-son-ea³ was on board soon
afterwards & reported the same with the addition that the ship was
large, and had on board 100 men. He also said the people who had
seen them, were three of a party belonging to Cape Smyth, who had
left this two months & a half ago, and had now returned – I was
hurrying on deck to make some enquiry on the subject, when the
impossibility of the story became so impressed on me, that I went on

¹ Maguire is probably quoting from John Simpson's journal. This estimate for the
range is reasonably similar to Edward Belcher's estimate of 176 yards for bows he saw
near Kotzebue Sound a quarter century before (Belcher, 1861, p. 139).
² 'Tikiraq' is the name for Point Hope; 'Tikirarmiut', for the members of the Point
· Hope society.
³ 'Erk-sing-era.'

deck more for the purpose of telling our informant, that he was acquainting us with stories that were not possible – I say not possible from Knowing that Point Hope offered no protection for a Ship to winter – Another strong reason against it was there being no Ship to be found there – For if either the Investigator, or Enterprise had come out of the Ice. They would no doubt have made their way to the South . . .[1]

Wednesday [February] 2[d] A wooding party under M[r] Wright were employed bringing in fire wood from Martins Isl[an][d] . . . The event with the Natives today was contradicting the story brought of the Ship wintering at P[t] Hope, they have found out the story to be untrue & seem anxious to set us right about it – This being the Anniversary of three of the officers, and myself sailing from England in the Orinoco, I was invited by them to celebrate the occasion, by a dinner in the Gun Room – where we passed a pleasant evening, recounting over some of our adventures on the passage out – We have a Native who is a nice lad, and has always been most friendly, sleeping on board, by invitation tonight – I think he was for some time afraid to do so, but has mustered up courage sufficient at last. The object in occasionally allowing one or two to sleep on board, as a great favour, has been, to give them confidence and let them see, more into our habits, which must tend as much as anything, to raise us in their estimation – During the night it blew very hard from East true – quite shaking the Ship. As this wind blows into the bay, and lowers the depth of water, it does not cause us the same anxiety, that a Southerly gale does, as a continued gale from that quarter, brings the open water close to the Ship –

Thursday Feb[y]. 3[d] Our friend Sable skin & wife paid us an early visit this morning, his wife had been on board the day previously and told us in evident distress poor woman. that her husband had taken an additional wife into his establishment – and on seeing him outside this morning, I was willing he should remain a little time there to show him that his consequence had not increased with us – Doct[o][r] Simpson enquired of Ak-sin-ra[2] – a very intelligent man, he is what might be termed a Chief & is a great friend of ours – He said that the story was true, and that bye & bye, he likewise should take another wife to his house – So it appears to be nothing unusual with them –

---

[1] This may have been a garbled third- or fourth-hand account of having seen the *Amphitrite*, a much larger vessel, during the summer.
[2] 'Erk-sing-era.'

My own idea of it is that any man can have two or more wives, as he pleases, if he is a sufficiently expert hunter to support them, but in a community where they have to rely upon their own intrepidity, to provide for their subsistence – One wife and one or two children, which is generally the content of their family, is as much as the ordinary sort of man is able to sustain – Some few are more expert than others, and these are the Chiefs, merely from the influence their character gives them, with the party they live & hunt with. We could not understand Mrs. Sables story of the second wife, and put it down as some temporary arrangement, it appears however that the woman in question is the widow of the man who was lost on the ice floe in December last – that I described some days back,[1] having sent for her to come to the Ship, and receive some presents in consideration of her loss. She appears poor woman to have done very well in this instance, as our friend Sables appears to be better off than any of the others.[2]

We had fewer natives along side than usual – The Stammering Man whose behaviour is reported to be much improved, by his own people, came down to the Ship, And as we have established our point of Keeping him away to as great an extent as one can expect to do with a savage, I requested Lt Vernon to have explained to him through one of the Natives, that he must go away, and that when we please that he should be allowed to remain along side the Ship, he would be sent for – Understanding this he went away very much pleased with the prospect of being friends again –

The Evening was mild and clear, I accompanied one or two of the Natives half way up to the Village, and could not help being struck with the desolateness of the view from our station – The whole circle of the horizon round, showing nothing for the eye to pitch upon, except an occasional ice hummock – And the rise of Point Barrow – Spit, on which Noo-wook is built – which alone distinguishes it from the ice horizon – the View in every other direction being unbroken – As the low shores of the Mainland are not distinguishable – . . .

Saturday Feby 5th . . . We had a visit at a very early hour from the old chief, who as usual was admitted on board at once. He brought a very small piece of Venison, for which he asked something very exorbitant, and on being refused his demands, seemed inclined to

---

[1] Maguire's entry for 18 January 1853.

[2] John Simpson (Appendix Seven, p. 525 below) identified only four men at Point Barrow with two wives.

give it to me – however, on second thoughts he told his wife to bring it away with her. Having previously asked one of the officers whether he should go home or not, on which he was told, that he was quite at liberty to please himself, and by going, I presume he did – He has of late become such an intolerable beggar, that I have been obliged to cease giving him anything, as I found him here every day, without ever offering to assist us, in any bartering, or being of any use beyond begging – And that he has indulged us in to an immense extent. As this was a night that we intended to Keep up with a Masquerade, and some dancing & singing & [e]t^c I intended inviting him to stay and partake of the fun, his early departure saved me the trouble of inviting and entertaining him and his wives no small one, when all the inconvenience one is put to on their account is taken into consideration. Aksunra[1] was on board also, he was invited to remain for the evening, as were several children & women who were outside of the Ship.

It struck me as flattering to us, to observe what confidence the unprotected part of these people place in us – At all times of the day, we have children about us, and our earliest and latest visitors, are generally females who continualy [sic] appear with their children, to place more confidence in us than the men. Except occasionally we have not many men waiting round the Ship – Our Men seem to have a natural dislike to them, and they receive little encouragement – I very often remark upon this subject to the officers, and find their opinion generally to be, that the men are ungrateful, and are of no use, accept to beg – whereas the women are Kinder in their natures, mend our peoples mocassins, & skin clothing, and show some sign of gratitude for the presents they receive – I have been several times very much Amused to see our Men on pea soup days, bring up all the remains from the lower deck, in a large tin can, and take it out on the ice, & place it between a party of women, who set to work devouring it in handsfull, whilst the honest Jack, walks up & down with his hands in his pockets, looking out under his eyes occasionally to see that all was going on in a fair scramble –

I asked a party of six or seven into my cabin this evening, to give them something to eat previous to their Amusements – Ak-sin-ra[1] was the only male of the party, the remainder were his wife, two other females, & some children – I sent him on deck during the time

[1] 'Erk-sing-era.'

167

of their visit, to give each of the Natives on deck, a small piece of tobacco. This appeared to give general satisfaction, and lead to the promise being made of spreading our name for goodness amongst all the 'Nations' far & wide from Point Barrow – He and his party seemed well pleased throughout, & when in the cabin spoke of the tales he would have to tell to his bartering friends when he met them, of all the wonders he had seen amongst us – I told his wife that in six Months, the ship would be going away, she expressed how much it would be regreted at Noo-wook – on this I replied that they would be very glad, but she decided the question by saying they would miss our tobacco very much – which is not unlikely – Aksinra entered fully with the evenings Amusements, getting up to dance with our people – following the Motions in the 'fishermans dance', like the others as directed by the leader – Our party broke up at 10 P.M. our Visitors and selves well pleased with our entertainment, which was much added to, by some well sustained characters amongst the officers – . . .

Sunday Feby 6th . . . I am sorry to find that notwithstanding all the attention and care that has been paid to the subject, the Scurvy still continues amongst some of the Seamen, and in some of a very healthy appearance in their first winter – those who have been a second & third are not to be so much wondered at. The diet of the Ship is now ample and excellent, those attached with scorbutic symptoms being on entirely fresh food & vegetables – Scurvy is a disease that is thought cannot exist in the present day, when its character is so well understood, And specifics against it known – In our case we find the contrary, as it remains notwithstanding the free use of all Known ante scorbutics –

The day remained threatening wind [sic]. We had very few Natives about or on board. The old chief was again Amongst the latter, he brought his piece of Venison with him, and this time sold it for some tobacco – I was engaged at the observatory all day, and therefore allowed him to remain on deck unnoticed which I hope will have the effect of keeping him more at home – . . .

Monday – Feby 7th . . . The expected event of a visit from the Natives from Point Hope 'tik-a-rams',[1] talked of for the last few days, took place today, in the visit of a Chief[2] accompanied by two

---

[1] 'Tikirarmiut.'
[2] He is later identified by Maguire as 'Sam-ma-ru-ma'.

nice looking young women his wives[,] – he was himself a pleasing, spirited, looking man, about thirty five years of age – & had travelled as he said to see the ship, having heard at Point Hope of our being here – He recognised Doctor Simpson, as having seen him before, about Hotham Inlet,[1] and asked for Mr Martin,[2] the former 2nd Master of this ship, he was also familiar with the name of Captain Moore – As I anticipated, he had no information of any ship seen to the South[wa]rd And as I was anxious to cultivate a good understanding with him, in consequence of our boats going to the South[wa]rd Amongst his people in the summer, I invited him down to the cabin, & made him some presents, with which he appeared much pleased, I found that he had been fifteen days on his journey, and that the sea was open all along the coast to the Southard – As it is at present to the Westward of Point Barrow, and to the southard by Cape Smyth,[3] he did not appear to have been familiar with ships, which I account for by the lowness of the land about Point Hope, detering the Whalers from approaching it, otherwise in the Latitude during the summer, they are in great numbers – He spoke also of his people being badly supplied with tobacco, which would not be the case on a part of the coast frequented by the American Whale Ships –[4]

It would appear that this man, was a poet in his way, as he favoured us with a long extempore song, which included the name of the Ship & also my own – After which he stroked his stomach down several times, expression of great friendship, then he got up & came to me, fixed his forehead against mine, and used it as a fulcrum, to rub his nose several times across mine, a ceremony not very agreeable, in his heated state, from singing – One of the Chiefs of this place[,] Ark-sin-ra[5] – was of the party, which no doubt tended very much to place him at his ease amongst us, otherwise they are inclined to be mistrustful on the first visit. This man also saved us a world of trouble, explaining the different uses of things in the cabin,

[1] An embayment of Kotzebue Sound.

[2] Henry Martin served aboard the *Plover* from 1848 to 1852 under T. E. L. Moore. 'Sam-ma-ru-ma' probably met them in the winter of 1849–50, when the *Plover* was wintering at the Choris Peninsula in Kotzebue Sound. In both that instance and this one he would have travelled through territories occupied by other Eskimo societies. For comments on such winter travel see above, p. 128, n. 1.

[3] This would have been a wide lead between the pack ice and the shore fast ice, not open seas.

[4] It was not until the 1860s that American Whaleships began to make frequent close approaches to the American shore north of Bering Strait.

[5] 'Erk-sing-era'.

& other wonders to him, that he saw in the ship – He appeared more surprised on being shown a looking glass, than I have seen any native previously, and looks upon me as a conjuror – After devoting several hours to the interview I made a motion for the deck, which was speedily understood by Ak-sin-ra – who led them off very well pleased . . .

Tuesday – Feb^y – 8th . . . This was the day appointed for the Stammering Man to be allowed to come along side the Ship, he made his appearance in the forenoon apparently in his best clothes and behaviour, and went away after remaining about two hours – The Chief from Point Hope was on board with his wives, but as he seemed troublesome, returning some tobacco he had received for a pair of mocassins, I ordered them to be given back, but not to be bartered with again, by any person on board. He soon afterwards went away, as well as many others, who seemed to be attracted by the novelty of his company – . . .

Wednesday – Feb^y – 9th . . . I have not seen fewer Natives along side the ship, Any day previous than today, what the occupation, or pursuit is, that keeps them away, I have not found out, but I feel much obliged to it, and hope it may continue to keep us clear, of the tiresome set of beggars – I had the old chief in the cabin for an hour in the afternoon – with his two wives and little boy – he comes on board almost every day for the sole purpose of begging, he never has anything to barter, so I conclude that he would not come in very cold weather, on the chance of an invitation below, except for the object of begging – I have confined myself to asking him below, & making him a small present once a week – We had a companion of the Chief from Point Hope on board also today, the officers invited him to the Gun Room – And the only information, they received from him, was there being a large Ship some where to the South[wa]rd with very little men on board[1] – whether we have mistaken their little for few – or most likely it is one of many such stories, these people have Amongst them, from the habit of repeating from one to the other, without reference to date. As in this case, if the story just mentioned was traced to its source, it would prove to be some American Whaler visited in the summer by them –

[1] This may have been a third-hand reference to the small trading vessel, *Swallow*, of Hong Kong that wintered in Saint Lawrence Bay, Siberia, in 1850–1. Apart from that, the *Plover* was the only other ship to have wintered in the western Arctic (Bockstoce and Batchelder, 1978a).

The day throughout has been overcast, giving our observers a holyday [sic] for getting their arrears of work up – I took a walk towards the Village in the evening accompanied by a few women & children returning home. I received most hospitable invitations to go to sleep for the night. I was glad to find that one of them, considered us as susceptible of charity, as she pointed out a little boy as having no Father – but the little fellow looked so fat, that I thought he has not as yet begun to feel his loss –

We had two useless dogs about the ship that were led out in the evening to be shot, however the first one, taking a great many ball to dispatch him, Doctor Simpson gave the other some Hydroceanic [sic] Acid, which speedily put the other one out of pain – to the great surprise of the Natives, who were evidently unacquainted with poisons, they called it bad water, and spoke more of it afterwards, than I had remarked them to do of anything previous – they afterwards begged to be allowed to take the skins to make gloves, which request was readily complied with – . . .

Thursday Feby 10th Gloomy weather, with the hazy appearance experienced here preceeding a Southerly gale, the boy Ki-o-wa told Mr Wright before breakfast that the Ice would all go out from where it did before, in two days . . .

The Tik-Ki-ra′me′ (Point Hope) Omelik (Chief) Sam-ma-ru-ma was on board with one wife, the other having gone on the ice on a sealing excursion – He described to Doctor Simpson (whose journal, I copy) the barter that takes place between his people and the Asiatics, who understood him to say that he gave the Martin (Sable), Fox, Wolverine, Wolf, and other Skins & sometimes whale oil & fish for Kettles, tobacco, beads, & Knives, I have some doubt about Bear skins, and I think they must also receive Walrus teeth[1] from the Tchuk-chi or Tsau-chieas, as they call themselves – He said he had only one Ne′-wak[2] or bartering friend at this place, and that he brought three kettles to barter getting (Kupwik) wolverine skins in return – He was lively and musical today, & sung of the good name he should give the ship on his way down to Point Hope, which will be of benefit to our boats in the Summer trip to Cape Lisburne – The officers speak of these Point Hope people and of the natives to the South generally, in terms of praise, in comparison with the Natives

[1] Other sources say that walrus ivory was traded *to* the Asiatics.
[2] The term for the association of two trading partners is *niuviriik* (Burch, 1970, p. 50).

171

at Point Barrow. The former express gratitude for favours received, accompanied with a degree of modesty, particularly the females – While the latter are spoken of as bold, impudent, and as ungrateful as need be . . .

Saturday Feb[y] 12th . . . The stillness & beauty of the day, seemed to attract an unusual concourse of Natives towards the Ship – The Stammering Man (now allowed alongside) being of the number. He appeared most axious [sic] to be allowed on board, but this I had no intention of complying with – However on thinking the Matter over, I came to the conclusion of giving all the Natives [(]about seventy) a dance & allowed all of them on board for two hours in the afternoon – A small present of tobacco each commenced the entertainment, when they were invited to dance, the Point Hope man opened the ball, and proved himself quite proficient in the art – eclipsing the Noo-wook men, who I presume saw their inferiority & did not offer to succeed him. The women however were all alive, and Kept us Amused for some time with their several dances – when another small donation of tobacco closed the party and all returned home. The Night was clear & fine tem[perature] −37 [−38.3°C].

Sunday Feb[y] 13th The days at this time lengthen apace – the sun rose this morning at 9 Am – Mean time – giving quite a cheerful aspect – were we not forcibly reminded of the weakness of his rays as yet, by a temperature of −25 [−31.7°C]. After church service, all the officers Amused themselves taking Lunar distances between the sun & moon – when some excellent observations were made –

We had an average number of Natives round the Ship, but fewer were allowed on board than usual. On their going away in the Evening, the officers were much mortified to hear that the boy Ki-o-wa, a great favourite with all, was detected by the Corporal of the Watch, stealing a pair of seamans sea boots, he had them rapped [sic] up in a pair of skin trowsers under his arm, and was taking them out of the Ship – This was the more ungrateful, as Doctor Simpson had but just bought the trowsers for, & presented them to him, having two days previously, given him a coat also – His adopted Father Sable, having stripped him on some misunderstanding occurring between them – Every favourable construction that was possible was put upon the act, without being able to account for it – The boy offering only the very poor excuse of not knowing they were there, which it need not be said Amounted to an impossibility – This act of ingratitude, from a lad who had been treated both by the officers &

172

Men with the greatest Kindness & immediately after having been clothed by the Ship, when stripped and turned out of the house of his adopted Father, is so much in character, with the general behaviour of these people that we now cease to be surprised at it, and only regret that we have such an unamiable specimen of the human race, in a state of Nature to deal with . . .

Monday – Febru^y 14th In the forenoon the people were employed bringing on board provisions from the house, and overhauling the gunners store bin – The afternoon when the weather admits is now devoted to foot ball, as a means of Keeping the people off the lower deck for more than an hour – It also makes an agreeable & wholesome exercise, required at present from the strong disposition to scurvy, that still manifests itself amongst the crew – We had fine clear weather with a low temperature . . .

This being Valentines day Doctor Simpson who had received from our Kind friend Mr Barrow[1] of the Admiralty, several humorous engravings for winters Amusement, previous to our leaving London – gave the people on the lower deck a very agreeable surprise this evening, by sending each a Valentine, s[e]lected by him as nearly in accordance with their characters, as he could, and addressed after the Manner of Seamens letters in general, naming the ship the individual had last served in, with the addition of a few trys here & there, until Icy Cape, Point Barrow, or some such warm sounding name closed the catalogue – The perfect secrecy with which the joke was Kept, made it the more appreciated the only previous notice given, was an advertisement in the Weekly Guy, for a few additional hands in the post office, refering [sic] candidates to Mr Johnson Post Master – The only gentleman of that name on board being the Serjeant of Marines, was of course obliged to take office without being in any way admitted into the secret – This morning while he was absent attending me round the lower deck, one of Doctor Simpson's accomplices (only three in number & officers) pasted a large placard of Post office on the Serjeants door, where he found it much to his surprise on his return. And I am told 'hardly knew how to feel, not understanding the joke, but no doubt concluded there would something come out of it – [']

In the Mean time the letters, had been placed in two bags, so as to extend the surprise over a double length of time, when shortly after

[1] See above, p. 60, n. 4.

the people had supped, a bugle sounded, announcing the arrival (by the Main Hatch way off deck) of a mail at the post office. Mr Johnson was now made aware for the first time of his duties – And on issuing the Valentines, which were of a very gaudy description, such as one seen displayed in cheap print shop windows, and well adapted for the people they were intended to Amuse – The effect was equal in the fullest extent, [sic] to that wished, by the pains taking contrivor of the plot – Which was concluded with an allowance of grog to wash down their Valentines, and no doubt pleasing thoughts caused by them, of our own happy land, where ones thoughts are more apt to roam, from the contrast with our present dismal abode –

We had not so many natives as usual today, The old Chief came down with his two wives, and the Chief from P^t Hope with a like number, the latter by invitation, to take leave of us previous to his return (named for tomorrow,) and to receive a promised present of tobacco to smoke as he went along, for which as we remarked, he said 'thank you,' a word unknown amongst the Natives here – He received many expressions of friendship, and took his leave – . . .

Thursday Feby 15th Calm clear weather, with low temperature −25 [−31.7°C]. Mr Gordon was away in the forenoon with a party for wood – And in the afternoon seemed to be the leader at foot ball also – Our friend from Point Hope paid us another parting visit, evidently put up by the people here to beg of us, what he wanted, as previously he had not done so – he told us they had no guns at Point Hope, and that he should like a small one meaning a pistol to show them – he then asked for a preserved meat tin, to cook in on his journey, this I considered rather unreasonable, as he came here to dispose of Copper Kettles, his wife was not idle either, as she asked for & received, some needles, & tobacco, but a comb and one or two other things we were unable to supply her with – The Man received nothing, as I considered his parting gift had been bestowed yesterday –

Doctor Simpson had a good deal of conversation with one of the Chiefs, as to the time the rivers on the coast hereabouts begin to run, And as the account he has received, makes it to be early in May – quite a month sooner than I anticipated, it has brought the thoughts of my intended journey to the Eastward forward, and set me about making some necessary arrangements.

The sun set in a haze which increased with a little snow drift in the evening, making it unfavourable for our astronomical observations –

Wednesday Feby 16th . . . We had very few Natives at the Ship –
Ak-sin-ra's[1] wife – Ne-pak-tik (the man who took the supplies on
shore to Lieut Vernon's party, at the time the ice carried the boats
through Moore's channel)[2] his wife and another woman were taken
below by some of the officers – It appears the conversation turned
upon thieving, when one of the women said that liars, and thieves,
slept badly on the earth when dead, and also that they got bad water
to drink, by this it was supposed they had an idea of a future state
after death – This idea however is much set aside, by our finding out
from Mr Wright that he had told this same woman – something
similar to what she decribed – These people confirmed a statement of
Ak-sin-ra's as to the time the river emptying itself into Dease's Inlet
began to flow, what is said to be some time in May, and that they
have whales here in April – they also stated that in March there were
none but women at Noo-wook, the men being out hunting, and that
they took advantage of that time, to be loose in their conduct. None
of them appear to have been so far to the Eastward as the River
Colville – . . .

Thursday Feby 17th . . . Very few Natives about the Ship. The boy
Ki-o-wa was alongside dressed unusually well, which we have
remarked on occasion before, with people who wish to ingratiate
themselves with us – it would appear they attach a good deal of
importance to dress. As Mr Hull asked one of the Natives some time
ago, whether he would go with him to Cape Smyth – when the man
agreed, but Mr Hull was to put on his coat with the dress buttons,
and they would get up a dance for him – The boy appeared rather
abashed, and endeavoured to get into conversation with a former
friend of his, our cook who was chopping wood under the stern – but
it was of no avail – The man very properly took no notice of him –

Friday [February] 18th . . . We had rather an increase in the
Number of Natives today. The old Chief being amongst the early
arrivals – As I had not entertained him for more than a week, I got
him down to the cabin in the afternoon – when Doctor Simpson
endeavoured to take advantage of the opportunity to get some
information from him of the River Colville, and the probable time of
the opening of the rivers on the Coast – But without much result, his
mind was occupied about two requests he had made from me,
previous to a hunting excursion he was going to take for a month.

---

[1] 'Erk-sing-era.'   [2] See Maguire's entry for 25 September 1852.

The [sic] was for the loan of one of our best dogs, to drag the deer back for us and the other was for gun powder, both of which I civilly declined complying with, but gave him a small present of tobacco, with which he was obliged to be content. My time is now a good deal taken up in arranging places for my intended journey along the land to the Eastw[ar]d . . .

Saturday – Feby 19th There is an improvement in the weather today but the wind keeps up too strong, to admit of walking outside, with any degree of pleasure . . . Doctor Simpson understood from a Native today (the tattooed man) that they had once seen a whale here in March. And they always appeared near this place in April – when they are taken. In March and April several birds appear, but '(Kee-wait-pi-via)' May is the bird month . . .

Sunday Feby 20th The wind and weather remained the same as yesterday so there was no walking outside, and in consequence of one [of] the Natives stealing the top of the therm[omete]^r case from the post at some little distance from the Ship, none were allowed on board for the whole day, except Ak-sin-ra,[1] whom I ordered to be admitted before church service, contrary to our general custom. Today however, I had made up my mind to ask him, to accompany me on a journey along the coast to the Eastw[ar]d, to act as our interpreter, with the Natives we might meet and to explain that our intentions were good – in fact to satisfy the inquisitive disposition of these people, and when assured that our visit was not to be attended with any ill consequences to them, they would be likely to give us very little trouble –

Doctor Simpson who knew my wishes spoke to the man upon the subject, on the upper deck, previous to my coming up. And I found him cogitating over it, when I did – He seemed undecided, and said he must talk to the people at Noo-wook before he promised – But on being told that he would receive a great quantity of tobacco, a cutlass, and a saw, he seemed inclined to go –

Church time coming on soon afterwards, Doctor S. thought it would tend to remove a mystery out of his mind, if he were allowed to be on the lower deck, when the prayers were being read – And seeing no objection to it, he was brought down, and seemed to sit without much wonder – We did not attend to it afterwards, from the difficulty of making a savage understand such a subject, with a very

---

[1] 'Erk-sing-era.'

indifferent command of the language – I had him down to the cabin and showed him articles he was to get in the presence of Doctor Simpson, who acted as the friend of both parties – This made the thing all clear enough, as far as promising went. It seems that he was leaving the Village tomorrow for two months to kill deer[1] but now he would return in half a moon to be ready to accompany me – He was going to take his wife, and two children to the hunting ground, where he described they slept in small snow houses – very low and arched –

We afterwards got him into a train of conversation about the Village, and the coast to the South and West. It was very amusing to see him, on being asked to count all the houses at Noo-wook – he first expended [sic] his own ten fingers, then his little daughters & then his wifes, keeping a sort of hold over them all, then Doctor Simpsons, and finally as many of mine as he required to make up fifty four. The number there – he was then going on to count the number of families – their numbers in each house – When I broke the thread of his idea, by some inappropriate question. He named the occupants of twenty six – amounting to 131, from which we concluded 250 to be near about the population of Point Barrow.[2] (Some further information on this subject – Doctor Simpsons journal) – 'We probably saw the whole force of the male population capable of using a bow, on the day they made the demonstration against the Ship, Amounting probably to 86, to which add 36 women. There would be left 114 children & old people – I had previously learnt that a good many people had died in the Autumn of last year, more I believe than the usual number – that being their sickly season – and since then there has been but three births – One more being expected in two months time – Cape Smyth he said contained forty huts which at the same rate would give a population of 210. Icy Cape is the next settlement excepting two or three places where there are from three to five huts. Allowing Icy Cape together with them, to have 200 inhabitants, and Point Hope to be equal to Point Barrow. The whole population including these two points would not exceed one thousand souls.

[1] Caribou (*Rangifer tarandus*).
[2] John Simpson (Appendix Seven of this volume, pp. 507, 525) gives the population of Point Barrow as 'near 290' and elsewhere as 309 in 1853.

Estimated Point Barrow –	290	
Population Cape Smyth	210	averaging three hundred people to
Icy Cape &		
intermediate	200	one hundred miles of coast line
Pt Hope	290	

Total[1]	990	

He also enumerated seventeen whales, having been taken by the Natives of Point Barrow last season – & all of a large size – when asked if they were as long as the cabin was wide, he said they were each as big round, we had imagined they might be the small white whales, spoken of in Artic [sic] Voyages – But I believe not common in this sea – at least I have not yet seen one – In answer to the question how many men had two wives at Noo-wook – he named three[2] – and at Cape Smyth five – he also mentioned another man at Point Hope, who had five, . . .

<u>Monday Feby 21st</u> . . . An important proceeding connected with our operations, took place this morning, in Mr Seath the carpenter commencing to build a sledge for our journey to the East[war]d I also told off the crew of seven men – eight is to be the number, but I am sorry to say, that out of our crew of 41, I had a difficulty in selecting 7 men, and required 8, this is caused by so many that would be very well adapted for it, being rendered unfit, from having been attacked with scurvy. However I have no doubt of being able to make up our efficient number. And those that are left will be in a very good condition to do all that is requisite about the Ship –

A woman from Cape Smyth who has constantly been in the habit of bringing us fish for barter, arrived today, and was the only native allowed on board, the 'tabboo' still existing from yesterday, until the top of the The[rmomete]^r is brought back – She brought seventeen pound weight of small fish, that are caught at the ice edge by jigging,[3] as I have before described, they were purchased from her as usual, and she remained about the deck I have been in the habit of

---

[1] Ernest S. Burch, Jr, on the basis of more thorough analysis (1980), has estimated that in 1840 600 people lived from Point Belcher to Point Barrow, 425 from Cape Beaufort to Point Belcher, and 900 from Cape Thompson to Cape Beaufort (including the settlement of Point Hope). Some of the difference in numbers may be explained by the recent famines in the area. See Maguire's entry for 30 August 1854.

[2] John Simpson (Appendix Seven, p. 525) estimated that four men at Point Barrow (Nuvuk) had two wives and the same number at Cape Smyth (Utkiarvik).

[3] Probably tomcod (*Boreogadus saida*).

making her a small present of beads & needles, as an encouragement to renew her visits, this day was an exception – In the afternoon she was discovered by the look [sic] man, to have wrenched two radiating Thermometers, (used by Doctor Simpson, and Kept when not in use, in a case hung to the Stantion [sic] of the Standard compass.) off their stand, and was making her way to the gangway to get out – endeavouring as she went to conceal the Ther[momete]^r under her skin coat – Fortunately the only injury they sustained, was the breaking away of the part of the glass back by which they were suspended & which cut her hands severely. This is one of the many instances of ingratitude we have almost daily experienced from these people – so much so indeed that we have ceased to feel so much on the subject, as at first, seeing there is nothing redeeming in their character – or any means that I can see of presenting their following such practices – except in keeping a vigilant look out, to avoid it –

In the afternoon our hands amused themselves at Foot ball, a game that has become quite a favourite, and is very beneficial to their health . . .

Tuesday Feby 22^d The weather very unpleasant, a strong breeze from N.E. (M[a]g[neti]c) with heavy snow drift, no going out of the Ship. Bringing snow to the Ship for thawing, repairing the ice wall, building the sledge, and altering a tent for our intended journey, were the employment for the day – The snow drift preventing the wished for game of foot ball. Very few natives about, our friend Sables, who has been of late comparatively a stranger was in the cabin – he is too stupid, or else always thinking of what he can get out of you – to give any information . . .

Wednesday [February] 23^d . . . We had about twenty Natives along side of the Ship, and in board – I have for some time had a wish, to see the mode of the Esquimaux living on the hunting grounds, at this inclement season of the year, As a great Number have gone from Noo-wook. I spoke to the man Ne-pak-tok[1] on the subject of being my guide to the old Chiefs establishment out there, and he seemed willing to comply, but as he is considered a stupid fellow, and not likely to be very strong in our defence in case of requiring aid, he has not been accepted – He is always treated by us with consideration, from his having taken the provisions on shore to the boat party when obliged to take refuge on the spit, on the first night the Ice made . . .

[1] Elsewhere, 'Ne-pak-tik'.

179

Thursday Feby 24th . . . our travelling preparations are going on with, the sledge is thought to be very big, but I have every reason to be satisfied with it and its progress – in the forenoon the people were employed bailing out the pump well, the afternoon according to our routine was given to making & mending clothes –

The Hard working man I-wak-em[1] has been selected by my companions on the journey to the hunting grounds, (Mr Gordon), to be our guide, and is inviteded [sic] to sleep on board tonight, whilst in my cabin in the afternoon, by some accident he got talking about a large dog he had seen on board a ship, with long hanging down ears – Doctor Simpson who was present, seems to think the Ship was the Enterprise, seen two summers ago off Cape Smyth, and Point Barrow, when there was a good deal of ice in shore and the Natives could not get their boats off to her – but that off Dease's Inlet, where I-wak-em happened to be with a party in one boat, and our friend Sables in another, there being less ice and a calm, they went on board and stopped some time, during which the Ship moved only a little way – and ultimately disappeared to the East . . .[2]

Saturday Feby 26th Aurora extending from West to S.E. the wind had moderated, having clear fine but very cold weather. Lieu^t Vernon with one man as a companion, walked across the bay to the Main land distant about 5 miles, to see if any deer were to be shot. He saw some but could not get within reach of them – one travelling tent was got up and tried today, and a few more alterations made in it – The Carpenter progresses rapidly with the sledge – And I am glad to find, has great confidence in the plan[.] It is drawn from [that] given by Lieu^t now Com^mdr McClintock, in the Arctic blue book . . .[3] On the upper deck where the sun shone through the stern door of the housing, on the Ships side, it was observed to thaw, being the first time it was observed this year.

As we were to have a theatrical performance this evening, the Natives were allowed on board in greater numbers than usual, they were as I have before remarked, mostly women & children, the Esquimaux men, seem to receive little encouragement from our people. The widow woman, who lost her husband on the ice, that I mentioned some time ago, as having made a considerable present to,

---

[1] The brother-in-law of 'Sables'. Elsewhere, 'I-wat-sa'.

[2] The *Enterprise* was off Dease Inlet on 1 and 2 August 1851 (Collinson, 1889, pp. 14–145).

[3] See Great Britain, 1852c, p. 186.

and desired to come again at the end of a month – came today, but as we know that she had in the mean time, become the 2^d wife of our friend Sables, who is in no need of charity – I had explained to her, that so long as she was without a husband, the Ship would make her a present, but now she was married again, she must not expect it – her second visit, did not make so favourable an impression as the first, as she told many untruths, and tried to deceive us about her marriage –

The performance of the Farce of the 'Original' was the Amusement of the evening, And was excellently got up, & as well performed as could be, doing just credit to all concerned in it, the principals being Mr Gordon the Manager who took the part of Jack. Nonpareil. and Mr Hull that of Colonel Detonator. It certainly had the effect intended to the fullest extent, that of enlivening the monotony of our scene, where, were it not for the Natives, who Keep us pretty well on the alert to prevent their running away with everything from us, Our life would be dull indeed, and felt the more, from the smallness of our numbers, it is under such circumstances, and indeed in Navigating these seas, that one becomes able to appreciate the company of a consort, or rather in our case the want of one. Although clever writers have not been wanting, to say, that of two ships employed on discovery, or Arctic Search, that the want of energy in the Commander of one Vessel, may keep the other back – And recommending emulation, each being allowed his own course – From what I see of Arctic service, no such principles should be disseminated, as far as separating two ships forming an expedition is concerned – quite the contrary, as no man in a ship in imminent danger when alone, can feel the same confidence, as when he looks out at his consort and say's, well if we are destroyed we have something to fall back upon, and many other, strong arguments, that nothing but experience can point out, may be made use of, to prove the advantage of two ships over one, in distant service such as we are on –

We had about twenty Natives on board, only two men out of that number, the rest women & children, and as most of them were known to have been away from home all day, & must be very hungry, they were fed with some bread dust & condemned preserved meats, which they seemed to relish uncommonly – We had a clear star light no Aurora Visible before Midnight –

Sunday Feby 27. – a fine clear day, but still a little too much wind to go out with any comfort. We had several Natives along side from an early hour, our friend Sable Coat of the Number, but whether his patience failed him, or his dignity was hurt at not being allowed on board, he did not wait until after church service, when a few were allowed on board – The water clouds in the offing looked closer today than usual, and had something of the appearance of the smoke ascending from the Numerous chimneys of a large town, when viewed from a distance in dull weather – Our trip to the hunting ground is fixed for Tuesday.

Doctor Simpson discovered from the boy Ki-o-wa's mother today, that since his disgrace here, in being caught stealing, that he has set out for Point Hope, with his newly adopted Father – He also understood from her that the 'Nuna-tag-mutes' the tribe next East of us,[1] do not frequent the Coast in the winter, and that their summer huts are of Reindeer skin, which we consider as a sign they have not much open sea work, or they would be of Sealskin – She told him also that the Indians of the Colville live in the interior, and only frequent the mouth of the river in the Summer, this I considered as favourable news, as on my journey, it would be rather against our success meeting with many natives – . . .

Monday Feby 28th Fine clear weather. The Forge was got up this morning to make the iron work for the sledge – Our time is now principally taken up, in making preparations, for our intended sledge party to the East[wa]rd. I have arranged to leave tomorrow morning on a short excursion into the interior, to visit the natives from this place at their hunting grounds . . .

Tuesday, March 1st [1853] I left the Ship this morning accompanied by Mr Gordon Mate, two seamen & a native guide, with a native sledge to carry our tent & provisions, drawn by six dogs – An account of the journey will be found with the rest of my journals,[2] which I keep apart from this as being connected mainly with the Ship – Any remarks relative to Natives, [e]t^c mentioned here during my absence from the Ship, I take from the journal of Doctor Simpson – as on all former occasions, the Ships log furnishing me with the necessary information, as to the movements on board – The employment on board was principally connected with preparations

---

[1] More correctly, probably, she was referring to any Eskimo society that lived nearby in the interior (see above, p. 117, n. 2), as John Simpson has indicated (Appendix Seven).

[2] These journals have apparently not survived.

for our extended journey – The Blacksmith working about the sledge, & Sailmakers preparing the tent – The radiating Thermomet^r showed a difference of 33° from the shade.

At-Ka-na the very old man, mentioned previously as a sort of Doctor[1] amongst his tribe was on board today and received a present of tobacco. It is not known whether it be from his age or experience, but he seems to be esteemed as the Chief Doctor, and is seen frequently to operate in a mesmeric style upon the others, passing his hand over, and blowing upon the affected parts – . . .

Wednesday March 2nd . . . 'The Man called "Tattoo" (from his face being much marked in that way, in straight lines from his mouth towards his ears –)[2] saw the Enterprize and had some "ak-lu-na" (rope) tobacco (Negro Head)[3] given him – Doctor Simpson tried his old friend (At-Ka-na) the Noo-wook Doctor, who was also on board and appeared very communicative, whether he knew of Mr Simpson's visit to this place in 1837, but he evidently did not know of it, or had not heard, as he was most probably Eastward at the time, and they might have been Cape Smyth people or others with whom Mr S. communicated –[4]

They seem in great glee in consequence of being successful in catching seals yesterday – They told with becoming seriousness whilst on board yesterday that the Father of the Man acting as my guide to the interior, had died, but it was not altogether an unexpected event, though perhaps somewhat sudden, as he was a man advanced in years . . .

Saturday [March] 5th . . . We had a good number of natives alongside, Amongst whom was a tall man we had met in the boats at Icy Cape. He had a piece of Amber slung round his neck, which he offered for barter, striking his breast and making it understood, that if worn, it would keep off all coughs [e]t^c from that important part of the human

---

[1] 'At-ka-na' was a shaman, or *angatquq*, who would have been employed in curing illness and in other relations with the supernatural (Spencer, 1959, pp. 299–315).

[2] John Murdoch, who lived at Point Barrow from 1881 to 1883, wrote (1892, p. 139): Tattooing on a man is a mark of distinction. Those men who are, or have been, captains of whaling umiaks that have taken whales have marks to indicate this tattooed somewhere on their persons, sometimes forming a definite tally. For instance, Añoru had a broad band across each cheek from the corners of the mouth . . ., made up of many indistinct lines, which was said to indicate 'many whales'.

[3] Negro head tobacco was a twisted form of sweetened cake (Cavendish) tobacco which was popular in Britain. See above, p. 100, n. 2.

[4] Judging from Thomas Simpson's narrative (1843, pp. 152–63), it seems more likely that he visited with people from Point Barrow (Nuvuk), not Cape Smyth (Utkiarvik).

frame[1] – The other Natives described this substance as found floating on the sea in this neighbourhood, sometimes, but that it is plentiful in the pools of snow and rain water, on the main land to the East[wa]rd . . .

Sunday [March] 6th The wind having risen during the night at E.S.E. with a good deal of drift, the day was not by any means pleasant, yet the Natives mustered to upwards of twenty around the ship, eighteen of whom were allowed on board after church Service – Amongst them much to her astonishment the 'stammerers' wife, who was afterwards taken down into the Gun Room, she and the two who accompanied her, vied with each other in describing the Coast as far to the South West as Point Hope, leaving the impression that there are very few grown up Natives of this place, who have not made the journey either in the winter or summer time . . .

Monday [March] 7th . . . As anticipated the stammerer made his appearance amongst the few natives alongside, in consequence of the Kindness shown to his wife yesterday, seemingly expecting to be allowed in – At 4 P.M. I arrived along side from a weeks trip into the interior, having reached to Lat 70°52′ & Long 157°31. S 40° W. 38 miles[2] –

Tuesday March 8th . . . The old chiefs wife was on board & expressed her sorrow that I had not seen Omig-a-loon. She also said the Narwhale is seen here but not the Walrus.[3] This must be because the food is different here, from that which the latter Animal finds at the Sea Horse Islands . . .

Thursday [March] 10th It blew strong from the West (true) with snow drift during the night – In the forenoon we were employed lashing the runner sledge together, and stowing the sledge boat, made out of duck or board in its place – The whole has been constructed on the plan submitted by Command[e]^r McClintock to the Arctic Committee, and I was much gratified, on weighing the runner sledge & boat, to find that ours exceeded his in weight only

[1] Phylacteries of this sort were often obtained from a shaman (*angatquq*) when an illness occurred and were used to prevent its return (Spencer, 1959, pp. 282–3). John Murdoch (1892, p. 61) reported that amber could be found on the beaches nearby. This piece, or a similar one, is now in the collection of the Museum of Mankind, London (Snow, 1858, No. 176).

[2] Maguire had reached close to the northern end of Peard Bay.

[3] Maguire must have misunderstood her. Narwhals (*Monodon monoceros*) reach Point Barrow only rarely (Bee and Hall, 1956, pp. 159–61), but walrus are found there regularly.

three pounds – being 160 & 163 lbs. This is the more creditable to Mr Seath, the Carpenter, as his Materials were drawn from a source which left him no choice, the result has proved him to be well adapted for the situation he fills – The day was boisterous with heavy snow drift throughout, which was not sufficient to keep the Natives from visiting us in considerable numbers – We had two old women on the lower deck all day, cleaning & repairing our deer skin tent blankets . . .

Friday March 11th Beautifully clear weather, the first for some days. A wooding party under Mr Gordon in the forenoon, and repairing the ice wall round the Ship in the afternoon, were the Employments for the day. I tried an experiment with spirits of Wine, and tallow for cooking, to test their relative merits from which I fancy the latter has the advantage, our cooking apparatus requires some alteration, which is being made – We are endeavouring to procure a few more deer skins to complete our tent blankets, as yet without much success . . .

Saturday March 12th . . . We have been in the habit throughout the winter of admitting a certain number of natives every day averaging from twelve to fifteen – And as they seemed to me, to be always the same set, and many of them having nothing to recommend them in the way of usefulness, I have become quite tired of seeing their hulking bodies sloping about our deck for eight or nine hours daily, employing one man at least to look out after them. I have given orders today to reduce the number admitted, preparatory to a still further reduction, as the spring advances, when our necessary duties in preparing the Ship for sea, will give ample employment to our small crew, without the unnecessary addition of looking after a set of Natives, whose only object in visiting us is to get all they possibly can, without giving anything they can avoid in return. We had a good many round the Ship, and more men amongst them than usual. We have now good daylight at 7 P.M. . . .

Sunday March 13th Calm clear and cold weather, a good many natives round the ship, and a few on board after church service. I had Sables in the cabin, as he is now without doubt the principal and only Chief left at Noo-wook. All the rest having gone to the hunting grounds, in pursuit of the Rein deer[1] – I endeavoured to get some information from him, but as usual his head was occupied about the

---

[1] Caribou (*Rangifer tarandus*).

chances of what he was likely to benefit by his visit, and I found him unable to comprehend my meaning about anything.

I received the unpleasant news from the Surgeon this morning that one of the best men (certainly the second) of my sledge crew would be unable to go the journey, from the effects of scurvy, and also that another man a marine, was in the like condition – All our arrangements for this journey are very up hill work, as we have every thing to prepare for ourselves, from very limited resources, added to this, out of a crew of forty one, we have been obliged to make changes, over & over again, to get any settled crew. I have made a fresh selection today, as I suppose from the most healthy, I hope they will answer the purpose, but I cannot avoid having some feeling of doubt on the subject.

The question as to the scurvy remaining amongst our crew, under such a liberal diet, when compared with the earlier, & not so well provided voyages . . . – And with my imperfect Knowledge of the subject, the only conclusion I can arrive at is, there is some cause, independent of the food, that we have not been able to detect[1] – that has tended to produce it, in such an unusual degree as we have been affected – a few small pieces of Venison were brought to the Ship today & purchased . . .

Monday March 14<u>th</u> . . . A good many Natives about the ship, I remarked a number of strange faces Amongst them, for the most part men – We have procured sufficient deer skins to furnish our tents fur blankets,[2] I am sorry to find they exceed the weight of Command<u>r</u> McClintock's estimate by nearly one half – but we cannot attempt the journey with less covering – Our travelling arrangements are now nearly complete, they have given quite a stir, to our people – As both sides of the lower deck assumed a busy scene, every body being employed, one way or another, connected with the sledge equipment . . .

Tuesday March 15<u>th</u> We have at this time 14 hours daylight from 5 Am to 7 P.M. the weather keeping very cold temp[eratur]<u>e</u> −25 [−31.7°C]. Not many Natives about & few on board, we had the good fortune to procure eighty pounds of Venison[3] from some men from Cape Smyth. This is the first that has been brought to the Ship in any quantity, And was very welcome. In the afternoon the runner

---

[1] This is not true. Vitamin C is only obtained in food.

[2] McClintock's estimate was 45 pounds of fur blankets for one officer and ten men (Great Britain, 1852c, p. 184).

[3] Caribou meat.

sledge was got out board, in order to secure the side stantions, preparatory to it being loaded for trial tomorrow – In the evening I personally examined the spare clothing, Knapsacks, & Arms of the sledge crew – supplying each with ten rounds of Ammunition . . .
Wednesday. March 16th Slight snow drift. Double Arch of Aurora to the North. I feared the state of the weather this morning would prevent our intended trial trip with the sledge, but as it was almost necessary, from the near approach to the time for departure on my journey to the East[wa]rd, the severity of the day, it was thought, would be a good trial, and not worse than we have reason to expect – And after breakfast the loading of the sledge was commenced with – In weighing each article of the equipment, I felt much regret in finding our weight so much in excess, of those of Captain Austins expedition[1] – And with all our endeavours to keep them down they Amounted to 217 lbs per man, to be dragged, this I was aware from the experience gained by the travelling parties on the East side, was too much by at least 10 lbs, to make an average journey –

At 1 P.M. everything being arranged we started, the wind and snow drift continuing and very nearly in our faces – Several of the people who came out to see us off were touched with frost bite in the face – We were obliged to 'spell o'' frequently, to allow the men to examine each others faces, no one escaped, but by placing the hand on the affected part, circulation became soon restored – My intention was to travel outward for four hours, and encamp for the night, so as to try all our, sleeping, cooking, and clothing arrangements returning to the ship in the morning to make such alterations as were found necessary, previous to our setting out for good – Our heavy load made our progress necessarily slow, averaging at most over a very smooth surface, one mile an hour, the sledge appeared strong in all its parts, and easily dragged, reflecting high credit on the constructor Mr Seath, our Carpenter – at 5 P.M. being four hours and a half from the Ship, we encamped on the ice between Gig's and Whale Islands.[2] The tent was damp previous to leaving the Ship, and had now become so hard frozen & shrunk, that it was with difficulty we got it spread, sufficiently to shelter us, by this time the wind had moderated a good deal – the temperature remaining at −21° [−29.4°C]. Our cooking Apparatus was found to answer very badly,

---

[1] See above, p. 118, n. 1.
[2] Approximately five miles from the *Plover*.

and required a thorough alteration, and many other little wants, showed the benefit of this trial trip – We found the deer Skins Kept us sufficiently warm without the sleeping bags, but few of the party slept from the confined size of the tent, caused by its being so badly spread –

March 17th Thursday The morning turned out calm & clear but very cold temp[eratur]^e −30 [−34.4°C]. Our breakfast was prepared with great difficulty owing to the defects in our special cooking lamps. The tent I found would not suit, for the intended journey – the canvas being too heavy and when frozen was quite stiff and unmanageable this together with its weight, nearly double what it should be, showed the necessity of making a new one from lighter material – By 9 Am we had packed and started on our return. I took a course direct for the Ship – leaving Mr Hull in charge of the sledge – Mr Gordon with his Auxiliary crew had been ordered to meet us – And as they passed at a considerable distance outside of me – I experienced one of those instances mentioned by Captain Parry, of the distance that sounds are heard at very low temperatures – As my attention was called by hearing voices distinctly, in conversation, when I could scarcely discern his party on their way out to meet the sledge – I got on board in an hour and a half, the sledge party not arriving for two hours more. When the sledge was unloaded, and all hands were allowed the afternoon in quiet, a comfortable dinner of Fresh Venison having been previously prepared, to celebrate the festival of St Patrick – The song afterwards went round, and all appeared to enjoy the day, as a respite previous to the labours of our intended journey. I had the pleasure of the officers company at dinner in the cabin, our fare being much the same . . .

Friday March – 18th Thick gloomy and cold weather, we commenced cutting out a new tent from ships duck at an early hour, and put as many hands to work about it, as could be employed, alterations were at the same time taken in hand with the cooking apparatus & lamps that were pointed out to us on our trial trip – Very few Natives about . . .

Saturday [March] 19th . . . Our preparations for the sledge journey gives occupation to almost every one And they are going on with satisfactorily [sic] – one of the Cooking apparatus was ready for trial this evening, and Answered moderately well . . .

Sunday March 20th Lt wind & fine clear weather – as the day advanced it became gloomy – Some hands were employed during the day to complete the tent and sledge boat – Very few Natives on board – we are in want of deer skins to complete our tent blankets but cannot procure them – Our friend I-wat-sa came down as the others were leaving and was allowed to sleep on board. He appears inclined to join our travelling party to the East[wa]rd, and with the absence of Ark-sin-ra[1] (who promised to be my guide, but who it seems there is little chance of our seeing), I will be rather glad of his company – 'He reports the arrival of two "Nunatagmutes" at Noo-wook with their wives, who have brought deer skins to sell by his account they have never seen guns, and are desirous they should see ours fired – He was altogether very communicative but half he said could not be understood – Among other things he spoke of a great battle between the Cape Smyth, and Point Barrow people – in which the latter were victorious – having lost only three men to fifteen of the enemy, this occurred when he was a child – he has no idea of his own age which must be about 22 – Death he thinks is bad "Apparently because life is good" & he seems to have no idea of a future state –[']^2

Monday – March 21st A L^t air from the East[wa]rd tempe[ratur]^e −34 [−36.7°C] this morning was fine & clear – A good many natives were round the Ship, but only a few admitted – The new tent was pitched this morning & found to answer very well, & weighed one half as much as the stout canvas one – our travelling preparations still going on with, and not by any means complete as yet – As one of the men with me on the trial trip of the 17th has been disabled from a frost bite in the feet, I have thought it advisable to delay our departure until the temperature rises a little more, to avoid a repetion [sic] of such mishap. In the afternoon the wind increased with snow drift, which would have prevented any party travelling, and this is the day I had fixed upon to leave the Ship. We are still deficient in deer skins, our friend Iwatsa has been entrusted with tobacco & sent to Noowook to endeavour to procure them –

Tuesday March 22nd The temperature has risen to +12 [−11.1°C] with dull weather. In the forenoon we were visited by some strange Natives from the S.W. the people here called them Nuna-tag-miuts,[3]

---

[1] 'Erk-sing-era.'

[2] This is no doubt a quotation from John Simpson's journal.

[3] These people may have been remnants of the Kuulugzuarmiut society, people who lived in the Meade River drainage and who had been dispersed by famine a number of years before the *Plover*'s arrival at Point Barrow. See above, p. 117, n. 2.

who these said people are, we have not been able thoroughly to make out, except that their name signifies living on the land – from which we conclude they are a tribe of Esquimaux who do not live on the sea coast – This specimen of them was nothing different in appearance from the people here, they described their homes being three or four days journey off – And their jaws appeared to have suffered much from frost bite on their journey. They had a few deer skin coats and few fish, to dispose of, but were not easily satisfied in a bargain –

Our attention is chiefly taken up with preparations for my intended journey – they are getting on with favourably . . .

Wednesday March 23^d . . . As my departure is fixed for tomorrow morning, the loading of the sledge was commenced with after breakfast & completed by Noon – By making our alteration, in taking nine men instead of ten and one officer, besides the Esquimaux guide & myself – I have been enabled to reduce the weights to 201 lbs a man[1] A reduction that I hope will admit of our making fair average journeys We had the usual attendance of natives about the ship, but few were on board. Our guide Iwatsa arrived in the evening ready to undertake the journey. The evil disposed of the Community of Noo-wook, it seems have been trying to frighten him from going with us. By saying they intended to follow & murder us when we slept including himself amongst the number – However it appears to have had little effect upon him – As he merely told the story without any apparent fear on his part and advised the men not to be let on board during our absence – One of the Men of my crew has been reported unable for the journey this evening – his place has been taken by a young marine but just discharged from the list with pains in limbs & scurvy –

Thursday March 24th At 8 Am our sledge parties were all ready to start, they consisted of nine men, a native guide and myself for the large sledge, victualled for thirty days, and accompanied by an Auxiliary party under Mr Gordon (Mate), with 4 men and two Native sledges drawn by 8 dogs, provisioned for ten days and carrying for the extended party 8 days, making up our resources to 38 days. Mr Hull 2nd Master accompanied me to make astronomical observations to fix some points of the survey and to return to the Ship with the Auxiliary party. The morning turned out dull & unpromising, the wind springing up fresh from the East[wa]rd with

---

[1] McClintock's average was 207¾ pounds. See above, p. 180, n. 3.

heavy drift against us, gave no hope of making a good journey the first day – A large number of Natives had assembled to see us set out, without showing any ill feeling, but wishing to show them, that we were fully prepared for defence, in the event of carrying their before threatened attack into execution, our men left the Ship, with their muskets slung and ready for immediate use – Previous to starting the party seemed very solicitous to have a name for the large sledge – And after revolving one or two over, I named her the S[t] Patrick, as the first trial cruize [sic] took place on the 17th of March – And the mottot 'Nabockliah' never 'mind' was adopted in allusion to our opinion of the threatened attack of the Natives –

At 9 Am we set out Amidst the good wishes of our remaining companions, and shaped a course to pass outside of the Islands. This was the first time I had left upon any excursion that I felt any increased degree of Anxiety about the ship during my absence. The report brought by 'Iwatsa' our Native guide, who I knew was not in the habit of repeating idle stories, made it evident that the subject of our force being separated by detached travelling parties, had been talked over by the Natives at Noo-wook And I felt sorry to find our residence amongst them for as long had produced no better feeling – From this cause I was not quite satisfied at leaving the Ship, while a doubt existed as to their friendly intentions. On the other hand I almost considered it a duty to show them, that we were capable of defending ourselves in small parties, and were not to deterred [sic] by their threats, from travelling along the coast, as we found it necessary. If this point was not established, our position, confined to the range of the Ship by a tribe of unarmed savages, would not be very flattering to our Characters notwithstanding great caution is necessary, to prevent any disagreement and at the same time to avoid giving them the idea, that we stood in any fear of them.

The object of my present journey is to examine the coast line to the East[wa][rd] for traces of the advance of the Expedition under Captain Collinson, and more particularly Harrison's Bay, which the former party from this Ship, searching the Coast for Sir John Franklin in boats, under Lieut, now Commndr Pullen, was unable to do from the shoaling of the water – I also have a wish to examine the Mouth of the Colville River, not visited by the discoverers 'Messrs Dease and Simpson'[1] or Commandr Pullen[2] – with the hope

[1] In 1837 (Thomas Simpson, 1843).
[2] In 1849 (Hooper, 1853). See Appendix One below.

191

of being able to clear up a report received from the Natives of this place by Comm^ndr Moore in 1849 – that two boats containing white people, and armed with muskets had entered a river on the Coast called the Kok-puk, and the crews had been murdered by the Natives.[1] This Kok-puk from the description I considered as not unlikely to be the Colville –

As this journey proved a failure from the sledge, breaking down on the second day in consequence of the wood in the Runners not being of the proper quality, to stand the weight & strain it was subjected to – I continued my journal of the Ships proceedings, mentioning the day of my return – The wind and snow drift continued heavy during the day – our party with the sledges made but slow progress against it, and encamped on Doctors Island at 5.30 P.M. During the night it blew very strong, and the wind shifted to the westw[ar]d, broad side on to our tent, giving me fears as to its holding on or of our being able to travel the following day.

Good Friday March 25th Water clouds from North to S.W. a good many Natives about the Ship, but only a few admitted after church service – Our sledge party proceeded at 9 Am from Doctors Island and passing Rultand [sic] Island[2] steering S E by E true for the mainland, the large sledge broke down as mentioned yesterday at 2.30 P M – As I saw there was no hope of our being able to make it fit to continue the journey, I sent Mr Gordon back to the Ship at once, to unload his sledges & return at all speed with empty sledges, to convey the loading of the broken one to the Ship – our party encamping on the ice, to wait his return – The weather continued stormy at S.W. with snow drift, the temperature fluctuating –

Saturday March 26th At 3 Am Mr Gordon arrived at the Ship with the information of my sledge having broken down.

Nearly a dozen Natives were alongside in the forenoon,[3] and there was no difficulty in procuring two sledges and dogs, to assist our own in bringing back the provisions – Although they were not made acquainted with the occasion for which the sledges were required, lest they should make some exorbitant demand for this use – and they seemed to go home well enough content to await their return to the Ship, before they got the promised reward of 'Tawac'.

Iwat-sa our guide who returned with Mr Gordon, held no

---

[1] See above, p. 34.
[2] These are the easternmost of the Tapkaluk Islands.
[3] Maguire is no doubt drawing on details from John Simpson's journal.

communication with them around, and did not even show himself until ready to start, when he asked for a sword, and laid aside his own Knife – Why? does not seem very clear, but he evidently treats his own people with suspicion and distrust – At 1 P.M. Mr Gordon Again left the Ship on his return to my party & met us at 6 P.M. on our return, as we had patched up the sledge in the mean time, sufficiently to enable us to load her again, & commence our return – Some of the men who returned with Mr Gordon were rather done up, but eighteen hours dragging & walking was sufficient to account for it – And was a great trial – A little rest rewarded them again – The united sledge parties halted for the night on Rutland Island. The night was remarkably fine but cold – . . .

Easter day – Sunday March 27th We set forward from our encampment at Rutland Island at 9 Am. the Morning was fine & clear, but very cold temp[eratur]^e −13 [−25°C] – A moderate breeze from the Westw[ar]^d with snow drift prevailed during the day – making the travelling against it very disagreeable – at 1 PM Mr Gordon reached the Ship, the main party with the big sledge travelling much slower did not arrive until 3.30 – I was glad to find from Lieu^t Vernon that the natives had behaved very well during the absence of so many people from the ship – and showed no disposition to take advantage of it to be troublesome, however efficient arrangements had been made, in the way of keeping the same Number of people on duty, as when all hands were on board, to prevent any such conduct on their part extending to an inconvenience – . . .

Monday March 28th Aurora from East to West the arch through the Zenith. The morning calm & clear, a good many natives around from an early hour – Bringing snow to the Ship and repairing the ice wall, were the Chief occupations for the day. Arrangements for another journey on a reduced scale with native sledges are being made. The party is to consist of three sledges, drawn by two men & four dogs each, making with myself and a Native guide a party of eight – We hope to carry twenty five days provisions, and to accomplish from 13 to 15 miles a day, in which case we can make as long a journey, as the large sledge in so much shorter time – Several alterations in the way of reducing the equipment for 11 to 8 men, are necessary, and are going on with – . . .

Tuesday [March] 29th Morning fine and clear – Bringing provisions from the house – And making the necessary alterations, for our renewed sledge journey were the employments for the day – The runner sledge St Patrick, is being repaired for any work about the Ship, but will not be used again for travelling purposes. We were fortunate enough to procure a small supply of Fresh fish 15 lbs. today, brought from the Natives in the interior, And we are told that a large quantity of Venison may soon be expected from the same quarter – These suppliers are looked for anxiously by us, as a means of preventing the scurvy from again breaking out to any extent – We are Now I am glad to find comparatively free from it – having but two cases, of an extent to Keep them from duty – . . .

Wednesday March 30th . . . I have considerable difficulty in procuring an additional sledge and dogs for my journey, a great many have been sent into the interior to procure fish and Venison, much wanted at Noo-wook as they appear to catch very few Seal just at this time, from the open water being farther off than usual – And there is less appearance of a water Sky, than at any other time during the winter – As the dogs food is principally frozen Seals blood, we have not been able to procure any supply for our journey, And will be much inconvenienced in consequence – Clearing the Springs from Snow was the Chief employment for the day – The travelling party were engaged reducing the tent equipage – . . .

Thursday [March] 31st . . . The Morning was fine & clear. The temperature Keeps low during the Night – & rises with the Sun. We observed the suns effect in thawing today (to any extent) for the first time, on one of the quarter boats turned bottom upwards on the davids & covered – Drops of water were oserved to run from under the cover – owing to the black colour of the boats bottom absorbing the heat – but before they could fall, they formed into Icicles from the boat, showing the effect in the first case of the suns rays acting on a large surface like a boats bottom, and in the second the intensity of cold still existing to congeal water in a falling state, when it would have the most power to resist its effects – Some of the Natives remarked on observing it, and told us that in two months more the snow would be all gone – I then asked one of them, (who I designated by the title of the 'big thief' from his well known propensities) when the Ice would go out, he said three months, as I know this was a month sooner than we had seen it here ourselves, I concluded they anticipate these changes a little –

I had fixed upon this day to make a second attempt at my journey, but was unable from the want of a third good sledge & dogs. I am now promised one by 'Sable Coat' tomorrow, and hope to get away on Saturday Morning. We have had a good many Natives about the Ship today, all very quiet and orderly – Our guide Iwat-sa came down in the evening but as I was not going away tomorrow I recommended him to go home for another night, when the poor fellow – very innocently showed me two little leather bags fast to his waist belt. Each about the size of a small waistcoat pocket – And a pair of moccasins – implying that his arrangements for a month were completed in them – And as he seemed to wish very much to be allowed to remain, I did not refuse him – These people have certainly an advantage over us in the lightness of their travelling equipment, and they understand the method so well of Keeping their skin dresses and moccasins dry on a journey, which we fail in, from allowing the snow drift to accumulate about us, this when not thoroughly got rid of, on going into the tent & getting between the skins turns to wet and makes it very disagreeable –

Advantage was taken of the fineness of the evening & absence of Natives to get the crew out on the ice to fire at a mark with muskets – . . .

Friday April 1st [1853] Clear fine weather – Three native sledges, and twelve dogs were observed this morning crossing the bay from Noo-wook towards the hunting grounds in the interior, this information gave me but poor hopes of being able to procure the dogs necessary for my journey, our want seems to have happened at a very unfavourable time, as all the dogs & sledges are employed bringing in the proceeds of the last two months hunting, as yet no Venison has arrived, although we hear of great quantities – I am afraid when it does come, it will be all devoured by themselves in consequence of the scarcity of food, mentioned before. They tell us that they are living on whale blubber at present – and 'eat very little' which being interpreted means they have very little *to* [sic] eat.

As I have failed in procuring the necessary quantity of dogs food from the Natives, & the Amount required at the rate of two pounds a day each, for twelve dogs, is very considerable, we have set about making up the quantity today from our own resources, which include (for that purpose) a small quantity of Goldners (condemned) preserved Meats. And as we have a large supply of Salt Beef, and are not using any of it, from its bad quality, 160 lbs of it, have been half boiled to be taken on trial, as I find from our guide, that the dogs become much less particular in their food on a journey. He also tells me they will eat Seal and Whale blubber, although while on board

195

they will not touch either, the Natives themselves eat the latter with much apparent relish – The quantity Amounting to 600 lbs is now made up from the three mentioned descriptions, and is packed ready for starting in the morning if I succeed in getting another sledge & dogs in that time, if not I must postpone my departure for two days more, as Sunday intervenes – . . .

Saturday April 2nd . . . I looked anxiously this morning for the arrival of the promised sledge from my friend Sable Coat, but was disappointed, An addition of one dog to our train made me think of setting out, but the badness of our sledges & weakness in dogs, taking the length of our journey into consideration, decided me in remaining two days longer with the hope of picking up some additional aid in that time –

Although the wind was light from the South[wa]rd the temperature did not take its usual rise with the Sun – having risen only to −28 [−33.3°C] at Noon, the day would have been very severe for us travelling, but that of itself would not have stopped us.

We have not had so few Natives about us for months as today, I supposed the low temperature kept them away, it was thought also that the absence of so many away with sledges, was reason for their scarcity – it is a change we feel no regret at, as small parties are always more civil & obliging –

Our guide I-wat-sa has been sent home this evening, as we do not start tomorrow, if he is allowed to live amongst us too much, I am afraid the novelty may loose its charm, and we, his services, which I set much value on at present . . .

Sunday April 3^d . . . At 4 Am. our friend Sable Coat arrived along side with his promised sledge, & three dogs, he was admitted in board, and afterwards on to the lower Deck, but as I found he was not settling himself for sleep, I sent for him into the Cabin, when he immediately without waiting to be asked, expressed his determination to sleep on the Sofa, which he did soundly for nearly 4 hours – After I had given him a share of my breakfast, (at which he used a Knife & fork, with less awkwardness than could have been expected) we accomplished a successful barter, for his sledge, and the use of the dogs for one month, for which he received a very good hand saw, and went away, apparently well satisfied –

My arrangements are now quite complete, and I purpose leaving in the morning. Mr Hull with a Native sledge accompanies me as an Auxiliary for three days, merely to report how we got on, to make observations for the Survey, and concert a place for meeting on my return – The low temperatures of the last few nights have rather surprised me, as we had been calculating on milder weather from the Native accounts, indeed it seems fortunate that we have not been exposed to it, as I fear it would have laid some of our party up with with [sic] frost bite, former experience showing that we are rather liable to it.

We have had a good many Natives about, and after church service, several were admitted necessarily from having assisted us with dogs – In the evening the sledges were got out board & loaded ready for the morning, the dogs tolled off into gangs, the Captains of the sledges drawing lots for choice – Our Number of dogs, counting three half grown, amount to 16 for the most part very good – Were it not that I fear some of the owners of them, might change their minds and take them away, I would wait a day longer for a milder temperature, but as it is, I think it most prudent to start whilst I am so well provided. I was glad to find the temperature did not fall during the night, to the same extent it had done, for the last few days –

Monday April 4th at 8 Am I left the ship with three Native sledges, 6 men & a Native guide on a journey along the coast to the East[wa]rd, Mr Hull 2nd Master accompanied me as an auxiliary with an additional party of four men, the particulars of this, will be found in its place, in a book kept specially, for all journeys undertaken from the Ship.[1] I continue the journal of the Ship during my absence, as on former occasions, obtaining my information relative to the Ships duty from the log, and that of a general and more interesting nature, from the journal of Doctor Simpson, who has at all times laid at my disposal, the fruits of his own observations . . .

Friday April 8th . . . A Moderate number of Natives were along side and amongst them To-ko-la-rua the stammerer who came armed with his bow and quiver. He sent an arrow to a distance of 140 yards into a mound of snow, on which some of the officers had a shooting target: but he gave his arrow so high a flight, that it was doubted if he could have exceeded that distance . . .

Sunday [April] 10 . . . A Raven was observed to pass the Ship, which is the only bird seen here since October last – At a little after

---

[1] Maguire travelled to a point a short distance east of the Colville River delta and returned to the ship on 29 April. His journal of this expedition has apparently not survived.

Noon Mr Hull arrived on board, giving a very good account of the passage of my party, but his own including himself came in, three with snow blindness, one with a sprained Ancle [sic], and one stiff in the ham –

Monday April 11th The weather continues mild but cloudy with a light wind from E.S.E. – New Moon – Kat-te-tá-wak (A-wak (whale)[,]^1 getting up provisions, and endeavouring to dig out the boundary chain from the ice, were the employments for the day – Some open water yesterday was visible from the Village but there is no appearance of it from the ship today –

Tuesday April 12th Overhauling the spare suit of sails, and digging out the boundary chain, gave employment for the day – In the afternoon a balloon (of Mr Shephards construction) was sent up, as the wind was from the Westw[ar]d, it went up with the breeze to a great height, & must have been carried a considerable distance before it fell – A good many Native sledges were observed to arrive from the hunting ground laden it was hoped with Venison. A net was bought from a Native today remarkable for its neatness being made for small fish – of 'balein' [sic] (whalebone) scraped down very fine, smaller than one seine twine, but flat & stronger. Dr Simpson procured a very nice bright specimen of Iron pyrites but he could not discover where it is brought from but most probably from the hills to the South[wa]rd . . .

Wednesday April 13th The hopes of Venison from the arrival of so many sledges yesterday were dashed today by none arriving from the Village. Nor did any of those Natives who returned yesterday show themselves – There was another net sold today, accompanied by a scraper in the form of a piece of a knife neatly fixed in a bit of ivory, having something the form of a 'spoke shave'^{2} and a 'gauge' for regulating the size of the meshes – This is a flat piece of ivory seven inches long, cut away at one edge so as to leave two small projecting horns at the requisite distance from each other for the size of the mesh^3 – This is seemingly less convenient than a plain flat piece of wood or ivory, as each loop of a mesh must be taken off before the

---

^{1} John Simpson (Appendix Seven, below) recorded this as the usual time for returning to the coast from caribou hunting in the interior to prepare for whale hunting.

^{2} This would have been a 'whalebone shave', an implement used for cutting long, thin strips from plates of baleen. These strips were used for lashings, for twice in net making, and for shavings that were used as insulation between the soles of a boot and the skin stockings (Murdoch, 1892, pp. 173–4).

^{3} This was not a mesh gauge but rather was a net shuttle, or 'needle', for holding unused twine while making the net (Bockstoce, 1977, pp. 56–8).

next goes on, whereas with the plain gauge, the meshes slide off to the left with more ease and rapidity, without interruption to the Knotting of the succeeding ones . . .

Sunday April 18th A.M. A water sky to the Westw[ar]^d on the hands going outside to work in the morning, it was observed that the ship had been risen by the ice forward 7 inches – and remained stationary abaft in consequence of her rudder projecting after under the surface of the floe & holding her stern down – By this change the ice wall is of course thrown out of employment, And looks a most unpictures-que ruin – The crew were employed for the day removing the snow covering from the upper deck – the late mild weather having done away with its benefit –

Our Visitors today were not numerous, one of the earliest was our friend Sable Coat, who has lately paid a visit to Cape Smyth – He says the people there talk of whales & birds having been seen lately – Most likely it was farther to the South[wa]rd off Icy Cape.[1] The patriarch of the Village old At-Ka-na has died within the last few days – Dr Simpson who had bought a head dress from him some time ago was told by sable [sic] today that it was bad for him to keep it[2] and supposed it of a piece with their practice of breaking articles used by the deceased, and leaving them out with the body . . .

Wednesday [April] 20th . . . Not many natives about, they speak of having seen two or three whales – The crew were employed for the day, carrying away the rubbish from the Ships side, and relashing the runner sledge. Mr Hull left the Ship at 6.20 P.M. to meet my party as previously arranged –

Thursday [April] 21st The morning was as usual cloudy, but about Noon the sky cleared giving more than usual sun shine – but the radiating Therm[ometer]r rose no higher than +48° [8.9°C] whilst the temp[eratur]e in the shade was +6 [−14.4°C]. with a fresh breeze from the N.E. – We had but few natives about today. Those outside were again much pleased by having their pipes lighted with a burning glass – Lt Vernon received an account from a woman yesterday, that there had been seven births at the Village since we came here, and only two deaths besides the man lost on the ice. But they all say a great many died in the Autumn (August). The crew

---

[1] The first bowhead whales (*Balaena mysticetus*) and beluga whales (*Delphinapterus leucas*) and snow buntings (*Plectrophenax nivalis*) could have been at Point Barrow by this date.

[2] Personal property was usually left with the corpse (Spencer, 1959, p. 253).

were employed in the forenoon cutting a hole in the ice, for drawing water for the use of the Ship, that at the tide hole having become oily from some blubber or grease being thrown about it . . .

Friday [April] 22nd . . . not many natives about today, they bring a report of open water & whales. The outside Sentry also received the intelligence that the people of the Village do not expect the ice to go out this year. And that they intend to Keep their Venison back and starve the ship until we are obliged to give large prices for the deer[1] . . .

Saturday April 23d The strong breeze continued all day from E.N.E. The Natives report that whales have been seen in great numbers, but they will not pursue them until the Moon wanes – One of the men caught a Hudson's bay Lemming with double claws to the feet.[2]

Sunday April 24th . . . Few Natives about – They talk of expecting the old chief and others in from the hunting ground – In the evening heavy water clouds were observed from N.E. to S.S.W. . . .

Tuesday April 26th . . . Five Native sledges were seen advancing slowly from the land towards the Village, apparently heavily laden. They were met by a number of people – and in the evening there appeared a great stir at the huts, the people being collected in Knots, supposed to be unloading the sledges, and gossiping – Later in the evening (Ark-sin-ra,[3] the man who had engaged to be my guide on the journey to the East[wa]rd but had not Kept his word) was observed coming towards the Ship, and some of the officers went out to meet him, he explained that unusual luck in hunting prevented his coming to accompany me – His coming to the Ship before going to the Village seemed dictated more by friendly motives, than objects of gain –

Dr Simpson has been catching a host of small animals of one species,[4] he supposes them the same as those he found in a seals stomach some time since – his method of taking them is by letting down a large tin to the bottom through the tide hole with some meat in it . . .

---

[1] Similar threats were given to Kashevarov's party (VanStone, 1977, p. 42) in 1838 and to the Signal Service expedition in 1882 (P. H. Ray to chief signal officer, August 1882, Records of U.S. Weather Bureau, National Archives, Washington, D.C.).

[2] This is the collared lemming (*Dicrostonyx groenlandicus rubricatus*) (Bee and Hall, 1956, pp. 57–74; P. H. Ray, 1885, pp. 102–3).

[3] 'Erk-sing-era.'

[4] These could have been one of several species of calanoid copepods (Frost and Lowry, 1981).

Wednesday April 27th . . . The old chief (just returned after an absence of two months to the hunting grounds) accompanied by sables [sic] paid an early visit this morning – the latter brought a small shoulder of Venison, the other Nothing – As many as forty sledges with Ninety three people were counted going from the land to the village today – The sledges seemed both high and heavy . . .

Thursday [April] 28th . . . Ark-sin-ra brought down a whole deer this morning (Making the first brought to the Ship) and received the value in tobacco with which he seemed well pleased. Another man soon appeared with with [sic] another for which he received a larger price according to its weight, and he too was well pleased seeming to think the price proportionate although it is impossible he could understand the weighing, especially with a steel yard – The old chief brought down one also, but hung on for a long time in the hope of getting an adze, however he at last took the tobacco, but turned it over and asked to choose the plugs – It was [a] matter of surprise to see so few of the rabble about, but in addition to their being tired most of them are suffering from snow blindness – Passak the old chiefs adopted boy who was on board actually cried for some time with the pain – The Quantity of good meat bartered today was supposed to be 300 lbs – weight . . .

The *Lemming* was killed today by a dog, it having escaped from its cage, on showing it to the Natives they said it fell from the sky,[1] but Ark-sin-ra says it is a larger sized animal of the same sort which falls from the clouds, & is white like paper – He was understood to have seen them fall in some particular state of the Air, which he describes as gloomy with an east or sometimes a S.E. wind! Dr Simpson presumes this notion arises either from the migration of those animals, or their habits of burrowing at some particular season with which these people are unacquaintted [sic] – 9 sledges and 16 Natives were observed returning to Noo-wook from the hunting ground –

Friday April 29th At 3.30 Am I arrived along side from my journey to the East[wa]rd after an absence from the Ship of twenty five days – Although at a most unseasonable hour for such a ceremony, as all hands must have been disturbed from their comfortable beds, my party was received by all the officers & Ships C^o with that good

---

[1] A century later Robert Spencer reported (1959, p. 34), 'The myth persists that the lemming comes from the clouds . . .'

feeling which generally prevails in the service we are engaged in – Sweeping the snow from the housing, and carrying snow to the Ship were the employments for the day – Several deer were bought today besides pieces, although not many natives visited the Ship – Amongst those on board was Ken-na-via one of the old chiefs sons who had received a small present of tobacco about a month since from Doctor Simpson, today he brought a return of some venison, but as he did not see him immediately, he could not withstand the temptation of the Tobacco, and sold it to the Ship – . . .

<u>Saturday April 30th</u> The morning was thick & hazy a good many natives made their appearance at an early hour & I was glad to find brought during the forenoon as many as eight carcasses of deer – which they bartered for tobacco, and in one instance a butchers Knife procured two – This supply has come in most seasonably, as the crew generally speaking are still disposed to scurvy, several new cases having shown themselves since my return, Amongst them two of my late travelling party who I considered, as healthy as any of the party. Doctor Simpson visited the town today, accompanied only by Arksinra, & was civilly treated, he found very few people idle, as on our former visits, the generality of the men were employed getting the baidars[1] ready for the approaching whaling season, & the women as busy sowing [sic] and stretching the skins for covering them – The old chief joined him in Arksinra's[2] hut – They seemed to eat heartily in each others huts, and to have very considerable apetites [sic], the food they seem fondest of is whales flesh – This may partly arise from their having been accustomed to deers flesh for two months while hunting, and are now glad of the change, as we certainly are for the deer –

The huts are all almost buried in the snow drift, leaving the entrance to the greater number of them level with the surface. They still Keep the lamps burning, so that the huts are very warm, this seems necessary in order to melt sufficient snow for drinking. It was observed that the quantity melted was not sufficient & they still eat a good deal of snow – The open water was not visible from the top of the huts – and at the distance of two miles or so, the hummocks of ice seemed very heavy beyond which they say the whales are very numerous – Ark-sin-ra & the old Chief returned with Dr. S[impson] on the way, they wanted to know how it was that the people on board

---

[1] Umiaks.   [2] 'Erk-sing-era.'

were not like their blood relations, and being told we came from different parts of the country they asked if we were very numerous, to which for want of a better explanation, our numbers were compared to the sand on the spit, and our ships to the larger pebbles, all of them seemed to understand and believe it. The great woman chief Pick-to-ria of course figures largely in all our movements, sending us where she thinks fit – The idea of a Queen is to them unintelligible, unless when they understand that her son is to govern after her, from which they consider that Pick-to-ria merely governs until her son is able to take the reigns of government into his own hands. The crew were employed for the day, removing the ice wall from round the Ship, and preparing the ice gear. I paid Iwatsa (my late guide) off yesterday, he returned to the Village in high glee, with a hatchet, a pursers shirt, and about one pound of tobacco – given to him for his services – The Natives lately returned seem all suffering very much from snow blindness – A strong breeze from the East[wa]r^d sprung up in the night – temp[eratur]e +20° [−6.7°C] –

Sunday-May-day [1853] The morning was overcast but mild, there were a good many Natives about but none admitted until after church service, previous to this several more carcasses of deer had been procured to tobacco – We now begin to think that we shall be able to obtain a supply sufficient to last us, until the bird time arrives. The radiating Therm[omete]^r rose to +63 ″17.2°C] at Noon and at 3 P.M. stood at +56 [13.3°C]. Four more sledges were observed returning to the Village from the land, laden as usual, we hoped with deer – After dinner I took a walk along the spit, and was glad to see the suns effect is showing out its outline[.] Night fine & calm with a clear sky and bright twilight temper[atur]^e +6 [−14.4°C].

Monday May 2nd . . . The crew were employed for the day running a saw cut round the stern of the ship as close as possible, from the tide hole at the port gangway, to the opposite side to allow the ship to free herself should she be bound under it by her rudder abaft. The Natives were not so numerous today but I remarked more men amongst them than usual – Mr Hull and Mr Wright visited the village, they observed nothing unusual, the Natives busy preparing their baidars, they preserve their walrus skins[1] by burying them under snow. Venison is still brought in considerable quantities, we

---

[1] The umiak covers were probably made of bearded seal (*Erignathus barbatus*) skins, not walrus skins (Murdoch, 1892, p. 337).

have been enabled to increase the allowance to 2 lbs and 1½ each day alternately, under this arrangement the preserved meats have been checked altogether, for the benefit of the crown. The salt provisions the men are allowed to draw if they wish, and if not, they have been given to understand they will be paid for them – I have adopted this course, as seemingly the most fair, in the absence of any precedent, or circular on the subject. And as the Venison has been purchased with condemned tobacco of an old date, I considered the government would not be at any less under the present arrangement.

Tuesday May 3<u>d</u> The radiating therm[omete]^r rose to +60° [15.6°C] while in the shade the temp[eratur]^e +17° [−8.3°C]. The work of cutting the ice round the Ships stern to free her rudder, has proved very heavy and troublesome, the ice in parts being 7 feet – thick, when the first circular cut round her stern was complete, the Ship rose aft 2½ inches with the piece hanging on to her, and in doing so jammed the saws so tight the piece will have to be broken away to clear them –

Not many natives about – they are supposed to be very busy getting their baiders ready for launching. I have lent two whale lances[1] for a month to two very civil and friendly chiefs – One is considered to be a more powerful man, than the one we have thought the chief – perhaps the latter has been thought so from being a greater bully – In doing this I had a wish to show them our willingness to assist them, and I also want to try their honesty, and see if they have any thing like principle about them –

Wednesday [May] 4<u>th</u> The fine weather continues, the highest temp[eratur]^e today was +14° [−10°C] the radiating The[rmomete]^r +65 [18.3°C] – Venison is still brought to the Ship, nearly as much from Cape Smyth as from Point Barrow – The Natives are about in considerable numbers, but they are well behaved – our friend Sables it is said is going to launch his boat tomorrow.[2] We have accounts that the

---

[1] Maguire's lances would have replaced the Eskimos' lances that were twelve feet long and tipped with razor-sharp spatulate flint heads (Murdoch, 1892, pp. 240–2). These lances were used to hamstring and then to kill whales which had been struck with a harpoon and which therefore were towing a number of inflated sealskin floats. It is debatable whether Maguire's lances would have been more effective than the flint-headed ones.

[2] The whale hunt was shot through with precise rituals. 'Angunisua's' ('Sables's') boat would not have been launched until he, the boat captain (*umialik*), had made sure that all of the whaling gear had been cleaned and overhauled, that his crew members had received certain gifts, and that a suitable spot for the boat had been chosen at the edge of the lead in the ice. Furthermore, the crew members had to have new clothes and the umiak a new cover. These and many other procedures, too numerous to mention here, had to be carefully executed to insure a successful hunt. See Robert Spencer's ethnography (1959, pp. 332–53) for a full explanation.

people at Cape Smyth have killed a whale – and that the open water is nearer to the Village . . .

Thursday May 5th . . . The crew were employed as on the last few days freeing the Ships stern – which was so far completed today as to allow her to resume her old line of flotation, which will I hope, have the effect of easing her stern frame from the weight of the floe. Doctor Simpson & Mr Gordon paid another visit to the huts today to visit our friend Sable Coat, who it appears is very anxious to procure the loan of a whale lance similar to those already lent – but as they are out on a trial of their honesty, I have not made up my mind to trust any more, on such uncertain chances – The officers were well received, and saw the glass of an old pair of spectacles given by Mr Gordon to Sables, reset in wood after their own fashion[1] They went afterwards to the hut of the old man we call the water chief, from his accusing us of stealing the water in Sept[embe]^r last (see this journal 13th Sept[embe]r 52) He is one to whom I have lent a whale lance. In his hut there was a whole carcass of a deer, Which anyone who felt inclined cut a junk off. There was also brought in a quantity of boiled seal which they seemed to prefer. In this hut there was a wooden mask,[2] to each side of which two bones were attached to rattle when it is shaken. The countenance carved on it was Esquimaux of a comically ugly aspect but wonderfully true in the proportion of length and breath [sic], preserving the usual prominence of the cheek bones. The open water was not visible from the hut, owing to a line of ice hummocks running N.E. true at the distance of two miles from the point, intervening – Four birds were seen today and described as long in the wings like swans – however they were thought to be either geese or gulls[3] – . . .

Friday [May] 6th . . . Mr Gordon was dispatched this morning with a party of seven hands and all our dogs to bring one or two good spars of drift selected at Doctors Island 7 miles distant.[4] He returned at 4.30 with one of the largest, although the day was particularly unfavourable – After buying several deer today, considering we had as much as we would keep good, after the thaw commenced, the barter was stopped,

---

[1] Presumably as snow goggles; see, for instance, Murdoch (1892, pp. 261–2).

[2] This may have been a dance mask (*sakimmak*) that was worn by a whaling captain at the festival celebrating the end of the whaling season (Spencer, 1959, p. 294).

[3] Perhaps they were whistling swans (*Olor columbianus*) or snow geese (*Chen caerulescens*).

[4] This would have been one of the today's Tapkaluk Islands, not the present Doctor's Island, which would only have been a half mile from the *Plover*. The confusion arises from Ernest de Koven Leffingwell's rearrangement (1918, pp. 93–100) of the place-names in the area.

and two were allowed to be taken away without being purchased . . .
We had a good many natives on board, who all seem to rejoice at the
strong Easterly wind, as it will blow the ice off the land, & favour their
whale fishing[1] – A strong Easterly wind prevailed during the night –
Saturday May 7<u>th</u> . . . Ark-sin-ra with his wife were the only natives on
board. He brought intelligence to 'Iwatsa' my late guide who slept on
board last night, that the baidar he belonged to was launched, and his
place was unoccupied, on hearing which he set off without a moments
delay, showing that their services are claimed on some stronger terms,
than we were aware of existing amongst them – Our friend Sables
launched his boat today also, making the two first for the season.
Doctor Simpson understood from Ark-sin-ra today, that he was one of a
party in a boat who ventured beyond the Colville to meet the Kang-ma-
li[2] people, and he seems to have had a close view of the Islands of Return
Reef, and the tents on or near them – He distinctly described the Nigh-
a-li or Colville as emptying its waters into the sea by four channels, and
that the Nuna-tagh-miuts live in the country above the point at which
these channels diverge. The crew were employed in the afternoon
washing their clothes, and in the evening the bedding was aired on the
upper deck – Water sky[3] from N.E. to S.W.
Sunday May 8<u>th</u> . . . The old chief was on board today begging tobacco,
but he was not successful, as it was well known he had plenty. Doctor
Simpson showed a volume of the Museum of 'Animated Nature' to
'Ark-sin-ra' yesterday to see if he would recognise [sic] the tusk of the
fossil Elephant or Mammoth, which he did besides the Rein deer, great
Northern diver, and others – He was altogether so taken with the
numerous pictures of Animals and birds in the book that he asked & was
allowed to take it to his hut, first giving his assurance that he would
return it clean & unsoiled with either grease or blubber – His wife
accordingly brought it on board this afternoon and said it had been
shown to a great many people – Ark-sin-ra frequently asks for things

[1] An easterly wind would open a lead of water along the northwestern coast of Alaska
and allow the bowhead and beluga whales to migrate past Point Barrow toward their
summer feeding grounds in the eastern Beaufort Sea.
[2] These would have been the westernmost sub-group of the Mackenzie Eskimos who
annually met their western neighbours at Barter Island and who, before the advent of the
Hudson's Bay Company near their territory, traded stone lamps, wolverine, wolf, dall
sheep (*Ovis dalli*), and beluga whale skins in return for whale and seal oil, baleen, walrus
ivory, walrus hide rope, and seal skins (John Simpson, Appendix Seven below; Smith,
1984).
[3] Dark streaks on the underside of clouds, indicating the presence of open water or
broad leads in the floating ice.

that are known to be of no use to him, but he says in excuse he wants to show them to his bartering friends amongst the Nuna-tag-mutes, whom these people meet annually about the Colville river[1] – We hear of two boats being still out after whale, but no accounts of their success . . . Monday May 9th . . . Our work of commencing to get the Ship ready, may be dated from today. The crew were employed getting the chain cables up, and holding a careful survey on them, and a small party with all our dogs made a commencement spreading a light covering of sand from the Ship towards the channel, to hasten the process of thawing for our passage out. Ark-sin-ra was on board today, and wanted a piece of rope which I did not give him, as I had lent him a whale lance I thought that a sufficient share of our favours – He described very cleverly that about the beginning of the Moon of July, the 8th or 9th – the ice outside of the spit would go away in one floe, whilst that inside where we lay would be made into holes by the sun and dissolved by the numerous rivers flowing from the land – And without being asked he said the gravel which the men were spreading would ensure the speedy thawing of the snow and ice over which it was laid – We have not very many natives about us at this time, making preparations for the Whaling excursions Keeps them all pretty well employed –

Tuesday May 10th Water Sky from N.E. to W.S.W. The whale boat was hoisted in board this morning to repair – And be prepared for her voyage to Cape Lisburne in July – The crew were employed digging out the cables fast to the shore, and to the floe, and propping them up on pieces of driftwood. The weather was fine today, but too cold for favouring the process of thawing, the temp[eratur]e in the shade not rising above +25 [−3.9°C]. And in the afternoon we had a strong breeze from the East[wa]r[d] which effectually put a stop to it –

The native accounts of whales are that those animals are abundant – Our friend Sables struck one, but lost his throwing spear[2] and line – The Cape Smyth people are reported to have caught (or struck?) three – Ark-sin-ra goes out tomorrow for the day, but some of the others remain out two days at a time, it is supposed they somewhat resemble the fishermen on our own coast in that way, who when the fish are abundant stay on the water until the crews are tired out.

Iwatsa came on board today his boat having returned – And brought with him a piece of crumpled paper on which he had drawn an outline of Dease's Inlet according to his own idea, for the benefit of M[r] Hull the 2[d]

[1] At Nirliq.
[2] Maguire is in error here. Eskimo whaling harpoons were thrust, not thrown.

master, who is about to make a short exploratory trip along the Coast as far as P^t Tangent. At the same time he excused himself from going in the capacity of guide to the party, in consequence of his engagement in his boat. But brought his half brother as a proxy, candidly saying that his other brother, had on one occasion been a thief at Noo-wook, but that this one would be perfectly safe from any such conduct with him . . .

Wednesday – May 11th A strong breeze from the East[wa]rd with slight snow drift – Today a commencement was made with the holds, and a survey on the remains of every species of provisions, & slops – As the examination of the latter had to be carried on in my cabin – I thought the best thing I could do was to get out of the way, and hearing about the same time that the Natives had caught a Whale. I made up my mind to visit the scene of slaughter, and with Mr Gordon as a companion started for the open water at 10 Am – our route took us close past the Village, at which we did not stop. The old Chief as we passed abreast of his habitation, came down and asked where we were going, and on being informed, returned with the idea, I supposed of looking out for our return, to receive or at least beg for some tobacco. A well trodden sledge track pointed to the direction of the open water,[1] which we found to be about 4 miles West (true[)] of Pt Barrow beyond a heavy range of ice hummocks, through which a rather picturesque track leading over the parts the most easy to pass [sic] – on reaching the open water which we found to Easterd to E.N.E. and W.S.W. we found three baidars hauled up on the ice, the stability of which they appear to have every confidence in, as the crews were returning to the Village to sleep – leaving all their fishing implements and gear in charge of one man, who seemed a guard for all – One boat only was afloat, the crew seemed standing on a floating piece of ice, on the look out. The ice to the South[wa]rd seemed open, and I supposed the open water in that direction extended most probably to the Mouth of the Straits[2] – Its Northern extent, it would be interesting to be able to conjecture, as the wind blowing so constantly as it has done from that direction, must clear a large space of water, if the ice should happen to be broken.

Both on our way out, and in returning we met several sledges loaded with the Whale blubber [e]t^c and to so much account do they seem to turn every part of the Animal, that on arriving at the place, they had cut

---

[1] This is the trail that the whaling crews had cut to allow them to drag their umiaks to the lead edge.

[2] Maguire is referring to Bering Strait (Bockstoce and Batchelder, 1978b).

it up – a small scrap of blubber about ½ AH weight[1] was the only remains we could discover – It had evidently been a small one, as the bone[2] we saw was not more than two feet long – This would perhaps account for their being able to make all of the whole of it as food – Walrus tusks appear to be bartered by these people to their neighbours to the Eastw[as]rd –[3]

Thursday May 12th ... Not many Natives about & very few on board. The old chief as usual begging, but little compassion was bestowed on him. 'Our friend Sables about a week ago lost his second wife, whom it appears he scolded well and she took to the land for it, but it is supposed she will turn up at Cape Smyth – This appears to stand as a joke against him, as the others seem amused when she is asked for.[']^{4}

Friday May 13th ... Not many Natives about[.] Sables and his wife were on board and saw some wonders amongst which were six cases of American Tobacco, and the interior of the Fore Hold of the Ship, prepared for restowing – Mr Hull & Mr Wright set out in the evening on a surveying journey along the Main land as far as Dease's Inlet & Point Tangent. 'Iwatsa' came on board to pass the night – he gave some of the officers the names of three sorts of whale caught here – two of which they kill as good for food and oil,[5] but the third they let pass by – (Fin back?)[6] He seemed to describe this as a savage beast that destroys the young of the other Kinds – The Natives reported birds today at the Village & Dr Simpson saw a flock at 11 P.M. passing to the Eastw[ar]^{d} some distance astern of the Ship –

Saturday May 14th ... I was glad to join Doct[o]^{r} Simpson and Mr Jago in a walk to the open water, visited by me on Monday last, the more so as I had gone out on that occasion without a compass or a sounding line, both of which I was anxious to use at the edge of the ice – We took Iwatsa

---

[1] Fifty-six pounds.

[2] Baleen.

[3] Walrus are uncommon in the eastern Beaufort Sea. Their tusks and hides would have been valuable to the Mackenzie Eskimos.

[4] Maguire is presumably quoting from John Simpson's journal. Patrick Henry Ray, who lived at Point Barrow from 1881 to 1883, wrote (1885, p. 44): 'Polygamy is not common, being confined to the leading influential men; even then [the second wives] are taken into the family more as assistants for the first wife, as she rules over them, treating them as servants.'

[5] There is considerable morphological variation among bowhead whales (Braham *et al.*, 1980). The Eskimos of northwestern Alaska distinguished between two basic types, with a number of subdivisions. It is likely that 'Iwatsa' was here referring to both the *ingutuk*, a short, round, fat whale, and the *usingwatcheak*, a larger, more attenuated whale.

[6] He is probably referring to the gray whale (*Eschrichtius robustus*), *agviluak*, a whale which is well known for its pugnacity.

for our guide and took the same beaten track as before – In crossing the
heavy hummocks before mentioned I tried to get soundings, with 10
f[atho]ms the length of our line, but failed.[1] – The appearance of the
water was now quite changed from the wind blowing on the land and
closing the ice – looking nothing more than a confined pool or lake
surrounded by ice.

There was only one boat – afloat, our friend the Chiefs, we found her
lying along side of a mass of ice, the crew all seated in their places, while
the old man sat above on the ice as if to command a better view – His
crew consisted of seven people besides himself, his largest wife making
one, six seem to paddle double banked, leaving the harpooner and
steersman single at the extremes – We stopped with the old man a few
minutes, and on leaving he made the usual enquiry for tobacco, and
today, I informed him, I had not none, he asked if my companions were
similarly circumstanced & when told they were, he said he would come
to the ship very soon –

Returning we stopped several times to inspect the different (oo-mi-
aks) boats hauled up and now numbering as many as ten or twelve[2] –
The fitting of these boats considering their means are very ingenious
and well arranged. They seem to carry in them, and about their persons
certain articles as charms, that are supposed to be lucky in their pursuit
– Most of the boats I observed had the skin of a crow – either flying from
a staff or lying on the seats[3] – About their dresses they have also
frequently the head and neck of a crow seen on the centre of the back –
and on their breast large pieces of crystal. This custom we have
frequently observed amongst them, and when they have been on board,
they have frequently shown us small pieces of different coloured
stones, and amber, sown about their dresses, that they suppose favour
the chase of particular Animals – such as deer, and seals [e]t[c4]

Each boat seems to contain a sort of register of the Number of Whales
that have been Killed from it. We remarked the first in the old Water
Chiefs.[5] It consisted of a bundle or string of pieces of Vertibra [sic] of a

[1] Maguire was therefore two miles or more west of Point Barrow.

[2] In the 1882 and 1883 whaling seasons there were about twenty whaling crews in all at
Nuvuk and Utqiarvik (P. H. Ray, 1885, p. 101).

[3] The Eskimos employed a number of amulets to insure success in whaling: raven
skins, stuffed lemmings, wolf skulls, and seal vertebrae (Murdoch, 1892, pp. 438–9;
Spencer, 1959, p. 339).

[4] These were hunting charms. Some were sewn directly on the outside of the clothing,
and others were carried in small bags under the clothing (Spencer, 1959, p. 282).

[5] Elsewhere, 'O-mig-u-a-a-rua'.

seal – with a skull of the same animal attached to it. I counted the pieces and found there were twenty four – which we were given to understand was the number the owner had Killed – The inflated seal skins attached to each harpoon seems to be two in number, sometimes by description they attach a third, but in each boat five in all are carried. The one next to the Harpoon is slung by a strong double thong, one part fast to either end, acting as a span to keep it athwartships, then there is a long coil of line of the same kind carefully stopped with fine strings of whalebone and at its end is the second seal skin, fastened on. We supposed the first is intended to offer as much resistance as possible when dragged by the Animal underwater, and the second is more of a float to show his position in order to follow him up.[1]

Coming back past the Village we had some pressing invitations to visit the huts which we declined but a crowd followed us a good way down the spit – The stammerer being as usual annoying & almost demanding tobacco – There were also more people round the Ship today than usual, in consequence of the open water being so limited, as to give them idle time to spend about the Ship.[2]

Sunday May 15th Dull and hazy weather, no thaw going on – After church service few Natives out of a considerble assemblage were admitted, but we had none of our acknowledged friends amongst them except M[rs] Sable who was brought below by some of the officers & seemed to afford them considerable Amusement. The change of wind to N.E. had induced many to go out to their boats. The weather has been cloudy all day with a heavier fall of snow than usual – In the evening there was a fresh breeze from N.E. accompanied with snow –

Monday [May] 16th A more favourable day for thawing than we have had for some time, the temp[eratur]e at 3 P.M. rising to +44° [6.7°C] but fell later in the day on a breeze springing up from the N.E. Ark-sin-ra and several women were on board but had no news to tell, except that with the full moon we should have plenty of birds – He was showed some of the cases of Tobacco and seemed so much struck with them as Sables had been – Indeed the astonishment of the discoverers of Peru at sight of its treasures could not have exceeded these peoples

[1] At Point Hope Froelich Rainey learned (1947, p. 257) that in the nineteenth century three floats were used, the first two to tire the whale, and the third to bob on the surface, indicating the whale's position to the hunters.
[2] When adverse winds or currents closed the leads in the ice, thus preventing the hunters from reaching the whales, the umiaks were hauled back to stable, shore-fast ice and left under the care of one man, while the crew returned to the village to rest.

when they viewed the Tobacco – He also informed us that last nights wind had not opened the ice, that it was now drifting to the South[wa]rd crossing against the land floe

The Employment of the crew has been getting provisions off and stowing the Fore Hold. The Carpenters still at work on the Whale boat – In the night we had a light fall of snow. Temper[atur]e 20 [−6.7°C].

Tuesday [May] 17<u>th</u> . . . We had a good many Natives round the Ship today but none on board except the 'Old Chief' & the 'Water Chief' with their wives – as the deck was much lumbered from clearing the after hold –

During the time the men were hoisting up the casks I was much amazed fancying to myself what an excellent custom house officer the old chief would have made. His eyes seemed to include every thing, not a movement escaped him, at the same time not appearing to be so engaged. To Keep them out of mischief during the time the men were at dinner I invited the whole party to the cabin, and with the assistance of Doctor Simpson and Lt Vernon amused them, by showing them swords and other articles, at which they as usual expressed great wonder, but did not according to their custom say they had none like it, implying they were quite ready to be supplied by you. They are all very anxious for tobacco to barter away to the East[wa]r^d in the Summer.

Lt Vernon recollected today that Captain Moore always spoke of the Kak-ma-le as the native name of Point Barrow, and Ko-pak the name of the river Colville, but in these we now find he was mistaken – By the report of the Natives of this place, confirmed by my journey, there can be no doubt the Kok-puk is the MacKenzie, and the Natives agree in calling the East people 'Kang-ma-lee' from the name of the country near the mouth of the McKenzie [sic]. Lt Vernon therefore suggests that the story reported to Captain Moore last year at Port Clarence by a Native of King's Island, to the effect that Captain Collinson was wintering at Kang-ma-le was true in as much as in the Summer of 1851,[1] two baidars containing men, women & children belonging to Point Barrow, boarded the Enterprize off Smiths bay[2] 50 miles east of this, and left her when a breeze sprung up and the Ship proceeded to the East[wa]r^d *towards* [sic] Kang-ma-li. This is so far

---

[1] Collinson wintered at Walker Bay on the west coast of Victoria Island in 1851–2.

[2] August 1 and 2, 1851. Collinson was surprised to find that one of the Eskimo women had a doll that he had given away the year before, probably at Point Hope (Collinson, 1889, p. 145).

satisfactory as it shows that news of any strangers approaching any part of the coast from the East[wa]r^d of Colvill [sic] River to Port Clarence will become known and may be gleaned up from the Natives on any part of the Coast.

<u>Wednesday May – 18th</u> We had two very fine eider duck brought to the Ship yesterday, making the first for the season. Today a very fine specimen of the Male King Eider[1] duck was brought, which Doctor Simpson has endeavoured to skin, but finds the difficulty of getting rid of the greasy substance inside of it, almost too great, to ensure any success, in the plumage retaining its original beautiful tints –

Ark-sin-ra was on board today & when in Lieut Vernons cabin Doctor Simpson happened to ask him if he had ever seen any boats along the coast such as we are now repairing on deck, when he said he had near the Colville – Finding that Doctor Simpson by turning over the leaves of the Blue book containing Command^r Pullens journal, was able to describe the occurrences that took place, Ark-sin-ra unwittingly gave a detail of the whole affair, which quite corresponded with the written account even to the wind – By which it appears our friend the old Chief 'Omigaloon' with his Hudsons bay gun – is the man described in Com[mande]r Ps journal[2] – This had been conjectured on board on our first seeing him, from his answering so well to the description, but it was then supposed not likely, from our fancying this people did not extend their journeys so far to the East as Point Berens – Ark-sin-ra said the old chief took a large number of men with him to follow the boats, but he could not tell what they wanted, of course! Ark-sin-ra was of the party left behind with the women and children. He was evidently very uneasy & perhaps thrown off his guard when he told of the whole affair, but the officers supposed that he thought, if the book told them so much, they must be also acquainted with every circumstance by the same means, and that he was doing no harm in acknowledging the facts. By his account Sables was on the land in Another direction – He says they left the post standing erected by Commd^r Pullen, and made no mention of the provisions having been disturbed – Doctor Simpson is inclined to think from his manner that he was not of Omigaloons party on the occasion, as he did not find him trip in repeating what he had *heard* not *seen* [sic] – He seems to think

[1] *Somateria spectabilis.*
[2] Great Britain, 1852a, pp. 28–9. See also Appendix One below, p. 452.

though they followed up so far they were in terror of the guns – Ark-sin-ra from the first was very anxious to learn the names of Pullen & Hooper, but he was not told, until he had identified them in the most minute way –

Our employment today was clearing the Tiers, and repairing the whale boat.

As our supply of Venison procured from the Natives is sufficient to allow of its being issued at the rate of 2 lbs a day for each man, advantage has been taken to stop the issue of lime juice, pork, preserved potatoes, and a further reduction of from one, to two [sic] pounds of bread each man a week, this precaution has been taken in the possible contingency of having to pass a second winter at this place without receiving a further supply –

Thursday May 19th The first clear day for several, but the temperature in the shade did not rise above +24° [−4.4°C]. An average number of natives about and a few of the principals on board – The old Chief of the Number, he appeared very sullen and informed me when he was going away, to which I gave my consent willingly & He met Doctor Simpson outside and expressed much friendship towards him, and invited him to the huts tonight, tomorrow, or any time he pleased.

The Natives speak of a great many flights of birds passing over the Village, they bring a few to the Ship to barter, parting with them readily for half a leaf of tobacco each . . .

Friday May 20th . . . We had a good many Natives about the ship, most of whom soon afterwards left as they saw numerous flocks of King duck[1] coming in from the South[wa]r^d. Mr Jago walked out on the ice for four hours with a gun and computed that he saw a hundred flights of these birds, but none passed near enough for him to shoot them.

The Natives watch the direction the birds take and run to the nearest point they expect them to pass over, and crouch in the snow until they are passing over, when they dexterously throw their trap to entangle them – and seldom fail to bring down one – The instrument[2] used is common all along the coast and both sides of Bherings straits, and consists of eight or ten pieces of ivory, slung by as many cords nearly a yard long, all of which are united in the hand, so that when thrown the balls spread out and turn over one or more birds in the flock, bringing them to the ground –

---

[1] King eider. [2] This is a bird bolas.

Doctor Simpson remarked a man outside wearing a small canvas bag, with an address written on it with ink – The Chief trader – in the Russian settlement – Nor^th America. This of course caused considerable curiosity on our parts, and on making further enquiries, the man told us he had the paper at his hut that was originally in the bag – on which we dispatched him with promises of a large reward in tobacco if he brought it to us – Some hours afterwards he returned with two torn pieces of paper, complaining that his little girl had destroyed the rest – they contained fortunately the most important part of the information to us of the whole paper – Viz. the date – the Ship – and her position, which turned out to be H.M.S. Investigator off Point Drew – August 8th, 1850.[1] So far this is very satisfactory as it shows that Capt[ai]n McClure was making the inshore passage whereas previously we had imagined he had taken the ice to the N.E.[2]

---

[1] Point Drew is the eastern point of Smith Bay, sixty nautical miles east of Point Barrow. Three Eskimos visited M'Clure's ship, the *Investigator*. They were part of a group on shore that was living in ten tents, having arrived there only three days before, presumably on their return from the trade rendezvous at Nirliq. M'Clure wrote (Great Britain, 1854a, p. 25) that he 'made a few presents, and gave them a letter to be forwarded to the Russian Fur Company [Russian–American Company], and made sail to the eastward'. Unlike most of the British ships, M'Clure's carried a competent interpreter, Johannes Miertsching, a Moravian missionary who had worked in Labrador.

Three days later M'Clure met 'O-mi-ga-loon' ('the old chief'), who was carrying his musket:

The head man possessed a gun with 'Barnet 1840' upon the lock; this he obtained from the Russians. As a fair specimen of the observation of these people and their aptitude for trade, the following may be taken. Seeing that we cut the tobacco into pieces to give in exchange for their fish (salmon trout), they began to do the same with the fish; this, however, we would not admit, so they were obliged to come to our terms. During the afternoon, while standing along a long flat island, observed a flag (a pair of seal skin inexpressibles) upon a lofty pole and a quantity of natives around it; we stood for them, but when the boats were pulling in they appeared to regret their temerity, for down came the seal skin and away they ran. Shortly gaining courage they returned, and as we approached, arranged themselves in line upon the beach and commenced extending their arms above the head (typical of friendship), which being answered from the boats, perfectly assured them of our amicable intentions. Upon landing they evinced a most manly confidence, rubbing noses, and embracing most vigorously. These were very cleanly, so that the operation was not so unpleasant as it otherwise might have been. Through the interpreter, Mr. Miertsching, we learned that these people had never before seen a European, or had they the smallest article of European manufacture about them (Lieutenant Pullen's boats they observed last year, but they were some distance off, and consequently had no communication).

(Great Britain, 1854a, pp. 26–7).
The Eskimos' description of their encounter with Pullen directly contradicts Pullen's own account (see Appendix One below).

[2] M'Clure had, in fact, stood northeast toward Banks Island and had run into a cul-de-sac – and was very lucky to have escaped (Great Britain, 1854a, p. 28).

The whaler[1] is still under repair, and the forge at work about her iron work. The tiers have been Kept clear for two days to air, and have been thoroughly whitewashed. The crew have been employed today restowing them. In the evening it became overcast the wind veering to East – it afterwards became foggy. temp[eratur]ᵉ +12 [−11.1°C].

Saturday May 21st The morning was fine with sun shine, but the temperature in the shade remained low for the day – We had a good many natives about and the old chief and his wives on board – I was endeavouring to find out from him whether there were any more pieces of paper similar to that brought yesterday, at the Village – offering large rewards of tobacco for any such – on which he first dispatched his boy, and then one of his wives after what we supposed some other paper received, it turned out to be only part of an old Song book (American)[2] which I explained to him did not speak to us – at the same time I gave him a good present of tobacco to enhance the value of paper Amongst them. It was very Amusing to hear how well the old fellow had Pullens name today, and to make it appear what friends they were, said that Pullen had given him beads – when Dr Simpson good humouredly answered him and you gave *him*! Arrows!! in return [sic] – They all seem now to wish to deny any participation in the chase of our boats on that occasion, even our friend Iwatsa when asked today if he were one of the boats crews, answered that he did not know.[3]

Arksinra was in the cabin today and drew a chart from Point Berens to the extent of their bartering journey to the East which we found to agree with Sir John Franklins account of the two tribes meeting at barter Island – where the Western people exchange Kettles, beads, and large Knives of Siberian Manufacture, for furs, deer skins, and small knives of English make – He also gave us an amusing account of the mistrust existing between the two parties, and said that his party never slept while they were in sight of near [sic] the others, as they were afraid –

It now appears pretty clear that these people from Point Barrow

---

[1] This was not, in fact, a boat for hunting whales, but rather, a heavy open boat, pointed at both ends.

[2] American whaleships did not reach Point Barrow until 1854 – and had only infrequent contact with the natives of Bering Strait from 1848 to 1852. It is most likely that this book came from one of the British searching vessels.

[3] See Appendix One below.

216

are those described as the western Esquimaux,[1] an appellation we were always in doubt who to apply to, imagining the journey to the East[wa]r^d far for these people, considering the nature of the coast, which is very much exposed, and their baidars when deeply laden are not calculated for a sea way – in addition to this the season of open water appeared to me of too short duration to admit of the distance being effected by them – These difficulties he explained away by saying they took their baidars away on sledges a month before the sea thaws and they cut off all the exposed parts of the Coast by making an inland navigation through lakes & rivers of which we knew nothing previously[2] . . .

Monday May 23d . . . We have had no natives on board today, forming almost a singular instance of such absence since we have been here – There were very few outside, we were told the men had all gone out in their boats after whale as the late strong breeze had eased off the ice.

Mr Hull and his party returned at noon – He has examined the shores of Elson's bay, without meeting any thing different from that laid down by Mr Simpson, in his examination of Dease's Inlet he found it to be a deep bay running to the South about 20 miles from the last point laid down by Mr Simpson, returning by Point tangent, the chain of Islands from our present position were traced, and angles obtained for putting them on paper. He has been unfortunate in his weather, but on the whole the journey has been successful.

Tuesday [May] 24th . . . We have few Natives about they seem to be all engaged either in their baidars after whale, or crouching about the ice and spits, lying in wait for the numerous flights of birds passing, over today – It is the first time I have witnessed an Arctic migration of birds,[3] their numbers are astonishing, looking round the horizon, it seems at times to be thronged with them, when looked at with a glass they appear to be flying in streams, and in different directions, but I suppose they are making for the open water, and the localities

[1] A term that was apparently derived from Franklin's narrative of his boat expedition along the north Alaskan coast in 1826 (Franklin, 1828 – see, for instance, page 130).
[2] Probably through a portage from Elson Lagoon, via Teshekpuk Lake, to Harrison Bay.
[3] These would have been king eider ducks (*Somateria spectabilis*) and common eiders (*S. mollissima*), as well as oldsquaw ducks (*Clangula hyemalis*), glaucous gulls (*Larus hyperboreus*), and probably yellow billed loons (*Gavia adamsii*) (Rosenau and Herter, 1984).

they resort to for breeding – A few only came within gun shot of it the Ship, one a male King Eider was shot by Mr Gordon – Several natives have spread themselves out on the ice, in expectation of being able to throw their nets over them but failed . . .

Wednesday May 25th . . . Ark-sin-ra with his wife and one or two others were on board, he says the huts marked by Sir John Franklin on the coast near to Flaxman's Island belong to the Eastern people and he described them as being without roofs[1] – There are also two on Flaxmans Island. He confirmed the report of the old chief having been on board The Investigator off Point Berens.[2] In the afternoon we had some large flights of birds passing to the N.E. . . .

Friday May 27th Magnetic term day . . . We have had very few Natives about, I conclude they are all engaged in their whaling pursuits – The night was cold and gloomy with a strong breeze from the East[wa]r^d.

Saturday May 28th . . . The Ship continues to leak slightly, averaging about ⅜ of an inch in twenty four hours. This is not much, still it is more than I wish to see, considering the lightness of her draft, and being free from pressure or strain – We have more natives about today than usual & more allowed on board, the old Chief and his two wives amongst the Number, he always seems to be spying about and watching closely what is going on in the Ship – with a look of greediness about him, that one would fancy the possession of the whole ship would barely satisfy . . .

Sunday – May – 29th Royal oak day.[3] On this day twelve months ago I sailed from Honolulu in H.M.S. Amphitrite – And as we have been as successful in that time as our wishes lead us, viz. wintering at Point Barrow we have reason to be satisfied. I hope, whatever my orders may be for the next twelve months, that I shall be able to carry them out as successfully . . .

The Natives were about as usual. And some on board after Church service – Arksinra and his wife of the Number. I had thought it probable that a deep channel similar to the one we are lying in (Moore's)[4] would be found at the opposite extreme of the chain of

---

[1] See Franklin 1828, map five. If these abandoned houses had, in fact, been built by the Mackenzie Eskimos, then their territorial range would have been somewhat greater than is generally thought. Barter Island is generally considered to be near the westernmost limit of their territory (Smith, 1984, p. 348).

[2] See above, p. 215, n. 1.

[3] Celebrating the restoration of Charles II on 29 May 1660.

[4] Today, Eluitkak Pass.

sand spits that guard the bay from Point tangent to this place a distance of 32 miles and Mr Hull in his examination of them fancied the appearance of the ice indicated a good depth of water, where it would be much more desirable to winter than at this place, both an account of there being a better supply of drift wood, and the distance from the Natives just sufficient to ensure you from annoyance. Ark-sin-ra on being questioned today as to there being a channel, destroyed our hopes by saying only boats could pass through, of this fact I hope to be able to satisfy myself personally when the season is a little more advanced –

The people at Noo-wook have killed several bears[1] within the last ten days, and have brought a small quantity of the flesh to barter, which no doubt would have been eaten with more relish, had our supply of Venison been less abundant – They have also brought several of their thigh bones and seem to be aware of the good properties of the marrow in producing hair. The bones on being broken do not have the same appearance as the marrow bones of other Animals, being cellular, and the marrow is in the fluid state. Their paws have been brought also more as a curiosity than for any value they possess.

Monday May 30th . . . We have had a few natives on board. I showed Ark-sin-ra & his wife, agreeable to an old promise, all the beads we have on board for presents, their astonishment was greater than I expected, particularly as the beads are very inferior, and none of them the colour or description they fancy, being the refuse of what the Natives to the South[wa]r^d seemed to place no value on – I seemed to rise very much in their estimation from being the possessor of such a treasure, although I always disclaim being the owner, and endeavour to explain to them that the things belong to the Ship, but this is a hard matter for them to understand – Nothing connected with my position in the Ship seemed to give them any idea of it, equal to the beads – Although strange to say they will give nothing for them in exchange, prefering [sic] tobacco to every thing else – He went away repeating how he would talk of them all along the Coast, and his wife described to us that when she slept they would be before her eyes –

I had Sables and his wife in my cabin afterwards, he seems intent

---

[1] Polar bears (*Ursus maritimus*). These bears may have been drawn to the coast by the odour of the whale that was being butchered

upon making a long journey to the South[wa]r^d, and talks of Cape Prince of Wales – where I have offered to give him a passage in the Ship. Today I endeavoured to explain to him on paper the difficulty he would have in getting back across the mouth of Kotzebue sound, which I think has left him in uncertainty as to going in the Ship – He proposed also to accompany our two boats in his oo-mi-ak to Point Hope or Cape Lisburne, but I explained to him that our boats would sail very fast and that he would not be able to keep up with them – . . .

Tuesday May 31st . . . The Natives are about as usual, but very inoffensive. 'Iwatsa' in conversation with some of the officers, seems to have said, that when the Natives came down to attack the Ship, bad men offered themselves to murder some of the officers first, by getting hold of their arms & sticking them with their knives – He was told in Answer that if any body belonging to the Ship had been Killed, that (Noo-wook) their town would have been levelled to the ground, and as he did not understand whether this threat was meant in a past or future sense, he told the people in Noo-wook that we were going to do this, And some of them asked me along side the Ship today, if such were the case. I laughed at them very much, at the same time I was sorry Iwatsa had not a better opinion of us – He came to the Ship this evening and was coldly received in consequence.

Wednesday, June 1st [1853] . . . As three or four different specimens of small land birds have been procured by the officers – The larger birds have not come as yet very near the Ship, at present our supply of Venison is so very plentiful, they are not much sought after or missed. In the evening two of the old chiefs sons came along side with a sledge, on their way along the Shore to the Eastw[ar]d for the purpose of hunting the young fawn, they seemed but poorly provided in the way of provisions and covering – A piece of Whale blubber and about 10 lbs of Venison wrapped in an old piece of cotton canvas – With their bows and arrows, was all the sledge contained[1] . . .

Thursday June 2d . . . The health of the Ships Co which has been very precarious for the greater part of the winter, has become quite restored since they have been on Venison diet – And we have had no one on the sick list for several days –[2]

---

[1] 'O-mi-ga-loon's' sons' absence from the whale hunt is puzzling. It may have been that 'O-mi-ga-loon' considered that all the whales had passed Point Barrow and hence hunting would be fruitless; it is also possible that a death had occurred in the family, thereby prohibiting them from the hunt.

[2] Because of the vitamin C that the fresh meat provided.

Friday [June] 3d . . . Messrs Hull & Wright went to the village today, to get Ark-sin-ra to put up some marks of his own, on the spit leading to the S.W.d from Pt Barrow towards Cape Smyth for the survey, Our own marks being pulled down the moment we are out of sight – The officers received no incivility, and Ark-sin-ra went out and did what they wished, requesting Mr Hull to tell me he had done so – We have not had many natives about us for the last few days. Those we are most intimate with seem to be too busily engaged to come near us at present. This I look upon rather as a relief than otherwise – . . .

Saturday June 4th Settled clear summer weather – Messrs Hull and Wright went away this morning with a sledge and one man carrying their instruments to take angles at the station on the spit between Point Barrow and Cape Smyth – for the survey – They returned at 6 P.M. having executed this service without any molestation from the Natives – At Point Barrow they found two summer tents erected, after the thaw regularly sets in, I suppose the winter huts are found to be damp, And not so convenient as the skin tents. I took the Angles at the South base station as they went on, in the event of the Natives pulling down the marks again – . . .

Sunday June 5th Another beautiful summers day, the thaw is now going on in good earnest, and we watch its progress with the same interest, one would do in seeing his prison clear away. We had more natives than usual about the ship, the old chief whom we have not seen for some time was of the number accompanied by his two wives – They were admitted on board after church, having waited very patiently outside for several hours – The old mans wife brought me a seal skin water proof coat she has been making for me and as it required some alteration she took it back again. I gave the Chief a leaf of tobacco as he has not been so regular in his begging visits, he seemed at first afraid that it was payment for the coat, and was not satisfied about it, until he came to me a second time to understand fully that it was given to him. Afterwards the wives were sent home, I supposed to hurry the alteration in the coat. As he remained on board the whole day, I was curious to know what he did with himself, and asked the Quarter Master late in the afternoon what he had been about – when I was informed that he had been bringing in small articles from the people outside to be disposed of, & levying a small tax upon each besides 'Kadging' begging from every body for tobacco. This is not a profitable source with him, as he is not a favourite with any –

There is a small space of clear open water under the stern, where the tide when running strong makes in a whirlpool. And on the West side of the ship where the strength of the sun strikes, there is a good deal of overflow, small pools of fresh water are beginning to form on the ice, from which the Natives drink abundantly. The luxury of a good drink of water with them such a rarity seems to be fully appreciated –

Tuesday June 7th . . . We had more than the usual number of Natives along side this evening, and on their going away I counted forty people and six sledges. The day for the most part has been hazy.

Wednesday June 8th About twenty minutes past five this morning I was awoke by the Quarter Master of the watch David Dunstall rushing into my cabin in a fearful state of excitement and reporting in a convulsed manner the [sic] he had had a dreadful misfortune, and to my horror heard that he had shot a native by accident along side the Ship.

My first enquiry as to his being dead, was followed by ordering him to call the Doctor, and hurrying on deck & outside the ship found the unfortunate man was shot through the head, and must have died instantaneously.

The previous account of the system that I have endeavoured to carry out, to avoid such a calamity as I had now before me, will of itself give some idea of the sorrow I felt, which was greater than I had over cause for in a rather lengthened service at sea.

The mans state, who had been the cause of this unfortunate event, was sufficient to explain that the act was an accident and in making the necessary enquiries as to how it occurred – I found that several natives had arrived along side the Ship at a little after 4 Am. And although it was well known to them to be a time they were not allowed to be there. The watch on deck could not prevail on them to go away. When the Quarter Master took a fowling [piece] belonging to one of the officers, that happened to be on the after part of the Quarter deck loaded with shot, and saying to one of the men of the watch, that he would see if he could not frighten them away, went out with it in his right hand, and motioning them away, it went off and lodged the contents of the barrel in the back part of the poor mans head.

The party consisted of five men, three women, and a child, with a sledge, who on the accident occurring ran away, two of our men followed them to endeavour to explain it was an accident, they succeeded in overtaking the women, but no entreaties could induce them to remain.

After deliberating with the officers as to our proper mode of proceeding it was thought best to remove the body to such a distance from the Ship, that the Natives could advance to it without fear of us, and not give them any pretext for coming nearer. This was immediately done and the body laid out in two clean hammocks, and a large quantity of tobacco placed beside it, with the hope of its being taken as a friendly intimation. After this was done, and the boats brought down close to the Ship to prevent mischief, all we could do was to hope that some of our friends would still have sufficient confidence in us to come down and give us an opportunity of explaining the melancholy affair.

In this expectation we were not disappointed as two Chiefs came down immediately, having previously exerted their influence to quell the rage of the people on the alarm being given at the Village.

They came on board without showing mistrust of any kind and one of them Ark-sin-ra a very intelligent man was fortunately able to comprehend how the accident took place. Great pains were taken to show him that the nature of the charge was shot intended for birds not for men.

When this impression was established no time was lost in requesting them to return immediately and explain the whole circumstance, which we found afterwards they had done.

By the time they had reached the body on their return many natives had arrived there from the Village, amongst them the wife and friends of the unfortunate man, who I was glad to find had no children. They all sat down and appeared to be deeply engaged in conversation for about two hours, we supposed hearing our explanation, when a man came from them to the Ship, and asked for a long line for a number of people to drag the sledge, & on being provided with it, he returned.

They afterwards seemed to examine the body, and his own deer skins having been brought down, he was wrapped up in them & placed on his sledge, and a little before noon the procession moved off with the body across the ice for the Cemetry [sic] on Pt Barrow. There were only five people who accompanied the body, four men and one woman (the wife) who was the leader of four who drew the sledge, and one man followed – Early in the forenoon the old Chiefs wife came on board apparently in great distress as the dead man was some relation of hers, she informed me that her husband was on the water looking after whale, but that he had been sent for, and would return soon, she remained a very short time, I sent a message by her for Iwatsa my former guide who has been a good deal on board, and understands us better than most of the others.

He arrived soon afterwards, and during the day, a few men remained alongside, but as they were for the most part of those that have not been friendly with us, our people were kept on board to avoid any treacherous retaliation.

We had also the wife of another influential chief (misua-ga-soon) on board the whole day, her husband was on the water but very friendly to us, we understood from her as well as Iwatsa that the people were divided in opinion as to revenging themselves on us for the accident, And in the evening one of the Chiefs who had been the first down in the morning came on board with his wife and confirmed the same story – While he was on deck, I remarked that he and Iwatsa looked now & then, anxiously at the Village, from which I concluded they were not certain whether we should be attacked or not. They told us the people at the Village would do no work for five days nor would the women sew, & remarked that we ought not have any hammering on board for the same time.

As I was most anxious to show every sympathy in our power, the Caulkers at work on the Ship outside were ordered to cease work, and the Ensign hoisted half mast the meaning of which was explained & understood by them.

After they left in the evening the arms & guns were loaded, and such arrangements made as were considered necessary in the event of an attack. I did not expect one from the fact of the Chiefs or their wives having been on board in the day, and the tribe divided were not likely to make such an attempt.

The night seemed to favour them had they meditated such a thing, as it came on a thick fog at ½ past 10 P.M. & remained until 4 Am. being the first time we have had one for a continuance since we have had the sun constantly about the horizon –

Thursday June 9th Early in the forenoon we had a visit from the four Chiefs who with their wives were assembled in my cabin, and with the assistance of Mr Vernon & Mr Simpson the Surgeon, the whole unfortunate affair was gone over again which seemed to be perfectly understood, and they gave us to understand that they had

224

been using their influence at Noo-wook to prevent any ill feeling that might arise in consequence of the death of their country man – the people were all good and did not intend taking any revenge upon us for the accident. The Chief had also previous to his coming on board, made a speech to a large number outside, many of whom had accompanied him to the Ship, and remained all day very orderly, but in consequence of a hint from one of the Chiefs our men were not permitted to go much amongst them.

The party in the Cabin became rather hungry about noon and the Chief asked for some Venison, the rest at the same time pinching in their stomacks [sic] to show they were very empty, My apologies for having none cooked were waived by their saying it was better without, and on a large joint of Venison being set before them raw, the ample justice they did it and part of another, made me form the opinion that a cooks labour would have been lost on them. Seals flesh they told us was better cooked, but Venison did not require it – Shortly after this plentiful meal, and they had been made a considerable present of tobacco, and as the large party outside seemed to expect something similar – the Chief was told it would be impossible to give to everyone that came, but to the wife & other people residing in the same house, large presents would be made to express our regret at the occurrence – The chief promised to bring them at the expiration of five days, the time of mourning according to their custom – The man mentioned above as a relative of the deceased explained to us that he came to show he bore us no ill-feeling –

Previous to the whole of the party outside going away, I went out amongst them and was much pleased with their apparent Kindness, I might say sympathy, feeling as I did truly sorry for the accident, after having avoided many real causes for such an occurrence, to have it happen on an inoffensive man at a time when we had established a good understanding with them, was in every point of view it could be looked at, most deplorable – And seemed like undoing in one moment what it had taken ten months forbearance to establish –

The party throughout the day although numbering amongst them some of the most troublesome, behaved themselves in a very orderly way, & returned home in the evening without any instance of ill will towards us being shown[1] –

[1] The Eskimos of northern Alaska believed in collective responsibility for murder (Spencer, 1959, p. 7). Some of the deceased Eskimo's relatives may well have been in consultation to decide whether a murder had occurred and whether therefore to seek

Friday June 10th This was a cold raw sort of day from the breeze, but the sun shine was warm & pleasant. We had none of the Chiefs, and very few men near us today but several women & children were alongside & on board.

We were told the men were all on the water, and none but women were left at the Village – Iwatsa was on board most of the day & was told he might sleep on board but he considered it better to go home, fearing some one might steal his tobacco . . .

Saturday [June] 11th . . .

We had only five or six women and a child along side today, they tell us they are all out fishing,[1] and they seem very anxious as to their success, although not actually in want of food at present – unless they kill a whale or two in the course of the next fortnight, their food will be very short – In the Middle of the day a man came from Cape Smyth with a large seal skin to barter, of the sort much prized at present for making soles for water moccasins, and although offered a good price for it, he preferred taking it to Point Barrow – . . .

In the evening an old woman came down with a pair of moccasins for one of the men, and told us with apparent satisfaction that our friend Sable's had Killed a large whale, so I conclude there will be great rejoicing at the Village tonight –

Sunday June 12th We have had a strong gale from the N.E. all day, which has prevented the Natives from going out, and left them at leisure to pay us a visit in larger numbers than usual. After church service Ark-sin-ra & several others were admitted, Amongst them a man who before the late accident occurred was never thought of being allowed on board & who I have mentioned very often before as the Stammerer, giving us a great deal of trouble, but at the present time I wished to establish a general amnesty and forgetfulness of the past if possible. No objectionable conduct occurred either in board or outside the Ship, and the late unhappy event will I hope pass over without giving us any serious inconvenience –

Monday June 13th . . . At 9 Am. as anticipated the friends of the unfortunate man shot by accident came to the Ship, Numbering as many as ten men & women. They were all shown down into the cabin, where after again expressing our deep sorrow at the event,

---

retribution from the English. It may well have been Maguire's explanation and gifts – as well as the intercession of the four *umialit* – that prevented further bloodshed.

[1] Whale hunting.

they were made large presents of tobacco, a Knife each, some beads & other useful articles, the Wife is a very young woman and seemed in unaffected grief, which the large presents she received did not dissipate, we must hope that time and a continued Kindness on our part will have the effect of alleviating her sorrow. Ark-sin-ra – one of the Chiefs before mentioned – accompanied them, and appeared to think we had done all that lay in our power for the present. The party of mourners left the Ship for Noo-wook soon after receiving their presents – We have had an average number of natives along side and in board, all expressing themselves friendly & behaving very orderly . . . I was glad to see Iwatsa come down to sleep on board after the other natives had left, as he had refused the offer to do so since the accident occurred, although previously he had considered it a great favour being allowed to do so. I was afraid he had lost that confidence in us, I have been so anxious to establish, and which the late event has been but too much cause to shake. The weather continued windy with snow occasionally during the night.

Tuesday June 14th . . . The Natives are about us again as usual, there appeared to be several strangers amongst them today, one woman I recognised as having seen at Icy Cape when we were stopped there in the boats. We had a larger number than usual in board including Amongst them several of the Mourning party of yesterday. We hear that some have gone on the water today, although the wind is too strong for them to venture far . . .

Wednesday [June] 15th . . . We hear the old Chief has caught a whale, he will be quite elated at his success. Ark-sin-ra was endeavouring to explain to us their system of sharing the animal when Killed, from which we could make out very little, beyond their being a great deal of confusion, and cutting, making it necessary for the proprietors to use all their strength to secure their share. After they are satisfied in that way, I believe they are very generous, and leave the rest for those who like to take it away –[1]

We had a good many Natives on board & Amongst them our

---

[1] Before the 1870s (when commercial considerations began to change the traditional sharing practices) the division of the whale's parts was worked out between the crews that had assisted in its capture – with the choice parts going to the *umialik* and crew that had first struck the whale. Robert Spencer (1959, p. 346) has written:

Trouble, if it arose, came as the result of divisions between crews, one umealiq taking the view that his crew had had a greater part in the capture than the first boat would admit. Moreover, some crew members would claim special shares, and their insistence might lead to dispute and occasionally bloodshed and murder.

widow as I must call her in future – I have requested the men to show her all the sympathy in their power by making her small presents from time to time, of such trifles as they will not miss, and will be to her a great acquisition.

Our former friend Kiowa the intelligent boy who got into disgrace for stealing the pair of boots in the winter, came down in the evening with some message from his adopted Father, Sable Coat, he told us the water had come much nearer to the land, from which I conclude there has been a disruption of the land floe. The Carpenters are still employed caulking the Ship outside, the crew have been refitting the rigging and taking the rafters off, used for the housing –[1]

Thursday June 16th . . . The Natives are alongside as usual, I fancy they beg more steadily since the poor man was killed, a slight alarm took place in the dinner hour, on a woman outside being detected stealing an empty preserved meat tin, several natives on board immediately ran out of the ship, and strange to say, the only party that remained, were the family of the deceased man who did not seem to have thought of going – Although the day has been clear with sun shine, the temperature in the shade rose no higher than 34° [1.1°C] . . .

Friday June 17th . . . We have a great many natives about us today, as the open water is very confined, the number in board was much increased also, we have altered our system in that respect, and put up with a good deal of inconvenience from having so many about our deck whilst so much work is going on in order to do away as much as possible with the unfavourable impression caused by the late accident. We had a visit from the old Chief who asked me in rather a mysterious way to go to my cabin, when there, his secret was that he had been talking a great deal in our favour to the people at Cape Smyth and Point Barrow, for which he requested without much ceremony some tobacco and a Knife, of the former I gave him a moderate present, with which he seemed satisfied & soon afterwards asked to go on deck. We have had no trouble with the Natives today. They report the open water as very confined, but it has neared the land considerably . . .

Saturday June 18th Waterloo day – etat 38 years – The wind was

[1] The noise from the caulking mallets and general carpentry must have distressed the Eskimos: during the whale hunt it was considered essential to do no hammering or to carry out other noisy activities, lest the whales be frightened away (Murdoch, 1892, p. 274).

from the Westw[ar]^d this morning, with dull weather but not cold, as the wind from this quarter brings in the ice the Natives are not able to be on the water in pursuit of their favourite occupation Whale fishing, we have consequently more of their company than is quite agreeable, although they all seem very quiet, and whilst here appear to bear no animosity for the late fatal accident. The temperature in the shade rose to 35 [1.7°C] at noon. The radiating Therm[omete]^r showing 82° [27.8°C]. We have had some small flights of birds pass over the Ship today for the first time for several days, and a few specimens of land birds have been brought by the Natives – We have now as many as five different species but none of them are new. We are deficient in books of description on ornithology, but we fancy we we [sic] have met with a duck here that has not been described . . .

Sunday June 19th A fine warm morning, without the aid of the sun, as it shone out only at times until Noon. The Natives for the present have no employment on the water as the ice has closed in, we have as usual in such cases an extra member alongside – –

Relative to the unfortunate event of the Native being shot along side the Ship on the morning of the 8th instant – I have thought it better to allow a certain time to elapse, previous to making the necessary enquiry as to the cause of the accident & the unauthorized use of fire arms by the Quarter Master on the occasion. And not wishing to pronounce singly on the conduct of the man, for taking the life of a fellow creature, I called to my assistance the four principal of officers [sic] in the Ship to form an enquiry on the subject, and after hearing a full description of the occurrence, The officers as well as myself were unanimous in acquitting him of all intention of firing the gun, yet his conduct was much to blame, firstly, for resorting at all to the use of Fire arms without *orders* or *necessity*, and secondly, for gross negligence that having done so he was not careful to ascertain that it was loaded – For which conduct I have disrated him to an A.B. and recommended his being discharged from this Ship for a passage to the Commander in Chief in the Pacific, for his disposal by the earliest convenient opportunity –

The Natives behaved very quietly along side all day, Although they were in large numbers – Their appearance going towards the town in a body in the evening was very formidable thrown up by Mirage . . .

Tuesday [June] 21st . . . There is no water sky today, and the Natives tell us the ice is quite close, from the Westerly winds. The

old Chief was on board & spoke of going away to the East[wa]rd[1]
which I was very glad to hear, it seems the time for their setting out,
is after the water forms in lanes between the edge of the ice and the
land. Doctor Simpson heard from Ark-sin-ra today that he had met a
woman at the Colville River[2] Amongst the tribe called Nuna-tag-
miuts, who had been on board this Ship in the winter of 1849–50 at
Kotzbue Sound[3] – From her account it appears they have a
communication by the rivers of the interior, from Hotham Inlet to
the Arctic Sea at the River Colville quite independent of that by the
coast.[4] Ark-sin-ra was also acquainted with the name of Chamisso
Isl[an]d & some of the Rivers of Kotzbue sound but had never been
there . . . As the wind was fresh from S.S.W. I suppose the Natives
were afraid of the stability of the land floe, as We observed four U-
mi-aks being drawn to the land from the open water.[5]

Wednesday June 22nd . . . We have not so many natives about us as
usual and I do not hear of any disruption of the land floe to account
for the O-mi-aks having been brought in. Ark-sin-ra brought down
Doctor Simpsons Therm[omete]ʳ stolen several months since, it
appears to have [been] buried with a preserved meat tin in the snow
and to have been lost sight of until the thaw has shown it up, & Ark-
sin-ra hearing of its existence succeeded in getting it back (although
we had given up, as broken or destroyed) for which he has been
rewarded by the owner. The man who got so good a thrashing from
Hayden the Qu[arte]r Master on our first arrival, came along side &
was admitted today, my present object being to do away with the
unfavourable impression caused by the fatal accident of the 8th by
the most conciliatory measures we can imagine. Many more being
now allowed in than formerly and Amongst them some that would
never have been under other circumstances.

The crew are employed refitting the rigging and preparing the
Ship for Sea. The small boats intended for Cape Lisburne are being
painted, and their arrangements made complete . . .[6]

Thursday June 23d . . . We hear from Noo-wook of a great

[1] On a trading voyage to Nirliq.
[2] At the Nirliq trade rendezvous.
[3] The *Plover* was wintering at the Choris Peninsula.
[4] For a compilation of the various travel routes from the upper Noatak River to the Arctic slope see Burch 1976.
[5] The whaling season was over.
[6] For a cruise to Cape Lisburne in the weeks before the ice would release the *Plover*.

dance[1] being in contemplation, I feel sorry that we shall not be able
to witness it as some unusual ceremony is described as taking place,
when the performer is either tossed on a large skin, or else it is held
while he dances on it. We have been visited today by the Father of
one of the Chiefs (Sables) a very old man and quite a cripple from
Rheumatism. His appearance was much care worn, but his features
were good and intelligent, we have not had any of the principal
people down, I suppose they are engaged in the ceremonies about to
take place. The present seems to be another idle time with them
while there is no open water, and they are waiting for the thaw to be
more advanced previous to setting out on their bartering expeditions
along the coast to the East[wa]rd . . . a sledge with two Natives
called alongside on their return to the Village from the land, where
they have been for two days trying to catch the young Fawn, without
any success. The[y] had killed a few birds and describe the rivers as
all running off the land in large streams. We had a continuance of fog
throughout the night.

Friday 24th June This has been the finest day we have had for for
[sic] some time with a clear sun shine since 6 Am. These fine days are
generally followed by fogs & unpleasant weather, which does away
with a good deal of the enjoyment of them, anticipating what is to
follow. We were visited this morning by the old chief, and his two
wives, the former dressed unusually well in honour of visiting us, or
as it was suggested by one of the officers, it was his mode of putting
her coat in the market. Ark-sin-ra was also on board with his wife,
they speak of setting out for the East[war]d in ten days. I am very
glad of it, as the fewer we have here when our boats are going away
the better. Their great dance takes place tomorrow, and it is to be in

---

[1] This was the festival, *nalukataq*, that marked the end of the spring whaling season
– which was potentially the most productive hunting project of the year. By the end of
the whaling season tons of meat, blubber, and other whale products could have been
stored in the Eskimos' underground cellars that were dug into permanently frozen
ground. The festival's events centred around the membership of the *qazgi*, a
ceremonial house, the membership of which was linked by kinship. Those *qazgit* that
had successful whaling crews in a particular season held the festivals. The events took
place out of doors at a particular open space belonging to the *qazgi*. The first day's
ceremonies were contests and games that were held in the lee of overturned umiaks.
Members of other *qazgit* arrived for games and, later, feasting, when the successful
umialik distributed the delicacy called *muktuk* (whale skin and blubber). The second
day of the festival was somewhat similar to the first and included a blanket toss from
walrus hides (Spencer, 1959, pp. 350–2). See also John Simpson's account in
Appendix Seven below, p. 513.

231

the open airs, not in the dance house, as Ark-sin-ra when asked about it today told us we should be able to see it from the Ship –

The crew are busily employed preparing the Ship for sea, this day being particularly favourable for the purpose a good many are at work painting the Ship outside. In the afternoon the Carpenters mate had a small gimblet stolen from him while he was at work on the Quarter deck, which caused a little stir to be made amongst our visitors without our being able to get it back, strong suspicion existed against the Chiefs Senior wife, but she was too experienced a hand to be frightened out of it . . .

Saturday June 25th . . . We have had more natives about us today than I expected, supposing they would be all too much interested with the dancing. We could see the crowd collected round with our glasses a little to the left of the Village, and occasionally the performer was observed over the heads of all the rest, this dance is quite novel to me, and I am not aware of having seen a description of it, from what we are able to make out of the Natives account, a great many people stand round holding a large Walrus hide in their hands, on which the dance takes place, while it is thrown up and down in a similar way to shaking a carpet, and it is to be supposed the agility of the dancer is displayed in being able to keep his legs. Ark-sin-ra made some casual remark relative to the festival, connected with the dead, but we could not comprehend his meaning, but we supposed it might [be] a ceremony connected with their religion. As a great many of them have appeared during the time in their best clothes, which they look upon as showing great respect. The night was dull & gloomy with the wind from the S. E.

Sunday [June] 26th A strong breeze from the East[wa]rd with fine weather. We heard yesterday the dancing was to be continued again today, but the Chiefs (O-mi-ga-loons) party which seems to have been a mistake as he came down early this morning & was allowed on board before church, as well as Sables and his wife who are also of his party, whether the open water caused by this wind has put it off or not I could not make out. We understood that three O-mi-aks were launched today and they say there is open water. The sky is not so well defined as we have had it previously, but this strong breeze for a continuance must open a considerable space of water.

After church a few Natives were admitted. They all seem to speak of their intended departure to the East[wa]rd. Ark-sin-ra said yesterday, they do no work now for ten days and enjoy themselves, they then make preparations for their journey and start in fifteen days. One man told us today that he was going in ten days. The old chief was accompanied today by the wife who suspicion fell upon, for stealing the Carpenters Gimblet on Friday, and she was not let on board, he appeared a little annoyed at first, but seemed or pretended to forget it very soon, & she went home – I heard from one of our visitors that a woman had a severe fall in the dancing yesterday and had injured her shoulder. The same informant seemed much surprised when I told him I had seen the dancing, as he mistook my meaning supposing I meant himself, my description of what I had seen would have answered for all equally as well as for him . . .

Monday June 27th . . . The track of the rivers off the Main land are now clearly discernible as they enter the bay ice, which will cut off the Communication with the main land on foot, in a little time. There is a curious feature in this bay ice, now becoming apparent as the snow thaws, and exposes a coating of mud on the ice, which it is supposed to have received in its formation, as there was a strong breeze from the East[wa]rd at the time, which we have always found to increase the current and in this case drifted the pancake ice in its formation on a muddy & shoal bottom into the bay, where at last the intensity of the cold set it fast. This seems a reasonable way to account for it. But the Natives inform us it is the effect of the wind blowing the gravel & dust off the Spits. Whatever has been the cause, the effect must prove very favourable to our release by hastening the process of thawing.

We have had a number of Natives about the Ship and in board, some of the latter, known to be of indifferent character, & whom we have been lately at variance with. Two or three large Eggs (goose & swan's) were brought along side this morning, making the first we have seen for this season. The water Chief as he is called was on board today & as he is not a frequent visitor, I am always glad to see him, particularly as his influence is equal if not greater than any other man here. On his going away I gave his wife an empty potato case, which he strapped on his back & walked away with looking a droll figure. Iwatsa came down in the evening to sleep, and brought us the welcome news of a great deal of the land floe having drifted off, bringing the water very near the Village. The ice outside of the Spit East[wa]rd is almost completely covered with water from the melted snow, the cracks not being sufficiently open to allow it to drain off.

233

<u>Tuesday June 28th</u> . . . Ark-sin-ra arrived earlier than his usual time, bringing us the intelligence, that it would be necessary to be on our guard of the Cape Smyth peoples Knives along side the Ship as they were unfriendly. This I was of opinion proceeded chiefly from a man who was on board yesterday belonging to that place and claimed relationship with the deceased native (shot) of which I was not aware, he has come again today & professes great friendship, and as it is politic to keep him in the same mind, I gave him the same present other distant relatives had received. Sables has been on board also, but did not remain long as he was anxious to join the old Chiefs dancing party which takes place today,[1] he seems to have made up his mind to accept my offer of giving him a passage to Cape Prince of Wales as he has been asking many questions about where he is to sleep, and such like – We have been Employed taking down the house on shore built from our spare spars, and getting them stowed in board. The carpenters have taken the Launch under repair, she was dreadfully cut about by the Natives Knives as Mentioned last Autumn – And a party are employed repairing the sails which are bent as they are finished.

<u>Wednesday June 29th</u> . . . The old Chief came down at an early hour accompanied by a man & his wife who were stopping, at his hut, he described them to me as Nuna-tagmiuts, but we found they came from Icy Cape, which they described as having 9 winter huts, which should give a population of about 50. I had them to the cabin and made them some presents. The man was old, dirty, and disagreeably covetous. His wife was young and pretty and we were told she is his daughter also, being the first instance that had come under our notice of incestuous intercourse.[2]

In the middle of the day which cleared up and gave us a little sunshine, Ark-sin-ra & Sables came down. The latter was still harping on his trip to the South[wa]rd in the Ship, and was anxious to see his destined house or cabin for the passage – And being shown the Sick bay he seemed very well satisfied with it. There was a long consultation afterwards in the cabin, with the three friends Omigaloon, Sables & Arksinra over the chart, as to the distance from Point Hope to Cape

---

[1] This would have been the whaling festival of the *qazgi* to which 'O-mi-ga-loon' belonged.

[2] According to Robert Spencer (1959, pp. 62–3) incest occurred very rarely in northwestern Alaska, and when it did occur, it engendered opprobrium. Maguire may have misunderstood the man's relationship to the woman.

Prince of Wales, and the difficulties Sable would have to contend with in returning by Kotzbue Sound as he would have to do. It was remarkable how well they comprehended the charts when their ideas were turned to it, but if I had asked them a question at another time and brought them to a chart when their mind was else where, it would have been difficult to make them understand any thing about it.

The result of the council was that sables would go to Cape Prince of Wales in the Ship, and take his chance to get a passage back in some whaler from the Straits to Point Hope – Which I considered was a very adventurous step for him, & shows them not devoid of enterprise. I walked a little way with them toward the Village, the Chief told me I could not go there, when I asked him if the people were bad, he said only one man was so, to which I answered and at the same time showed him I had no Knife or arms about me, that I was not afraid of our man. However if I understood them right a file would set this individual all to rights, which I suppose will be arranged.

Thursday June 30th A fine clear morning with a moderate breeze from the East[wa]rd. We had a visit as early as 6 Am from Ark-sin-ra & Sables who came down to tell us the Cape Smyth people intended to attack the Ship. The Noo-wook people would not join them and declared in our favour. I thought more of this report than usual as they left the Ship immediately afterwards, saying that no one from Noo-wook would come to the ship for the day, and they took with them a few people who had already assembled round. These reports of attacks coming every other day makes it very tiresome, and were it not for the loss of life on their part, that would attend one it would be better to have the attack over & be done with this constant state of suspense. The day remained very fine & we were left to the enjoyment of it without disturbance from the Natives, two or three only coming down who have described the Cape Smyth people as very bad.

In the evening the old Chief and Sables came down[,] the former no doubt with the hope of extracting presents for his pretended friendly interference. But their avidity is so great and insatiable, that I have almost lost patience with the system of expecting a reward for every imagined service. Tonight I told him I should be very sorry if the people came down to attack us, but if they did a great many would be killed, as I explained to him we should fire at them, and not over

235

their heads as on former occasions. He endeavoured to make out that he wished to fight on our side, but this I took no notice of, and he went away without being able to make out any case for receiving a present – Sables remained behind with his wife for two or three hours but no information of their movements was gained from him. After he left the arms were loaded and every arrangement made to prevent surprise, a thick fog favouring such a design if intended.

Friday July 1st [1853] A beautiful clear morning with a light wind from the East[wa]rd. Our accounts from the native today are more pacific. Ark-sin-ra & Sables say they told the hostile party to come down and attack us and they would find us ready for them which appears to have made them change their minds. The Natives have not been allowed to come nearer to the Ship than the spit today, as I have got quite tired of the reports of attacks day after day, without any Kindness on our parts having the effect of producing any friendly feeling, except in those who have received presents of tobacco, & they expect a renewal on each occasion they make out of befriending us. I endeavoured to have explained to them today, it would be better they kept away altogether, & we should be spared the pain of hearing so many unpleasant accounts of those who are evil [sic] disposed. And if they came to attack us we should be ready for them. This tone has not been previously tried, and as our former views have been dictated with a view of Keeping up a friendly intercourse at a great sacrifice to convenience, I hope keeping them away for a day will have the effect Kinder acts have failed to produce.

Our work is now all done, and the Ship ready for sea, our next business of importance will be getting our boats away to the South[wa]rd. The prospect to seaward is not very promising, as the land floe is still of some extent, & the open water very limited. I hope the next week will work a change in our favour. The boats are quite ready, & the provisions are being carefully packed. We find on getting every thing off from the Shore, the Natives have stolen our three Top Gallant Masts, the Carpenter has been employed making a Fore Top Gallant Mast which was ready for fidding in the evening . . .

Saturday July 2nd . . . The Natives of whom only a few have come down, were allowed along side as usual, and several in board, they all seemed very demure & on their best behaviour, and no more reports of dissatisfaction. The Cape Smyth people who were so ill disposed have gone home, leaving the Noo-wook people in active preparation for their intended summers excursion to the Eastward. We hear they are to start in about five days time, a most agreeable piece of information to us. I have been very anxious for some days past to send Mr Hull away for a day or two, to get a few angles for making a more complete survey of them. But the constant state of agitation we have been Kept in by the Natives, has prevented my doing so. I have now deferred his departure until after the Natives set out, as they take the same line he would be returning on, & his meeting so large [a] party is as well avoided – Ark-sin-ra with his wife & Iwatsa came down in the evening, the latter to sleep on board, and the former to return the whale lance I lent him two months ago. As he seems to be the most disinterested in his friendship towards us, I made him a present of it, Begging him whenever he met of any of our country people along the coast to befriend them, And not to let his people steal from them . . .

Sunday July 3d . . . I forgot to mention yesterday that we had bought a Native O-mi-ak for something less than three pounds of tobacco, they are very light, and I have been anxious to get two of them in case of anything happening to our own boats. We had none of the leading characters from Noo-wook down today, except Ark-sin-ra who came in the evening, he speaks of coming down & pitching his tent along side the Ship tomorrow, on his way Eastward. We had a laughable scene on the ice with the Esquimaux one of whom fell into the hole over his head in pursuit of an old preserved meat tin thrown there purposely by one of our men, who seemed bent on making a little Amusement. I sent the sufferer away with a present of tobacco which had the effect of turning the laugh on his side, which was certainly much against him previously, although he looked a very wo-begone [sic] figure notwithstanding. The open water has nearly disappeared today from the wind blowing on shore, but the progress of the thaw on the ice must be very rapid.

Monday . July 4th . . . A party of Natives were observed early bringing their O-mi-aks towards the Ship, and the old Whaling chief called along side on his way to the East[wa]rd[1] to return the whale lance I had lent him some two months since. And as he has been a less frequent visitor and therefore the less troublesome, I made him a present of it. His party consisted of four O-mi-aks, they were

---

[1] To the trade rendezvous at Nirliq.

secured on sledges and seemed easily drawn by 2 people. Five or six small (truck) sledges carried their barter which appeared to be seal and Whale blubber. These were drawn by the dogs & women, the men keeping charge of the O-mi-aks, but at considerable cracks & bad places to pass, they Mutually assist each other. I accompanied the party some distance from the Ship, to observe their system of travelling, which seemed expeditious while they were moving, but they made frequent halts to smoke, and before I left them, although near their place of encampment, they eat [sic] a hearty meal.

In the Evening O-mi-ga-loons party brought down their O-mi-aks & pitched their tents close to the Ship, although after our usual time for admitting them, a large party were allowed on board, as I wished to distribute some printed notices prepared for the Eastern Esquimaux, Amongst them,[1] previous to their setting out to meet that people. Each person charged with papers received a present of tobacco, some buttons (with the names of the Ships engaged in Arctic search engraved on them) & other small trifles to keep them in mind of their charge, which they faithfully promised to pass on. I redeemed a long made promise to the old chief of giving him some gun powder, I had considerable qualms of conscience in doing it, but I hope it may have a good effect and produce confidence by showing we had no fear of them. I was fully aware that he had a sufficient quantity by him for all mischievous purposes, as his gun when in our possession was found well loaded with ball cartridge.

I landed afterwards as well as several of the officers to Visit them in their huts, we were Kindly received, but wishing to lay in a stock for their journey, they begged for tobacco most unmercifully.

Repairing the main sail & preparing sledge gear [e]t^c for the boats has been the employment for the day/

Tuesday July 5th A fine morning with the wind at West. The Natives migrating to the East[wa]rd occupies all our attention. We have now eleven O-mi-aks at the Ship, four went on the day before yesterday, and there are two at the Next Island making 7 in all, and taking an average of three men for each would give fifty, but counting women

---

[1] After the Nirliq rendezvous was over, some or all of 'O-mi-ga-loon's' party must have continued eastward to trade with the Mackenzie Eskimos at Barter Island, Alaska – because a year later a group of Mackenzie Eskimos passed one of these printed slips to the *Enterprise* in Camden Bay, Alaska (Collinson, 1889, p. 315). See below, p. 427, n. 3.

& children more than double that number of individuals have gone. And there are a good many who have not yet started.

It appears to be a tour of pleasure as far as the Colville River, where they meet the friendly Nuna-tagmutes [sic] who they seem very fond of & speak in raptures of the dancing & eating they enjoy[1] togeather [sic] from thence a select party extend themselves to barter Island, leaving much of their lumber & perhaps smaller children until their return, the women go on until a day's journey or so,[2] of meeting the Eastern people, when the men advance & conclude their business as expeditiously as possible. The journey from the Colville occupies them about 10 days, which they seem to make against a contrary wind, as their return to Pt Berens only occupies two days & they speak of sleeping that time in their boats. The journey from this [sic] to the Colville is ten days allowing them ten more to enjoy themselves with their friends the Nunatagmiutes, it would bring their depature [sic] for the East[wa]rd on the 25th of July which Doctor Simpson has calculated from the party who followed Com[mande]r Pullen at Pt Berens on the 5th of August[3] being then on their return from barter Island. The time of their annual visit never probably differing more than three days. From this it may be concluded that the Esquimaux make ⅓ of their summer journeys by the time a ship or even Ships boats become available, which gives them a season so much longer at a time when the weather is usually very fine. Were it otherwise and they confined themsevles to the season of open water only, their excursions must of necessity be very limited. Their return for the winter, takes place as we experienced last year, about the 10th of September.

Our friends who encamped last night have given us the benefit of their society for the day, their object in so doing, is to beg tobacco a pursuit they have been most diligent in, but their success has not been great, as the presents given last night were the last. We have now a very large party on the spit, but they all move forward in the morning. Our employment has been preparing the boats provisions, and getting everything ready for their departure, but the continuance of a Westerly wind gives us no hope of open water at present.

[1] See John Simpson's description of the trade rendezvous at Nirliq in Appendix Seven below, p. 505.
[2] See Appendix Seven below, p. 538.
[3] Pullen gave the date as 11 August 1849 (Great Britain, 1852a, p. 27).

Wednesday July 6th A fine morning with the wind still from the Westw[ar]d. Our neighbours on the spit all moved forward at 4 Am. And were succeeded by five more O-mi-aks. They halted at the Ship for a final begging match, and made an attempt to steal some rope, to leave a parting impression of their unchangeable propensity. They moved forward during the forenoon, and took advantage of the favourable breeze to set their skin sails, which must lighten their labour much in dragging. I avail myself in this place of an interesting remark from Doctor Simpson's journal, relative to this people. 'The indulgence with which children are treated by these people has been a subject of frequent remark to us. Lately we had an instance of it in a small boy who not receiving at once something he asked for, went for a piece of wood with which he struck his friend & cut him over the eye. This was taken in very good part by the man and some time after the child was seen attempting to repeat the blow. This indulgence in childhood must affect the character of the full grown men and indeed they act towards us in a similar way first begging for tobacco & then threatening us if it is not given. However, if their feelings are easily excited in this absurd way, they have a merit of great patience and good humour under privation, and I am inclined to believe they are by no means vindictive, or in general capable of bearing malice long, as the Red Indian is described to be.'

The provisions were placed in the boats when afloat today and I was glad to find they did not bring them deeper than good sailing trim. We are only waiting for a change of winds to open the ice, when they will be started.

Thursday July 7th The wind is still from the Westw[ar]d moderate with occasional snow showers. We have laid out a bower Anchor to the S.W. as we have nothing to Keep us off the Shore with the winds from that quarter. I made an excursion across the bay today to the point where the spit of Pt Barrow joins the main land, called by the Natives Pering-ni-ak[1] in our chart & summer camp. I was accompanied by Doctor Simpson & Mr Gordon[,] Mate[,] with one Seaman, my object being to find out the best available track for the boats, and

---

[1] This is the site of Pirginik, an ancient occupation site which is shown as 'Pergniak' on some charts and is known archaeologically as 'Birnirk' (Ford, 1959). It is at the base of the Point Barrow sandspit (about three miles from the point itself), a place where vast flocks of eider ducks, returning to the south in the summer, cross from the Beaufort to the Chukchi seas. In the nineteenth century, as today, the Eskimos used this as a summer campsite to catch large numbers of ducks with their bolas. Its standardized spelling today is Bernirk (Orth, 1969, p. 127).

to observe the state of the sea ice & position of the open water. The travelling on first leaving the Ship appeared impossible for the transit of boats, from the depth of the pools in which several holes occurred and the uneveness of the surface, but after a little time we pronounced it practicable. We found two families encamped on the land, one from Cape Smyth, the other from Pt Barrow, the latter being somewhat of old acquaintances. The man accompanied me out on the sea ice for two miles to the Westw[ar]d but I found the late Westerly wind had completely closed the ice, having no water to be seen in any direction. Which made me form the idea of taking the boats over the ice to the South[wa]rd until we fell in with it. Whilst I was away Doctor Simpson went shooting round the pools, 'he found birds of the snipe Kind,[1] and a few of similar habits pretty numerous – And a good many of the long tailed duck[2] were feeding in one of the ponds, several geese & a few eider duck were seen on the wing – He did not see a flower – only a few grasses & a plant the leaves of which the natives sometimes eat, it is not yet in bloom'[3] –

On arriving on board arrangements were made for the departure of the boats to the South[wa]rd.[4]

Friday July 8<u>th</u> The day was fine with little wind shifting gradually from West to North. All our work for the day has been preparing the boats, getting them lashed on the sledges & the provisions stowed on Native sledges to accompany them. I have arranged to go with an auxiliary party of ten counting myself & Mr Seath the Carpenter, to be provisioned for six days, taking four in addition for the boats, so as to start them with their original supply of 34 days. I hope the wind will favour us & open the ice, otherwise we shall have a long drag.

Saturday July 9th The morning was dull with a light wind from the N.E. at 7 Am. I left the Ship with the two boats[5] & three sledges carrying their provisions, to convey them to the open water. Our party made twenty in all. The two boats crews and their officers Lieut Vernon & Mr Gordon Mate making ten in addition to my Auxiliary party of the same number. As we were all armed, and the Natives very much distributed about the country, we had no fear of

---

[1] The common snipe (*Gallinago gallinago*).

[2] Oldsquaw (*Clangula hyemalis*).

[3] Maguire is no doubt paraphrasing from John Simpson's journal.

[4] Maguire estimated (Great Britain, 1854a, p. 182) that from 4 July to 7 July 1853, 150, with 27 to 30 umiaks, passed the *Plover* heading east. The winter-time population of Nuvuk was approximately 300 people.

[5] A gig and a whaleboat (Great Britain, 1854a, p. 183).

any interference on their part. When we got clear of some deep pools near the ship our progress was very good, until the Sledge on which the gig was carried began to complain & in passing over some rotten ice, the boat fell through it & in extricating her the sledge was broken beyond all repair. Under these circumstances I thought the most expeditious mode of proceeding was my returning to the Ship with Mr Seath the Carpenter & one man to carry back the old sledge with the dogs, and construct a new one as quickly as possible leaving the rest of the party to await our return. Our delay at the Ship was little more than two hours, so that we were again moving forward with the boats by 3 P.M. And reached the Spit about 4.30. We found here a much larger assemblage of Natives than we were prepared for, but they were not uncivil & rendered us good help in carrying the boats across to the sea ice, over the shingle spit, a little more than a tenth of a mile in width, which we should have had much difficulty in doing by ourselves. The party numbered over sixty in all, 3 of them being Cape Smyth people & the remainder Point Barrow. After the transit across was effected in which it required great vigilance to prevent theft, they were all made happy with some tobacco, and we proceeded on to the South[wa]rd to increase our distance as much as possible from them before we encamped. We were followed by a few troublesome characters who, I found it difficult to shake off, and when every other argument failed, they said they were going our way & of course had as much right to it as we had. We found the ice very irregular & bad for getting the boats along, as we proceeded to the S.W. & did not halt until 11 P.M. when we imagined we were far enough to be clear of the Natives, but we had plenty of them at our encampment. However, they all went away on being desired by Lieut Vernon when we wished to sleep.

Sunday July 10th Wind N.E. & weather cold & cloudy – According to my previous custom I continue the journal of the Ship unbroken although not on board. Copying any information the Ships log does not afford me from Doctor Simpsons journal.

'Since the breeze has sprung up from the N. E. a water sky has been apparent in that quarter, gradually extending itself to West but from our Mast head it only looks like a lane of water. There are but few Natives on board today.'

The party with the boats proceeded at 11 Am for Cape Smyth keeping close along shore. Two Native companions from Noo-wook left us here to return, pretending their wives would be very anxious about them, but in reality they had a dislike to being seen with us by the Cape Smyth people. The first part of the days journey was a little difficult for the gig, but we soon got on to good ice, and got on fast, accompanied by Natives most of the way.

At 4.30 we arrived at the Village of Cape Smyth & at a time that I wished to get on as fast as possible to avoid the annoyance of the Natives, the sledge carrying the whaler broke down & obliged us to stop to repair it. This was done without any interference & no thefts, thanks I suppose to the experience gained by our team in twelve months of such watching.

When we proceeded from Cape Smyth, a little display of feeling took place. The Natives who had previously assisted in dragging the boats, all ceased togeather [sic] & looked on to see if our men could get them on without assistance, who finding themselves left in such a way were rather put on their mettle, and they stepped out in good earnest, which the others seeing were glad to assist again. We halted at 11 P.M. two miles South of Cape Smyth –

<u>Monday July 11th</u> Fine weather with the wind from N. E. The employment of the crew on board was getting water off & other small jobs. Very few Natives were about.

The party with the boats started at 11 Am & found the travelling pretty good. We had natives about our encampment all the time we slept & many of them slept in the open air. We were joined by two native O-mi-aks on their way to the South[wa]rd, one to Icy Cape & the other to some river emptying itself into Peard bay.[1] Two hours after starting we heard a report from a Native that Sables was Killed, this was afterwards modified to his going to be Killed the next day, this report had the effect of taking away our Native guide 'Iwatsa' as he is the brother of the intended victim's wife & was anxious to go back and protect her. This I could make no objection to, however much I regretted his going back, which I felt to be a great loss to our boats.

At 5.50 we halted at a place the Natives told us was the best adapted for launching the boats, & where the water seemed at a

[1] The Kugrua River, presumably. In today's nomenclature Peard Bay merely comprises the waters that are enclosed by the Point Franklin sandspit and by today's Sea Horse Islands. To the British, however, Peard Bay was the waters between Point Franklin and, approximately, 'Refuge Inlet' (Walakpa Bay). It should also be borne in mind that in the British nomenclature the 'Sea Horse Islands' were the low sand islands between Point Belcher and Point Franklin, whereas today they distinguish the sand islands southeast of Point Franklin.

distance of two miles from the shore. In order to satisfy myself as to the practicability of it, I walked to the sea accompanied by Lieut Vernon, & although we were of opinion the water was very tempting, the hummocky nature of some parts of the ice was considered impassable for our boats and left us uncertain as to the best steps to be pursued, as by carrying the boats further South we increased our distance from the water, and would lose the assistance in Natives that we had now with us, and who all spoke of this being the best place to launch them. I was fearful of stoving them, otherwise there appeared to me no objection, as the water seemed very open & had the appearance of running along shore in the desired direction. On reaching the encampment I was quite uncertain to our future proceedings and determined to sleep on it, before deciding what was to be done. The night was wet, with the wind Easterly.

Tuesday July 12th The wind inclines to the S.E.d. 'We had but few Natives near us and one of them whom we know by the name of Union Jack[1] from a coat he wore in the winter, made of a flag, was inclined to make himself disagreeable & was sent away by Mr Hull the Commanding officer. This is the same man who took a prominent part in treating badly the men who by invitation visited the Village in the winter. He is also a Cape Smyth man & is spoken of as one of our enemies by the Noo-wook people. One of the visitors invited Doctor Simpson & Mr Hull to the Village as there are but few people there now. He expressed the sentiment so common amongst his people that they will be sorry at our departure as tobacco will be scarce. This is the true state of the case as we have no hold on their affections. The women who are slaves to a great extent at home like us best as they are treated with as much civility as their husbands & even more so, as they are more communicative & less inclined to steal, besides which they are well paid for their sewing which is necessary to us.' The employed [sic] on board, has been getting up Iron work from between the tanks to complete the survey of the Warrant officers stores –

At 7 Am Our party with the boats were ready to move forward and as the weather was favourable, I decided to attempt the transit to the water from where we were, and started assisted by a large party of Natives & sledges, which enabled us to clear the boats of every

[1] 'Ne-lick-tua' or 'Ne-lick-tuma'.

244

thing, and by great caution & good fortune they were launched & shoved off by noon, with a favourable breeze which they held for 8 hours, a time I had considered almost sufficient to take them past the last floe.[1] The Natives returned with me to the shore to receive their well earned award of tobacco, which I had much satisfaction in giving them as they behaved and assisted us admirably. I now retraced my steps towards the Ship with the Auxiliary party, passed Cape Smyth without any trouble from the Natives, and halted for sleep 1 mile north of it at 8 P.M. The night turned out Calm with heavy rain.

Wednesday July 13th 'The wind came round to the West[war]^d today and Keeps at that point with fine weather. Sables with his boat & crew with all their travelling baggage came on board this morning. A dread of the Knives of the Cape Smyth (Oat-Kea-rum)[2] people having prevented his sleeping the last two nights he came to the ship to be out of the way – as his life is threatened now that his friends are absent from Noo-wook, for having cheated a Cape Smyth man out of an axe or some such article.[3] He was told he had better pitch his tent on the spit, but as it would have the appearance of taking a part in a personal quarrel on the part of the Ship besides protecting a swindler who was only threatened by one man, it was suggested to him that he might feel himself safe enough with his body guard at Noo-wook & he with[d]rew again to the Village in the Evening with his boat & most of the baggage –'

I arrived on board at 1 P.M. with the Auxiliary party all well except one man who had been more or less unwell from cold all the time he was away – I was accompanied to the Ship by two Cape Smyth families who had rendered us good assistance all the way with the boats. I invited them to return with me in consequence, to receive some more useful presents, than I had it in my power [to] give them when away – They had every Kindness shown them &

---

[1] Shore fast ice.
[2] The village of Utqiarvik.
[3] Ernest S. Burch, Jr (1974) has explained how in northern Alaska in the nineteenth century there was a clear distinction between feud and warfare. The putative case of the Cape Smyth people attacking the *Plover en masse* would properly have been considered warfare, the object of which was the annihilation of another population. Robert Spencer (1959, p. 79) has written that 'offenses relating to property would not result in killing'. 'Angunisua' ('Sables') therefore was probably already involved in a feud between family groups which had been touched off by a murder, as Maguire's entry for 9 February 1854 indicates.

were sent to sleep in one of our tents pitched on the spit quite loaded with presents, & they returned home the next day . . .

Thursday [July] 14th The wind is still westerly and light, with rather cloudy weather. The depth of the water between the ice and the Shore prevented the Natives coming off today, who however were by no means numerous. 'There is a Native bitch on board which was purchased at "Garesk"[1] in the spring of /51 which has always shown great affection not only for her own young but has been known to add to her family by stealing others. At present she has a litter nearly the same age as those of her daughter now a year old & she manifests the same regard for all. In the beginning of the winter when the other dogs were afraid to trust to the new ice she came to the Ship from the Island & carried to her brood then half grown a piece of blubber. Today she has appeared restless & seems to entertain an instinctive dread of the ice on which her house is placed along side the ship, and tonight has carried one of her grandchildren through the water about four inches deep and brought it on board. The ice is now so rotten that several of our men have fallen through lately & it would seem that the bitch has some foreshadowing of her location being in danger of giving way beneath her.'

Friday July 15th The breeze this morning and all day was about E.S.E. weather rather cloudy as it has been for several days and the depth of the water between the Ship & the Shore prevents many natives visiting us. 'Whilst calculating on the progress the boats might have made with this favourable breeze a party of people were observed coming down the spit from the village and various surmises were made of what their object could be in coming down at eight o'clock in the evening soon after they were made out to be tracking an O-mi-ak & sixteen heads were counted in all by Doctor Simpson, whose astonishment on seeing with the glass Mr Gordon get out of the boat was so great that he could not believe his eyes & immediately asked the Corporal of the Watch who verified the matter, and ran down immediately to report it to me. I went without loss of time to meet them, not in an enviable frame of mind as may be supposed, but when I found the full number of the party I was comparatively easy – It appears that on Wednesday night finding the ice closing on them they managed to get the boats on the floe and fancied themselves safe through drifting to the North[wa]rd. The ice

---

[1] Today, Unalakleet, Alaska, on Norton Sound.

continued to press in towards the land crushing the floe and piling it up to nearly twenty feet in hight [sic] and at length the floe gave way beneath them & the gig was partly filled with the pieces & could not be withdrawn further towards the land. The Whaler a lighter boat was also stove and as she could not be brought further the whole party were obliged to make the best of their way to the shore before the ice would ease off as it seemed inclined to do and leave them on detached pieces. Fortunately the danger so imminent was of that slow but overwhelming nature that they had time to provide themselves with three days preserved meats & their arms & Ammunition – And still more Providentially fortunate they met with no impassable lanes of water through a distance estimated at six miles to the beach in Peard bay – Coming to an Inlet they found Natives by whose boats they were able to cross & met with no obstruction on their way to the Ship. Arrived at the summer camp (Pering-nieng)[1] they found several native tents from whose inhabitants they asked for a boat to bring them on by the lane of water along the beach to the ship, but finding them divided in inclination to comply and consulting together & Lieut Vernon observing a woman, herself friendly disposed, to be in great trepidation directed the party to uncover their arms. This demonstration of readiness to assist had the happy effect of settling the question in their favour, and the man, Union Jack,[2] who was supposed to be the most evil disposed was also the one who showed most alacrity in getting the boat. After this their progress appears to have been uninterupted' –

Such is the account of the misfortune. which I have copied from the journal of Doctor Simpson, as being more to the purpose than any one I could produce, at all events until I receive the journal of Lieu[t] Vernon which is not yet complete.[3] None of the party are able to give as they consider any idea of the overpowering force with which the land floe was slowly cracked beneath them, crushed into fragments and piled up to a hight [sic] the lowest and most guarded estimate of which was 18 feet [sic] –

The loss of the Ships boats is a heavy misfortune, but when it is considered that the whole party have found their way safely to the Ship, one is too much rejoiced to give a look of regret after the boats which could not have been saved. L[t] Vernon speaks in high terms of the crews, not a man of whom expressed any opinion about deserting

---

[1] Pirginik. See above, p. 240, n. 1.   [2] 'Ne-lick-tua' of Cape Smyth.
[3] Vernon's report is Appendix Five below, pp. 495–7.

the boats until he had decided on doing so, when he concludes from their manner, they thought it was high time, And he describes them as obedient, cool & intrepid from the beginning of the danger until their arrival on board.

On their return they found the naked body of a woman & child & having mentioned the circumstance to some natives they immediately said they must be those of the widow & her child whose husband was lost on the ice in the winter & who afterwards became the second wife of Sables. He was said to have treated her badly and she ran from his hut in consequence, becoming a victim to exposure when seeking an asylum down the coast.

Sables is still on board & told Doctor Simpson today that his life was threatened by four men in consequence of the old chief (O-mig-a-loon) having cheated some one out of an axe. This seems improbable and he is most likely to have been the cheat himself. Our Employment for the day has been airing the spare sails, and getting the sail bins well scraped dry, after the thaws . . .

Sunday July 17th . . . I have had serious thoughts of dispatching a party in a Native O-mi-ak to Keep our appointment at Cape Lisburne,[1] but in weighing the matter maturely, & consulting with Lieu^t Vernon (who was most anxious as far as he was personally concerned to undertake the trip) and also with Doctor Simpson whose judgment is always clear, I gave up the idea, as no means in our power could reach Cape Lisburne by the appointed time – And the Ship having to wait for the return of the party would delay us to a time that would render it impossible to regain this place as a winter station in the event of it being so ordered. With these considerations and a present prospect of an early release, I have thought it best not to divide our small force at a time when the services of every one may be required to extricate the Ship – But to take the earliest opportunity of going south as we ought to do to get supplies.

In the afternoon Sables made up his mind to return to Noo-wook having heard I suppose that his enemies had gone elsewhere, but his excuse was to get food which could be as easily sent for. In fact it may be said that not being 'Victualled on board' he was starved out. This rainy weather too rendered his habitation under the Forecastle uncomfortably wet – . . .

Monday July 18th A fine day with the wind at N.W. The Surgeons

[1] To rendezvous with the *Plover*'s supply ship.

report this morning I was sorry to find included two cases of sore gums from scurvy. And as he recommended exertions being made to procure birds in the absence of any other fresh food, I sent a party of two men with an officer immediately to the neighbouring Island, who returned in six hours with eight duck which were placed at the disposal of the Surgeon for the use of the sick. A party of Natives from Cape Smyth visited the Ship, and wishing to establish a good feeling in that quarter, I made them a present of some tobacco. The Natives from Point Barrow who were on board spoke confidently of the Ice easing off to the North[wa]rd but I could see nothing of it myself. Nor could Mr Hull the 2^d Master from the masthead. Some of the officers speak of an observable motion in the hummocks outside, but I have not remarked it. Our employment has been lashing our spare spars on the ice chock outside – Roping a gaff top sail – and repairing the dingy – In the evening a shooting party were again dispatched who returned at 11 P.M. with six duck –

Tuesday July 19th . . . The Natives are now to a certain extent cut off from the Ship, by the depth of water between us & the Shore, making it necessary to have a boat to Keep up the Communication – We had a few down from the Village, but they bring us nothing to barter. A few birds were procured from some Cape Smyth people, the only thing of the sort we have had for several days. Our Noo-wook refugee Sables came again at noon with his wife & boy to take up their quarters on board. He appears to be a new man, as his enemies for the present have desisted in their pursuit of him, and have gone away on the land to hunt.

We have got one of Halkets boats[1] set up for the use of our sportsmen, it is very convenient and admirable in its contrivance, but here the Native O-mi-ak is fully as light, draws as little water, is capable of accomodating a large party, & seems to be preferred. Our Employment of the day has been getting the stream chain in & stored away, and securing & covering the booms preparatory to hoisting in the launch.

I have been endeavouring since the return of our boat party to procure a good Native O-mi-ak or two, but with no success as they seem to part with them very reluctantly.

[1] The Halkett boat, designed by Lieutenant Peter Alexander Halkett in the 1840s, was one of the first inflatable boats manufactured in England. It was nine feet six inches long and four feet nine inches wide and was made of black waterproof canvas. Halkett boats were carried on several of the Franklin Search expeditions (Jones, 1958, pp. 154–8).

Wednesday July 20th . . . Sables who I sometimes call our refugee comes occasionally to sleep on board, with his wife & boy, whether for the purpose of avoiding his enemies, or of more perfectly establishing his passage to the South[wa]rd in the Ship, is not certain . . .

Friday July 22d . . . We have but few natives come near us at this time and we receive no information from them. Our refugee Sables slept on board again tonight. He has been installed in what was originally intended for a sick bay, but used as a storeroom. He was promised it during his passage in the Ship to South[wa]rd, & I did not intend to allow [him] into it until we started, but the wet state of the decks today, induced me to change my mind . . .

Saturday [July] 23d . . . Very few Natives about us. The widow of the poor man who was Killed lamented to me today the prospect of the Ship going away. I could not kept [sic] thinking that she had good reason to recollect the Ships Visit, but I feel assured there is not any ill will borne to us by her or any of her family, whatever others may feel on the subject. We are in a state of preparedness for taking advantage of the first opening the ice may give us – to make our escape. A shooting party went away in the evening & returned at 11 P.M. without getting a bird. The temperature of the Ice is 34° [1.1°C] which of itself must have a considerable affect in thawing the ice . . .

Monday [July] 25th . . . The Natives brought us a report this morning that our boats that had been deserted, were drifted near the Shore at the Sea Horse Islands and their contents taken from them by the Natives. The tobacco & other things will have made a fine prize for them, which I am sorry for, as getting possession of so much valuable property to them, might give them an idea of attacking small parties for a similar booty.

There has been no end of the reports flying about the Ship today, all originating in one brought also by the Natives, that some of them had heard a ships guns firing to the West[wa]rd in the offing. Our people seem to have amused themselves enlarging this into a steamer setting up Rockets & other such unlikely things. About 11 P.M. we had a good deal of drift ice setting past the Ship, but not sufficiently close or heavy to strain the cable. The night was dull with a breeze at N.W.

Tuesday July 26th The same weather with a West wind. I left the Ship after breakfast this morning in our Native O-mi-ak, accompanied by

Doctor Simpson, Messrs Hull & Wright & four seamen, intending to cross the western spit and go as far down the coast as Cape Smyth to observe the state of the ice. We paddled across the bay & tracked along the Spit to the Summer Camp where we usually cross, but we found the ice did not offer the slightest lane of water, although there was a perceptible Northerly drift in the ice in shore. But the hummocks & heavier ice outside was stationary. The Natives a few of whom only are remaining told us the ice was all leaving & we should have a lane of water next day. There did not seem a sufficient certainty of this to induce me to remain for the chance, and after devoting some little time to shooting and getting our dinner cooked we returned to the Ship.

The Surgeons report of the state of the health of the Ships C^o is unfavourable, a tendency to scurvy having again shown itself, & only a month after a plentiful supply of Venison which lasted two months – This week nine cases are under treatment, all very mild at present with the exception of two to whom it has been found necessary to issue preserved vegetables, although our supply is by no means adequate to our wants. When it is considered that the present is the most favourable season of the year for procuring additions of game, fish, [e]t^c and the one at which scurvy least often shows itself, the necessity of getting other supplies becomes very apparent – without doing so another year passed on our present resources would be attended with serious results in those whose disease is barely Kept in check at present. As the position we occupy is five miles from the land, we have not been able to procure any of the wild vegetables & scurvy grass[1] that ships have usually found in this climate – the benefit of which has been fully appreciated. We also expected a good supply of birds at this season, but very few have been procured, the Natives require for themselves nearly all they Kill & our sportsmen have met with but indifferent success –

Wednesday July 27th A calm fine morning. It afterwards became dull & misty, with light V[aria]ble winds. There is some loose ice in the bay, that sets backwards & forwards with the tide, without its coming near the Ship in a heavy body. In the afternoon as the bay was perfectly free from ice, a party of officers & men under Lieu^t Vernon went to haul the Seine but they met with no success. Doctor

---

[1] Scurvy grass (*Cochlearia officinalis*) is a circumpolar coastal plant, the leaves of which can be used as an antiscorbutic (Hulten, 1968, p. 499).

JOURNAL OF ROCHFORT MAGUIRE

Simpson & Mr Jago have been preparing some printed notices to be left with the Natives at this place, in the event of our not getting back here again, if ordered. A large mark has also been erected on the spit close to our winter station – With a suitable notice. The evening became wet & we had a hope of a breeze from the Southw[ar]^d, but it came from West –

Thursday [July] 28th . . . one passenger Sables came down this afternoon in his baidar & sleeps on board, he seems to think the ice will soon be gone – We have not many other Visitors at present, as they have few O-mi-aks disposable to come down in, & the open water in the bay cuts them off from the Ship if travelling on foot . . .

Sunday [July] 31st . . . Just before church time a young native & his wife paddled off on three inflated seal skins,[1] after making several vain attempts, & no person who saw them when successful could accuse of them of being wanting in nerve to venture themselves as they did [sic] Mr Hull went across the bay this morning in the small boat, to watch the state of the ice, & returned in the evening reporting a lane of water close in shore as far to the south[wa]rd as he could see. This makes the best piece of news we have heard for some time, & promises an early departure – our passenger Sables & his suite came down in the afternoon with their provisions for the voyage & baggage – Madame looked overheated & greasy as if she had been participating largely in the preparations for departure – The evening was fine and a breeze sprang up from the E.S.E. –

Monday August 1st [1853] A fine clear morning with a light breeze from E.N.E. In consequence of the favourable report brought back by Mr Hull yesterday of the lane of water extending along shore to the South[wa]rd I left the Ship in the Launch at 7 Am accompanied by Mss^{rs} Gordon & Hull to examine its extent and see whether it offered us an outlet, and also to sound along shore to find how close we could approach in the event of necessity. Every thing seemed favourable to our purpose and I fully expected to get underweigh on returning on board but on approaching Cape Smyth I had the mortification to find the lane of water to terminate so close to the shore as not to allow the passage of a Native O-mi-ak. This is one of the disappointments connected with ice navigation that try ones patience, & requires to be borne with in addition to other perplexities we are liable to even

---

[1] I have been unable to find other references to this method of transportation in northern Alaska. George Lyon saw this means of transportation at Southampton Island in Hudson Bay (Lyon, 1825, opposite page 55).

under favourable circumstances – From the Cliffs on which the Village[1] at Cape [Smyth] stands, about thirty feet above the level of the sea, there was no water to be seen either along shore or in the offing – The ice to the Westw[a]rd outside of the land floe had a perceptible drift to the North[wa]rd and the Natives led me to suppose it would not be long before a lane of water would make to the South[wa]rd. Under these circumstances there was nothing to be done but return to Ship where we arrived at 7 P.M.

We found very few natives at Cape Smyth, and those were mostly old people. The town is about ¼ less than Point Barrow, and the situation I should think is much inferior, as the houses are built on a foundation of grass & swampy earth, which at this season is so sodden with wet, as to fill the passages leading underneath the houses with water, from which cause they are not very habitable And for their Skin summer tents, they are obliged to have a flooring of bords [sic] to Keep them off the wet. We met with no interruption from the people, and no sign of bad feeling was shown towards [sic] –

We have had very few natives on board today. Our passenger Sables is at the Village, the boy Kiowah is left in charge of the property. He gave L[t] Vernon some account of the Natives taking our boat[2] on shore from the ice, by yoking on numerous dogs to her. He said they were afraid to break her up . . .

Tuesday. August 2nd . . . Our passenger Sables came down to day and Doctor Simpson finding him in a communicative humour, touched upon the subject of the descent of the Noo-wook people upon us in the early winter – He said the Chief 'Omigaloon', Arksinra, himself and some of their adherents were against the movement, but being reproached with cowardice were obliged to join the others, and that when the great gun was fired he became so alarmed that he ran to the ship & threw down his bow & quiver, and then exerted himself to dismiss the people to their homes. This was probably true as he and the others of the peaceful party were the only ones acquainted with the destructive nature of fire arms and were consequently more afraid of those weapons which they knew we possessed in abundance . . .

Wednesday August 3[d] A good deal of light ice drifted into the bay

---

[1] The village at Utqiarvik at Cape Smyth, the present site of the town of Barrow.

[2] The boat was abandoned near Peard Bay by Lieutenant Vernon's party on 13 July 1853.

and past the Ship until 8 AM. When the wind veered to N.E. and the fog cleared away, leaving a fine day but no open water to be seen to seaward, which prevented my making another excursion in the boat to Cape Smyth, to see if any change had taken place in the ice. However, I dispatched Mr Gordon across the bay in the small boat to observe the state of the offing at Cape Smyth on his return he reported the ice in the same position as when visited two days previously, with the same northerly drift in that outside the land floe. He procured some Eider Duck & two small seal, the latter from the Natives at Cape Smyth who catch them in great numbers on the ice at this season and in the absence of any other sort of fresh food appear to be relished by our crew. Lt Vernon took the Launch to the town in the afternoon for a turn of water, being the first time that any of our boats have been there since last September.

Sable's Father was on board today as well as yesterday. Doctor Simpson asked him his age and he told him three score. This is the first native who has been able to tell his age. He also said Atkana who died some time ago was grown up when he was a very little boy, and Omigaloon was a lad when he was a man. The joints of all his fingers and his right Knee are stiff and deformed, probably from an attack of Rheumatism, and he says he has been in that state for ten years, and that it was brought on by working hard with an adze, probably a chill after being overheated at work.

The night was fine with a light wind from N. E. which Keeps the ice closely packed outside of us . . .

Sunday August 7th The continuance of an Easterly wind induced me to start in the launch this morning to examine the state of the ice about Cape Smyth. I left at 7 Am accompanied by Doctor Simpson & Mr Hull & with a favourable breeze soon reached our destination. In passing to the South, we observed the ice to be much opened from the late Easterly wind, and althought [sic] it was still fast to the shore about Cape Smyth, there was a lane of water leading out of sight to the South[wa]rd running parallel to and at about the distance of a mile from the shore. I walked some distance to the South[wa]rd of C. Smyth & thinking the chance of getting out worth the trial, I made up my mind to return at once and make the trial. Coming back the wind had veered to the North East which obliged us to beat. In standing in shore we picked up two Natives who we offered a passage to Point Barrow, but after making a stretch out and back, they were glad to be landed, being unaccustomed to the sensation of a boat under a press of sail, besides the spray flying over them, for which their skin dresses are badly adapted. In passing Noo-wook Doctor Simpson raced up to call our passenger Sables who was quite ready, & we got on board by 7 P.M.

As soon as the Launch was hoisted in, we weighed and left our Anchorage[1] that had afforded us security for eleven months and three days, being seven days later than Sir E. Parry left Melville Island in the year 1820. At a little after 9 P.M. we passed the City of Noo-wook the population of which seemed to have abandoned the insides of their houses & taken to the tops of them, to gaze upon the novelty of a ship sailing past there And to lament over the departure of their much prized 'Ta-wac'. Our Ensign was hoisted out of complement on the occasion, although I much doubt if it was understood. We now shaped our course along shore for Cape Smyth & passed it about 10.30 with a favourable wind and the prospect of a lead of water as favourable as we could wish . . .

<u>Monday August 8th</u> Our breeze gradually fell away after midnight, and at 2.30 I witnessed the unpleasant sight from the Fore Castle of a S.W. breeze travelling to us over the water, which soon took us aback, and made our situation far from agreeable, as we had a very narlow [sic] channel to beat in, with a thick fog & very heavy rain for about two hours, when we had clear weather but a contrary wind, with which I was sorry to observe by the grounded ice in shore, that we did nothing more than hold our own against.

At 9.30 Am a party of natives were observed coming off from the Shore, in a boat, I have mentioned previously our having heard that one of our boats had been dragged by them to the Shore. They now brought her off, as might be supposed stripped of every thing, however we were glad to get her in any shape, having no outside boat except the Dingy, and her good qualities in a sea way being well known & appreciated by all on board – We gave in exchange for her a native O-mi-ak & some tobacco, with which they took their leave of us. The man who had got possession of all the boats valuable cargoes, is well known to us, but he of course did not make his appearance and I believe what the other Natives previously told us, that he was afraid to break the boat up, or we should never have seen her again.

---

[1] This was a year in which the ice opened unusually late. In the nineteenth century whaleships usually counted on arriving at Point Barrow in the third week of July.

The weather during the day was calm with light v[aria]ble airs from the S.W. to which our sails were trimmed & braced about a thousand times to endeavour to gain a mile or two, but without doing any good as we found the current taking us back at the rate of 1½ miles an hour. At 6.30 P.M. seeing we did no good, and all hands requiring a little respite, we made fast to the largest floe piece within our reach until some change should take place in our favour. Whilst fast we found the Current setting us N.E. 1 mile an hour.

Our passengers are very quiet & desire to make themselves useful. They have had several serious alarms from the Ship coming in contact with the ice. A few Walrus and Narwhals[1] have been seen & two or three large flocks of ducks.

A 8 P.M. a light breeze springing up from North we cast off and made all sail, steering to the South[wa]r^{d} & S.E. as the ice allowed us for Peards bay [sic]. The sameness of this coast renders it difficult to distinguish one point from Another, but we supposed ourselves off Refuge Inlet on this day of our detention.

Tuesday August 9th We continued to run on with a light wind from N.N.W. with comparatively open water, but at times a very thick fog until 3 Am when the closeness of the Ice & thick weather made it necessary to shorten sail, & go very easy. At 4 Am we seemed brought to a stop. As the land floe was forced to extend unbroken from the shore to a distance of Nine Miles, and the ice to the West[wa]rd seemed too close for us to penetrate in that direction.

At 6 Am. an opening offering to the S.W. we bore up for it under easy sail, and after sustaining some heavy shocks with the ice, succeeded by 8 Am in forcing the Ship into comparatively open water, which increased as we advanced, and enabled us to shape our course for the Sea Horse Islands. At noon we had very little ice in sight, & were enabled to fix the Ship by observations, which placed us in Lat 70[°] 53['] & Long 158°05' Cape Franklin bearing N 74°W 12 miles.

At 45 minutes past noon we observed the Sea Horse Islands bearing S.S.W. (Mag[neti]c) but for some time mistook two remarkable hummocks on the main land in Peard bay for the northernmost Island (Cape Franklin)[2] but in drawing in shore discovered our mistake & hauled out for Cape Franklin West, and

---

[1] These were probably beluga whales (*Delphinapterus leucas*).
[2] Today, Point Franklin. See above, p. 243, n. 1.

shortened sail, as I intended landing there to put up a notice, of our having passed to the South[wa]rd in the event of any boats having been dispatched from the Ship waiting for ours at Cape Lisburne, but on getting off the Cape the wind was blowing too strong and rather more on shore than off, and the water too shoal 3 f[atho]ms to admit of my doing it. We consequently shaped a course under all sail along shore for Icy Cape keeping a good look for boats passing as long as the land was distinct. The Hummocks in Peard bay that we mistook for Cape Franklin, are a little higher, bare on the sides as if worn by the wash of the sea, and a little hollow on the top, whilst the Cape is like several hummocks placed togeather with sloping sides and all green with the vegetation.

In the afternoon the wind increased to a strong breeze with a good deal of sea, which was quite a novelty after being shut up for twelve months in the ice. Our passengers seemed to suffer a good deal from sea sickness, but bore up against it with a great deal of good humour. In the first watch we passed some loose pieces of ice, but the constant day light of this Lat. enabled us to avoid it. Our rate of travelling was now increased to 7 knots, which might be set down as the Plovers maximum. At midnight we had the wind registered 7 in force & calculated ourselves to be nearly off Icy Cape –

Wednesday August 10th In anticipation of having to haul up a little after passing Icy Cape, the Top sails were single reefed at 1 Am. and at 2 Having by our reckoning rounded Icy Cape we shaped a course S.W for C[ape] Lisburne & saw no more ice.

At 9.15 The cheering report of a sail standing in for the land was made, and soon afterwards Mr Gordon pronounced her to be a Man of War. This seemed to me to be too much in accordance with our wishes to be true. And I determined not to be disappointed, by disbelieving her to be so as long as possible. However, after the usual Amount of conjecture & opinions, she turned out to be the Amphitrite now hove to in our hawse, and on passing under her stern we had the gratification of receiving three Cheers from her crew, who seemed a vast host in our eyes unaccustomed for some time to see so large a number togeather [sic], our native passengers seemed to be much surprised at them, And perhaps the sight gave them as great an idea of our power as it was possible to convey to them. I went on board the Amphitrite a little after 11 Am. And was Kindly received by Captain Frederick and the officers. We found they had been laying off for our boats three weeks, and were beginning to have some Anxieties about us, when we made our appearance – Which seemed to be very opportune as they were on their way to Icy Cape to dispatch a boat party to Point Barrow. And as their boats are not adapted for such a service, or the crew accustomed to it, I consider it very fortunate the attempt was not made.

The news from England which most nearly concerned us, was that of the Rattlesnake coming out under the Command of my friend and help mate in the Herald for six years, Henry Trollope,[1] to be stationed for one year at Port Clarence, and bringing suitable supplies for us for the same time. The orders for the Plover for the ensuing year were discretionary as to remaining at Point Barrow, but as the case in point had not been provided for in the orders, viz– that of being obliged to leave from the ill health of a portion of the crew, but on their being removed & a good supply of provisions received, being able to return again. I thought our doing so was the course pointed out by the general spirit of my orders, and I made up my mind to do so if Possible. However as Port Clarence must be gained under any circumstances our course was continued for Cape Lisburne.

The Rattlesnake's late date of sailing[2] from England made it necessary to have a ship sent on before her to meet our boats, and for this service only the Amphitrite had been dispatched, as she brought nothing for us except 500 lbs of pemmican – And a few Carpenters stores – Our letters & every thing of interest or importance were in the Rattlesnake, and the general opinion seemed to be that she would be very late. I spent an agreeable day on board the Amphitrite talking over the events of the past year and returned on board at 9 P.M. The wind had gone down considerably so that our rate of sailing decreased by Midnight to ½ a mile an hour.

Thursday August 11th We had light variable winds through the night. As I was invited to breakfast with Captain Frederick & to bring our Native passengers on board to see the big Ship, I sent word to them to put on their good clothes and to be ready to pay their visit. When I went on deck a little before 8 Am I found them all ready, and dressed in the extreme of Esquimaux finery, so much so, that their appearance on going on board the Amphitrite made a very

[1] Henry Trollope had been Maguire's shipmate as a lieutenant aboard H.M.S. *Herald* from 1845 to 1851.
[2] The *Rattlesnake* left England in late February.

favourable impression. As they are really very fine specimens of their race, and appear in strong contrast with the wretched natives about Cape Lisburne. They were shown all over the ship, and treated as may be supposed with the greatest Kindness, notwithstanding which, I am told Sables who is naturally of a nervous & suspicious disposition, felt ill at ease particularly when the crew went to quarters and drew their Cutlasses. The large ten inch gun on the poop attracted its share of attention, and Sables was induced to take the measure of it, by putting his head into the Muzzle. In the evening the young men – Iwatsu,[1] Ne a wala joined the dancing in the waste [sic] & seemed to enjoy it uncommonly – But Sables seemed to think himself more secure in the Vicinity of the officers and sat on a gun near to where we were smoking –

We returned on board about 9 P.M. And as we were approaching Point Hope where our Point Barrow friends had decided upon landing, I made them a present each of something useful, either a saw or a small axe and good supply of tobacco, and sent them to bed, in very good spirits, and told them to be prepared for leaving the first thing in the morning. We now shaped a course to pass close outside of Point Hope[,] distant about twenty six miles, and ran during the night S.S.E. with a light wind at North.

Friday August 12<u>th</u> Our progress along shore to Point Hope was very slow. We did not sight it before 7 Am. & at 9.30 an O-mi-ak was observed coming out from the settlement, and soon afterwards came alongside. There was some shouts of recognition between our Point Barrow passengers and these people as they came up, but our passengers were too busy preparing for their departure to loose [sic] much time in conversation with the new comers. At 10 Am Sables and his crew took their departure with most cheerful looks but saying they were very sorry. The Point Hope people paddled away at the same time to the Amphitrite, laying some distance outside of us. We now steered off to close her, and I went on board to spend the day, the two vessels running S.S.E. with a light wind from the N.N.W. which shifted to N.E. in the evening after I returned on board, and came on thick with a misty rain.

<u>Saturday</u> [August] 13<u>th</u> After Midnight the wind veered to East & freshened to 5 in force. The rate of sailing averaging 5 knots. Steering S.S.E. at Noon – our Lat by observations was 66.63 and

---

[1] 'Sables's' brother-in-law; elsewhere, 'I-wat-sa'.

Long 168°32′ there being no bottom with 24 fms. In the afternoon we lost the wind & by 6 P.M. we lay with our head to the South[wa]rd, becalmed.

Sunday [August] 14th At 6 Am a breeze sprung up from N.W. with a thick fog in which we ran for the day in close C° with the Amphitrite, the wind gradually freshening throughout. During a break in the forenoon & afternoon Mr Hull obtained some flying sights which with our reckoning gave us our position sufficiently near to run for the Straits.[1] The Fair way rock (Diomede Isl[a]^{nds}) bearing at noon S10W49 miles. Our Lat was found to differ from the Amphitrites 12 or 13 Miles hers being to the North[wa]r^d placing her farther off which was afterwards accounted for by their allowing that much for current against them. Our Lat by double alt in the afternoon agreed nearly with our D.R.[2] which satisfied me we were near the truth. As we approached the straits the wind came from N.N.W. which blowing against the current, caused the usual short hollow breaking sea peculiar to this place. The Amphitrite was obliged to yaw about to Keep astern with us, Although she had only her Top sails, single reefed set, we were under all sail. A whale ship was observed to the East[wa]rd in a break of the fog, standing in towards the land under cruising sail.

At 6 P.M. the Amphitrite hauled up across our stern as I supposed to lay to and wait for a clear [sic], she reefed Top sails & Sounded. As I considered we should not be able to Keep in C° with her laying to from our leewardly qualities, & seeing that by the time we had shortened sail, and reefed we should have been out of sight of her, I continued on feeling pretty confident of getting through safely, with a deep sea lead going and a good look – Although the weather at times was exceedingly thick, and the Ship always steers badly, but running with a following sea, her course certainly cannot be calculated nearer than a point, which running for a passage only ten miles wide with imperfect sights & a strong current makes it uncertain which side of the channel you may be. About an hour after leaving the Amphitrite the weather cleared up so as to enable [us] to see to the distance of a mile, and soon afterwards we observed the Amphitrite to be again running but keeping some distance to the Westw[a]rd of us. At 9 P.M. the loom of the land about Cape Prince

[1] Bering Strait; a narrow and difficult passage, which, if attempted from the north, almost always includes a contrary current.
[2] Deduced reckoning.

Wales [sic] was made out, which we endeavoured to Communicate to the Amphitrite by night signal, but it was not made correctly, although understood by her. Captain Frederick thought however that there was no certainty of its being the land and continued his course to the South[wa]rd. We considered ourselves to be well through the Straits by 11 P.M. and hauled in E by N for Port Clarence – & lost sight of the Amphitrite.

Monday – August 15th At Daylight we observed the land from Cape Prince of Wales extending to Cape York & hauled up N.E. to close it. Soon after 5 Am. two Whale Ships were observed at Anchor near the Entrance of Port Clarence. On passing them at 8 Am. The Captain of one of the Ships came on board. His Ship the Levant of Sag Harbour,[1] had been in the Arctic Sea the last season, & during the winter in the Southern Hemisphere, he sailed to 68° South Latitude and got amongst some Ice there, but saw nothing except sperm whale for the capture of which he is not fitted, returning north[wa]rd he had touched at Chatham Island[2] where he laid in a stock of Vegetables [e]t^c for his crew, & touching at another Island in the tropics for water made again for this quarter. He has got 1,200 barrels of oil & wants 2,300 more. He gave us an account of an American Whaler being wrecked on the Coast of Asia some where about East Cape last Autumn[3] – And that the crew had been hospitably supplied by the Natives during the winter –

As the wind had nearly died away to a calm, and the Amphitrite had only now hove in sight from the mast head, I thought we could not employ the time it would take her to reach us, better than in endeavouring to get some fresh potatoes or any other supply out of these vessels. The gig was accordingly sent on board and succeeded in getting a supply for present use – and a promise for the next day of a considerable quantity – I wished also to get a boat, but they seemed reluctant to dispose of those they had, except for a very exhorbitant [sic] price. Our boat had returned at 11.30 Am and the Amphitrite having about the same time entered the Harbour, we proceeded in C° up Port Clarence for the Anchorage near Grantley Harbour. At 1 P.M. the Amphitrite anchored, but as we were to leeward it was 2

---

[1] Sag Harbor is on Long Island, New York. The other ship was the bark *Harriet Thompson* of San Francisco (San Francisco *Commercial Advertiser*, 1 October 1853).

[2] Southeast of New Zealand.

[3] The *Citizen* of New Bedford was wrecked on 25 September 1852 near Cape Serdze Kamen, Siberia, northwest of Bering Strait (Holmes, 1857).

oclock [sic] when we came to close inshore of her in 4 fms. The Launch was immediately hoisted out, and sent with a party to haul to seine, to endeavour to get some fish for our sick. Captain Frederick came on board, and in conversation relative to the reprovisioning of the Plover – He told me that he had made up his mind not to allow us to go to Point Barrow again. This determination of his surprised me not a little as it seemed so much at variance with his ideas of last year, which seemed to avoid all interference or taking any responsibility upon himself as to our movements when he really had orders relative to the ship. But this year he had none, and had come to Behrings strait only for the purpose of communicating with our boats at Cape Lisburne, as it was considered the Rattlesnake could not be in time. The launch returned at 8 P.M. having caught a small basket full of fish, but acceptable to our patients suffering from scurvy.

Tuesday August 16th In consequence of Captain Frederick's determination relative to detaining the Plover at Port Clarence, I took a letter on service to him this morning pointing out what my views on the subject were. He had in the mean time ordered a survey to be held on the Ship by the Carpenter & officers of his ship and on the health of the crew by the Medical officers present. Carrying out the survey on the Ship Kept the crew busily employed for the three days it lasted, as the head room in the fore peak had to be entirely cleared as well as the magazine and other places, that gave a great deal of work.

The launch was sent to the Whale Ships visited at the mouth of the Harbour yesterday, to procure a further supply of potatoes, onions [e]t^c And returned at 6.30 with a very good supply . . .

Wednesday [August] 17th . . . Another whale ship arrived at our Anchorage this evening. She came in for water. I met her Captain on board the Amphitrite where he had gone to consult the Surgeon in consequence of part of a cap in snapping a gun flying into his eye, causing him severe suffering for five or six weeks previously, a piece of the cap had in this time worked itself through the eye ball & had come out underneath, but it was supposed by the medical officer, that there was still some part of it remaining in the eye – The sight of which was much impaired but not destroyed, and I believe it was thought that with care it might be preserved. The information he gave relative to the success of the Whale fishing this season, was not very encouraging, as he described the weather & [sic] unusually foggy, and there was a great deal more ice met with than usual, but he remarked that it was of a much lighter character than he had been in habit of meeting in other years – Which I considered in some measure to agree with an opinion I have formed, that the season was an unusually mild one, but the absence of strong winds had left the Ice more undisturbed than usual.[1]

Thursday August 18th On going on board the Amphitrite this morning, I heard from Captain Frederick the result of the officers opinions on the survey of the Ships hull Which were to the effect that the Plover was unfit to be exposed to heavy weather or to content [sic] with ice, from this the Master Mr Crane dissented, and gave his opinion that she was fit. But as the attention of the surveying officers had been called (to a letter of mine written last year – wherein I state the Plover to leak considerably) previous to their commencing the survey – And the order also stating that it was a very late period of the season, which I begged to state was not the case – I urged the point of the Ship being perfectly equal to encounter the probable casualties of a passage to Point Barrow on which Captain Frederick came on board the Plover to hear the officers opinions here on that subject, and as they were of the same opinion, he decided to provision the Ship and to allow us to proceed according to my request – My arrangement was to complete the Ship for sixteen months, viz twelve months for our own consumption leaving four for the use of any parties that might fall back on us from the vessels in advance[2] – In the afternoon we were busily employed receiving coals and making arrangements for our departure, which I thought had better not be delayed, as I had no hope of the Rattlesnake reaching Port Clarence in time to be available for us this season.

Friday August 19th A very fine day with a moderate breeze at E.N.E. We were visited by a few natives but they seemed an unusually poor set. We got a small quantity of Venison & some fish

---

[1] In 1853 there were more than 150 whaleships cruising in the Bering Strait region (Bockstoce, 1986, p. 348). Maguire was right: strong spring gales can be as important as a mild spring in clearing the sea ice from the Bering Strait region.

[2] H.M.S. *Enterprise* and H.M.S. *Investigator*. The *Enterprise* was, at that date, heading back toward Bering Strait from Victoria Island. She was, however, stopped by the ice and forced to winter 250 nautical miles east of Point Barrow in Camden Bay, Alaska. M'Clure had abandoned H.M.S. *Investigator* in the spring of 1853 on the north coast of Banks Island during his third winter on that expedition. The crew walked to the safety of ships that were wintering in the eastern Arctic; thus they became the first men to traverse a Northwest Passage.

from them, with a good deal of trouble. The attention of every one was much taken up, receiving & stowing away provisions & coals. The men recommended to be removed by Medical survey, seven in Number, besides one invalid from rupture, and the man Dunstall who shot the Native at Point Barrow with Mr Wright midshipman, were discharged today to the Amphitrite for conveyance to England. And we received the same number of her crew who volunteered for Arctic service – Amongst the men removed by survey were the Sergeant of [and] Corporal of Marines, the only two remaining amongst the crew who had come out from England with the ship. They were both excellent characters, and a great loss to the Ship. Doctor Simpson is now the only person remaining who left England in the Ship.

As the crew of the Amphitrite gave a theatrical performance tonight at 7 P.M. to which we had all been specially invited, we ceased our labours of stowing holds a little earlier to allow our people to get the coal dust off themselves in time to appear – And on returning on board at ½ past 10 every body seemed to be much pleased with their evenings Amusement – The piece was the farce of Box & Cox concluding with a new Pantomime prepared expressly for the occasion entitled Fun, Foolery, Frolick & Mirth. The performers were composed of the crew and I believe all the arrangements were made by them, which seem to have been much to their credit.

Saturday [August] 20th The weather continued fine with light Easterly winds – Our employment of receiving & stowing away provisions was continued and completed today, leaving us all ready to take our departure, but as there was still a good deal of writing to be done, I arranged to wait a day longer to allow time for all accounts to be made out & transmitted – The wind shifted to S.W. in the afternoon, and afterwards died away, and in the 1st watch we had the wind from N.E. with fine clear weather –

Sunday August 21st Towards 8 Am the weather became misty with the wind from East, in force 4. The occupation of everyone today seemed to be writing letters, and in the evening, taking lease of our Kind friends in the Amphitrite, who had not spared themselves in supplying any of our little private wants to best of their power. At 6 P.M. The Top Gallant yards were got across and the cable shortened in. My public correspondence was closed about the same time & forwarded to the Senior Officer with a message of my intention to sail on the following morning –

The night was overcast & misty with the wind at E by N.

<u>Monday [August] 22nd</u> The morning was misty with a fine haze at E by S blowing straight out of this deep Harbour.

At 3.30 Am we weighed and made all sail, leaving the Amphitrite to calculate the probable length of our passage, as we had done the year previous, one day sooner, the 21st After the sail was made and the course shaped for the Entrance of the Harbour, I went below to lay down, and in a hour the officer of the watch reported what he called a likely sail for the Rattlesnake, as this seemed too good news to be true, I hardly dare hope it would prove so. However on coming on deck and looking at her, I could not but agree with Mr Gordon's report, she had all the appearance of a vessel that certainly was not a Whaler. And after a great many doubts and fears, mixed with a degree of uncertainty that was painful, we had the extreme gratification of making her out to be the Rattlesnake, and it was quite gratifying to witness the pleasing effect it had upon all on board, who were previously more or less dejected at our going away without our letters, and but poorly provided for another winter – As the Rattlesnake had to beat up some four or five miles, I left in the gig at 8 Am. Accompanied by Doctor Simpson Mr Jago to pull on board, having the Plover hove to in her present position, to be the better able to communicate the Rattlesnake's No. [number] to the Amphitrite. I was delighted to find my friend Trollope quite well, and I was soon satisfied as far as letters were concerned by receiving more than I had present leisure to read.

The two Ships Rattlesnake & Plover anchored togeather [sic] under the spit at Point Spencer at 10 Am – And set to work at once to supply & receive our provisions, clothing & stores [e]t^c sent from England. All of which were of the best quality & much needed by us. We had also a quantity of special comforts supplied, in the way of Wine, Port & Sherry, preserved Vegetables, onion powder & a French preparation of vegetables called Julienne, which of themselves seemed a guarantee against our being visited by Scurvy in the coming winter. Amongst other benefits, conferred upon us by the Rattlesnake were two Bullocks, which were now killed for our use, and as many live Hogs & fresh potatoes as we could conveniently stow. Providing stowage for all these good things, & reading our letters Kept every body well occupied for the day, which was gloomy & inclined for rain, the wind light from S.E.

<u>Tuesday August 23rd</u> The morning was fine & clear. Our work con-

tinued without ceasing for the day, and left us by 6 P.M. ready to proceed again on our voyage. But as it would take an hour or two to make out the necessary receipts [e]t^c, and the night turning out very wet, I arranged not to sail until daylight. A further change took place in the crew at this time, five men who were anxious to return home being allowed to do so in the Amphitrite, while they were replaced by men from the crew of the Rattlesnake.

Wednesday August 24th The rain ceased after midnight and a fine breeze sprung up at S.S.W. with which we weighed at 3.30 & ran along the land under all sail for Bherings Strait. At 10.35 the Fair way rock bore West and at Noon Cape Prince of Wales bore East (true). The wind had fallen very light at South, but the Current seemed to be setting the ship rapidly to the North[wa]rd. At 1.30 We we[re] boarded by a boat from the American Whale Ship 'R. Morrison' of New Bedford. She was laying to a Kedge, waiting for a wind to take her over the current to the South[wa]rd We received no intelligence of any importance from him, except that he considered this season to be a month later, than any former one he had experienced. We gave him some news papers and all the information we could, as to where we had seen whales, the position of the Ice to the North[wa]rd [e]t^c.

After the Whale boat shoved off we found on sounding the Well, that by some oversight a great deal of water had been allowed to accumulate in the Ship from not pumping her out at the proper time, and as I feared it might have reached the bread stowed in bulk in the Fore peak, It was cleared out and found to have escaped injury – At 8 P.M. We were taken aback with a shift of wind from N.N.W. & tacked every four hours, keeping in the stream of the Strait –

Thursday August 25th We continued to work to the North[wa]rd with the wind at N.W. Moderate & fine, Keeping about the Meridian of the Strait, to get all the benefit of the Northerly current – at noon we were in Lat 55°20' & Long 157°50' Point Hope bearing N12°E. 123 miles – At 3.30 In standing to the West[wa]rd the land of East Cape was observed S.W. and an hour afterwards the Diomede Islands S. by E. We had no change during the night, which was fine but a little squally.

Friday [August] 25th The day was moderate & fine but no change for us in the wind which remained steady at N.W. At Noon our observations placed us 55°41' Lat – and 167°23' Long, Point Hope bearing N.11°E 101 miles. After 8 P.M. The wind veered two or three points to the North[wa]rd with some heavy squalls.

Saturday [August] 27th Very little change in the weather. The wind has inclined to draw to the West[wa]rd for the day. Which has induced me to stand to the North[wa]rd although at the expense of getting out of the stream of current, as the wind did not allow us to lay up for Point Hope by three points, and standing into the Entrance of Kotzbue [sic] Sound seemed to place us out of all current.

Sunday [August] 29th Standing to the North[wa]rd all night. The land was observed at 2.30 Am about Cape Thompson – bearing N30°W. and by 8 Am we lay becalmed, drifting towards the land. I had been induced to close this shore, to get into the current marked on the chart as setting to the N.W. along the land, but whether we were not sufficiently close in or not to get into this stream, we certainly did not experience it, as we lay becalmed for the day & found the current setting North, true at the rate of about 1 mile an hour – At 5 P.M. we were favoured with a light breeze at S.W. and stood to the W.N.W. along the land for Point Hope. The wind increasing moderately with thick hazy weather.

Monday August 29th At 3 Am. we had run our distance for Point Hope, and as I wished to pass close to it, to pick up our Native friends from Point Barrow that we had landed there previously, We hauled in and at 3.30 made Point Hope, which we continued to work up for until 7 Am firing guns occasionally to attract notice – When finding there was no appearance of any boat putting off, We bore up under all sail, along the land for Cape Lisburne, Point Hope bearing S56°E 4 miles. The wind did not favour us for more than two hours, when it veered again to the North[wa]rd and we beat along the high land for Cape Lisburne. At 11 P.M. it having been previously calm a light wind sprung up at East with which we steered to the North –

Tuesday Aust 30th An Easterly and S.E. wind allowed us to make a good run to the North[wa]rd the Lat. ob[taine]^d at Noon 69°25′ Long 165° Icy Cape N50°E 89 miles – Cape Lisburne in sight S.5°W. The new hands who had lately joined had their arms issued to them today, and our number of muskets having been increased by 4. Every Man is now armed with one except the Cooks and Stewards – At 7 P.M. the wind headed & obliged us to take in our stud[din]^g sails & we continued for the night at N by E the wind at East –

Wednesday August 31st Sailing by the wind At E we came up with some streams of loose ice at 3.30 Am and continued our course until 10 Am. when the ice becoming closer we tacked to the S.E. to gain more open water. At noon the lat ob[serve]^d was 70°42' and Long 161°30' Point Barrow bearing N.68 E 111 miles. We found a current in the last 24 hours setting N 42°E 16 miles – Throughout the day which was very fine, and in the afternoon nearly calm we were surrounded by an immense number of Whales and Walrus. And it seemed to me that a Ship in pursuit of the former would have made a fine harvest in our position – without incurring much risk from the ice, as it was very light & open. During the afternoon we did little more than drift to the N.E. with the current at the rate of about 1 mile an hour – At 8 P.M. we were favoured with a light breeze from the South[wa]rd & Steered under all sail N.N.E. by E through loose sailing ice. Whales & Walrus still numerous particularly the latter, which might be said to be in swarms –

Thursday September 1st [1853] After midnight the ice became a good deal closer, obliging the course to be frequently altered to avoid coming in contact with it – At 2 Am I was awoke by the noise of the Walrus, a peculiar sort of hollow or deep grunt and knowing from it that the ice must be very thick round us, I went on deck and found soon afterwards that it was necessary to take in the Stud[din]g sails and look round, the ice becoming of a more heavy character than I had previously seen. By a good deal of pushing & driving to the S.E. we succeeded by 7 Am in reaching open water & steered E by S for two hours when we made the land about Wainwright Inlet and shaped our course N.E. for the Sea Horse Islands the wind blowing Moderate at S.W. and the weather very thick but occasionally clearing off sufficiently to show us our distance off the land.

At Noon Point Belcher bore East 4 miles, our course was now North along the shore of the Sea Horse Islands – Just about this time we experienced Another of those extraordinary low barometers, which caused me some anxiety at this critical point in our passage particularly with the wind at S.W. But fortunately it passed off as the former had done at Port Clarence, without producing any violent wind, a more moist state of the atmosphere with fog & heavy mist being the only changes observable –

About 2 P.M. the weather becoming a little clearer, some winter huts[1] were observed on the low land abreast of us, which we soon afterwards recognised as the Southern of the Sea horse Islands,[2] on which provisions had been buried by Captain Moore in a boat

---

[1] Probably the village of Atanik, northeast of Point Belcher.
[2] See above, p. 243, n. 1.

expedition to Pt Barrow in 1850.[1] Seeing two O-mi-aks pulling out for us the Ship was hove to, to allow them to come up, when we found that most of them were old acquaintances from Cape Smyth. They came on board in their usual boisterous way, and did not loose much time in expressing their wants in tobacco [e]t^c No intelligence that could be relied on, of the state of the coast to Point Barrow could be obtained from them, and their boats becoming endangered by the ice getting closer they were sent off – & we pursued our course for Point Franklin under what appeared as not very favourable circumstances, the ice in the offing being very thick & close in with the land.

The weather again became very foggy & the ice so close that it was with some difficulty we avoided coming into collision with it from the rapid way in which the Ship was drifted over the ground by the current & many of the heaviest pieces of ice being aground made this set the more perceptible – In this way we were carried stern on to a piece 27 feet high, of a cubical form sloping from one corner to the opposite, the bowsprit which I fully expected to see rigged in, was saved by a smaller piece Keeping the Ship of[f] it, and we drifted clear at the rate of 2 miles an hour. As we approached Point Franklin which is very shoal & with night coming on and thick weather, I would gladly have made the Ship fast to some of these grounded masses, but we were carried along at too rapid a pace to afford a chance of our doing so without running great risk of getting separated from some of our people – between 7 & 8 P.M. we were passing the Cape in from 4½ to 6 fms & hauled out under easy sail to clear the Shoal water until 8.30 P.M. when we shaped a course for the depth of Peard bay – N.N.E. and had a clear run for six hours which was quite contrary to my expectations, and I supposed we should have an a[n]xious night, & be much baffled with ice – The weather was cold and foggy with the wind at N.N.W. (true) –

Friday Septr 2nd At 2 Am. we were again stopped by the ice and obliged to steer again to the S.E. to avoid a heavy stream. the wind had also veered to W.N.W. which made it difficult for us to steer a free course through sailing ice – At 3 Am the land was observed in Peard bay – the wind shifting to N.W. & North, we could do no more than beat along the edge of ice extending from the land to a distance averaging five miles – The lane of water we were in being from two to three miles wide – At 10 Am the weather being very clear and no appearance of a lead into the land which I was anxious

---

[1] See Appendix Two below.

to close, to avoid being beset in the event of the wind shifting to the Westw[ar]ᵈ. We bore up for the slackest part of the ice S.E. and continued boring in shore until near noon, when we were brought to a complete stand still by some heavy ice, and as it would require some time to warp the Ship through it, sail was shortened to allow the people to get their dinner – After which the warps were laid out and the ship warped into slacker ice, when sail was again made in shore the soundings decreasing gradually from 12 to 4½ fms. At 4.30 we were close in shore and no lane offering in our course the ship was made fast for the night to a large irregular field of ice which was aground, 8 or 9 miles to the South[wa]ʳᵈ of Refuge Inlet.[1]

The wind today has been N.E. and from snow which fell constantly in the morning, it changed to rain in the afternoon which continued. The principal variety has been three bears seen since 3 Am when I was called to see the first, and was only up in time to get a glimpse of him. In forcing through the ice, one remained within shot a considerable time and Doctor Simpson made several attempts to get his rifle off, but by some unusual fatality it snapped until we had passed out of range – 'At present we have no great prospect of getting on unless a good breeze spring up from the East[war]ᵈ or S.E. to open the way for us. The current is an element in the question which seems difficult to determine the value of in opening or closing the ice.[']'[2]

Saturday Sepʳ 3ᵈ The wind during the night veered to the East[wa]ʳᵈ S.E. and S. W. and at 1 Am we had a lane of water along shore which gave us a promise of making a few miles. But it cost us more than four hours to extricate the Ship from a natural dock in the floe into which she had been warped. And on the wind shifting to the opposite point our position being to le[e]ward, and the young ice having formed round us so as materially to obstruct boats passing, it was not until a Kedge anchor had been laid out to windward of the floe, that the ship was got clear, in time to avoid being sealed up in our dock, by the ice drifting down before the wind. This was a lesson in the business of securing a ship, in the ice which on another occasion I should profit by, a dock in the floe is a very desirable thing to have as a retreat in case of necessity from pressure, but to be avoided when it is of importance to be ready to move as expeditiously

[1] Today, Walakpa Bay.
[2] It is not clear from whom Maguire is quoting, but Dr John Simpson's journal is the most likely source.

as possible. Having warped out to our Anchor we made sail weathered our late tro[u]blesome harbour by a scrape, and ran alongshore to the N.E. in a very promising lead of water – over an average bottom of 4 fms – At 7 Am. We passed two summer tents pitched on the summit of the cliff, – And soon afterwards the weather became so thick we lost the clear lead of water, and got lead so close in shore that we were obliged to make fast to the grounded ice in 3½ fms. The wind soon afterwards shifting to N.W. would also have tended very much to check our further progress.

As soon as the Ship was made fast, Mr Hull the 2nd master accompanied by Doctor Simpson went away in the gig to sound in shore, and to ascertain our present position by the land & on their return I found the water in shore was too shoal for our purpose, and that we were about one mile to the South[wa]rd of Refuge Inlet – The post erected by Mr Shedden[1] on its Southern Cape was found standing. We were also made aware of the unpleasant fact of having taken the wrong lead in the fog, by seeing a lane of water not ½ a mile outside of us running paralell [sic] with the coast, as far as could be seen, but to get into this it was necessary to go back about half a mile which the ice prevented our doing at present and were obliged to remain under our disapointment [sic] & await some changes in our favour – At noon we had a fresh breeze from West which obliged us to furl sails & make all secure. during the afternoon the ice closed round leaving us in a pool of water. The night was clear, the wind light at N.W., sky cloudy.

Sunday Sept[r] 4th There was no change in our favour this morning, and we were obliged to submit with our best patience to another days detention – The weather has been clear today giving a good view of the ice all round. The lane of water outside is still open and can be traced nearly as far as the eye can reach, but the wind at N.N.W. and the close state of the ice round us prevents our moving for the present – As our distance from Point Barrow was now much less, than (by retreating we should have found) the open water our fate lay between getting to our destination or wintering on the exposed beach we were lying off, the latter event being canvased by us for the first time today. After Noon. Several parties of men & officers went on

[1] Robert Shedden, the owner of the yacht *Nancy Dawson* (see above, p. 27), set up a post nearby in 1849. It is likely that this one was set up by T. E. L. Moore during his boat expedition to Point Barrow (Appendix Two below) in 1850. See also footnote 3 of Appendix Six.

shore to stroll about the Lakes on the Shore, and as they carried their guns a good many ducks and geese were procured, although it was the Sabbath and not generally kept by us in that way, our present state of inactivity & the rareness of such an opportunity was the reason for its being allowed – We were visited by some Natives from the huts passed yesterday, in an o-mi-ak, they brought a little venison for barter, and on going away stole a small brass lanthorn which was missed soon afterwards, and on their being followed in our small boat, were quite prepared to give it up when she got to them – In the evening we were favoured with a light promising breeze off the land, which I hoped would open a road for us before the morning

Monday 5th of September The wind during the night veered from N.E. to E.S.E. and at 3 am to S.E. when we commenced to warp the ship astern to place her in an available position, to make sail and endeavour to force her through the belt of ice between us and the open water, but this attempt failed from the closeness and heaviness of the ice forming too great a resistance for us to force through. And after 8 or 9 hours hard labour, the ship was again made fast to the floe we cast off from in the morning. The wind had in the meantime shifted to the West which would most probably close the lane of water outside, and made it necessary to relinquish the idea of doing anything further for the present – In the afternoon I left the ship in the gig accompanied by Doctor Simpson & Mr. Hull to sound close along shore and examine the state of the ice to the Southward. We found the sounding irregular, but in places the beach was sufficiently steep to allow the ship to be hauled within her own length of it, which was so far satisfactory, as with the present unfavourable state of the ice for advancing, I thought our chance of lightening the ship and hauling her up where we were, was preferable to that of getting out again to the South[wa]rd – After pulling a little better than a mile to North[w]ard we came to Refuge Inlet, which to people in our position had a most vexatious wanting in depth of water, otherwise its appearance was every thing that could be desired, and is a beautiful sheet of water, having two entrances but both so shoal that it was with difficulty we got the gig inside, although outside there is a depth of 13 and 14 feet close to – We landed on the North side of the Inlet in consequence of using some natives approaching us from the high bluff in that direction with whom I was anxious to communicate. They proved to be from Cape Smyth and seeing the ship under sail in the morning had come down the coast to see us. The 'headman' was an old acquaintance of mine, who had made himself very useful and friendly when we transported the boats over the ice in July. We ascended the highest point of land near where he pointed out to us, that the coast was open from Cape Smyth to Point Barrow, and that the lane of water outside which we had been unable to reach would lead to it. He proposed returning on board with us, which I willingly acceded to, and also brought a companion for him, with the hope of getting some useful information from him [r]elative to the ice, but from our not understanding their language sufficiently he proved of no use. However I am inclined to think we give them credit for more knowledge in that way than they possess, and for shipwork their experience [is] of not of much value. On returning on board at 3.30 p.m. the wind had increased to a fresh breeze from the S.W. with thick unpromising weather, the ice closed very much round the ship and in shore, but the lane of water outside was still open, though very foul. As we could do nothing at present but wait for a change in our favour, the sails were furled and the Ship made as secure as possible for the night. On the South point of Refuge Inlet there is a post left standing which was erected by Mr Shedden in the Nancy Dawson Yacht to point out the position of some provisions buried farther to the South, but the natives informed us that the bottle and paper had been taken away by some of their number –

Tuesday September 6th The ship laid without any disturbance from the ice during the night, and at day light 3 Am we commenced warping towards the lane of water outside, and after some hours labour got to the edge of it, but the wind blowing right on to the ice, made it necessary to lay out a kedge Anchor to haul sufficiently to windward to make sail. In doing which we found it dragging, & to avoid being drifted amongst the ice again, the warp was cut, and fortunately we succeeded in weathering the floe & gaining the outer lane by 8 Am – when we bore up under all sail & had two hours very pleasant sailing, when the weather became so thick that we lost the proper lead, and at 10 Am. Although abreast of Cape Smyth, we could see no lead to the open water in shore, and the lane we were in was found to be taking us too much off. I endeavoured to force through the slackest part and if possible get in shore, but in this attempt we became beset and drifted to the N.E. – At half an hour after noon whilst the crew were at dinner a partial clear in the weather showed us open water to the North[wa]rd and before we could warp the Ships head in the desired direction, Point Barrow was observed and the heavy grounded hummocks off it, the current setting the ice in which we were beset rapidly past them –

On getting into a little slacker ice all sail was made to bore toward them, either to force our way through or to make fast to avoid being carried off the land. The closeness of the ice as we drew near the grounded masses precluded any hope of the former, and the rapid rate the current was carrying us past, made the approach to the hummocks a business of some hazard in the event of being carried in collision with them, however, the wind having gone round to the North gave us the power of Keeping along side a large grounded hummock in 7½ fms & twenty feet high whilst warps were run out and the Ship secured. The current continued to set past us at the same rate, carrying some heavy ice with it, from which the ship sustained some severe pressure not to say 'nip', the port quarter boat although topped up to a great hight [sic] was with difficulty saved by the quarter being pressed against a square & perpendicular part of the berg quite thirty feet in hight [sic] which we warped ahead of – And the wind coming round to the East[wa]rd of North brought us rather under the lee, and had the effect of checking the current, not before a large piece that had been reported to me as setting down upon us fortunately taking the ground on our bow in such a position as would have saved us a good deal of pressure had it continued, but the ice was becoming more open & the Ship lay for the night very quietly with rather more strain on the stern warps from the wind, than the current brought from the opposite direction.

The natives of Noo-wook must have made us out as soon as we could distinguish the Land and came off in their boats – In the mean time our C[ape] Smythe [sic] friends on board had become very nervous and seemed anxious to get on shore, until the fresh arrivals re-assured them. Our Visitors included all the principal people many of whom were admitted on board while the ship was being made fast. Amongst them was Omigaloon[,] the Water Chief,[1] and Arksinra[2] with their wives, we were rather surprised to see them back so early from their Eastern journey, in comparison with last year, and whether it was an anxiety to have another look at the Ship, as difference in the reason caused it, I have not been able to understand – They soon mentioned having performed all our requests relative to

---

[1] 'O-mig-u-a-a-rua.'   [2] 'Erk-sing-era.'

distributing the printed notices and buttons amongst the Kan-ma-li[1] or eastern people, who had in their turn promised to give them to the MacKenzie River tribe (Ko-pug-mun)[2] who we hope will give them to any White people they meet. Arksinra further informed Doctor Simpson that they had a great deal of dancing and were on friendly terms with the Eastern people, but that none of them had heard or seen anything of Captain Collinson's ships,[3] or any other in the sea near their country.

He also described being Kept without sleep for five days & nights out of the ten he spent at the Colville among the Nuna-tag-mun, in consequence of the many things he had to tell & to show them from his winters intercourse with us – Among the greatest novelties were some spirits of wine, & Lucifer matches. He has this time been able to procure a gun at Barter point which has the date of 1850 on the lock, two other men have also got guns so that there are now at Noo-wook four guns all H. Bay's[4] – at present there is a pressing demand for gun powder, but tobacco is not forgotten – Ark-sin-ra at my request consented to stop on board, as he is to show us an available opening through the grounded ice by which we may gain the open water –

Wednesday Sept[r] 7th The officer of the Watch M[r] Gordon reported a clear passage through the hummocks ahead of the Ship, at 2 Am. and as the wind was directly fair through, there seemed to be nothing more necessary than to cast off & run into the open water – which was done with the earliest day light at 3 Am. when we stood in for Point Barrow & had to make a few tacks to get sufficiently to windward for entering the channel leading to our Anchorage. The wind being fresh at North East with some loose ice about, kept all

[1] These people were the westernmost sub-group of the Mackenzie Eskimos, with whom the Point Barrow people traded at Barter Island. One of the messages, dated 4 July 1853, reached the *Enterprise* when a group of Mackenzie Eskimos arrived at Camden Bay on 2 July 1854 (Collinson, 1889, p. 315).

[2] The 'Ko-pug-mun', the Kupugmiut, were the sub-group of the Mackenzie Eskimos who lived in the lower Mackenzie River delta (Smith, 1984, p. 348).

[3] The *Enterprise* did not reach Camden Bay, Alaska, until 14 September 1853 (Collinson, 1889, p. 301).

[4] Hudson's Bay Company guns. The guns that were purchased at Barter Island from the 'Kan-ma-li' would have originated at the Company's trading post, Fort McPherson, which had been established in 1840 on the Peel River. 'O-mi-ga-loon', however, who as early as 1849 was reported to have owned a musket (see Maguire's entry for 17 September 1852 and p. 82 above, n. 2), seems to have claimed to have purchased his gun from the Indians.

hands pretty busy working the ship so as to gain as much as possible.

By 4.30 we were passing the settlement on Point Barrow and had a number of spectators for whom we hoisted our colours. In running down the channel there was great difficulty in seeing the marks, owing to the late snow obliterating everything. From this cause the ship took the ground on the Southside of the channel, but was warped by a Kedge until she lay afloat at 8 Am. when the crew went to breakfast, half a pound of preserved meat being allowed them each, in consideration of a hard mornings work, and a days in perspective. The launch was hoisted afterwards, and the work of Kedging continued until the ship was brought into six fms. and in a position from which we were able to put her again under canvas, which was done at 11 Am. when we stood into the Harbour & Anchored at Noon in 3 fms where I purposed remaining until the rudder was unshipped, previous to hauling into shoal water for our winter's berth.

After the sails were furled & the ship made snug, the crew went to dinner at 1 P.M. when I felt very thankful for the successful termination of our voyage, which had presented in its course, almost every obstacle met with in Ice navigation, all of which had been overcome by good fortune more than management as we are all mere novices at such work, but have certainly on this occasion got a little insight into the business, and gained some valuable experience – though the poor old Plover has never had such a thumping before and bears the marks of some heavy bruises, and strange to say she leaks less now than when we started, which the carpenter thinks a mystery, and shakes his head very profoundly on the subject.

The wind in the afternoon hauled more to the East[war]^d and the sea became more & more open, so that at last the ice outside the hummocks formed a line several miles to the N. of our last nights position, leaving a space of open water along shore to a breadth of 15 miles – The hummocks form a continuous line the same as before, but the loose ice being removed several openings are distinguishable in them – Our Native friends put off to us in the forenoon but went on shore when told we were too busy to receive them, a pleasing contrast to their conduct of last year – Arksinra and our Cape Smyth friends were put on shore at their own request early in the afternoon. The weather continued cold with a fresh wind at East.

Thursday Sepr 8th The wind continued to blow hard from the N. E. with gloomy weather. I was anxious to get the ship into her winter position without loss of time, so as to be able to have the boats people available for collecting a store of driftwood for building a store house, and for fuel – We commenced by unhanging the rudder, and laying out a Kedge Anchor and warp in the direction of our intended berth, but when the ship was moved to it, after carrying away a new warp and bringing a very heavy strain on another, the wind was found to be too strong to secure the ship as we wished, the starb[oar]^d anchor was let go & cable veered to 30 fms, the ships quarter being steadyed [sic] to the end of the spit, to prevent her being swung & whirled round her anchor as she has been twice by the strong weather current. All is now left for calm weather.

We had six boats full of Natives alongside, but only Arksinra was allowed on board. He stayed only a short time, and on going away told the others we were too busy with the ship, but tomorrow when the vessel would be close to the beach they should be allowed on board. They brought small quantities of Rein deer Meat & fish but wanted large prices. Arksinra says they have plenty of skins but they are not made up yet for sale – So it is supposed though at high prices we shall not want for moccasins or gloves.

Friday Septr 9th The N. East wind continued in full force today and there was no attempt made at moving the Ship. The Top Gallant yards were sent upon deck, & commencement made for the housing in by lashing the spare main yard fore & aft. The boats crews were engaged preparing the boats for an intended excursion along the Islands for the double purpose of sounding for a ship passage between & to collect spars of driftwood – The moment the ship is secure and the wind moderate. The line of hummocks remains & the smaller pieces have been packed into a great portion of the lane between Noo-wook and the grounded masses – No doubt this breeze has in a measure checked the N.E. current as the water is considerably below the usual lead, and as the wind lulls one may expect it to flow in its usual course with accelerated velocity and compensate for this check.

The Natives came off as expected in considerable numbers, but most of them retired early from becoming sea sick, the short motion of the ship riding across a strong weather current with a short jerking sea was very peculiar & proved too much for the equanimity of many of their stomachs – Although a few did not suffer at all and others after the first effects recovered themselves – Arksinra with his family and the Stammerer remained after all the Native boats had left & had to be put on shore in a ships boat –

277

Arksinra was much edified by seeing several boxes opened which had been sent to me by Mr Barrow & others – The exhibition of a hind quarter of beef excited a good deal of astonishment and convinced them that our stories of the large deer in our country were no fables – All their enquiries about the family of Sables whom it will be recollected we took to Point Hope have been answered, and they look forward to his telling them in the winter the wonders he saw on board the Amphitrite, and they seem especially interested in the fact of his seeing a gun into the muzzle of which he put his head, which was the ten inch carried abaft the Ships Mizen mast –

Saturday September 10th The wind from N.E. continued today with unabated force, bringing to mind the hard hearted wind we experienced at Icy Cape in the beginning of August last year. The sky is clear with sun shine temp[eratur]^e 25 [−3.9°C]. A good many coals had been started amongst the casks stowed round the Sylvester[1] in the Main hold, some people have been employed getting them up & clearing the stove for use – preparing the boats has occupied the Carpenters as well as the forge which had to be got up for that purpose. The crew were allowed the afternoon to wash their clothes, when advantage was taken to issue the warm clothing received from the Rattlesnake, which includes many useful articles we have not had before – Amongst the articles was a new form of seal skin cap or 'helmet' which will be very valuable in the winter. The jackets are improved by having outside pockets which the previous ones had not and the cork soled cloth booths [sic] will be a very necessary comfort for the men to wear on the lower deck, as the moccasins with every care get sloppy when taken into the warm parts of the ship – indeed the whole supply is very liberal, but not more so than is required.

Sunday September 11th The breeze continued and the sea today was covered to a great extent with sludge ice, but the Natives seem to think it is not yet the setting ice of winter. Although the temperature of the water has fallen to 29 [−1.7°C]. They are very anxious for a calm as they cannot get out in their boats to catch Whale at present, and they are very short of that necessary part of their food. They seem to have caught only one Walrus this summer.[2] In the afternoon

---

[1] The hot-air stove. See Armstrong's account (1857, pp. 609–14) for details of its operation.

[2] This shortage was not due to the harvest of walruses by the crews of whaleships; that hunt began in earnest only after 1865 (Bockstoce and Botkin, 1982).

the wind and some alteration in the set of the current brought the ship near to the position I wished to occupy & in order to save further trouble, warps were run out to the shore to keep her there. The sludge ice continued to form and drift past with the current.

Monday [September] 12[th] The same cloudy weather blowing almost a gale from N.E. with star shaped small flakes of snow. The continuance of the sludge ice to form, has made me despair of getting away to the East[wa]rd in the boats as our experience with it last year has shown us how helpless a boat becomes when hampered with it. And we should be doubly so returning with rafts in tow, I have [made] up my mind not to attempt it unless a change takes place.

Two O-mi-aks returned from the East[wa]rd today,[1] their good management of them attracted our attention, and they seemed to incur not a little danger of being swamped in the sea way between the Islands & crossing Moore's channel.[2] Each had a small sail set in the bow which kept the boat before the waves, and the bow and stern paddles were kept in constant action – notwithstanding which they must have taken in some water & would have taken in more but for a Kai-ak secured to each side of the O-mi-ak which gave them stability & not only brakes the seas & prevented their crests toppling in, but also prevents the rolling – Not many Native visitors today – The Carpenter is still employed preparing the gig, as she has many small wants to be supplied after her complete rifling by the natives. There is still some sludge ice on the surface of the water, but it is not so thick as yesterday. The stream chain has been run out N.W. to the spit and the ship secured very nearly in her winter position.

Tuesday September 13th Rather less wind but sludge and pancake ice continue to form & drift past the Ship. The boats are provisioned and ready for our trip but I fear there is not much chance of a change to allow it. The crew has been employed clearing the main hold, and unreeving the running rigging. We have had a good number of Natives on board today, they talk of a dance at Noo-wook. They are very anxious for a change of weather as they have not been successful this summer in capturing whale: the winter will probably be one of some hardship with them if they do not succeed in capturing some before the frost sets in – They evidently expect a cessation of the

---

[1] Returning from the summer's trading, hunting, and fishing expedition no doubt.
[2] Today, Eluitkak Pass.

present weather and tell us this ice will not last. Another O-mi-ak arrived today from the East[wa]rd

<u>Wednesday</u> [September] <u>14</u>th The weather continues cold but with less force of wind at N.E. The crew were employed lashing the spars for the housing, and making an alteration in the stowage of the spirit room to make room for the officers private stores, stowed, at present in the Gun room, so as to be enabled to get their stove placed. The carpenters have commenced erecting the winter round houses[1] & the blacksmith is employed at the forge making good the Sylvester funneling – Doctor Simpson with Mr Hull paid a visit to the Village, and were received with great civility, and the Natives wished to get up a dance for them. The sea to the West[wa]rd both within & beyond the hummocks seemed clear of ice, and the young ice on the North side of the spit was strong enough to bear their weight easily. The Villagers seem to be living on birds principally at present, and are not very successful in catching seals – The sludge ice continues to form & drift out of the channel, a brilliant arch of Aurora was observed tonight I believe from the first time this Autumn, coruscating and passing through the zenith.

<u>Thursday</u> [September] <u>15</u>th The breeze continued light from the N.E. and we had a good deal of sun shine. The crew were employed placing the rafters for the housing between the Fore & Main Masts, and preparing for housing in. The Carpenters continue about the winter round houses. And the black smith is still employed with the Sylvester funnel. The ice around is getting firm and there are only a very few small openings now left near the ship where the current ripple prevents the surface freezing over. Not many Natives about today & none of the Chiefs. The pin tailed ducks[2] are now collecting into flocks & seem on the move – At 9.50 P.M. There was a slight and sudden movement in the ice, which carried away both our warps fast to the spit –

<u>Friday September 16</u>th The wind still from N.E. and the sky rather clouded – the temperature is not so low but the ice today is firm enough for the Natives to walk alongside on it. By their account it is doubtful if this ice will remain. In fact it depends on the force of the next South[er]ly wind. The warps carried away last night were hauled in this morning. We are now at a stand with all our work, until the ice makes sufficiently secure for travelling over to obtain

---

[1] Around the hatches?   [2] Oldsquaws (*Clangula hyemalis*).

drift wood for building our storehouse. A commencement has been made to saw down battens for the housing from some small wood brought by the Natives, and the Carpenter is at work about the winter round houses. The blacksmith still at work at the Sylvester funnel. The weather is sufficiently moderate to allow the Natives to launch their boats, we hear of four being out today,[1] it is much to be hoped that they may be successful, otherwise they will be very hard up for provisions. Elson's bay is frozen over, with the exception of some pools where the tide ripple seems strong, but the channel outside leading to Point Barrow is quite free. Several flocks of duck are still hovering about open water.

Saturday [September] 17th The wind N.E. light & cloudy. Our employment today has been warping the ship into her winter berth. I did not intend doing it until the ice was considered fast for the winter, but the ease with which the ice is broken at present was the inducement. We did not get as close to the position of our house last year, as I wished from the ship taking the ground. But our present berth is a better one from farther along the spit, and from open water in case of another break up in the winter. And our head is N.E. (true) which will be more end on to the prevailing wind. During our operations several of the men fell through and got a thorough wetting, and Gray[2] had incurred some risk in skating, but after all fell in alongside the Ship – The Noo-wook people caught a Whale with its young one today – Four O-mi-aks that have been detained by the ice on doctors Island[3] came past on their sledges under sail.

Sunday Sept[r] 18th The wind remained at N.E. with fine weather. We had not many natives about, indeed I have had much satisfaction in observing their altered bearing this year in comparison with last. They are now civil and will do as they are told, enough has been said previously describing them in the reverse – Several boats are reported to be out after whale – And two other parties have arrived from the East[wa][rd] over the ice. There was an unusual low tide remarked by Doctor Simpson in his walk this evening, the difference the present level and the highest surf mark being 38 inches.

Monday [September] 19th The wind has increased again at N.E. and as the Natives cannot get out in their O-mi-aks we have an unusual number alongside. The old chief O-Mig-a-loon was very anxious for

[1] Hunting for bowhead whales presumably.
[2] H. R. E. Grey joined the *Plover* in 1853 as midshipman.
[3] Today, one of the eastern Tapkaluk Islands.

281

us to fire a great gun in the winds eye, thinking that it would alter its direction & favour their whaling – but the officers told the Natives the wind was unfavourable in consequence of their thieving propensities, a man having stolen a patent log towing line yesterday which was brought back by Erk-sin-ra today. We are employed today getting our sledges put together, and making dogs harness and tracking lines, to be ready for bringing wood to the ship as soon as the ice is quite secure. The distance this year from where it will have to be brought is between five and six miles, that in our neighbourhood & to that distance having been exhausted last winter – The carpenter is still at work about the winter round houses – And the blacksmith at the forge repairing the galley funnel.

Tuesday September 20th There is less wind today but the weather is cloudy. The ice was sufficiently strong this morning to allow of the bower chain being substituted for the stream N. W. going [?] from the Ship with 84 fms – We are now secured between that and our port bower to seaward with 33 fms. which I intend leaving down for the winter – The stream chain was hauled in & stowed away – Our first wooding party went away today under Mr Gordon to the first Island to pick up the remains of our last years wood stocks – The carpenters are employed sawing battens and building the winter round houses. The blacksmith is reducing the size of the fire places in the Cabin & gun room stoves – We had a good many people around today but chiefly women and children. The woman we call the widow whose husband was shot, told a story about a man having disappeared on the land deer hunting. It would seem he sank in a bog and they are at a loss to know whether he is dead, but her story was not very well understood –

Wednesday Septr 21st The wind continued all day light at East and increased in the evening veering to N.E. temp[eratur]^e +26 [−3.3°C]. This wind has not veered a point from between N.E. & East during the last fortnight. It is much to be hoped for the sake of the Natives that the weather may be moderate in order to allow them to lay in a good winters stock of Whale – The same may be perhaps desired for our own sakes, that having plenty of their favourite food, they may spare us some of their Venison.

The site of our new store houses was fixed upon today, it occupies some feet in length & breath [sic] less space than last year, at present our difficulty in getting on with it, is the want of wood, which can only be procured from a distance. And the ice is not yet trusthworthy.

The employment of the Carpenters & blacksmith was the same as yesterday, and a party have been collecting wood from the next Island – As many as ten boats were reported today to be out after Whale – still there was an average number of Natives about the Ship. There are still some parties on the Islands detained by the ice being too firm for their boats & not strong enough for their sledges.

Erk-sinra told Doctor Simpson a story today of having seen a Bear on the further ice yesterday quite close to his party & the outcry that was made for him to shoot it with his gun which was unfortunately where the dutch Man left his Anchor, at home – The next cry was for him to attack the Animal with the Whale lance given to him by the Ship, but the beast got off from that weapon also. He described the position of the boat to be by a stream of ice as Doctor S understood attached to the pack, beyond the interval of open water outside the hummocks he therefore infers that the N.E. current is not now so rapid as we experienced it in the Ship – The Whale are described as abundant but the weather unfavourable for striking them –

Doctor S. applied to Erk-sin-ra as one of the wise men of the tribe to get some account of the disappearance of the man spoken of by the widow yesterday. He confirmed her story, and after talking with several others, Doctor S found that the general account is that the deceased (Nebrona)[1] went out with two others one morning to hunt Reindeer, and that he disappeared[,] the whole party being then on good hard ground away from the vicinity of any pools, bogs, or rivers, and that when his companions missed him they searched carefully for him but their search was fruitless. The Natives therefore conclude that he was drawn into the earth by '*turn-gain*' (spirits) – It appears that these 'turn gain' are the spirits of men who are dead & that they live beneath the surface of the ground. They are frequently seen by the natives in dark and gloomy weather, their form being the upper half of men who are dead, but different accounts make them of gigantic or diminutive size – They spend most of their time in sleep and do not use any food, or if they do its nature is not known – All people who died become turngain[2] – There

[1] Elsewhere, 'Nebrua'.

[2] Ghosts of dead people were an element of the supernatural and were regarded with some fear. It was necessary to placate them if they made their presence apparent (Spencer, 1959, pp. 291–3).

283

are also other 'turn-gain' or spirits of the air which are not visible, but they sometimes strike people dead, their form is supposed to resemble birds – This is the first general account we have heard from these people of their belief in spirits or ghosts or of a future state of human existence – The latter is evidently one they do not covet as they all look upon death as the last greatest evil – This season is several days in advance of last – I left the Ship in the gig on this day last year & crossed Dease's Inlet returning on the 23^d.

Thursday September 22nd . . . I walked to the Village today accompanied by Doctor Simpson, I wished to see the state of the open water and to ascertain if it would be practicable for a ship to reach this place after the bay had been so long frozen over – The day turned out very thick & unfavourable for a good view, but from what we could see, the sea was still quite open & navigable to within a cable's length or so of our position – I was glad to find very few men at the Village, they were all out on the water after whale. We did not enter any of the huts. Some 30 or so women & children followed us but there were only 7 or 8 men. They told us one whale had been caught yesterday. Their lake of fresh water[1] is not yet frozen to the bottom, and we observed they had cut slabs of ice from the surface of the pools for winters use, in which the effect of each nights frost could be seen giving a peculiar structure to it when looked at edge wise –

A number of women went out towards Coopers Island this morning with several sledges to assist the parties there to return to the Village, we had therefore only a few visitors along side – We had a general muster with arms in the evening, and served out a supply of Ammunition in charge of each individual, we muster very strong with muskets this year.

Friday [September] 23rd The wind from N. E. with a lower temperature which we have been anxious for to increase the strength of the ice so as to allow our wooding parties to get away for wood. We are delayed much in our work for the want of it to build our house, but a few days of this temperature +20 [−6.7°C] will make the ice strong enough for anything. The winter round houses have been completed. The Carpenters are now employed placing doors at the hatch ways to be Kept shut by a pulley & weight – Mr Gordon and a

---

[1] This was probably the small pond at the northern tip of the Point Barrow sandspit.

party have been employed getting wood from Martins Island[1] and were rather successful. I omitted to mention two days ago, that the thievish propensities of some of our Noo-wook friends, one of whom was caught trying to unshackle the rudder pendants off the rudder triced up across the stern, has reminded us of establishing our boundary chain round the Ship, which has been got on with as fast as posts can be procured. No natives out in their boats today, the assemblage about the Ship was therefore considerable. those out yesterday saw a great many [whales] but succeeded in killing one only – Two boats lost their harpoons & gear in fish without capturing them –

Ark-sin-ra it seems made enquiries of M[r] Gray as to whether the Chief of the big ship, the Amphitrite had been told of him, & seemed quite modest when informed that the great 'omelik *Rederick*'[2] had been told of the Chief Arksinra[3] who was so good at Noo-wook. He had also an opportunity of seeing a cocoa nut opened which Doctor Simpson had reserved for him. He was very attentive in watching the process of taking off the husk and he thought highly of the Kernel and the milk, and at first seemed Amused with the appearance of the Monkeys face on the end of the shell but afterwards when it was given to him he did not seem to care about it in consequence of Doctor S. calling it a turn-gak or spirit at any rate he left it behind which he would not have done had he valued it –

In the afternoon three O-mi-aks came past the ship on sledges from the East[wa][rd] these togeather [sic] with several other sledges laden with Reindeer belong to the people who have been sometime detained on Coopers Island. M[r] Gordon's party seem to have been helping them along, when he as well as one of his men fell through the ice, which at this season is not considered more than a joke. He saw ten or twelve deer on their sledges . . .

Saturday September 24th This morning was fine with light snow the temperature has fallen to +10 [−12.2°C] which will I think secure the ice for the winter – The natives are unable to go out with the present wind – Omigaloon & Erk-sin-ra were amongst our visitors, the latter sold me his best sledge for a good saw & appeared very well pleased with this bargain. The ice was sufficiently strong today to

---

[1] The first island east of the *Plover*'s anchorage.
[2] Captain Charles Frederick of the *Amphitrite*.
[3] 'Erk-sing-era.'

allow a bower Anchor[1] to be taken on shore to which the cable was secured. We have also established our boundary line the same as last year to include the house and observatory. This I was anxious to get done before the work on the house commenced, as it prevented the natives from interfering with it. We have placed a few of the supports of the house, making the best shift we can with the wood within our reach – Our wooding party at Martins Island bring in a few loads of small wood the most of it only fit for burning. In the evening a small party came past with one O-mi-ak, a part of those detained at Coopers Island for five or six days. They seem to have been successful in catching deer & sold us two for a small saw. As they were going to pitch their tent close to the ship, I offered them the use of our upper deck under the Awning which they seemed glad to avail themselves of.

<u>Sunday</u> [September] 25th The morning was overcast but nearly calm. Our Native friends who slept on board were stirring soon after 6 A.M. & before 8 they were joined outside the ship by some of their friends from Noo-wook who seem to have persuaded the man that he had made a bad bargain for his two deer – As he returned the saw and said it was too small, on hearing which I ordered him to be allowed to take away his deer, and he took them and set out for the Village. This conduct caused some indignation of feeling on board, after his having received a nights hospitality on board, but I did not think much of it, Knowing there is a scarcity of food at present Among them – And it is of no use judging their feelings by our own standard –

After Church Mess[rs] Hull & Gray went to the village and were received with unusual marks of friendship. They were taken to the dance house[2] and several dances performed for their Amusement. After which they were made some small presents each, which I have been told is the custom to the South[wa][rd] about Grantley Harbour, wherever strangers visit their dance houses – Erk-sin-ra[,] who got a musket[3] on his last journey to Barter point,[4] but did not get any

---

[1] Bower anchors were the two largest anchors in a ship that were kept permanently attached to their cables. They were carried on both bows.

[2] The *qazgi*, which has been variously called a 'men's house', a 'dance house', or a 'ceremonial house', was used for a number of social and religious functions by the local family that owned it (Burch, 1980, p. 271). In large settlements, such as Nuvuk, there was more than one *qazgi*, reflecting the fact that more than one extended family resided in the settlement.

[3] See above, p. 275, n. 4.   [4] Barter Island.

Knowledge of the explosive powers of gun powder – on being visited, loaded it with powder and put a wad of something Mr Hull could not make out over it, and was going to fire it against the inside of his hut, as a 'feu de joie' on Mr H. visiting his house – who had hardly time to dissuade him from it – when he pointed it upwards through the sky light & fired to the Amazement of our officers, who thought there was a great chance of his burning some of the many faces peering down – when he exclaimed there is no shot [in] it! evidently supposing that powder of itself went for nothing –

We had a good many natives on board, they seem to bring nothing to barter, and our tobacco from being distributed amongst them in large quantities by our new hands, it seems to have lost its charm. In the afternoon a party went along the Islands to hunt bears, and returned at 8 P.M. with one,[1] they had killed another which was left on the ice to be brought in on another occasion. The night was calm.

Monday September 26th The day has been nearly calm & gloomy with a good deal of snow falling. The channel is frozen over from Point Plover[2] to within half a mile of Noo-wook, round which and to the S.W. there is still [a] lane of open navigable water – Several parties of Natives passed the Ship at an early hour to the East[wa]rd to hunt bears. And they returned at 8 P.M. Ark-sin-ra being one of the party – much elated at his success in shooting one or two with his gun.

Our first distant wood party left the Ship this morning under Mr Gordon, and returned at 4 P.M. bringing a very good load, but our sledge for such heavy purposes is too straight in the runners, and from the want of shoeing drags very heavy – some alteration in the way of oak battens to run on have been made this evening, which I hope will lighten the labour. The launch was taken on shore this morning and all the running gear, and the dingy stowed in here and

---

[1] Spencer wrote (1959, p. 273) the following about the division of a polar bear:
As soon as the hunters brought the carcass of the bear to the beach, the word was passed along from house to house. All rushed out to get a piece, bringing a knife and a container. The bear was hacked to pieces on the spot and each one took a section. There was considerable play on this occasion, blood being spattered over clothes and on faces. The hunter who had taken the bear held onto the hind leg while the villagers cut up the bear. When the bear had been cut to pieces, the hunter kept his joint and took it home. The bear was not previously skinned. Each one who took a piece tried to get some of the bearskin also. If large enough, this was made into mittens, if small, a piece was sewed to the mittens.

[2] Point Plover is the eastern tip of the Point Barrow sandspit, at Eluitkak Pass ('Moore's Channel').

covered over for the winter. The spare spars were also carried to the house and a commencement made to lash them in their places to support the roof [e]t^c. Mr Hull was engaged with a small party cutting out slabs of ice for building the observatory. Our runner sledge the St Patrick has been put togeather [sic] to be employed collecting fire wood near the Ship – The only water in sight from the ship now is a pool in the channel. Kept free by the strength of the current, there have been a good many of the small pin tailed duck[1] on it all day. Some of the officers have been very successful in shooting several of them, but the difficulty is getting them out of the water. I had the misfortune to get a dip this evening, in approaching too near the pool on the thin ice, and not thinking of anything except securing the game – We have had a good many natives about all quiet and civil. The night was calm, with snows –

Tuesday Septembe^r 27th . . . Nothing of consequence stirring amongst the natives, a good many have passed to the East[wa]rd hunting bears, but we have not heard whether they have met with success or not – They seem to have a superstition about the women sewing at this season,[2] as it is not considered lucky for their success in whaling – And any thing we want done in that way has to be performed out of sight of the men, or on board.

Wednesday Septembe^r 28th . . . The storehouse might be said to be finished this evening, it has been completed with much greater ease than I anticipated – The Carpenters & blacksmith have been at work making the doors and hinges which are not yet complete – A party of natives came past from the East[wa]rd in the evening, having killed two bears, they have been out for two days & one night without having slept much, and were looking much in want of it, they soon left promising themselves a blow out of it – the night is very windy N.N.W. temp[eratur]^e −3 [−19.4°C] –

Thursday September 29th The wind moderated in the morning, but the temp[eratur]^e remains at zero. Several small parties of Natives passed to the East[wa]rd at day light to hunt bears.

---

[1] Probably oldsquaws (*Clangula hyemalis*).

[2] In general the autumn whaling season was less circumscribed by ceremony than was the spring season (Spencer, 1959, p. 349); nevertheless it was clearly important to minimize noise during the fall hunt as well. Patrick Henry Ray (1885, p. 39) wrote the following about noise in the spring hunt: 'No work is done that will necessitate . . . any noise . . . Should their garments be accidentally torn, the women must take them far back on the tundra out of sight of the sea and mend them; they have little tents, in which just one person can sit, in which this work is done.'

<u>Friday</u> [September] 30th . . . 'A good number of people were about the ship early in the day but most of them went away soon' – 'Arksin-ra was on board & very patiently gave Doctor Simpson the words of a song, but as yet he cannot make any sense out of them' 'Hearing Mr Gordon play the flute he was quite at a loss to know how the music was produced, & after looking on for sometime he went and examined his fingers and making nothing of them to his satisfaction he proceeded to inspect his mouth to see if there was any peculiar mechanism about it, never dreaming of the combination of the make of the instrument and skill of the player' He thought it a good joke going away to go up to Doctor Simpson & shaking hands to say good bye, but he could give as equivalent expression in his own language . . .

<u>Saturday October 1st</u> [1853] The wind backed round to the East of South during the night, and the morning was very fine with a light air at S.E. – Mr Gordon left the ship at 7 Am with our distant wooding party & returned at 4.30 P.M. All the provisions and stores to be landed were sent on shore yesterday, and the house is quite full – Advantage has been taken of this calm mild day to get the housing cloth over the upper deck – As the native boats were out today after whale[,] we had mostly women & children about the Ship. The Sylvester stove was lighted for the first time this afternoon which had the effect of thawing the ice collected on the beams & drying up the decks. A large flight of duck probably the last we shall see[,] were observed to day by Mr Hull going to the South[wa]rd. I dont know whether they were rightly understood or not, but Mr Hull was lead to understand that the women were not wearing their beads today for good luck for those out after whale – The night was fine with the wind at East force 2 temp[eratur]^e +10 [−12.2°C] –

<u>Sunday October 2nd</u> The morning was fine & calm temp[eratur]^e +8 [−13.3°C] – The principal news of the day has been that three men belonging to the Village including O-Mig-u-a-a-rua the water chief have been taken out on a piece of ice while employed in setting their sealing nets – Some of their boats went out this morning to look after them with hopes of picking them up – A daughter of one of these men was down at the Ship & went home on hearing the news from Lt Vernon. This tends to show that news travels less surely from house to house at the Village where on such an occurrence all might be expected to be in commotion, than one would suppose; and that the ship, like a market place being a point where many meet, is

the best for hearing the news of the day. It does not appear that the boats had any success in their pursuit of whale yesterday, but there were several out on the chase again today – The Sylvester stove was lit again today – Messrs Hull & Gray [sic] walked to the main land after church they found the ice very smooth, & the land as yet very little covered with snow. They saw only a solitary Ptarmigan – A Native passed in the evening having killed another bear – . . .

Monday October 3d A water sky from N.W. to S.S.W. a fine morning with a light wind at N.E. Mr Gray left with a wooding party at 7 Am. The rest of the crew were employed securing the housing cloths and the Carpenters putting up gangway, bow and stern doors – There were not many Natives down. The report of the men being carried out on the ice has been verified today, but as it is drifting to the South[wa]rd the case is not considered hopeless, and they are expected to be picked up again – particularly if the wind changes to West – But they seem to say when they are drifted away to the North[wa]rd there is no hope – A calm night temperature −2 [−18.9°C]. No birds have been seen today – . . .

Tuesday Octob^r 4th . . . We have not had many Natives at the ship today, and there is no account of the unfortunate people who have been carried away on the ice. We hear of a party having left for the Main land to assist the return of some others –

As my orders for the ensuing year direct provisions to be buried at advanced positions along the coast, and as our work is now nearly finished and the season the best for the purpose – I have arranged to leave the ship on Saturday morning next for Cape Halkett which I look upon as the most prominent & extreme position that we can expect to reach being distant from the Ship upwards of ninety geographical miles – Where I purpose burying 4 tins of pemmican weighing 32 lbs each – And placing notices & marks on the different head lands between that place and the Ship – I have undertaken this duty myself, not from its importance as any officer on board could carry it out equally as well, but from Knowing the route thoroughly & being the only officer who does, I go merely to economise the labour & perhaps the privations of the party – Which is to consist of four Seamen with Mr Gray M[i]d[shipma]^n and two native sledges with four dogs for each – The night fine –

Wednesday October 5th . . . I have been engaged making preparations for the journey to Cape Halkett – Not many Natives alongside, they bring a few fish for barter – The three unfortunate men on the ice have not been heard of . . .

Thursday [October] 6th This day has been more windy than usual from E.N.E. A good many natives about us, but no intelligence from them of the poor people adrift on the ice. Those who visit the ship seem to treat the matter lightly, or as I thought today, perhaps we do not understand their method of grieving – I bought a very good sledge the best we have ever been able to procure from these people. It is quite new, but is shorter than the general run. I was obliged to give a new saw as I required it for the journey. The walls (ice) of the observatory were finished today, & the beams of the roof (flat) laid across – . . .

Friday October 7th . . . The observatory was finished today under the superintendence of Mr Hull – A house of that kind built with great care with ice of moderate thickness, taken from the surface of the water when undisturbed by wind would have a very good effect and appear quite a crystal palace. We had a few of the Chiefs down today. Erksinra Amongst the number, the three people on the ice have not been heard of. Our employment today has been stacking wood, and preparing for my journey – Everything for which is now arranged and the sledges stowed ready for the morning. The wind continued fresh during the night –

Saturday [October] 8th The breeze from N.E. Continues, I had doubts during the night from hearing the strength of the wind about starting today, but when I have made up my mind to go, I don't like being put off. And left the Ship at 7.30 Am. provisioned for sixteen days for Cape Halkett – At this time of the year the ice is smooth and as yet it is only thinly covered with snow so that we ought to make good progress & be able to see the form of the coast line – A wooding party under Mr Gordon started with us and as our route lay togeather [sic] for five miles we Kept Company.

I continue the journal of the Ship as has been my custom when away. Doctor Simpson kindly furnishing me with his, from which I have on these, and all occasions borrowed largely, & for which I am much indebted to him, for many valuable remarks. We had but few Natives about the Ship today. Most of them women, it is feared there is but little hope now of the three men who went adrift on the ice making the land again – The report is that ice has formed over the interval between the land and the hummocks –

Sunday October 9th . . . A Moderate number of Natives were alongside – mostly women and children – Erk-sin-ra came rather later than usual & asked to stop after the others – After the officers had dined he was brought into the Gun Room & took a glass of wine which he enjoyed very much – he had a cigar also which he equally relished but did not smoke it out saving the remainder for another occasion – He seemed to have a special mission on board today – (The result or object I copy verbatim from Doctor Simpson's journal) as he was understood to say he had been deputed by the people at Noo-wook to ask me (Doctor S) if on their making a suitable present I could by any means change the wind so as to bring back to land the water chief[1] & the other two men who were taken out on the ice – He was of course made to understand that I possessed no such power –[2]

I have no doubt that this application has its source in the explanations that I have attempted to give him of the office I hold in the ship the use of the Medicines in the dispensary – These he no doubt understood imperfectly though he had seen from time to time the use made of cupping glasses [e]t[c] and comprehending but little gave me credit for more than natural powers. But it is ever thus with a 'Medicine Man' among the uncivilized, they are sure to connect his office with their own superstitions, hence the request today to do something to change the wind –

Several of the Natives were occupied today in fishing for small fish letting their hooks and line drop through a hole in the ice – It seems evident this is a season of scarcity of the favourite food, the whale, as they are all making greater shifts than they did last year. Those who went to the main land have remained later, those who went to the East[wa][rd] came home earlier, & several have gone lately to the rivers to look for fish – From these & other circumstances Doctor S concluded that last season was one of unusual abundance the Point Barrow people having Killed seventeen Whales and that this is one of the opposite Kind as they have taken only five – Probably the line of ice hummocks grounded off the point is one great cause of their want of success this season – The Ship gave a jerk tonight which appears to be caused by the ice separating from the sides of the vessel & allowing her to rise in her bed –

Monday October 10th . . . M[r] Jago accompanied by one man went to the mainland but saw no deer – Very few natives down. Erk-sin-ras wife was on board, she said he was at the Village today – 'A big

---

[1] Elsewhere, 'O-mig-u-a-a-rua'.

[2] The attempt to pay Dr Simpson for changing the wind demonstrates that the people believed him to have the superior power of a shaman (*angatquq*).

Doctor'[1] employed drumming a pain out of a mans belly. It would appear his art is not an unprofitable one as he is paid for his services in skins [e]t^c . . .

Tuesday Oct 11th . . . We had not many friends on board today but a good many visitors, some of them lately arrived from the mainland – Nepaktok[2] Enu-grua, the man who came on board at the beginning of last winter & took provisions to the spit for Lieut Vernon & the boats crews was among the new arrivals – His wife gave the officers some fish as a present which were accepted and paid for as if bartered, as they go into the common stock of the Ship, but the sentiment that prompted the gift was not an interested one. One of the others a girl belonged to the party of the man Nebrua, she confirms the story of his being stolen by the evil genii of the earth 'turn gain'[3] – There is something which Doctor Simpson cannot yet comprehend, which seems like his having had a forewarning in a dream of such an event occurring to him – or his having been told by others that such would be his fate – . . .

Wednesday Octob^r 12th Weather fine with a light air at North, Our visitors today were neither numerous nor influential. Most of the people appear occupied in fishing along the high water crack with a hook & small whale bone line . . .

Thursday [October] 13th A fine clear day with a light wind at North. Early this morning Erk-sin-ra having heard of the theft which took place yesterday afternoon procured the stolen articles and brought in on board before 8 o clock. It was the tripod of the Az[4] & all instrument[s] left on the top of the observatory after observations –

By an accidental turn in the discourse with two young native girls, Doctor Simpson was able to learn, that one of them was newly born or 'carried in the hood' at the time of Mr Simpsons visit to this place in 1837. Erksinra had heard something of it but he could form no idea of how long it was ago.[5] Doctor S. hopes yet to lead him back

---

[1] For a full description of the shaman's curing process see Spencer's account (1959, pp. 306–8).

[2] Elsewhere, 'Ne-pak-tok'. See Maguire's entry for 25 September 1852.

[3] See Maguire's entry for 21 September 1853.   [4] Azimuth.

[5] Thomas Simpson (1843, pp. 145–64) visited Point Barrow in 1837. He travelled east from the Mackenzie River with Peter Dease and succeeded in mapping the 150 miles of unknown coastline between the farthest penetrations of Frederick William Beechey's and John Franklin's expeditions of 1826. Thomas Elson, one of Beechey's men, reached Point Barrow in the ship's barge, and Franklin, coming from the Mackenzie in open boats, reached as far as Beechey Point, east of Harrison Bay (Bockstoce, 1977, pp. 13–4). The British were apparently ignorant of Kashevarov's boat expedition to Point Barrow in 1838 (VanStone, 1977).

gradually to M[r] Elsons visit to Noo-wook and then to their ideas of a more remote antiquity, and any interesting traditions they may possess . . .

Saturday [October] 15th Wind South[er][ly] with hazy cloudy weather. Erk-sin-ra was on board and Doctor Simpson had some further conversation about M[r] Simpson's visit. When he told him the name of the cripple who drew his knife on M[r] S at Point tangent[1] – He also said that his Father had never visited the Kang-ma-li[2] – He sold M[r] Gordon a womans coat for beads: This was part of the payment he had recently received for his 'professional attendance on the sick' He enumerated eight articles he had received among which were a deer skin, a wolf skin, a pair of labrets, a string of beads, and a womans coat[3] . . .

Sunday [October] 16th The wind continued South[er]ly inclining to East very light & accompanied with mist – After church Doctor Simpson Lt Vernon & M[r] Hull paid a visit to the town, and as they wished not to have any dancing or hubbub they made a detour on the ice entering the village on the further side & thus escaped public notice – They made at once for Erk-sin-ras hut, and were received by him on the 'house top' – They had first to admire his new hut which is yet unfurnished with the usual sleeping bench – It is a little larger than any of the others being 15 feet by 10½[4] but only 5½ feet high in the centre, and the planks and beams are squared and finished with considerable care – He showed his peltry consisting of three Wolverine skins, a large number of Reindeer [caribou] skins young & old, a portion of white deer skin[5] which he says comes from the

---

[1] Simpson, 1843, p. 147.

[2] These were the westernmost subgroup of the Mackenzie Eskimos, with whom the Point Barrow people traded at Barter Island. It may well be that their trading activities intensified after the establishment of the Hudson's Bay Company post at Fort McPherson in 1840. On the other hand his father may simply have been one of those who chose not to go on the trading expeditions.

[3] 'Erksinra' seems to have been a shaman of considerable skill; payment for the curing of the sick was usually only made when a angatquq's ministrations were successful (Spencer, 1959, p. 308).

[4] In the early 1880s John Murdoch (1892, p. 73) recorded that 'the dimensions of a house were generally about 12 to 14 feet long and 8 to 10 feet wide'.

[5] If this piece was part of the mottled white skin of a *reindeer* – hence from Asia – it would have been very rare in northern Alaska and quite valuable. To have reached 'Erksinra' from the Indians (which seems unlikely) its origin in Alaska would probably have been the Russian–American Company trading posts, rather than the trans-Bering Strait native trade (in which some reindeer skins changed hands), which primarily involved Eskimos.

Ko-yu-kuk (Indians) of the hills & told the officers their relative values in Kettles and tobacco. A Wolverine & a Wolf skin are equal & each worth at Point Hope one large Copper Kettle & 20 heads of tobacco, but he gets them for Kettles of smaller size togeather [sic] with beads from the Eastern tribes, (Kang-mali-mun). He described as he had done once before the barter transactions at Barter Island[,] Knife in hand – But the most interesting article he exhibited was a *coat of mail*[1] made of pieces of iron or steel about three inches long and ¾ of an inch broad perforated at the sides & stitched togeather [sic] with leather thongs. The iron plates formed four circles round the body which they fitted closely allowing perfectly free motion. He put it on next his skin & over it a coat – then said he did not fear the thrust of a Kang-ma-li knife when thus protected – Doctor Simpson was curious to Know whence he had procured such an article, as it was impossible to conceive its being made in this country, but he said at once it came from Asia.

The officers received a message from the 'Water Chiefs' wife[2] requesting them to visit her which they complied with. The hut was quiet and on the part of the old woman there was no ostentatious but evidently a great deal of real grief which showed itself particularly in her red suffused eyes – She seemed to entertain some notion that the magnetic instruments at the Ship could be made to give some information about the ultimate fate of her husband – Doctor S. remarked that the hideous mask was missing which formerly hung over the entrance of the hut inside but he forbore asking about it – There was likewise a thin piece of thong carried four or five times round the hut and secured at the corners which had some connexion with their superstitions[3] – The time seems almost past now to expect the return of these unfortunates – yet the parties interested in them hope against anything just as is done in England about the Erebus and Terror[4] – yet who shall say they are already destroyed. A flock of ducks were observed near Martins Island[5] in the afternoon –

<u>Monday October 17th</u> Weather thick and wind rather fresh from

---

[1] In northern Alaska armour (made of overlapping plates) was used for protection in warfare, and in some tense trade encounters as well. The origin of this armour piece was probably Asia – for similar pieces were collected among the Chukchis (Bogoras, 1909, pp, 54, 161–8). Walter Hough reported a similar piece from Cape Prince of Wales, Alaska, and believed that the influence for this style of armour came from Japan (Hough, 1895, pp. 631–3).

[2] The 'water chief' is 'O-mig-u-a-a-rua'; his wife, 'Ma-to-mia'.

[3] See Maguire's entry for 5 November 1853.   [4] Sir John Franklin's ships.

[5] The first island east of the *Plover*.

N.E. Temperature 8 & 9 [−13.3° & −12.8°C] above Zero. We had a tolerable number of Natives today considering the badness of the weather − but nothing short of a gale at 40 below Zero [−40°C] would keep them at home. Erk-sin-ra was on board and Lt Vernon gave him a looking glass and Doctor Simpson gave him a piece of printed calico to make an over all coat, in return for his attentions yesterday, among which were a present to each of the officers of a wolfskin fringe[,] articles of value to him − Yesterday he pulled out a piece of tobacco Doctor S. had given him for his own use last year all of which he had not smoked − He told Doctor S he had not allowed any one else to use it according to his directions, & wished to know if he might give some to his wife now, so careful was he to follow Doctor S's injunctions as he understood them. The only caution he had been given was not to barter it as it was of a superior description but to keep it for his own use, which might include his whole family and a select circle of particular friends. He was very patient today in explaining the meaning of Native names of different places. Nu-wu-ak signifies a point of land − hence Noo-wook. Nek-si a fish hook hence the Sandy hook of Nek-si-ura the Cemetry [sic] on Pt Barrow at which Mr Simpson landed[1] & took possession of the country− A.D. 1837 . . .

Tuesday [October] 18th Winds N.E. with some drift − Mr Gordon left the Ship with a wooding party at 7 Am − and soon after leaving Doctor's Island on his return, espied my party coming up behind him on our return to the ship − Both parties joined afterwards arriving on board at 2.30 P.M. As advantage had been taken of a very favourable period for ice travelling (viz the month of October) before the snow attains a thickness to become an impediment, the journey to Point Halkett[2] had been performed without suffering many of the inconveniences of ice travelling − It occupied six days going and 5 coming back. The direct distance being about 100 miles, which gives an average of twenty miles a day on the return, independent of the extra distance gone over from not being able to travel in a straight line. As an account of this journey will be found in the Journal[3] book, I have only to mention here its results. The object having been noticed before on the 4th inst The provisions were buried as intended at Cape Halkett & two marks erected on the

---

[1] Simpson, 1843, p. 153. See map p. 84.
[2] Cape Halkett.   [3] I have been unable to locate this journal.

Island to point them out. Marks with notices were also placed on several prominent head lands on our return, for the guidance of any parties falling back. The absence of snow enabled us to trace the coast line all the way without difficulty. We saw a few ptarmigan and deer & traces of several foxes & bears, but did not succeed in getting a shot at any thing. And as far as carrying out the object of the journey, in compliance with my instructions, it was performed very much to my satisfaction –

We had only a small gathering today & nothing of importance transpired among the Natives. When Doctor Simpson asked Pannek-pa the wife of Erk-sin-ra the object of the line round Omer-a a-ruas[1] hut, she told him the people watched it constantly as when the Chief walked about the line would vibrate from the touch of an invisible spirit[2] – 'The last flight of ducks seen today.'[3]

Wednesday October 19th The weather was fine and sunny and nearly calm. Erk-sin-ra was on board early this morning with his congratulations on my return. He & some other natives had a good deal of discourse about the three men on the ice, from which it was understood that they thought the indications of the weather to be at present favourable – the S.W. West and N.W. (true) winds[4] they consider as such and they look for the wind springing up from the Westw[ar]d.

Two of the people – a son & sons wife of the water chief were on board, and there seems to have occurred something to relieve their

---

[1] Elsewhere, 'O-mig-u-a-a-rua', the 'water chief'.

[2] At Point Hope, Froelich Rainey (1947, p. 253) learned of a similar custom: When a man was lost on the ice his wife hung a pair of boots with grass or shaved baleen in-soles in her house, then stretched two lines across the room, one running in the direction from land and sea, the other at right angles to it, and a little lower. If the in-soles were flattened or appeared to move from day to day the wife knew her husband was alive. If the upper line sagged slightly towards the lower, she knew her husband had camped for the night. If the in-soles moved back and the upper line touched the lower one only slightly, she knew he had landed safely on shore. But if the in-soles moved to one side and the lines joined solidly, she knew he had died. Wives also wore their parkas in the house (this kept the husband warm). Sometimes they burned little pieces of driftwood wrapped in willow bark under their parkas. One man lost on the ice many years ago said, after he returned safely, that he could smell the burning willow bark under his wife's parka when he sat down to rest. The *inyusuq* (soul or life) of a man lost on the ice always returned to his home. Sometimes a woman saw or heard her husband enter the house and pass right through it. Then she knew he was dead.

[3] Maguire is presumably quoting from John Simpson's journal.

[4] These winds would have pushed the pack ice toward shore. See Maguire's entry for 5 November 1853.

minds to a certain extent as they appear quite cheerful today – Erk-sin-ra said whilst the man was alive the 'line' round his home would remain tense, as he walked about it would vibrate, but if he were dead it would hang slack – Doctor Simpson enquired of him if the It-ka-li or (Ko-yu-kuks) were cannibals but he said they were not – He then said he had heard of a people beyond the MacKenzie who had pursued a man, killed him & afterwards ate him – Doctor S thought he could also trace by him a fish Kettle that was stolen from the ship in Kotz-bue [sic] Sound and afterwards was bartered along the coast to the Kang-ma-li (Eastern people).[1] The crew were employed bringing wood from Martin's Island & banking up snow against the Ships side – The ice about the Ship is cracked a good deal in consequence of an alteration in the level of the tide – . . .

Thursday October 20 Wind N.E. with a very low tide since yesterday morning & the weather rather thick. The party from C. Halkett had the last of the good travelling until the snow becomes frozen hard – as walking is much impeded with the snow drift which is yet soft – But few natives down today – The old chief O-mi-ga-loon was one of them – Doctor Simpson asked him about his wife having see M[r] Simpson's party at 'Kul-gu-ra' (Black rock point.[2] Dease's Inlet) he said she had, but was then the wife of another man since dead, he showed Doctor S how the Natives crept in the shade to steal Mr Dease's spoons[3] – The Employment for the day has been cutting and stacking wood, and banking up snow round the ships side – cleaned & inspected the arms – The night was cloudy with faint moonlight –

Friday [October] 21[st] The day was fine with the wind at East temp[eratur]e −4 [−20°C] – We had some visitors from C. Smyth

[1] This kettle would probably have been traded to Nuatarmiut at the summer trade rendezvous at Sheshalik on Kotzebue Sound, then carried with them to their home on the upper Noatak River, then carried the following summer to the Nirliq trade rendezvous at the mouth of the Colville River, and then, perhaps, purchased by Point Barrow Eskimos, who carried it the same summer to the trade rendezvous at Barter Island, where it was sold to the Mackenzie Eskimos.

[2] Thomas Simpson (1843, p. 149) reported the existence of this rock at approximately 71°04′ N., 155°16′ W. in 1837, as 'the first and only rock seen in the whole extent of our discoveries (westward of Return Reef) – an angular mass of dark coloured granite'. It is now called Black Head (Orth, 1969, p. 140). See below, p. 541.

[3] Thomas Simpson returned to his camp near Cape Simpson from Point Barrow on 6 August 1837. He wrote (1843, p. 167), 'I now learned from Mr. Dease that the natives . . . had left him two days before; and, on departing, had helped themselves to some silver tea spoons and one or two other articles, out of his travelling-case, while he lay asleep in his tent.'

who brought a few fish & small pieces of Venison to barter – One of them an elderly man who had lent me a hand with the boats in July last, to whom I made some presents, was now apparently anxious to return the compliment, by presenting me with some Rein deer fat & some fish, but Knowing they did not take a refusal in such cases very much to heart, I did not accept them – Lt Vernon and Mr Jago walked to the main land to get a shot at a deer, but returned without having met any. At 9 P.M. very faint Aurora rays hardly distinguishable in the Moon light – Halo round the moon distant 20° –

Saturday [October] 22nd This has been a moderate breeze from the N.E. and a little hazy accompanied by slight drift. Very few Natives about today & no news – Mr Gray went away with a wooding party to Doctors Isld[1] The remainder of the crew were employed banking up snow round the Ship side – The carpenter fitting a scale batten for the tide pole . . .

Sunday [October] 23rd A fine calm & Sunny day. Doctor Simpson – Lt Vernon & Mr Gray went to the Village after church – They visited sable's Father first and gave him some tobacco for which he was very grateful – And looking in upon several others they met with kind receptions & found all the females very busy, serving & cleaning skins – A large party of Natives with five sledges passed from the Main land (East) to the Village – There was a remarkable cloud to the West and N.W. tonight, which gave an appearance as if the open water was close outside the spit. A light air inclining to the South came round at night to West & N.W. still very light –

Monday [October] 24th . . . A moderate number of Natives about and on board. Erksinra had screwed up part of his gun lock until he could not pull the trigger. It was soon put to rights for him at which he rejoiced very much. There is a report of deer being within a days hunt of the ship & it is thought Erk-sin-ra is going after them – The people seem to depend a good deal this season upon the fish and Venison brought in from the land, as parties are continually setting out to assist in bringing in what is already on the way or in procuring other supplies – They still try for small fish along the cracks in the ice but their success is indifferent – They also complain of having no food for their dogs – A party of Natives with an O-mi-ak on the sledge were observed to pass from the main land to Noo-wook.

Mr Gordon left the Ship at 7 Am for a turn of wood & returned at

---

[1] About 7 miles from the ship.

3 P.M. The remainder of the crew were employed banking up snow against the ships side – The Carpenters making a spare Top Mast stud[din]g sail boom – Returning from a walk in the evening I witnessed a beautiful display of the Aurora rising from Mag[neti]ᶜ North to the Zenith –

Tuesday October 25ᵗʰ . . . We had but few Natives today among them was a man who remembers Mʳ Simpson's visit to 'Nek-si-u-ra'[1] the Cemetry [sic] – on Pᵗ Barrow – And his wife[,] daughter to Om-i-ga-loons – wife who saw him at Pt Tangent[2] and another girl who were then children. They said they afterwards blackened their faces in token of joy when their first fears had subsided . . .

Wednesday October 26ᵗʰ The day has been clear and fine but the temperature low −18 [−27.8°C]. Among the Natives who visited us today was the man from Icy Cape with his wife, who brought the boat left on the ice in July to the land, and had the pillaging of the stores provisions [e]tᶜ left by both boats[3] – I did not give him a very warm reception, but he has promised to bring the tent tomorrow, & speaks of returning more things when the ice is better for travelling – I have been engaged sorting papers & arranging the many gifts of books and charts [e]tᶜ received from the Kind friend to all engaged as we are – Mʳ Barrow of the Admiralty – There is now a very perceptible diminution in the hours of day light, dark setting in very soon after 4 P.M. The night was calm & cloudy –

Thursday [October] 27ᵗʰ Dull – over cast weather with the winds at N. E. (in force 2). Several sledges were observed passing towards the

---

[1] See map 4, p. 84 above. Thomas Simpson landed there – two miles south of the point at the small hook (Niksurak) on the lagoon side of the sandspit – on 4 August 1837. He wrote (1843, pp. 153–4):

> One of the first objects that presented itself, on looking around, was an immense cemetery. There the miserable remnants of humanity lay on the ground, in the seal-skin dresses worn while alive. A few were covered with an old sledge or some pieces of wood, but far the greater number were entirely exposed to the voracity of dogs and wild animals. The bodies here lay with the heads turned north-east, towards the extremity of the point; and many of them appeared so fresh, that my followers caught the alarm that the cholera or some other dire disease was raging among the Esquimaux. We had landed half-way between a winter village [Nuvuk] and a summer camp [Pirginik] of these people, situated about three miles asunder.

[2] This was probably the encampment that Thomas Simpson encountered on 2 August 1837 near 'Black Rock Point' (Black Head) (Simpson, 1843, p. 146).

[3] See Maguire's entries for 15 July and 1 August 1853. It is possible that the boat's salvor was from near Wainwright Inlet, not Icy Cape; see Maguire's entry for 2 November 1853.

land & a Number of persons towards Cape Smythe we suppose after deer. Only a few Visitors for the most part families and Children . . .

Friday [October] 28th The morning was fine & clear with a light breeze (2) from N.N.W. The Icy Cape man of boat notoriety brought the gigs sails down today, it was quite whole & uninjured he was given some tobacco for it through Lt Vernon but not allowed on board. I was startled today by hearing my name called in the cabin & looking up saw Ark-sin-ra dressed in Lieuts undress Uniform with sword cocked hat Epaulettes [e]t^c he was delighted with himself, & went on deck & outside the ship to show himself to his astonished country people.

Mr Gray started at 7 Am with a wooding party temp[eratur]^e −15 [−26.1°C) & returned at 3 P.M. He seems to have got his face touched a little by frostbite coming back − travelling has now become comparatively heavy − The remainder of the crew have been pumping the ship out with a boats pump, & passing the water over the side in buckets. The Carpenters have been placing the screen around the Coppers − The Sylvester stove has not been lit today, as we find the Ship retains her heat much better this year than last. Doctor Simpson suggests the cause to her being more head or end on to the prevailing winds which she is by nearly four points of the compass − and the embankment of snow round her being more effectual than the ice wall of last winter − The night was calm & clear temp[eratur]^e −16 [−26.7°C].

Saturday October 29th Morning fine calm & mild. Erk-sin-ra was on board again today & a good many others leaving very few outside − At present the men are idling and the women are busy sewing − today two nets were placed under the ice to catch seals . . .

Sunday October 30th . . . Erk-sin-ra with his little girl were alongside at 9 Am and being favoured individuals were allowed on board before divisions & church, when a numerous admittance took place − Four of the officers paid a visit to the Village and were as usual received Kindly, but many of the men were absent laying down their seal nets, some of them were very successful last night − I sent a small present of tobacco to the poor old Whaling Chiefs[1] wife through Lt Vernon who speaks of her as becoming a little more reconciled to her fate Poor old creature, but clinging to the hope that they have been carried in with the land about Point Hope . . .

---

[1] 'Ma-to-mia', the wife of 'O-mig-u-a-a-rua' (the 'water chief'), who drifted away on the ice while hunting.

301

Monday October 31st This has been a calm fine day throughout with a low temperature −20 [−28.9°C] Very few natives about. Doctor Simpson was told by a woman today of her Father having been Killed by our friend Sables, she afterwards mentioned Omigaloon having made the matter up by a present of Wolfskins[1] −

Mr Gray left at 7 Am with a wooding party. The remainder of the crew were employed pumping the Ship out by hand pump. Doctor Simpson was busy all day preparing Mr Barrow's presents to the crew in the way of papers & periodicals [e]tc for distribution − The carpenters have commenced making two tables out of drift wood, for trial on the lower deck during the winter, as I imagined the absence of them must be attended with some inconvenience, when any of the seamen should feel inclined to amuse or instruct themselves in reading and writing . . .

Tuesday November 1st [1853] The wind for the last 24 hours has been light and variable, the latter is not very usual here − We had very few Natives on board, Omigaloon and Erksinra were however among them. These separately confirmed the tale of Sables having Killed a man some two or three years ago. From the latter Doctor Simpson understood Sables to be looked upon as a bully and a coward, to prove his cowardice his conduct in throwing down his arms when the Natives surrounded the ship was referred to . . .

Wednesday November 2nd . . . A larger number of Natives & on board & round about drawn out I supposed by the mildness of the weather − We hear of their having caught some seal, and of a party gone to Wainwright Inlet with the man of 'boat fame'[2] . . .

Thursday [November] 3rd This has been a thick dull day throughout, the temperature about Zero − wind from the East[wa]rd Mr Gordon left the ship at 7 Am. with a wooding party. He had some difficulty in making his way out & returned very late in consequence, he would have been much later had he not been assisted by a party of five Natives with dogs, who left the ship for the purpose of their own record early in the afternoon − They were brought on

---

[1] See Maguire's entry of 15 November 1853 for confirmation of this report. 'O-mi-ga-loon's' action implied that he and 'Angunisua' ('Sables') belonged to the same kin group, and, because of the collective responsibility of kin in regard to homicide, 'O-mi-ga-loon's' was an act of propitiation to avoid an internecine feud (Spencer, 1959, pp. 71–2). Maguire's gifts to the wife of the man who was accidentally killed on 8 June 1853 may well have been viewed the same way by the Eskimos. See Maguire's entries for 8 and 9 June 1853.

[2] See Maguire's entry for 26 October 1853.

board & regaled with fish, biscuit & tobacco & water & left in about an hour seemingly satisfied with their treatment – We had but few Natives about – Doctor Simpson & Mr Gray have been engaged bringing out a Weekly Guy to accompany & announce the first issue of papers sent out by Mr Barrow. The crew were employed banking up snow round the ship as high as the gunwhales [sic]. The Carpenters making the tables for the lower deck . . .

Friday Novr 4th The morning was fine & clear with a very light air from S.S.E. Mr Gray left at 7 Am with a wooding party & got back in good time. Rather a larger assemblage of Natives both in board & out. Early in the afternoon we were very glad to hear of the arrival at Noo-wook of our friend Sables and his party, landed from the Ship at P^t Hope early in August last[1] – In the evening the arms were cleaned inspected & loaded as the Natives are to be on board in any numbers tomorrow – Night overcast with snow, wind N.E. in force (2) temperature +9 [−12.8°C] –

Saturday [November] 5th A mild dull day – We had no work going on in consequence of the preparations for the Guy Fawkes entertainment, to which the Natives were invited, but they commenced arriving much before the appointed time which kept them waiting longer than was agreeable to either party. We had an effigy of Guy Fawkes attached to the gally Funnel from the early morning but inferior in design to that of last year –

Our Friend Sables party arrived about noon & were received with much welcome. They had of course a great deal to talk about, of the wonders they had seen on board the Amphitrite & the difficulties of their return journey – it appears they were obliged to abandon their O-mi-ak about half way between Cape Lisburne & Icy Cape – from not being able to drag her along – They seem to have started with her on a sledge from the neighbourhood of Cape Lisburne where they had been encamped for some days, in company with a party of Point Hope people. A part of sable's exploits at the time caused him to be looked upon less favourably by us, it appeared he assisted to murder a man whilst he slept, who had threatened him in some way, but had killed the brother of Sama-ru-ma[2] who visited the place last winter.

---

[1] See Maguire's entry for 12 August 1853. 'Sables' therefore had to have crossed two territorial boundaries on his return to Nuvuk, in a season when hostile attacks were expected.

[2] This was 'Angunisua's' ('Sables') second reported homicide (see Maguire's entry for 31 October 1853). 'Sama-ru-ma's' brother is elsewhere referred to as 'Ku-su'. See Maguire's entry for 4 April 1854.

They seem now to have made their arrangements togeather [sic], & while their victim was asleep in a summer tent between two wives, they pulled it from over them & with their Knives did the deed which was completed by one of Sable's party driving an arrow through his body. It appears that the victim was a man of influence well known to be of an evil disposition who had killed several men besides the one mentioned.

The most important news is that the three men taken out on the ice on the 2nd of October got on shore to the South[wa]rd of Icy Cape, but the water chief,[1] and another starved on the land & only the younger one of the three was saved. This was a very stout man who is now represented as reduced to a skeleton by his hardships – Their return journey occupied them fifteen days, and it appears that Icy Cape and a place to the South[wa]r^d of Wainwright Inlet, are the only winter residences between Point Hope & Cape Smyth that is on the sea coast. Neither at Wainwright Inlet nor the Sea Horse Islands were there any Natives[2] –

In the evening after dark we had a procession round the upper deck with Guy Fawkes mounted on the back of what was intended for a Horse, he was then lead to the gallows at some distance from the Ship & executed with the usual pitch barrel, and a display of fireworks – After which the Natives were admitted to a larger number than I had seen previously on board. But they had had so long to wait on the ice for admittance, they were in no great humour for dancing and it required an exertion to get them to Amuse themselves at their favourite pastimes – And were quite ready for the party breaking up at Nine o'clock when a further display of Fireworks took place for their gratification, but this part of the entertainment was cut short, by the box containing the fireworks becoming ignited by accident, when the mixture of Roman Candles, crackers & serpents [e]t^c made a very confused display – The Natives not knowing any better, I suppose thought it very fine – But Mr Gordon (the son of an Enginer [sic] Officer) and the Gunners Mate who had been for some days manufacturing them, were much annoyed at the accident – My impulse at the time was to laugh notwithstanding.

The Artificial Horizon lost in the boats was brought on board by a

---

[1] 'O-mig-u-a-a-rua.'

[2] The people may have been hunting and fishing in the interior at this season.

Native today, it was quite complete nothing having been moved from it, I can only account for this, either by their being afraid of it – or not being able to unscrew the iron bottle containing the Mercury – They readily gave it up for some tobacco –

<u>Sunday November 6th</u> . . . Very few Natives about – Lt Vernon walked to the Village alone which seemed rather to surprise them, perhaps fancying we were afraid of them. He saw very few people about & reports the last hunting party having come in from the main land – the rivers being to [sic] deeply covered with snow to allow of fishing – It is reported that the old Whaling Chiefs son has gone down the coast to look after the remains of his Father,[1] a piece of attention to the dead we had not given them credit for.

<u>Tuesday November 8th</u> A fine clear day with a light wind from S.E. A good many Natives about. A man & woman brought Lt Vernons sexant [sic] & a Blanket frock left in the boats for which they received a handsome present of tobacco – Lt Vernon walked to the Main land and saw a considerable number of deer, 'thirteen', but at a great distance –

We had a number of our old acquaintance of last year in the 'Weekly Guy' published today, by way of letting us know that he is still alive, though in some way superceded this year by the generosity of Mr Barrow who has sent a Number of papers & periodicals sufficient for a good, separate supply every week, from Nov[embe]^r to April – His idea on this subject is I think a happy one, by his wish the papers [e]t^c or weeks supply are first placed on the cabin table, from whence they go to the Gun Room, and then to the lower deck, so that people almost from the force of habit will take them up & perhaps obtain information & news of which they had been previously ignorant. But of our old friend the Guy I feel sorry that the means at the disposal of the Editor, are not in any way, either mechanically or literary, adequate to ensure Keeping up the publication with spirit – however we are promised an occasional number, when anything of unusual importance takes place.

Erk-sin-ra informed Doctor Simpson that the bartering place for the Natives to the South of us is some where in Hothams Inlet[2] – to

---

[1] Robert Spencer (1959, p. 253) reported that when carrying a corpse to a cemetery a man usually followed the body, brandishing a knife to frighten the dead person's spirit so that it would not return to its house. Perhaps 'O-mig-u-a-a-rua's' son was going to Icy Cape to do this.

[2] At Sheshalik.

which the people from Point Hope, Kotzbue [sic] Sound & all the
coast from Cape Prince of Wales resort, & there meet and effect
their exchange of goods with the people from the Asiatic coast –
The latter are described as crossing by the Diomede Islands to
Cape Prince of Wales whence they follow the coast into Kotzbue
[sic] Sound, which they cross at its narrowest part – The intercourse appears to be always friendly and the barter not effected
Knife in hand as Doctor S learnt from Tsan-chi of Ourel.[1] The
time of meeting is a little after Mid-Summer 'when the sun dips for
a short time blow [sic] the waves' which would correspond probably to the end of July or beginning of August. The Nuna-tagmun
attend these meetings & procure Kettles & Knives which the
ensuing summer are disposed of to the Point Barrow people. The
mode of transit from the Colville mouth to Si-sú-a-liung[2] (or place
of barter) is easily effected in the Summer by boats, Erk-sin-ra says
the Nigala or Colville is only a mouth of the main stream taking its
rise in the mountains & that another mouth called the Nuna-tu[3]
pursues its course to the sea in Hothams Inlet or Kotzbue [sic]
Sound near the place of barter – Doctor S thinks the Nuna-ta gives
to the inhabitants residing on it the name of Nuna-tag-mun – who
have hitherto puzzled him. The crew have been employed banking
up snow as high as the hammock nettings and the Carpenters about
the lower deck tables –
Wednesday November 9th . . . We had fewer Natives about today.
The old Chief Omigaloon confirmed the account given yesterday by
Erk-sin-ra & added the name O-ta-ka[4] to one of the Rivers
concerned – A small boy son of Sama-ru-mā, and his youngest wife
have accompanied sable's party from Point Hope, on some bartering
speculation, they return alone in a short time – It appears wonderful
two such young people undertaking so long a journey unaided, at the
commencement of the coldest season – . . .
Thursday [November] 10th A cloudless day with a light wind from
the Westw[ar]d temperature −16 [−26.7°C] We had a large number
of natives on board some five & twenty leaving about a dozen outside –
Erk-sin-ra was on board & talked again with Doctor Simpson about
the rivers. He said there was a small lake inland among the hills

[1] He is referring to the *Plover*'s first winter in the north (1848–9) when the vessel was
frozen at Plover Bay, near a Chukchi village. See William Hooper's account (1853) of
the winter.   [2] Today, Sheshalik.
[3] The Noatak River.   [4] Today, the Utukok River. See p. 307, n. 2.

behind Cape Beauford[1] [sic] from which a River flowed to the sea near Point Lay – but that it also received a stream (or gave?) which came from the Nunatak.[2] The first is called the Ko-pak[3] & the last the O-to-kak and these are the means by which the Nunatang-mun communicate with Obrona (Icy Cape).[4] He also mentioned the Ko-wak which falls into Hothams Inlet at its Eastern end, and when Doctor S mentioned the *Se-la-wik* he corrected him by calling it Si-la-wik or (See-la-wik) from which it appears the name was not strange to him although he said he did not know in what direction it is to be found, he also said the Nuna-tag-mun did not go on the saltwater to arrive at the bartering place in Kotz-bue Sound but only to the mouth of the Nuna-ta from which Doctor S infers the place called Si-su-liung (barter rendezvouz [sic]) is probably within the entrance of Hothams Inlet . . .

Friday November 11th Fine clear weather but very cold wind S.S.E. 1 to 2 in force. Lt Vernon and Mr Jago accompanied by Erk-sin-ra walked to the main land to try and get a shot at a deer but saw nothing . . . We had not many natives down today & no news was had of them.

Saturday November 12th. . . Mr. Jago has been engaged today printing notices to be sent down the coast with the point [sic] Hope – young people now at Noo-wook. The crew were employed clearing away the snow from the bower chain to the shore, cleaning out the tanks and bailing out the pump well. We had but few natives down today, a party with a sledge passed the ship at 8 Am. going to the East[wa]rd The night was Moon light with some haze only a very faint Aurora[.] Temperature −20° [−28.9°C] –

Sunday [November] 13th Clear fine weather the wind light but steady at N.W. The Natives were down in considerable numbers but were not according to custom admitted until after church – When Doctor Simpson & Lieut Vernon paid a visit to the village, they went to Erk-sin-ra's hut first and he accompanied them to several others – They saw the wife of the stout man[5] who was carried away on the ice,

---

[1] Cape Beaufort.

[2] The Utukok and Noatak rivers do not have the same source, although some of their headwaters are very close in the DeLong Mountains. There was a well-used overland route between the Noatak and Utukok rivers (Burch, 1976, p. 7).

[3] This may well be the 'Kugzuaaq' River (today, the Kugururok River), a tributary of the Noatak River, from which one could cross to the headwaters of the Utukok River (Burch, 1976, p. 7).

[4] Wainwright Inlet, not Icy Cape; see Maguire's entry for 15 June 1854.

[5] Elsewhere, 'Kai-a-tuna'.

and who is now at Icy Cape, and gave her some tobacco – on entering
sable's hut they found the inmates dancing, the only place in the
Village that seemed to have any life in it – They saw also an elderly
woman who had seen M[r] Simpson's party in 1837, & had received
beads & tobacco from them, her daughter who was then an infant is
the only person in the village besides Erk-sin-ras boy[,] now two years
old[,] whose age Doctor Simpson has been able to ascertain An old
woman died at the Village a few days ago and a female child was born
about the same time –

Monday November 14th . . . We had not many natives on board
today but among them was the second wife of a Point Hope Chief
Sa-man ru-ma who visited this place last winter – Doctor Simpson
through his knowledge of the Hotham Inlet tribe who are well
known by the Point Hope people was able to get some very
satisfactory information from her, as it agreed with what he had
been told by Erk-sin-ra & others of this place – She was well
acquainted with S etc – 'Ka-kok' and 'Ak-Koul-iak' who Doctor S
had known at Hothams Inlet,[1] besides 'Ang-a-blak'[2] the woman
'erksinra' saw at the Colville two years ago – she at once named the
rivers Se-la-wik, Ko-wak & No-a-tak or Nu-a-tak which Doctor S
remembers to be the one explored by M[r] Martin.[3] This is the Nu-
na-tak described by Erksinra & falls into that part of Hothams Inlet
under Deviation Peak, marked as not examined by Captain Beechy
[sic] – she was well acquainted with the place Si-su-a-ling[4] (the
barter rendevouz [sic] where the Koklit[5] people meet the Esquimaux and she has often been present at the bartering – She was
there in the summer of this year – Doctor S concludes by saying
that it is exceedingly satisfactory to be thus able to trace the inland
channel of communication and trade amongst the sections of a
people seemingly so remote from each other & offers a tempting
field for speculation & conjecture connected with the inhabitants on
both sides of the Straits . . .

Tuesday November 15th . . . Sables and his party came down pretty

[1] In the winter of 1849–50, when the *Plover* wintered at the Choris Peninsula in
Kotzebue Sound.
[2] She was, presumably, one of the Nuatarmiut from the upper Noatak River.
[3] These are the Selawik, Kobuk, and Noatak Rivers. Henry Martin, the second
master of the *Plover* from 1848 to 1850, made a sledge trip to the mouth of the Noatak
in February 1850 (Great Britain, 1851, p. 30).
[4] Today, Sheshalik.
[5] Siberian Eskimos.

early dressed in their best clothes, and in high spirits about something, he had been at the dance house & made presents there, and he had a circular mark on his forehead made with black lead which indicated as he informed us, that he was very glad. We have often remarked them with their faces marked in different patches, a very common way is to see, spectacles painted across the eyes, but we have had no explanation of them previous to Sables's – We had but few others on board the Ship – one old man seeing the people pump water up from the tanks in the hold & not detecting the pipe by which it was conducted became sadly puzzled about where it came from – He first asked if it was salt & had some given him & then he was told the man at the pump made it, as he is but little acquainted with hydraulics, he had no choice but to believe or disbelieve, it was thought the latter . . . Compared with last winter there is a great absence of water sky – a phenomenon as constant then as to lead us to the belief that the prevailing N.E. Current assisted to keep the sea open. The facts of the men carried out on the ice last year landing at or near Wainwright Inlet, and the three men who were carried off in the same way this year, being landed at or near Cape Lisburne would rather indicate a winter current in the opposite direction . . .

Wednesday Novr 16th . . . We had not many natives on board today but from Ersk-sin-ra & two others. Doctor Simpson received a casual account of the number of huts and inhabitants at Noo-wook which may be relied on – The number of huts is [blank].[1] The same as given last year but now there are five tenantless, and the entire population now is 309 of all ages being 166 males and 143 females which is something over the number made out last year, but then Doctor S did not take the census so carefully – The old water chiefs son has returned having gone only some distance beyond Refuge Inlet, where he met the survivor of the unfortunate party – The story now is that they landed a good way beyond Icy Cape & made their way to a store house where they found walrus flesh, but the old water chief[2] was too much exhausted to revive, & the third gave up on the road saying 'he should never see Noo-wook again' . . .

---

[1] John Simpson (Appendix Seven below, p. 506) gives the figure as 54 inhabited houses in 1852–3 and 48 in 1853–4 ('in consequence of the scarsity of oil to supply so many fires [lamps]') – as well as a few other houses 'which do not seem to have been tenanted for several years', and two ceremonial houses (*qazgit*).

[2] 'O-mig-u-a-a-rua.'

Thursday [November] 17th . . . Few Natives. All complaining of the scarcity of food;[1] they have however a good stand by in a dead whale cast on Coopers Island three years ago to which they make frequent journeys. One man borrowed an axe today to cut it with, for which he has promised us a share of his cargo for dogs food.

Some printed notices have been prepared for forwarding along the coast to the South[wa]rd with information to Commander Trollope[2] of the date of our arrival here for winter quarters, & of the intended positions for placing further information by travelling parties in the Summer. The Point Hope boy & young woman previously mentioned, and who are now on the point of setting out on their return (& for whom the papers were principally prepared) came on board together with Erk-sin-ra who acted as interpreter & explained that the papers given were to be distributed along the coast, with instructions that they were to be delivered to Capt[ai]n Trollope's ship either at Port Clarence or Point Hope, some were also given to be left at Icy Cape – . . .

Friday November 18th. . . We had many natives on board, I was very sorry to find that one of them had committed a theft in which he was assisted by several who I thought ought to have known better, but I suppose we must come to the conclusion that there is no cure for this propensity of theirs, however we had intended to give them a dance on board tomorrow which has been annulled, and the admittance to the ship will be more limited in future, to show them our disapprobation of such conduct . . .

Saturday November 19th The weather came on thick during the night and has remained the same all day . . . wind light at S.W. As many as 7 or 8 sledges passed to the Eastward in the early morning, going for the putrid Whale blubber on Coopers Island, which they are by necessity obliged to make use of – Not many Natives about and very few in board.

Doctor Simpson went to the Village alone for the purpose of seeing a man who was suffering from a severe cut in the leg, which he found in a bad looking state from a large slough in it – He saw

---

[1] This is the first mention of the famine which would last throughout the winter of 1853–4 and would result in the deaths of about 15 per cent of the combined populations of Nuvuk and Utqiarvik.

[2] Trollope was in command of H.M.S. *Rattlesnake* which was then wintering at Port Clarence.

also the man who is returned from his perilous adventure on the ice. He is now a remarkable contrast with what he was being emaciated & weak; whereas he was formerly the fattest man in Noo-wook – He told Erk-sin-ra a long story about his misfortunes, part of which only Doctor S could understand: it was to the effect that they were carried close past C. Smyth & along the land & got on shore near C. Lisburne, when they were in doubt whether to go to Point Hope or to Icy Cape, at one part of the tale he had to stop being overcome with emotion and cried outright. Doctor S. saw also the second widow who like Ma-to-mia (the Whaling Chiefs widow) is very sorrowful . . .

Sunday [November] 20th . . . Doctor Simpsons account yesterday of the unfortunate sufferer on the ice, brought to my mind our being able to afford him relief in the way of some nourishing food to recover his prostrated strength, Doctor S accordingly visited him again today after church, and took with him a good mess of preserved meats & a little Port wine, his account of him is less satisfactory as he imagines that his lungs are affected.

We had a good many natives about the ship but not many in board. Erk-sin-ra was one of them & brought down a woman with a pain in her thigh bone to be cupped by D^r S which was done. She brought a pair of gloves as a fee,[1] which were purchased from her. The old water Chiefs widow[2] was down also, poor creature, she says that at the Ship she is not sorry, but when in the house she is always crying – I send her forward to the officers cook who is a ready humoured good fellow & makes her forget her sorrow –

Monday November 21st . . . Doctor Simpson went to the Village again attended by two or three of our men who wished to see it, he found his patient much better today, & talking already of growing fat. His brother was admitted into the ship by Doctor S. in consequence of his admiring the ingenuity with which he had mended a broken teacup, by drilling holes through it and passing a great many turns of fine Whale bone through them looking when done, not unlike the way china is repaired at home with solder clamps. However he was found to have returned the attentions shown to his brother and himself by stealing the key of the store

---

[1] It was customary to pay a shaman (*angatquq*) for a successful cure (Spencer, 1959, p. 313).

[2] 'Ma-to-mia.'

house – Showing if instances were wanting ingratitude sufficient to damp any attempts at showing them kindness. Not many natives on board, the old chief[1] & Sables being part of them, I invited them to the cabin when they made a joint attack upon me about the scarcity of food at Noo-wook – which I was sorry it was not in my power to remedy . . .

Tuesday [November] 22d . . . Doctor Simpson went to the village as usual, having a companion or two from the crew, one of whom carrys the small Kettle containing his patients dinner – who seems to do well, but he has something seriously wrong in the right side of his chest, but the pain is more circumscribed than before – His brother was in the hut whom he said he had well scolded for stealing – A moderate number of Natives about – Atkana from C. Smyth & his daughter were on board, he is an unscrupulous beggar & never comes for any other purpose – his modest request today was for lead to cast a pipe – Two sledges returned from the East[wa]rd loaded with blubber. We are badly off for common oil to burn in our deck lamps, as we trusted for our supply to the Natives, and this year we have been unable to get anything from them . . .

Wednesday November 23^{d}. . . Doctor Simpson went to the village as usual and put a blister on his patients chest, which he seemed glad of, as he expects it to suck away the internal disease. Coming back Doctor S met a little girl who pointing to a small sledge stuck into the snow on its end – said she and her companion were frightened by it in the twilight taking it for a 'turn giak'[2] (ghost) Thus timid & superstitious to a degree they see a spectre in every shadow & 'hear a voice in every wind' as not a few people at home do – We have had a slight repetition for the first time of the Knife threatening work of last year from Stammering John,[3] who was refused admittance in consequence of his assisting in a theft on board a few days ago. A good many Natives left from in board & outside, I suppose from hearing him make use of some dreadful threat, which we happily [sic] for our peace of minds were ignorant of – however I suspect there is not more in it than talk . . .

Thursday November 24th. . . We had a few natives down and received a startling report of Sable's & four others having been

---

[1] 'O-mi-ga-loon.'

[2] According to Robert Spencer (1959, p. 300), a *tunarak* was a type of spirit that was involved in shamanistic power.

[3] 'To-ko-la-rua.'

carried out on the ice, which broke away in the night[1] but as the wind was blowing strong on shore nothing was thought of it

Although the weather was not favourable Doctor Simpson paid his usual visit to his patients at the Village, I was glad to find on his return that the people reported to be adrift on the ice were snug in their houses at Noo-wook – And he thought it an exaggerated [sic] report if not a false alarm – He had also met with a little playful opposition on his entrance to the Village by stammering Johns brother standing across his path & telling him he was not to go to the Village, Doctor S answered by saying he was not going near his house & passed on – Erk-sin-ra appears to have been [aware] there was something not satisfactory going [on] as he kept by Doctor S until he came away. They have had better success in catching seals lately . . .

Friday November 25th. . . We had a good many natives in board and about – I am glad to find they are beginning to catch a few seal. One man has been so unfortunate as to loose nine, as well as the net he caught them in,[2] by the ice breaking away –

Doctor Simpson went as usual to visit his patient, and had his attention drawn by a circumstance in keeping with strict superstitious observance – It was causing the seaman who accompanied him to desist from knocking the ashes out of his pipe against the floor of Kai-a-tuna's hut – *because no one must hammer in a dwelling where there is sickness or sorrow.*[3] Not to Knock the ashes out of a pipe but to be obliged to clear it with a pricker he mentions as carrying the matter to an unexpected degree of refinement . . .

Saturday [November] 26th The day has been dull and threatening the temperature rising gradually wind (3) at S.E. Doctor Simpson on

---

[1] The five were undoubtedly netting seals, See following footnote.

[2] Seals were netted in the winter and spring. There were two ways of netting seals: with vertically hung nets and with horizontally hung nets. The vertically hung nets (which are referred to here) were used in the early winter around cracks in the ice at night when there was little or no moonlight to allow the seal to see the net. Horizontally hung nets were used later in the winter and in the early spring, when the deep cold completely froze over vast expanses of sea, forcing the seal to keep small breathing holes open. The nets were suspended under these holes (Ray, 1885, p. 40; Sonnenfeld, 1957, pp. 43–60).

[3] It may have been that there had been a death in 'Kai-a-tuna's' house – in which case sewing or hammering would have been forbidden, lest the spirit of the dead person return to the house (Spencer, 1959, pp. 252–3). At such times, while the family was in its mourning period, they would have been allowed no visitors, but perhaps in the Eskimos' perception the British stood beyond such strictures.

his way to the Village to visit his patient & give him his usual dayly meal, was met by Erk-sin-ra's wife, who came to tell him that he was not to go to the sick mans hut today, as they were going to perform some miracle or ceremony of their own for his cure[1] – But that he was to go to Erk-sin-ra's hut instead, however as he had no business there he returned to the Ship – We had only a few natives around today, but there was a man & his wife in board from Cape Smyth, whom I have known as good people ever since my first visit here in the boats in /52. He brought me a present of two fish & would take no refusal – from his account they seem to be more fortunate in catching seal at Cape Smyth than they are at Noo-wook. Still he spoke of some people there having very little to eat. In the evening the wind shifted to W.S.W. and the temperature rose to +22 [−5.6°C]. A strong wind 6 to 7 in force with drift . . .

Monday [November] 28th The wind moderated this morning leaving clear and cold weather which continued throughout the day, the temp[eratu]r[e] −12 to 15 [−24°C to −26.1°C]. In consequence of two of the Petty officers setting the bad example of fighting on the Lower deck yesterday afternoon, one of them Ed [Edward] Sutton Q[uarte]r Master was deprived of his good conduct badge as he disobeyed an order given to him by Lieut Vernon in addition to the other offense, both of them were reprimanded afterwards in the presence of the Ships c°[mpany] . . . We had a good many natives about. We hear that they are now more successful in catching seal, but they are slow to acknowledge it, as any individual who is asked about their having enough to eat, invariably answers they have nothing to eat, and when closely pushed acknowledge to a little . . .

Wednesday Novr 30th . . . In the forenoon the crew were employed completing the clearance of our enclosure, and bringing provisions from the house to the Ship. In the afternoon until the school hour 3 P.M. they Amused themselves playing at football. Not many natives about. The old chief[2] with his large wife and Sables were in my cabin, our number was afterwards increased by Dr Simpson on his return from seeing his patient at the Village who appears not to have received the expected benefit from the native miracle workers, & was anxious for a renewal of Dr Simpson's treatment & diet. The wife of O-Mig-a-loon saw Mr [Thomas] Simpson the arctic explorer of

---

[1] No doubt they had decided to consult a shaman (*angatquq*).
[2] 'O-mi-ga-loon.'

(1837–38) at Dease's Inlet, and the Native O-mi-ak so necessary for the fulfillment of his enterprize was bought from her.[1] I read out of M[r] Simpson's book some of the particulars of this meeting, And she pretended to express a great deal of surprise, at the power the books give us of Knowing events we have not seen or otherwise heard of – But she was aware of this facility of ours before the present – . . .

Thursday December 1st [1853] A clear day wind from the S.E. 2 in force temp[eratu][r][e] ranging −15 [−26.1°C]. The crew were employed shifting the boundary chain on top of the snow bank. And examining & setting up our boundary lines round the spit. The

[1] This encounter took place at Black Rock Point (now Black Head) near Tangent Point on 2 August 1837. Thomas Simpson wrote (1843, pp. 146–8):

. . . we descried four Esquimaux tents, at no great distance, with figures running about. We immediately directed our steps toward them; but, on our approach, the women and children threw themselves into their canoes, and pushed off from the shore. I shouted 'Kabloonan teyma Inueet', meaning, 'we are white men, friendly to the Esquimaux'; upon which glad news the whole party hurried ashore, and almost overpowered us with caresses. The men were absent, hunting, with the exception of one infirm individual who, sitting under a reversed canoe, was tranquilly engaged in weaving a fine whalebone net. Being unable to make his escape with the rest, he was in an agony of fear; and, when I first went up to him, with impotent hand he made a thrust at me with his long knife. He was, however, soon convinced of our good intentions; and his first request was for tobacco, of which we found men, women, and even children inordinately fond. This taste they have, of course, acquired in the indirect intercourse with the Russians; for the Esquimaux we had at last parted with were ignorant of the luxury. Our new friends forthwith brought us some fresh venison; and, concluding, not without reason, that we were very hungry, they presented, as a particular delicacy, a savoury dish of choice pieces steeped in seal-oil. Great was their surprise when we declined their favourite mess; and the curiosity in scrutinizing the dress, persons, and complexions of the first white men they had ever beheld, seemed insatiable. They shewed us, with evident satisfaction, their winter store of oil, secured in seal-skin bags buried in the frozen earth. Some of their reindeer robes, ivory dishes, and other trifles were purchased; and I exchanged the tin pan, which constituted my whole table service, for a platter made out of a mammoth tusk! This relic of an antediluvian world contained my two daily messes of pemican throughout the remainder of the journey. It is seven inches long, four wide, and two deep; and is exactly similar to one figured by Captain Beechey at Escholtz Bay [sic], only the handle is broken off. Confidence now being fully established, I told them that I required one of the oomiaks, or large family canoes, to take us two or three days' journey – or sleeps, as they term it – to the westward; after which we should return; These skin boats float in half a foot of water. No ice was visible from the tents; and, from the trending of the coast, it was more than doubtful that our journey could have been accomplished in any reasonable time on foot. They acceded to my demand, without a scruple. We selected the best of three oomiaks; obtained four of their slender oars, which they used as tent-poles, besides a couple of paddles; fitted the oars with lashings; and arranged our strange vessel so well that the ladies were in raptures, declaring us to be genuine Esquimaux, and not poor white men.

Carpenters sheathing over all iron bolts showing on the lower deck. We had a moderate number of natives about but none of the Chiefs or our particular intimates were down . . .

Friday [December] 2nd A fine day with little or no winds – The crew in the forenoon were employed re-sanding the snow covering on the upper deck, and in the Afternoon playing at football. There is still a strong solar reflection on the horizon at noon – but it does not continue longer than about an hour. We had a strong number of natives down today, our friend stammering John was one of the outsiders, he is still under a cloud, for assisting at a theft before mentioned, and is not allowed on board, but contrary to his usual custom he was unoffensive . . .

Saturday December 3^d . . . We had a large number of natives on board, a man in the afternoon stole a knife and a preserved meat tin containing some frozen oil for trimming the lamps – he wore (or is supposed to have) a larger deer skin cloak which enabled him the better to conceal his prize. As soon as the mischief was found out those remaining were informed that none of them would be admitted on board until the things were returned.

This winter the same as last, the crew are supplied with hot water for washing on Thursday & Saturday afternoons . . .

Sunday [December] 4th . . . There were a good many natives down but not one on [sic] allowed on board in consequence of the theft yesterday – An alteration has been made today in the allowance of Coal dayly [sic] for the Sylvester stove, from thirty to forty pounds and to be lit two hours sooner at 10 Am instead of Noon –

The Ship in every way seems warmer this year than last, which I can only account for by the arrangements being more effectual, in cutting off the external atmosphere. The snow embankment outside, and the deck covering seem to be main defenders & so far are answering the purpose intended, better than those of last year –

Monday December 5th This has been the coldest day we have had this winter the temperature ranging about −30° [−34.4°C]. No Natives were allowed on board, but in the Afternoon Erk-sin-ra and another man brought down the preserved meat tin (that had been stolen) and asked for a description of the Knife in order to recover it also. They were allowed on board & remained about an hour. I walked for three hours along the Islands to the East[wa]rd and felt very little inconvenience from the low temperature. I followed the track of two Natives who had gone along early in the morning Seal hunting, & met them on their return, having met with no success. They were following an extensive tide crack (running past the second Island) in the hope of finding a space sufficiently open for setting their nets. As they seemed disposed to treat me with a full account of all their wants from food to tobacco, I parted company from them, not having the means of satisfying them, and on my return on board found that natives had all left from outside giving an unusual and lonely appearance, this is the second day that none have been admitted. I believe a singular instance since our arrival at Point Barrow . . .

Tuesday [December] 6th . . . A few natives down. Erk-sin-ra arrived about 10 Am. & brought the Knife (stolen) which removed the embargo from the admittance of the natives when a few were allowed in, mostly women as we find they do not steal. Erk-sin-ra was invited into the cabin, and made a present of tobacco for the trouble he had taken, in recovering the stolen articles, more than for the value of things which to us was nothing, but I think it best to keep up an appearance of setting a value on every thing we possess.

He seemed to speak despondingly of the great scarcity of food amongst the Natives at present. Doctor Simpson who was in the cabin tried to lead him back to a similarly bad year which seemed to be about five previous, namely /48 – Their wants at present do not seem exaggerated. Erk-sin-ra told us he gave a deer skin for about three or four lbs of Venison – . . .

Thursday [December] 8th A calm cloudy day, but not thick or [sic] was there any snow falling. The temperature very mild very few natives down, they informed us that those who went out after seal yesterday, had remained on the ice all night and had not returned as yet to No-wook – their success was not known, but the hopes were favourable.

A man died at the Village on the morning before yesterday, and a woman this morning which makes the third death there this winter besides the two men lost on the ice . . .

Friday – December 9th Weather fine and clear. The Natives had only partial success in catching seal yesterday but are out today again in great numbers – Doctor Simpson's patient Kai-a-tu-na who was so long adrift on the ice, is afflicted again with the pain in his chest, and Erk-sin-ra is engaged with him beating it away with a drum.[1] No sewing is allowed to go on [e]t^c in the Village on account of the

---

[1] 'Erk-sing-era', a shaman (*angatquq*), was exercising his curative powers.

317

woman's death yesterday. We had not many natives down today, and very few men amongst them . . .

Sunday December 11<u>th</u> . . . Erk-sin-ra arrived at the ship about 9 Am and being a favoured individual was admitted before divisions & Church – We knew that he had been attending Doctor Simpsons patient lately, and questioned him as to his present state which he reported favourably of – we were much amused at his informing us that the woman who had died, had not been treated by him, or the result would have been different – Another of Doctor Simpsons patients who has received a deep cut on his shin was down and dressed on the lower deck. As this was a case beyond Erk-sin-ra's skill he was content to look on approvingly and on one of the officers remarking that Doctor S. wore moccasins similar to his, implying that there was something professional in them, his modesty was put to the blush & he appeared much flattered. He told us a great many of the natives had gone out on the ice today to kill seal with spears[1] – A few were allowed on board –

Monday December 12<u>th</u> . . . A moderate number of natives about, but no particular news from them. I imagine the supply of food at present is a little better as we hear less complaints on that subject –

Tuesday [December] 13<u>th</u> . . . The Natives were not down in any great force today. Some of them reported the death of Kai-a-tuna – the man who was carried away on the ice and was the survivor of the three – poor man his has been a severe trial – at 10 P.M. there was an extensive halo round the moon.

Wednesday [December] 14<u>th</u> . . . The Natives had more success in the way of seals yesterday. Not many on board today, one of them told Doctor Simpson of fifteen deaths including children, from disease & disaster since the Ship came to Noo-wook – also that the last woman who had died, had a child taken or cut out of her, as her death was caused by child birth. And from some esquimaux superstition this is considered necessary & the child is laid alongside of the mother . . .

Thursday December 15<u>th</u> . . . The Natives were about in moderate numbers, the old Whaling Chiefs wife[2] was on board & in my cabin. I afterwards sent her forward on the lower deck where she was detected in the attempt of stealing a tin pannican [sic] . . .

---

[1] Maguire means harpoons, and he is referring to daylight seal hunting at cracks in the sea ice (in contrast with night seal netting).

[2] 'Ma-to-mia.'